The Churching of America, 1776–2005

The Churching
of America,
1776–2005

Winners and Losers
in Our Religious Economy

ROGER FINKE
and
RODNEY STARK

RUTGERS UNIVERSITY PRESS   New Brunswick, New Jersey, and London

Second paperback printing, 2006

Library of Congress Cataloging-in-Publication Data

Finke, Roger, 1954–
    The churching of America, 1776–2005 : winners and losers in our religious economy
/ Roger Finke and Rodney Stark. — 2nd ed.
        p. cm.
    Includes bibliographical references and index.
    ISBN 0-8135-3633-2 (cloth : alk. paper) ISBN 0-8135-3553-0 (pbk. : alk. paper)
    1. United States—Church history. 2. Christian sociology—United States. 1. Stark, Rodney.
II. Title.
    BR515.F56 2005
    277.3'08—dc22

                                                                              2004016429

A British Cataloging-in-Publication record is available for this book from the British Library

Manufactured in the United States of America

Contents

List of Illustrations

List of Figures

List of Tables

Preface to the Second Edition

The first edition of *The Churching of America* caused quite a stir. Peter Steinfels devoted a *New York Times* article (February 20, 1993) to review the apparent controversies surrounding the book and reviews of the book went far beyond the traditional disciplinary outlets of sociologists and historians. Receiving the 1993 Distinguished Book Award from the Society for the Scientific Study of Religion, the book has been praised by many. Sociologists have been effusive. Andrew Greeley described it as a "brilliant and revolutionary analysis of the social history of American religion" and Phillip Hammond (1993) agreed that it is a "wonderful, refreshing addition to the literature of both the sociology of religion and the history of American religions." Many historians also welcomed the book. Church historian Walter Sundberg (1993) wrote that "many of us are still mesmerized by the Mainline Tale" that religious decline is inevitable in the face of modernity. He went on to prescribe that "reading Finke and Stark is the best way I know to break the spell." John Wilson (1993) noted that the book is of "great significance in itself," but predicted that it would also be important for the "discussions it provokes, both within disciplines and among them." Robert Swierenga stated that the "authors convincingly challenge the biggest names in the field and show how an 'establishment' bias has blinded them to the real underlying pluralistic trends." But those who were convincingly challenged were less receptive.[1]

Writing in *Christian Century*, where he then served as the senior editor, Martin E. Marty (January 27, 1993) claimed that "Finke and Stark's world contains no God or religion or spirituality, no issue of truth or beauty or goodness, no faith or hope or love, no justice or mercy; only winning or losing in the churching game matters." Marty knew perfectly well that our major emphasis was on faith in God. On the very first page of the book we wrote, "to the degree that denominations rejected traditional doctrines and ceased to make serious demands on their followers, they ceased to prosper. The churching of America was accomplished by aggressive churches committed to vivid otherworldliness." That theme dominated the entire book. Although chapter one now clarifies how we challenge the existing historiography of American religion, addressing the most serious charges of Marty required no revisions or additions.

In any event, our primary reason for updating this book is that, just as the trends we charted in 1990 have continued, we have continued to learn about the fundamental features of religions and the whys and wherefores of strong congregations (Stark and Finke, 2000). Fortunately, although we have taken the opportunity to fix minor glitches, draw on recent historical research, and improve our databases, we have not needed to retract any of our major arguments. Moreover we have improved on the first edition by extending our analysis to African-American religion, a rich and remarkable story that once again shows how religious freedoms allowed upstarts to compete and churches to serve as organizational havens from outside intervention. As we updated the final chapter, we also included a new section on the ethnic religious communities of recent immigrants—a story that echoes those of immigrants building ethnic religious enclaves in the nineteenth century. Despite all of the changes and updates, however, the final message remains the same. The churching of America was accomplished by aggressive churches committed to vivid otherworldliness.

Once again, we are indebted to many colleagues for their advice, encouragement, and counsel—far more than we can list here. In addition to the many we listed in the first edition, we offer thanks to Helen Rose Ebaugh, Frank Lambert, David D. Hall, Phil Schwadel, Thomas Tweed, Jennifer McKinney, and John Wilson for generously sharing their expertise. We again want to acknowledge the contributions of the late Jeffrey Hadden and James C. McCann. Jeff first made us aware of the many decades of efforts by the National Council of Churches to monopolize radio and television time for religious programs. Jim McCann alerted us to Jernegan's work in the *Atlas of the Historical Geography of the United States*, and had an enthusiasm for the project that was exceeded only by our own.

Locating the necessary documents and books for the completion of this project required the assistance of many. With the completion of the second edition, our list has grown. We are indebted to librarians at numerous institutions: the Archives of the Archdiocese of Chicago, the Billy Graham Center Library and Archives, the University of Chicago, Concordia College, the Christian Theological Seminary, Franklin College, the Garrett Evangelical Theological Seminary, Loyola University of Chicago, the Newberry Library, the University of Notre Dame, the University of St. Mary of the Lake, Purdue University, Seattle Pacific University, the Southern Baptist Theological Seminary, the University of Washington, Penn State University, Princeton Theological Seminary, and Princeton University. Benjamin and Linda de Wit of Chalcedon Books in East Lansing, Michigan, located copies of many original sources for us, including James R. Rogers's *The Cane Ridge Meeting-House*, which unexpectedly turned out to consist mainly of Barton W. Stone's autobiography.

Illustrations for this book were taken from ten different collections and benefited from the advice of archivists from many others. We offer a special note of thanks to Doreen Fast, Cathy Koves, and Wendy McDowell, curators at the Billy Graham Center Museum, for their tireless search for the perfect pictures.

Finally, and foremost, we thank Terri and Lynne.

The Churching of America, 1776–2005

Chapter 1

A New Approach to American Religious History

We did not intend to make major revisions to the history of American religion, but unless reason and arithmetic have failed us, we have done precisely that. It seems appropriate, therefore, to begin this study with an explanation of how it took shape and why we were so often forced to challenge the received wisdom about American religious history.

The most striking trend in the history of religion in America is its growth—or what we call the churching of America. The backbone of this book consists of our attempt to explore and explain how and why America shifted from a nation in which most people took no part in organized religion to a nation in which nearly two-thirds of American adults do. Along the way we shall discover that the churching of America was not simply a rise in participation. Many observers have discounted the rise in church membership on the grounds that it was accompanied by a decline in acceptance of traditional religious doctrines. But this simply isn't so. Not all denominations shared in the immense rise in membership rates, and to the degree that denominations rejected traditional doctrines and ceased to make serious demands on their followers, they ceased to prosper. The churching of America was accomplished by aggressive churches committed to vivid otherworldliness.

We began tracing this trend in church membership with quite modest aims. We intended merely to provide more adequate quantitative evidence for the study of American religion and to resolve more fully such limited questions as: How religious was colonial America? Have church membership rates risen constantly over the past two centuries or have there been cycles of ups and downs? But as our work progressed we were drawn to some rather blunt questions about the characteristics of winners and losers in a free market religious environment that exposed religious organizations to relentless competition. To be more specific, we were led to ask questions such as: Why had the leading denominations of 1776 gone into such rapid eclipse by the turn of the century? Why were the Methodists and the Baptists able to win such huge and rapid victories, making them the dominant religious organizations during the first half of the nineteenth century? And then what happened to the Methodists? Why did their nearly miraculous rise soon turn into a long downward slide?

As we assembled and constructed evidence appropriate to answering such questions, we began to discover that many general historians of American religion seemed to be ill at ease with arithmetic and "borrowed" numerical claims from one another quite uncritically. We often found that the same wrong number had been repeated by one writer after another across the decades. Some of these errors have caused major falsifications of the past. For example, general historians of American religion have passed along patently absurd statistics about Catholic membership during the latter half of the nineteenth century. Having greatly exaggerated Catholic membership, each was forced to present a very misleading historical account, as we shall see in Chapter 4.

Having noticed these things for ourselves, however, we were better prepared when we encountered the findings of Douglas H. Sweet (1976). He reported that the characterization of the religious situation in the immediate aftermath of the American Revolution as the "lowest ebb-tide" in our history was used nearly word for word by all the leading authors from Robert Baird in 1844 to Sydney Ahlstrom in 1972. Having noted the common language, Sweet traced it to a common source—Lyman Beecher's autobiography. Sweet shows that Beecher's gloomy description of the period was at best reflective of the hard time on which Congregationalism had fallen. In fact, as we shall see in Chapter 3, the Baptists and Methodists were booming in this era and the ebb-tide characterization was a myth based on the concerns of an elite few.

We shall meet variations of this myth many times as the book goes along. Frequently, a lack of religious activity is asserted when all that is lacking is a preferred brand of religious activity. In Chapter 3 we shall see that the American Home Missionary Society claimed to be a nondenominational movement devoted to bringing religion to unchurched areas. Most general historians accept this claim. However, many of the areas pronounced as unchurched by the society abounded in Baptist and Methodist churches and were lacking only in Congregationalists, Presbyterians, and Episcopalians.

In similar fashion, general historians of American religion (as well as many specialists) have been content to trust the claims of proponents of the federated church movement that there was a severe crisis facing the churches in rural America. All report that during the first three decades of the twentieth century, thousands of rural churches closed for lack of members because of the rapid decline in the rural population caused by urbanization. And everyone agrees that this state of affairs is well described as "the lamentable over churching of many rural communities" (Sanderson, 1942, p. 318). But, as will be discussed in Chapter 6, far from shrinking, the rural population continued to grow substantially throughout the period. Although some denominations were closing rural congregations, others were opening new ones at such a rate that the total number of rural churches grew. The real concerns of the proponents of federated churches had to do with rural America's taste for "unsuitable" denominations.

By the latter half of the twentieth century, sociologists and historians scrambled to explain the sudden rise of the conservative faiths and the rapid decline of the more liberal "mainline" denominations. We will show that this trend was well underway two centuries earlier. The trend of growing upstart sects and declining mainline denominations has been in place since at least 1776. What everyone noticed in the twentieth century was a decline in the membership totals of the mainline bodies. But, long before this decline in membership, mainline market share (or percentage of all religious adherents) was showing a steady decline.

We offer more than an improved numerical profile of the churching of America, we also offer a new explanation. Whereas, "Great Awakenings" loom large in traditional histories of American religion, emphasizing sudden cultural change and new demand for religion, we stress changes in religious supply. As the state and local regulation of American religion declined, a growing supply of energetic clergy actively marketed their faiths, new churches arose without resistance, and a rich variety of new religious options emerged. Rather than searching for sudden shifts in religious demand, we will draw attention to how new religious freedoms changed the incentives and opportunities for churches, preachers, and revivalists. Ironically, the earliest accounts of American religion, written by European authors for Europeans audiences, gave extensive attention to the "voluntary principle" and the new "sect system" that were arising. They spoke with candor and detail about the new "religious economy" and the "competition" that arose as upstart sects were allowed to freely compete with the older religious bodies in America.

We will review a few of their comments and explanations before briefly introducing our own.

The Voluntary Principle Revisited

European scholars and church leaders visiting nineteenth-century America often used explicit market terms when they described the unique voluntary principle and the open competition that resulted from separating church and state. In 1834, when Andrew Reed was sent by the Congregational Union of England and Wales to assess American churches, he offered strong views about America's "Religious Economy": "Deliberately, but without hesitation, I say, *the result is in every thing and every where most favourable to the voluntary, and against the compulsory principle*" [italics in original]. Basing his conclusions on visits, interviews, and an extensive collection of quantitative data on churches, communicants, and ministers, Reed explained that "the ministry has been supplied with better men; the men have been better maintained. Churches have been revived where they languished, and they have been created in abundance where they did not exist" (Reed and Matheson, 1835b, pp. 137, 141).

Writing in 1837, Francis Grund, an Austrian who eventually became an American citizen, explained why the American clergy were so energetic: "In America, every clergyman may be said to do business on his own account, and under his own firm. He alone is responsible for any deficiency in the discharge of his office, as he alone is entitled to all the credit due to his exertions. He always acts as principal, and is therefore more anxious, and will make greater efforts to obtain popularity, than one who serves for wages." Like Andrew Reed, Grund used the language of economics to discuss this surge in religious activity: "The actual stock in any of these firms is, of course, less than the immense capital of the Church of England; but the aggregate amount of business transacted by them jointly may nevertheless be greater in the United States" (in Powell, 1967, p. 77).

Perhaps the most celebrated European visitor of the early nineteenth century, Alexis de Tocqueville ([1835] 1969, pp. 295, 296, 298) made similar observations. Like other European visitors he immediately noticed the "innumerable multitude of sects" and the religious zeal of the clergy and their members. He commented that "the religious atmosphere of the country was the first thing that struck me on arrival in the United States." When he asked others to explain this atmosphere, he reported that "all agreed ... the main reason for the quiet sway of religion over their country was the complete separation of church and state." De Tocqueville added that the "facts convinced me that I had been told the truth" and he later concluded that "any alliance with any political power whatsoever is bound to be burdensome for religion." Like Reed, Grund, and many other European visitors, de Tocqueville traced his explanation for the multitude

Cobbett's Observations on Taxes and Priests

The prominent and colorful English traveler William Cobbett (1818) explained to his neighbors and friends in England why churches supported by taxes and the power of the state hold little appeal to the people (in Powell, 1967, pp. 43–44, 46–47).

Taxes and Priests; for these always lay on heavily together ... I will, on these subjects, address myself more immediately to my old neighbours of Botley, and endeavour to make them understand what America is as to taxes and priests....

I have talked to several farmers here about the tithes in England; and they *laugh* ... they seem, at last, not to believe what I say, when I tell them that the English farmer gives, and is compelled [by law] to give, the Parson a tenth part of his whole crop.... They cannot believe this. They treat it as a sort of *romance*....

But, my Botley neighbours, you will exclaim, "No *tithes!* Why, then, there can be no *Churches* and no *Parsons!* The people must know nothing of God or Devil; and must all go to hell!" By no means, my friends. Here are plenty of Churches. No less than three Episcopal (or English) Churches; three Presbyterian Churches; three Lutheran Churches; one or two Quaker Meeting-houses; and two Methodist Places; all within *six miles* of the spot where I am sitting. And, these, mind, not poor shabby Churches; but each of them larger and better built and far handsomer than Botley Church, with the Church-yards all kept in the neatest order, with a head-stone to almost every grave. As to the Quaker Meeting-house, it would take Botley Church into its belly, if you were first to knock off the steeple.

Oh no! Tithes are not necessary to promote *religion*. When our Parsons ... talk about *religion*, or *the church*, being in danger; they

(continued)

mean that the *tithes* are in danger. They mean that they are in danger of being compelled to work for their bread.

But for the fact is, that it is the circumstance of the church being established by law that makes it of little use as to real religion. . . . Because . . . establishment forces upon the people, parsons whom they cannot respect. . . .

The most likely way to insure [a clergyman is both sincere and industrious] is to manage things so that he may be in the first place, selected by the people, and, in the second place, have no rewards in view other than those which are to be given in consequence of his perseverance in a line of good conduct.

And thus it is with clergy in America, who are duly and amply rewarded for their diligence, and very justly respected for the piety, talent, and zeal which they discover; but, who have no tenure of their places other than that of the will of the congregation.

of sects, the religious zeal of the clergy, and the grassroots support for religion to the separation of church and state, or what was commonly called the new voluntary principle.

Two of the earliest surveys of American religion, not surprisingly, used the voluntary principle to explain the unique religious economy of America. Initially written for European audiences, *America*, by Philip Schaff (1855), and *Religion in the United States of America*, by Robert Baird ([1844] 1969), invoked volunteerism as the cause of the unusually high level of religious activity and the growing number of sects in the United States. Swiss-born, German-educated Philip Schaff (1855, p. 11) quoted with favor an "impartial" Austrian editor: "The United States are by far the most religious and Christian country in the world . . . because religion is there most free." Baird ([1844] 1969, p. 409) devoted one of the eight sections of his book to explaining the voluntary principle. At the close of this section he concluded that the voluntary principle "has brought gospel influences to bear in every direction." For Baird and Schaff the "facts" seemed obvious: religious freedoms increased the involvement of the people and stimulated evangelical activity.

But Schaff and Baird were keenly aware of the charges coming out of Europe against the new voluntary principle. Schaff acknowledged that the "shady side" of the new sect system "changes the peaceful kingdom of God into a battle-field, where brother fights against brother" (1855, pp. 99, 102). Yet, both writers came to the defense of the new system. Schaff promised that the new system "will produce something far more grand and glorious, than Catholicism," and Baird devoted an entire chapter to address the "Alleged Want of Harmony Among the Evangelical Christians of the United States" ([1844] 1969, pp. 607, 610). He argued that many of the charges were based on "gross misrepresentation" and gave personal testimony on how the "enlightened members of one denomination respect and esteem those of another."

In the surveys of American religion that followed, however, the voluntary principle fell from favor and only the hope for denominational unity remained.[1] Despite the attempts of Sidney E. Mead ([1975] 1963), Franklin Littell (1962), John F. Wilson (1965), Frank Lambert (2003), and others to emphasize the transforming power of religious freedom, their views were submerged by the prevailing wisdom that competition was an unfortunate consequence of liberty. In his review of Sydney Ahlstrom's monumental history of American religion, Mead (1973, pp. 49–52) lamented that the "'Puritan Epoch' motif seems to provide the standard for judging the historical significance of everything in the religious history of the American people . . . while somewhat less than two pages are given to the sections on 'Church-State Relations and Religious Freedom.'"

Ahlstrom was not alone. Martin E. Marty, Winthrop S. Hudson, and others of this era all chose to ignore the organizational aspects of the history of American religion, including the rise and fall of denominations, and instead cast the history of American religion as a history of religious ideas. There is nothing wrong with writing histories of ideas, of course. But when general historians have done so, they nearly always adopt (at least implicitly) a model of intellectual "progress." Their history is organized on the basis of showing how new religious ideas arose and were progressively refined. Moreover, the standards against which refinement is usually judged are entirely secular—parsimony, clarity, logical unity, graceful expression, and the like. One seldom encounters standards of theological progress or refinement based on how effectively a doctrine could stir the faithful or satisfy the heart. As a result, the history of American religious ideas always turns into an historical account of the march toward liberalism. That is, religious ideas always become more refined (i.e., better) when they are shorn of mystery, miracle, and mysticism—when an active supernatural realm is replaced by abstractions concerning virtue.

This preference for theological refinement distorts the story in significant ways. First, it draws attention to the mainstream Protestant churches' efforts in reducing differences and seeking unity. After reviewing twelve church mergers between 1906 and 1940, William Warren Sweet ([1930] 1950, p. 424) proclaimed "there is hope for a better day." Twenty years later in the *Righteous Empire* Martin E. Marty (1970, p. 244) described the momentum of Protestant churches as "centrifugal" in the nineteenth century and "centripetal" in the twentieth. He explained that "they noted the limits of their competition and division, experienced frustration in mission around the world, and began to draw back together in the ecumenical, or Christian unity, movement." As we will see in Chapter 6, however, such optimistic assessments of unity required the general historians to ignore a rapidly growing number of conservative movements. Hence, when viewed through the lens of theological refinement, the growing sects and minority religions are consigned to historical insignificance.

More recent surveys of American religion have shifted attention from the Protestant insiders to the religious outsiders. This focus reveals the rich diversity of religious experiences in American history, offering an important corrective to previous surveys, but makes little effort to tie these experiences to a larger story. A new generation of historians has abandoned the model of theological refinement, but they now struggle to find a coherent thesis for explaining the disparate religious histories (see Tweed, 1997; Tweed et al., 2002). Like the nineteenth-century European visitors before us, we will use economic language to explain the new sect system and the churching of America.

In this book, the history of American religion is the history of human actions and human organizations, not the history of ideas (refined or otherwise). But this is not to say that we regard theology as unimportant. To the contrary, we shall argue repeatedly that religious organizations can thrive only to the extent that they have a theology that can comfort souls and motivate sacrifice. In a sense, then, we are urging an underlying model of religious history that is the exact opposite of one based on progress through theological refinement. We shall present compelling evidence that theological refinement is the kind of progress that results in organizational bankruptcy.

On Religious Economies

Some readers may shudder at the use of market terminology in discussions of religion, but we see nothing inappropriate in acknowledging that where religious affiliation is a matter of choice, religious organizations must compete for members and that the "invisible hand" of the marketplace is as unforgiving of ineffective religious firms as it is of their commercial counterparts. We are not the first to use an explicit market model to explore the interplay among religious organizations. Indeed, as we shall see in Chapter 2, Adam Smith did so very persuasively back in 1776. Economic principles will serve as tools for understanding religious change, but they imply nothing about the merits of such change.

We will use economic concepts such as markets, firms, market penetration, and segmented markets to analyze the success and failure of religious bodies. Religious economies are like commercial economies in that they consist of a market made up of a set of current and potential customers and a set of firms seeking to serve that market. The fate of these firms will depend upon (1) aspects of their organizational structures, (2) their sales representatives, (3) their product, and (4) their marketing techniques. Translated into more churchly language, the relative success of religious bodies (especially when confronted with an unregulated economy) will depend upon their polity and local congregations, their clergy, their religious doctrines, and their evangelization techniques.

The use of economic tools in no way suggests that the content of religion is unimportant, that it is all a matter of clever marketing and energetic selling. To the contrary, we will argue that the primary market weakness that has caused the failure of many denominations, and the impending failure of many more, is precisely a matter of doctrinal content, or the lack of it. That is, we will repeatedly suggest that as denominations have modernized their doctrines and embraced temporal values, they have gone into decline.

The primary value of analyzing American religious history through a market-oriented lens is that in this way some well-established deductions from the principles of supply and demand can illuminate what might otherwise seem a very disorderly landscape (as it indeed often appears to be in standard histories of the subject). Consider the following examples.

A major consideration in analyzing religious economies, as in the analysis of commercial economies, is their degree of regulation. Some are virtually unregulated; some are restricted to state-imposed monopolies. In keeping with supply and demand principles, to the degree that a religious economy is unregulated, pluralism will thrive. That is, the "natural" state of religious economies is one in which a variety of religious groups successfully caters to the special needs and interests of specific market segments. Religious variety arises because of the inherent inability of a single product to satisfy very divergent tastes. Or, to note the specific features of religious firms and products, pluralism arises because of "normal" variations in the human condition such as social class, age, gender, health, life experiences, and socialization.

In fact, because of this underlying differentiation of consumer preferences, religious economies can never be successfully monopolized, even when a religious organization is backed by the state. At the height of its temporal power, the medieval church was surrounded by heresy and dissent. Of course, when repressive efforts are very great, religions in competition with the state-sponsored monopoly will be forced to operate underground. But whenever and wherever repression falters, lush pluralism will break through.

Sociologists have long been fascinated with religious pluralism and its consequences for the religious landscape. Unfortunately, their grasp of both economics and history has been imperfect. The received wisdom is that pluralism weakens faith—that where multiple religious groups compete, each discredits the other and this encourages the view that religion per se is open to question, dispute, and doubt. Peter Berger (1967, 1979) offers the most eloquent and effective argument for this position. His early work is suffused with a very European belief that religious disintegration set in when pluralism shattered the "sacred canopy" of "one true faith" that inspired the universal piety we often associate with the medieval village.

Historical evidence says otherwise. There is ample evidence that in societies with putative monopoly faiths, religious indifference, not piety, is rife. Perceptions to the contrary are nostalgic error. As we shall see in the next chapter, in the Puritan Commonwealth of Massachusetts religious adherence probably never exceeded 22 percent. It is becoming increasingly well known that religious participation was very low in medieval Europe (Stark, 2003). And today, close inspection of the religious situation in societies where "everyone" is a Roman Catholic reveals levels of religious participation that are astonishingly low compared with those in America—the exceptions being places such as Ireland and Poland where the church has served as the primary vehicle for political resistance to external domination (Stark and McCann, 1989; Stark and Finke, 2000).

In addition to being based on bad history, faith in the power of monopoly religions is rooted in bad economics. We have already noted that the inability of the monopoly church, despite its sacred canopy, to mobilize massive commitment is inherent in the segmentation of any religious economy. A single faith cannot shape its appeal to suit precisely the needs of one market segment without sacrificing its appeal to another. Where many faiths function within a religious economy, a high degree of specialization as well as competition occurs. From this it follows that many independent religious bodies will, together, be able to attract a much larger proportion of a population than when only one or very few firms have free access.

A second, equally compelling, principle of economics also applies: Monopoly firms tend to be lazy. This is most evident when we look at the clergy. Whether it comes in the form of support or suppression, state regulation changes the incentives and opportunities of the clergy (Finke, 1990). In contrasting the American and European religious situations, Francis Grund (1837) noted that establishment makes the clergy "indolent and lazy," because "a person provided for cannot, by the rules of common sense, be supposed to work as hard as one who has to exert himself for a living" (in Powell, 1967, p. 77). The clergy must now openly compete for adherents and their churches now rely on the resources of the adherents, not the state, for survival. The survival of the churches and the support of the clergy are no longer ensured by state subsidies.

When applied to American religion, we will find that lifting regulations eases entry into the religious market. In other words, the start-up costs for new religions and new churches is greatly reduced. This principle is especially important for new religions. Whether they are new faiths favored by immigrants (e.g., Catholic, Lutheran, Jewish, Hindu, or Islamic) or religions developed on American soil (e.g., Disciples of Christ, Mormons, or Jehovah Witnesses), the lack of regulations allows them to start new congregations without facing persecution from the state. The autonomy of the local congregations also allows them to develop distinctive ethnic, racial, and religious subcultures that provide a wide array of services for their members. Chapters 4, 5, and 7 will show how churches can serve as the organizational foundation for the unique language, cultural, and political interests of their members. But the ease of entry into the religious market benefits more than the new religions. Low start-up costs allow new churches from any religion to quickly emerge in new or changing settlements. Because new churches can now arise without seeking permission from the state or existing congregations, the supply of religions quickly matches the demand for religion.

Lifting regulations also gives all clergy new freedoms. Regardless of pedigree, training, or support from the established religions, clergy are free to preach and seek a following. As we will see in Chapter 3, these freedoms unleashed a new supply of clergy in the young nation. Once again, Grund offers a pithy assessment: "The Americans, therefore, enjoy a threefold advantage: they have more preachers; they have more active preachers, and they have cheaper preachers than can be found in any part of Europe" (in Powell, 1967, p. 80). When the refined and educated clergy were unwilling or unable to serve an area, a host of self-supporting or poorly paid clergy would arise. Time and time again we will find these clergy opening new churches in areas of population growth and supporting existing churches in rural areas or small communities where only a handful of followers can be found. But we will also find that they can effectively compete for adherents throughout the nation and over time.

Finally, the deregulation of religion leads to a constant stream of new innovations. Throughout American history we will find that the upstarts are a source of innovations in music, communication, religious education, preaching, revival, and organizational strategies (Finke, 2004). The new freedoms unleashed entrepreneurial religions, churches, and clergy that sought new ways of appealing to the people. The flurry of new techniques, fueled by the power of their religious beliefs, resulted in the churching of America.

Rather than cloud the story of American religion with opaque economic terms, we will use basic market principles to explain the success and failure of religious organizations. However, we shall postpone more extended discussion of this and other details until the need arises in the chapters that follow. Now we turn to the empirical foundation for our study and preview initial results.

Data on American Religion

In 1962 the distinguished American demographer William Petersen published an essay on religious statistics in the United States in which he flatly stated that the "census in this country has no data on religion." In addition, Petersen lamented, few denominations possessed more than fragments of historical data on their membership, and they were of dubious reliability. Worse yet, the religious data from national opinion polls were "not an adequate substitute for official statistics" (1962, p. 166).

Although Petersen's essay was published in a journal for specialists in the social scientific study of religion, many of them sophisticated quantitative data analysts, no one raised the slightest challenge to his claims for they were not controversial. Unlike national census forms in Canada, and in many nations of Europe and Latin America, the United States Census has never asked citizens to report their personal religious affiliation. Hence, it seemed self-evident that quantitative studies of American religious history are precluded.

Fortunately, Petersen was wrong. At the time he wrote, an amazing array of "official statistics" on religion could be found in any well-stocked university library. Indeed the United States Census began to collect detailed statistical information from all American religious bodies—from the largest to the most obscure—every ten years from 1850 through 1890 (with a gap for 1880) and then from 1906 through 1936. Many eastern states also conducted their own census at mid-decade, and many of these include religious statistics. Furthermore, after federal and state governments ceased gathering religious statistics in the 1940s, private organizations soon filled the gap—although these data offer little more than membership counts.

How could generations of scholars have remained ignorant of what was clearly a massive census undertaking? Indeed, how could demographers, and especially their graduate students, fail to notice a whole shelf of books of religious statistics located alongside the regular census volumes? In fact they didn't overlook them—the books weren't missed, they were dismissed. We have since talked with many demographers who noticed these volumes while in graduate school, but in each case they were informed by faculty members that these statistics were nothing but junk that the census bureau should never have bothered with. Why? Because they were not based on tabulations of individual responses to a question on the regular census form. Instead, they were based on reports prepared by individual pastors or boards of elders. And, it was claimed, such people were not to be trusted. The figures would necessarily be hopelessly inflated.

These professors of demography seem to have known little about American religion and to have never bothered to examine the data with care. Hopelessly inflated statistics are precisely what are obtained when individuals are asked their religious affiliation. Ever since the start of public opinion polling in the late 1930s, surveys have found that approximately 85–95 percent of the population claims a religious affiliation.[2] More careful investigation reveals that for many, their claim to a religious affiliation amounts to nothing more than a vague recollection of what their parents or grandparents have passed along as the family preference. Consider that substantial numbers of students at major universities commit the most unlikely spelling errors when filling out a questionnaire item on their denomination. Can students who think they go to the Pisscaple Church have ever seen the word Episcopal? Or what of Presditurians? If one wishes to know which churches have how many members (that is, people sufficiently active to have their names on the membership rolls), one needs to visit churches and count the rolls. Or one can ask how many names are on the rolls. But it takes very careful and elaborate research techniques to calculate membership by summing the responses given by individuals.

Rather than being hopelessly inaccurate, then, there are strong prima facie grounds for thinking that these old census statistics are relatively accurate. But there are other strong indications of their accuracy as well. The first of these is that the numbers claimed by the churches are modest. The national rate of religious adherence based on the 1890 data is only 45 percent. Second, the data are extremely stable over space and time. Had there been substantial local misrepresentation, then the data ought to jump around between nearby communities, and they do not. By the same token, if they were inaccurate there should have been a great deal of inconsistency from one decade to the next, and there is not. Finally, the Bureau of the Census was very concerned with accuracy and provided extensive, sophisticated, and persuasive evaluations of its procedures.[3]

These volumes offer a glittering array of scholarly possibilities. For example, each set of volumes contains a carefully researched section reporting on the history, doctrine, and organizational features of every religious body in the nation, along with detailed statistics on such things as total membership (also separated by age and by sex), Sunday school enrollment, number of congregations, value of church property, amount of debt, total expenditures, ministers' salaries, contributions to foreign missions, and so on—presented separately for every state. In addition, statistical summary volumes organize membership data by counties and for all cities with more than 25,000 inhabitants.

To provide a glimpse of these materials, we reproduced two sample pages from the 1926 volumes. The first is part of a one-and-a-half page table for the city of Buffalo, New York. Here we can see the inclusiveness of the Bureau's definition of a religious body. In 1926 the Baha'is had one church and 15 members, all of them age thirteen and over. The

A page from the 1926 census of religious bodies showing a portion of the detailed membership statistics for Buffalo, New York. (From Bureau of the Census, 1930, vol. I.)

CITY AND DENOMINATION	Total number of churches [1]	MEMBERSHIP BY AGE [2]				SUNDAY SCHOOLS [3]		
		Total number [4]	13 years and over	Under 13 years	Per cent under 13 [5]	Churches reporting	Officers and teachers	Scholars
Brookline, Mass.—Continued.								
Jewish Congregations	4	7,500				2	22	530
Methodist bodies:								
Methodist Episcopal Church	1	810	789	21	2.6	1	24	375
Presbyterian bodies:								
Presbyterian Church in the United States of America	1	448	448			1	25	344
Protestant Episcopal Church	3	2,745	2,217	528	19.2	3	90	612
Roman Catholic Church	3	9,975	7,975	2,000	20.1	3	57	1,739
Unitarians	2	522	522			2	23	177
Universalist Church	1	295	268	27	9.2	1	16	45
Buffalo, N. Y.	341	351,907	236,275	75,677	24.3	261	5,201	66,037
Adventist bodies:								
Seventh-day Adventist Denomination	3	267	254	13	4.9	1	29	158
American Rescue Workers	3	53	36	17		3	4	37
Bahá'is	1	15	15					
Baptist bodies:								
Baptists—								
Northern Baptist Convention	25	6,265	5,904	194	3.2	25	534	5,322
Negro Baptists	5	2,383	2,285	98	4.1	5	71	856
Brethren, Plymouth:								
Plymouth Brethren I	1	52	52			1	9	100
Plymouth Brethren II	2	213	213			2	34	225
Catholic Apostolic Church	1	136	125	11	8.1	1	5	55
Christadelphians	2	77	77			2	8	36
Christian and Missionary Alliance	1	73	73			1	14	100
Church of Armenia in America	1	126	92	34	27.0			
Church of Christ, Scientist	3	939	939			2	111	594
Church of God (Headquarters, Anderson, Ind.)	1	40	39	1		1	6	50
Church of God and Saints of Christ	1	8	7	1				
Church of God in Christ	2	115	72	3		2	10	75
Churches of God, Holiness	1	105	80	25	23.8	1	9	70
Churches of the New Jerusalem:								
General Convention of the New Jerusalem in the United States of America	1	59	39	20		1	4	59
Congregational Churches	5	1,385	1,186	12	1.0	5	77	833
Disciples of Christ	8	2,534	1,674	70	4.0	8	196	1,987
Eastern Orthodox Churches:								
Greek Orthodox Church (Hellenic)	1	1,632	655	977	59.9			
Roumanian Orthodox Church	1	300	269	31	10.3	1	1	20
Russian Orthodox Church	1	2,550	1,800	750	29.4			
Evangelical Church	6	1,069	1,042	27	2.5	6	103	914
Evangelical Synod of North America	20	10,634	10,634			20	554	5,073
Friends:								
Religious Society of Friends (Hicksite)	1	30						
Jewish Congregations	14	20,000				1	16	300
Latter-day Saints:								
Church of Jesus Christ of Latter-day Saints	1	58	40	18		1	4	25
Reorganized Church of Jesus Christ of Latter Day Saints	1	107	100	7	6.5	1	13	45
Liberal Catholic Church	1	27	24	3				
Lutherans:								
United Lutheran Church in America	15	14,347	10,437	3,910	27.3	15	390	4,410
Evangelical Lutheran Augustana Synod of North America	1	406	258	148	36.5	1	12	101
Evangelical Lutheran Synodical Conference of America—								
Evangelical Lutheran Synod of Missouri, Ohio, and Other States	12	6,562	4,588	1,974	30.1	12	178	1,867
Lutheran Synod of Buffalo	4	1,525	942	263	21.8	4	70	669
Methodist bodies:								
Methodist Episcopal Church	27	10,667	9,494	548	5.5	27	801	9,451
Free Methodist Church of North America	2	140	140			2	21	288
African Methodist Episcopal Church	1	300	225	75	25.0	1	15	125
African Methodist Episcopal Zion Church	2	780	711	69	8.8	2	64	430
Colored Methodist Episcopal Church	1	80	75	5		1	8	60

See footnotes on p. 360.

Christadelphians had two churches and 77 members. The Swedenborgians, already split into two denominations, appear under the heading of "Churches of the New Jerusalem."

The second page is one of seven tables from the section devoted to the Methodist Episcopal Church. Summary statistics are given for several of the measures collected by the Bureau and are broken down by urban and rural territory. Notice how very disproportionately female the Methodists had become, having but 66.8 males for every 100 female members.

Initially, we believed that the Census Bureau began this massive work in 1890, but we soon discovered that they had actually begun in 1850, piggybacking the project on the regular census conducted that year. In addition to their other duties, local census supervisors (often U.S. deputy marshals) were asked to assemble a list of every organized religious body meeting in the community and then to visit each with a questionnaire. This was repeated in 1860 and 1870. For reasons that remain obscure, the census of religious bodies for 1880 was never published and now is thought to be lost. But publication was resumed in 1890. The project was then shifted to the sixth year of the decade in order to relieve the workload on the Bureau of the Census—so the next one was conducted in 1906, and again in 1916, 1926, and 1936. Unfortunately, the 1936 census was distorted by the decision of some bodies not to report and the efforts to conduct the 1946 religious census were suspended after a number of groups challenged its propriety.[4]

But even this wealth of data didn't allow us to make meaningful membership comparisons over the full span of American history or across all major denominations. We had to overcome three obstacles. First, we had to provide church membership estimates prior to 1890. Despite collecting many details on American churches by county and for each denomination, the 1850, 1860, and 1870 censuses failed to ask the number of church members. And, prior to 1850, they didn't collect any data on the churches. Second, we needed to have a comparable standard for church membership across denominations. The most serious difference was that some denominations, such as Catholics and Lutherans, count baptized infants as members, whereas many groups count only those who have given a testimonial or profession of faith. The final obstacle was finding

A page from the 1926 census of religious bodies showing a portion of the detailed membership statistics for the Methodist Episcopal Church. (From Bureau of the Census, 1930, vol. 2.)

METHODIST EPISCOPAL CHURCH

STATISTICS

Summary for the United States, with urban-rural classification.—A general summary of the statistics for the Methodist Episcopal Church for the year 1926 is presented in Table 1, which shows also the distribution of these figures between urban and rural territory.

In the Methodist Episcopal Church persons are received into full membership upon public profession of faith (usually after six months' probation) and a pledge to conform to the discipline and rules of the church. Baptism is required and those baptized in infancy must publicly renew their vows.

TABLE 1.—SUMMARY OF STATISTICS FOR CHURCHES IN URBAN AND RURAL TERRITORY, 1926: METHODIST EPISCOPAL CHURCH

ITEM	Total	In urban territory [1]	In rural territory [1]	PER CENT OF TOTAL	
				Urban	Rural
Churches (local organizations)	26, 130	5, 489	20, 641	21. 0	79. 0
Members	4, 080, 777	2, 212, 180	1, 868, 597	54. 2	45. 8
Average per church	156	403	91		
Membership by sex:					
Male	1, 518, 791	818, 438	700, 353	53. 9	46. 1
Female	2, 274, 615	1, 228, 612	1, 046, 003	54. 0	46. 0
Sex not reported	287, 371	165, 130	122, 241	57. 5	42. 5
Males per 100 females	66. 8	66. 6	67. 0		
Membership by age:					
Under 13 years	313, 840	164, 350	149, 490	52. 4	47. 6
13 years and over	3, 250, 505	1, 782, 927	1, 467, 578	54. 9	45. 1
Age not reported	516, 432	264, 903	251, 529	51. 3	48. 7
Per cent under 13 years [2]	8. 8	9. 1	9. 2		
Church edifices:					
Number	25, 570	5, 516	20, 054	21. 6	78. 4
Value—Churches reporting	25, 290	5, 358	19, 932	21. 2	78. 8
Amount reported	$406, 165, 659	$274, 162, 895	$132, 002, 764	67 5	32. 5
Average per church	$16, 060	$51, 169	$6, 623		
Debt—Churches reporting	5, 064	2, 286	2, 778	45. 1	54. 9
Amount reported	$42, 749, 854	$35, 971, 915	$6, 777, 939	84. 1	15. 9
Churches reporting "no debt" on church edifice	15, 346	2, 433	12, 913	15. 9	84. 1
Parsonages:					
Value—Churches reporting	13, 665	4, 362	9, 303	31. 9	68. 1
Amount reported	$60, 724, 434	$32, 057, 564	$28, 666, 870	52. 8	47. 2
Debt—Churches reporting	2, 041	976	1, 065	47. 8	52. 2
Amount reported	$4, 547, 967	$3, 159, 937	$1, 388, 030	69. 5	30. 5
Churches reporting "no debt" on parsonage	8, 805	2, 568	6, 237	29. 2	70. 8
Expenditures during year:					
Churches reporting	25, 790	5, 466	20, 324	21. 2	78. 8
Amount reported	$89, 422, 307	$57, 411, 370	$32, 010, 937	64. 2	35. 8
Current expenses and improvements	$68, 949, 285	$43, 038, 086	$25, 911, 199	62. 4	37. 6
Benevolences, missions, etc	$20, 462, 262	$14, 372, 684	$6, 089, 578	70. 2	29. 8
Not classified	$10, 760	$600	$10, 160	5. 6	94. 4
Average expenditure per church	$3, 467	$10, 503	$1, 575		
Sunday schools:					
Churches reporting	24, 730	5, 404	19, 326	21. 9	78. 1
Officers and teachers	382, 043	156, 744	225, 299	41. 0	59. 0
Scholars	3, 796, 561	1, 910, 259	1, 886, 302	50. 3	49. 7

[1] Urban territory includes all cities and other incorporated places which had 2,500 inhabitants or more in 1920, the date of the last Federal census; rural territory comprises the remainder of the country.
[2] Based on membership with age classification reported.

comparable data after the census quit collecting data on religion in 1936. If we could fill in these gaps, it would be possible to chart the churching of America for over two hundred years.

Extending the Timeline: Turning Pews into People

Our greatest challenge was developing accurate estimates of church membership prior to 1890. The lack of membership statistics in the mid-nineteenth-century census reports was especially frustrating. For every church in the nation, we know details such as the value of the church buildings and land, the number of organizations sponsored by each, and the seating capacity of the church. But we have no information on how many of those pew seats were ever filled. Because the 1890 census takers still asked about total seating capacity, the value of church property, and total membership, we were able to construct a statistical procedure that, in effect, turned counts of pews into counts of people. The details of such predictive models have been reported elsewhere (Finke and Stark, 1986). The logic involved was to construct a predictive model using 1890 data. The value of church property, the number of organizations, and the seating capacity were used to predict the actual membership of denominational groups in 1890. When this attempt turned out to be successful (Finke and Stark, 1986), we then applied the predictive models to the 1850, 1860, and 1870 data to provide the missing membership statistics. As a check on these results, we compared our national totals with estimates reported in Edwin S. Gaustad's *Historical Atlas of Religion in America* and with available denominational statistics. The match-up was very close, giving us confidence that our estimates of membership are adequate substitutes for the actual statistics.

Yet, even with these new estimates, we couldn't return to the late eighteenth and early nineteenth century, when the churches were responding to new religious freedoms and expanding into new frontiers. With the help of our colleague James C. McCann, however, we discovered two essential sources for constructing a reliable and detailed statistical portrait of religion in 1776. The first is the *Atlas of the Historical Geography of the United States*, by Charles O. Paullin, edited by John K. Wright, and published jointly by the Carnegie Institution of Washington and the American Geographical Society of New York in 1932. The second is a series of publications on colonial clergy and congregations compiled by

Frederick Lewis Weis, published by the Society of the Descendants of the Colonial Clergy (Weis, 1936, 1938, 1950, 1955).

The *Atlas* was one of the truly great team projects ever conducted by American historians. In 1903 the first outline of the project was proposed by J. F. Jameson, then professor of American history at the University of Chicago. Several years later Jameson became director of the department of historical research at the Carnegie Institution and serious work began. Those helping fashion this great mapping of American history make up a Who's Who of early twentieth-century scholars. For example, Frederick J. Turner played a leading role until his death and the mapping of American Indian materials was supervised by A. L. Kroeber. While some of the maps in the *Atlas* are unremarkable, having been based on well-known data, many others were based on extensive primary research (gathered over the nearly thirty years that the project lasted).

One of the most amazing of these original research projects involved an effort to identify and locate *every church congregation* in America for the period from January 1, 1775 to July 4, 1776! This project was directed by M. W. Jernegan, a University of Chicago historian who specialized in the colonial period (cf. Jernegan, 1931). How good are these data? They were produced by what appears to have been an exhaustive search of old documents, diaries, newspapers, and accounts to note every mention of a church and then to search out its location.[5] The procedures, described at some length by Jernegan, strike us as wholly practical, requiring simply the application of substantial resources—and these seem to have been plentiful at the Carnegie Institution during this time. In describing the data, Jernegan wrote that he probably could not be off by more than 150 churches—or less than 5 percent (and clearly he thought he had missed many fewer).

The *Atlas* reported on the total number of churches in 1776 (3,228), the number of churches for each denomination, and provided a separate map for each denomination, with a dot designating the location of each congregation. Nothing of their original work remained in the Carnegie Institution's archives, so we counted dots in order to recover the actual numbers of congregations for each denomination in each colony. Unfortunately, for some denominations, their density was so great in parts of some colonies that solidly black areas resulted and not even computer enhancement techniques were of any use in deciphering them. The map that gave the greatest difficulty was the one for the Congregationalists (see Figure 1.1). Clearly there are areas in Connecticut, Massachusetts, and New Hampshire that cannot be counted. When a denomination

CONGREGATIONALIST
1775-1776

One dot for each church (see text)

produced only one uncountable area, the problem was solved by sub-
tracting the counted dots from the total, since Jernegan reported the total number of congregations for each denomination. But when we were
unable to decipher multiple colonies we turned to one of Frederick Lewis
Weis's volumes on the colonial clergy for help.

The Colonial Clergy and the Colonial Churches of New England (Weis, 1936),
listed all men who had ever held pulpits in New England during colonial times. And in the last section of the book, the names were listed by
congregation, showing the period of tenure of each man to hold that pulpit
(there were, in effect, no female clergy in this era). This gave an independent list of all the Congregationalist churches by location. By elimi-
nating those not shown to have been occupied in 1776, it was possible
to create the missing Congregationalist statistics for Connecticut, Massachusetts, and New Hampshire. This volume, and others by Weis (1938,
1950, 1955) containing similar data for the other colonies, filled in the
blanks everywhere the dots were too thick to count. By comparing Weis's
lists with dot counts it was also possible to cross-check the sources. The
level of agreement between Weis and Jernegan was consistently very high
(see Stark and Finke, 1988). In this way it proved possible to reconstruct
a detailed portrait of the denominational make-up of America on the eve
of the Revolution. Finally, as will be explained in Chapter 2, we established a basis for estimating the number of members in a denomination
from the number of its churches.

The final two obstacles for charting and comparing church membership were far easier to overcome, though equally important. As noted
earlier, some denominations count children in their membership totals
while others do not. This might sound like a trivial difference, of interest only to statisticians obsessed with detail, but recall that because children
made up a very large percentage of the population in the nineteenth century, to include children in some denomination's membership totals, and
not others, results in serious biases. For example, since 39 percent of the
total population was under the age of thirteen in 1850, denominations
(such as the Baptists) that did not count their children would seem far
smaller than those (such as the Catholics) that included them, when they
might well have been of equal size.

To overcome this potential error, we use a correction technique that
was developed by denominational statisticians (Johnson et al., 1974). This

Figure 1.1. Jernegan's Map of Congregationalist Congregations in 1776, Showing the Uncountable Areas. (From Paullin, 1932, Plate 82.)

technique allows us to develop an adherence estimate for each denomination that includes children.[6] By factoring in children thirteen years of age and under for denominations that did not count children, we can now significantly reduce biases when making comparisons across denominations and over time. Not only does this measure give us greater confidence when comparing Catholics to Baptists, it also helps to standardize the measure over time as the percentage of the population under thirteen sharply declines. We should caution, however, that this measure does not include everyone who might have ever attended or once affiliated with a church. As just noted, this would produce a meaningless measure that includes the vast majority of the population. Instead, we are striving to determine the number of people, including adults and their children, who are *members* of a church.

The final obstacle was to obtain comparable contemporary data on church adherence. Here our choice was obvious. The most complete series of church and church membership studies were conducted by the National Council of the Churches of Christ in the USA in 1952, 1971, and 1980, and by the Association of Statisticians of American Religious Bodies in 1990 and 2000. Lacking the resources or the authority of the census bureau, the collections are far less complete and offer less detail, but they do provide comparable statistics on religious adherents. When supplemented with data from the *Yearbook of American and Canadian Churches* and other sources, we can offer estimates of the percent of the population holding membership in a local church.

1776–1980: The Churching of America

At this point it seems appropriate to present the primary fruits of our adventures with religious statistics. Figure 1.2 plots the overall trend in the rate of religious adherence for two centuries. This pattern can truly be called the churching of America. On the eve of the Revolution only about 17 percent of Americans were churched. By the start of the Civil War this proportion had risen dramatically, to 37 percent. The immense dislocations of the war caused a serious decline in adherence in the South, which is reflected in the overall decline to 35 percent in the 1870 census. The rate then began to rise once more, and by 1906 slightly more than half of the U.S. population was churched. Adherence rates reached 56 percent by 1926. Since then the rate has been rather stable although inching upwards. By 1980 church adherence was about 62 percent.

FIGURE 1.2 Rates of Religious Adherence, 1776–2000

This is the phenomenon we shall try to explain in this book. Why did the rate rise so greatly? Which denominations contributed most to the great increase in religious adherence, and which failed to benefit?

Disclaimer

We must emphasize that this book *is not* a general historical account of religion in America. Our aim is to place the history of American religion within a dynamic, interpretive model and to correct some major misconceptions. To do this does not require that we cover every significant topic or include every significant figure—indeed, such inclusiveness would have produced an exhausting work in which the model would have been buried in detail. Our decisions about what to include have been based on what is most pertinent to our analysis. Thus we give extensive coverage to George Whitefield and to Charles Grandison Finney in order to dispel claims about Great Awakenings, but we make no mention of two equally important figures, Dwight L. Moody and Billy Graham. Moreover, many religious groups of considerable historical and cultural significance are also essentially ignored, including Jews, Christian Scientists, Disciples of Christ, Jehovah's Witnesses, Mormons, Pentecostals, Unitarians, and the many Eastern Orthodox bodies. We also have paid no attention to nineteenth-century millenarian movements, to Mennonites, or to the Amish. Lutherans are mentioned only in passing. We have added several pages on African-American churches, but our account unveils only a small segment of the rich story that historians are now revealing.

We justify these omissions on the grounds that our primary aim is not to *describe* the history of American religion, but to *explain it*. To the best of our knowledge we have omitted nothing that would modify any of our conclusions.

Chapter 2

The Colonial Era Revisited

DAMN

[Nostalgia is the enemy of history.] No educated person any longer believes that the ancients were correct about a fall from a Golden Age. Yet
we frequently accept equally inaccurate tales about more recent "good
old days"—tales that corrupt our understanding of the past and mislead
us about the present.

Americans are burdened with more nostalgic illusions about the colonial era than about any other period in their history. Our conceptions
of the time are dominated by a few powerful illustrations of Pilgrim scenes
that most people over forty stared at year after year on classroom walls:
the baptism of Pocahontas, the Pilgrims walking through the woods to
church, and the first Thanksgiving. Had these classroom walls also been
graced with colonial scenes of drunken revelry and barroom brawling,
of women in risque ball-gowns, of gamblers and rakes, a better balance
might have been struck. For the fact is that there never were all that many
Puritans, even in New England, and non-Puritan behavior abounded.
From 1761 through 1800 a third (33.7%) of all first births in New England
occurred after less than nine months of marriage (D. S. Smith, 1985), despite
harsh laws against fornication. Granted, some of these early births were
simply premature and do not necessarily show that premarital intercourse
had occurred, but offsetting this is the likelihood that not all women who
engaged in premarital intercourse would have become pregnant. In any
case, single women in New England during the colonial period were more
likely to be sexually active than to belong to a church—in 1776 only about
one out of five New Englanders had a religious affiliation. The lack of
affiliation does not necessarily mean that most were irreligious (although

For generations of American schoolchildren this picture *was* the colonial era, supposedly an age of piety and faith: devout Puritans walk through the snow to church, many of the men bearing arms as protection against Indians. The schools chose not to hang portrayals of colonial revelers alongside those of the churchgoers. But Boston's taverns were probably fuller on Saturday night than were its churches on Sunday morning. (Courtesy of the Billy Graham Center Museum, Wheaton, Ill.)

some clearly were), but it does mean that their faith lacked public expression and organized influence.

In several colonies, especially Massachusetts, small religious minorities dominated public life to the extent that they gave the illusion of nearly universal membership. Indeed, because the Congregationalists were the established church in New England and drew support from all taxpayers, they sometimes placed their membership close to the total population figure. The Congregationalist minister Ezra Stiles, for example, set the number of Congregationalists in New England in 1760 at 445,000, or just about 4,000 persons short of the total population of the time (Sweet, 1939, p. 3).[1] Such optimistic counting, combined with the superficial aura of respectability sustained by legalized Puritanism, often badly misled visitors about the religious situation. The Church of England's Society for the Propagation of the Gospel in Foreign Parts reported that New England was the "only well-churched area in the American colonies" (in Ahlstrom, 1975, vol. 1, p. 215). Not only was there no well-churched area in America, however, but New England's religious adherence rate was not significantly higher than that of the Middle Colonies, and New Jersey and Pennsylvania had slightly higher rates than Massachusetts. What

were the denominational profiles of the colonies on the eve of the Revolution? Why, in particular, were so few of the colonists church members?

Religious Adherence

When M. W. Jernegan presented his detailed maps of churches by colony
and denomination in the *Atlas of the Historical Geography of the United States*,
he also listed the total number of churches for each denomination. Table
2.1 presents the totals by denominations for all 3,228 congregations. As
might be expected, the Congregationalists had the most churches and
the Presbyterians were a solid second. But many will be surprised that
the Baptists were already in third place, exceeding the Episcopalians
by two congregations. Interestingly, there were only five synagogues in
the nation by 1776: Rhode Island, New York City, and Georgia had one
each and two were in South Carolina. However, although counting dots
on the *Atlas* maps and consulting Weis's (1936, 1938) data on clergy allow us to break these denominational totals down by colony, even this
information doesn't answer the question of how many people belonged
to these congregations.

Historians of American religion have long noted that the colonies did
not exude universal piety. There was a general agreement that in the colonial period no more than 10–20 percent of the population actually belonged to a church (Sweet, 1947; Ahlstrom, 1975; Hudson, 1981). These
were offered as ballpark figures and were admittedly not based on actual counts. But more recent work by the highly regarded colonial church
historian Patricia U. Bonomi and her coauthor Peter R. Eisenstadt (1982)
concludes that the church adherence rate was 80 percent in 1700, 75.1
percent in 1750, and 59 percent in 1780. These estimates are so far outside the ballpark figures accepted by earlier general historians that they
would require an entirely different playing field. Indeed, the lowest estimate in 1780 is nearly three times higher than the highest previous estimate. Using the colonial church data collected by Jernegan and Weis
and various congregational statistics, we calculated totals that are in agreement with the ballpark estimates of general historians, but which, because they are based on some actual statistics, provide greater precision
and fuller detail.

To develop these membership estimates, the first step was estimating the average size of congregations in 1776, for then membership rates
required nothing but simple multiplication. We began by looking at the

TABLE 2.1
Number of Congregations per Denomination, 1776

Denomination	Number of congregations
Congregational	668
Presbyterian*	588
Baptist†	497
Episcopal	495
Quakers	310
German Reformed	159
Lutheran§	150
Dutch Reformed	120
Methodist	65
Catholic	56
Moravian	31
Separatist and Independent	27
Dunker	24
Mennonite	16
Huguenot	7
Sandemanian	6
Jewish	5
TOTAL	3,228

SOURCE: Paullin (1932).
*Includes all divisions such as New Light, Old Light, Associate Reformed, etc.
†Includes all divisions such as Separate, Six Principle, Seventh Day, Rogerene, etc.
§Includes all synods.

1890 census. Here the average Protestant congregation in the nation had 91.5 members. Surely they would have been smaller than this in 1776, because population density was commonly cited by religious leaders of the time as a primary barrier to sustaining churches. But if churches were smaller in 1776, how much smaller were they? This question caused us to search for any membership statistics that might have survived.

The Methodists have quite complete and apparently accurate statistics for this period. The 1776 *Minutes of the Annual Conference of the Methodist Episcopal Church* report a total membership of 4,921. If we divide this number by the 65 Methodist congregations reported by Jernegan, we arrive at an average of 75.7 members. This is closely matched by Baptist data. Rufus Babcock (1841) reported that the average Baptist congregation in 1784 had 74.5 members. In 1790, John Asplund reported the results of an eighteen-month, seven-thousand-mile journey (most of it on foot) to visit all the Baptist congregations, which he numbered at 867 with a total of 65,233 members, or an average of 75.2. Congregationalist statistics are reported by state associations since the national body was not formerly organized until 1871, and are relatively few. When the 1866 *Congregational Quarterly* assembled the scattered statistics, they found the average size of the congregation rapidly rising, yet still small. The congregational size had risen to 109 members in Massachusetts by 1830, but remained far smaller in the more rural states. In 1857, Maine reported only 70 members per church. Each of these averages would have been lower in 1776. Finally, Herman C. Weber (1927) reported that in 1826 the average Presbyterian congregation had 70 members.

Let us cautiously assume that the average congregation in 1776 had 75 members. If we multiply this by the 3,228 known congregations, we arrive at a total of 242,100 members. Factoring in children, in order to be comparable with later data, and dividing by the total population produces a national religious adherence rate of 17 percent for 1776. This percentage falls nicely within the ballpark limits, but holds two significant advantages. First, the estimate is based on an actual enumeration of churches and on an average congregational size supported by church records. Second, we can offer statistical profiles by colony and denomination.

Before turning to this profile, however, we should briefly explain why our rates vary so dramatically from Bonomi and Eisenstadt's adherence estimate of 59 percent for 1780. We first checked to see if they had located more churches than Jernegan. The opposite was true. Their estimate for 1780 was based on 2,731 churches, 497 churches fewer than Jernegan's total despite being four years later. The source of the significant difference was that Bonomi and Eisenstadt estimated that each church had 480 adherents, compared to our estimate of 75 members (or about 106 adherents) per church. Relying primarily on the reports of Anglican clergy responding to the Bishop of London's queries in 1724, they assumed that each colonial congregation has an average of 80 active families, with an average of 6 members per family for a total of 480 adherents per church. Even for the Anglicans, these clergy reports strike us as works of fiction. Although the immorality and incompetence of the Anglican clergy exiled in America might have been overstated by early historians, their sloth was not. The colonial Anglican clergy were a world apart from their distant bishop and faced little accountability for their behavior and even less for the accuracy of their reports.

Moreover these reports sent home to Britain bear little resemblance, not only to data reported by other denominations, but to fragmentary evidence reported to an American audience by Protestant Episcopal churches. Using the Protestant Episcopal General Convention reports for 1832 and 1841 and their *Church Almanac* for 1861, we found the average congregational size was 43 in 1832, 54 in 1841, and 67 in 1860 (Protestant Episcopal Church, 1832; 1841; 1861).[2] By 1890 the census reports that Protestant Episcopal churches averaged 106 members per church, only slightly higher than the average Protestant church.

At best, we might suggest that the estimates reported by Bonomi and Eisenstadt more accurately reflect the percentage of the population that claimed a religious identity or who had stepped foot through church doors at some time in their lives—just as 85 percent of the population today claims religious affiliation and church attendance. But Bonomi was clear that this was more than a religious identity. She would later write that "recent estimates suggest that a majority of adults in the eighteenth-century colonies were regular church attenders" (Bonomi, 1986, p. 87). Too much data, from too many independent sources, suggest that the estimates presented so aggressively by Bonomi and Eisenstadt are spurious.[3]

Table 2.2 offers a profile of adherence rates by colony and region. The rates have been rounded to the nearest whole number because the use of even one decimal place would give an unwarranted impression of precision. There is substantial variation, from as low as 7 percent in Georgia and 9 percent in Vermont and North Carolina, up to 26 percent in New Jersey, 24 percent in Pennsylvania, and 22 percent in Massachusetts. The rates for New England (20 percent) and for the Middle Colonies (19 percent) are essentially the same, but the rate for the Southern Colonies (12 percent) is substantially lower. This difference is partly an artifact of slavery.

In 1776 slaves made up 42 percent of the population of the Southern Colonies and they are included in the population denominators on which the adherence rates are based. But, in those days very few slaves belonged to a church. Jernegan himself wrote in 1916: "Though so many forces . . . were favorable to the conversion of slaves, progress was nevertheless exceedingly slow, and the results attained at the opening of the Revolu-

TABLE 2.2
Religious Adherence Rates by Colony, 1776 (in percent)

Colony	Adherence rate	White adherence rate
NEW ENGLAND	20	20
Maine	19	20
New Hampshire	20	20
Vermont	9	9
Massachusetts	22	22
Rhode Island	20	20
Connecticut	20	20
MIDDLE COLONIES	19	20
New York	15	17
New Jersey	26	26
Pennsylvania	24	24
Delaware	20	22
Maryland	12	17
SOUTHERN COLONIES	12	20
Virginia	12	22
North Carolina	9	14
South Carolina	14	31
Georgia	7	20
NATIONAL	17	20

SOURCE: The data in Table 2.2, 2.4, 2.5, and A.1 are based on a series of esti-
mation procedures described in the text. The number of congregations is estimated
from Paullin (1932) and Weis (1936, 1938, 1950, 1955); the number of members per
congregation is estimated from existing denominational totals.

tion were comparatively meager" (p. 526). In fact, the Church of England
held until well into the nineteenth century that blacks were not sufficiently human to be baptized and several British colonies imposed heavy
fines on Quakers for doing so (Stark, 2003). In addition, the formality of
worship styles, rigid organizational structure, and requirements of extensive religious instruction were significant barriers to the conversion of
slaves (Raboteau, 1978; Butler, 1990; Andrews, 2000).

For this reason the adherence rates in Table 2.2 have also been calculated using only the total white population in the denominators. With this taken into account, all regional differences disappear. New England, the Middle Colonies, and the Southern Colonies all have the same rate as the nation overall, 20 percent. In our judgment, the rates based on whites only are probably a bit too high—it is certain that some blacks were churched in this period. The true rates for the Southern Colonies, therefore, probably lay somewhere between the two rates shown.

If we now know approximately how many church members there were in each colony, to what denominations did they belong? The data on numbers of churches allow us to present regional profiles of denominational make-up (see Table 2.3). To the degree that it was churched at all, New England was a bastion of Congregationalism. The Baptists were second, followed by a scattering of Episcopalian, Presbyterian, and Quaker congregations.

Compared with the other regions, New England was very lacking in diversity. Not only was there no dominant denomination in the other regions, but there was strong representation by "non-British" denominations—German and Dutch Reformed, Lutheran, and Moravian—especially in the Middle Colonies. This too emphasizes that New England was well named, for it was equally lacking in terms of ethnic diversity— its limited set of British denominations reflected its almost exclusively British ethnicity. The 1790 census classified 82 percent of the population of Massachusetts as English, as compared with 52 percent in New York and 35 percent in Pennsylvania. Adding in Scots and Protestant Irish accounted for 90 percent of the residents of Massachusetts, but only two thirds of New Yorkers and just over half of Pennsylvanians. Even the Southern Colonies had considerable religious and ethnic diversity in this period. Interestingly, the immense success of Baptists in the South had already begun.

Appendix Table A.1 presents similar breakdowns for each colony. There are no real surprises here, but the data suggest that many historical generalizations are rather exaggerated.

As expected, Rhode Island is the most Baptist of colonies, but it wasn't very Baptist. Given that only about half of its churches were Baptist and that only 20 percent of Rhode Islanders were churched, only about one person in ten would have been a Baptist.

Next, examine the profile of the "Quaker State." Quakers made up only the third largest denomination in Pennsylvania, far behind the Presbyterians, and behind the German Reformed. Moreover, Quakers represented less than 5 percent of Pennsylvanians. Indeed, Quakers were more common in Delaware and North Carolina.

TABLE 2.3

Denominational Percentages by Region, 1776, Based on Number of Congregations

NEW ENGLAND (N = 1,039)	
Congregationalist	63.0
Baptist	15.3
Episcopal	8.4
Presbyterian	5.5
Quaker	3.8
Other*	3.6
MIDDLE COLONIES (N = 1,285)	
Presbyterian	24.6
Quaker	14.1
Episcopal	12.9
German Reformed	9.8
Dutch Reformed	8.9
Lutheran	8.6
Baptist	7.6
Roman Catholic	4.2
Methodist	3.8
Moravian	1.8
Congregationalist	0.3
Other*	3.1
SOUTHERN COLONIES (N = 845)	
Baptist	28.0
Episcopal	27.8
Presbyterian	24.9
Quaker	9.0
Lutheran	3.8
German Reformed	2.8
Methodist	1.4
Moravian	0.6
Congregationalist	0.1
Roman Catholic	0.1
Other*	1.2

SOURCE: See Table 2.2.
NOTE: Only 3,169 of Jernegan's 3,228 congregations could be located by colony.
*"Other" includes Separatist and Independent, Dunker, Mennonite, Huguenot, Sandemanian, and Jewish.

Founded by Lord Baltimore as a haven for Roman Catholics, Maryland was the most Catholic colony in 1776. But that wasn't very Catholic— about three people in a hundred.

In any event, what is most noticeable about religion in the colonial era is how poorly the denominations were doing. To put it another way, these firms had failed to make any serious dent in the market. Whatever their religious needs, preferences, or concerns, the vast majority of Americans had not been reached by an organized faith. What factors produced such a lack of religious mobilization? And was anything brewing? Were new firms about to inject new methods and energy into the religious economy?

To begin to answer these questions, it is important to realize that most colonial settlements, even in the eighteenth century, were part of an untamed frontier. Everyone knows that in the "Wild West" of the nineteenth century, towns such as Dodge City, Tombstone, and Deadwood were not filled with God-fearing, Sunday-go-to-meeting folks, but were

Appearing on the front page of *Harper's Weekly* in the early 1880s, these pictures served to authenticate nostalgic memories of colonial religion. The picture to the left was entitled "Early Settlers on Their Way to Church," and for the picture to the right the caption read "The Call to Church—Early Colonial Times in New England." (Courtesy of the Billy Graham Center Museum, Wheaton, Ill.)

wide open, lawless capitals of vice and violence. Why should it have been any different when the frontier boom towns were New York or Charleston?[4] It wasn't. On any given Sunday morning there were at least as many people recovering from late Saturday nights in the taverns of these seaport towns as were in church.

The Sociology of Frontiers

By definition, a frontier is an area of new settlement and rapid population growth. As a result, frontiers are populated with newcomers and strangers. Quite aside from whether those attracted to frontiers tend to be deficient in moral character, wherever large numbers of people lack social ties, or what are often called interpersonal attachments, the result is social disorganization.

The real basis of the moral order is human relationships. Most of us conform to laws and social norms most of the time because to do otherwise would risk our relationships with others. When we are alone, even the most respectable of us act in ways we would not were anyone present. People who have no relationships with family or close friends, or whose relationships are with persons far away, are essentially alone all the time. They do not risk their attachments if they are detected in deviant behavior, because they have none to lose. Even in highly settled, stable communities some people are deficient in attachments, and it is they who are apt to engage in deviant behavior. In frontier areas, *most* people are deficient in attachments, and hence very high rates of deviant behavior exist.

Moreover, in areas where people are constantly passing through and where most people are strangers and newcomers, it is very difficult to sustain organizations of any kind, be they churches, fraternal lodges, or political clubs (Berry and Kasarda, 1978; Wuthnow and Christiano, 1979; Welch, 1983; Finke, 1989). People are recruited into and kept active in such organizations through social networks—through their attachments to others who also take part (Stark and Bainbridge, 1980, 1985). Where such networks are lacking, group actions are more apt to take the form of outbursts of collective behavior, such as riots or mob actions, than to be structured and directed by formal organizations.

As a result, frontiers will be short on churches, and long on crime and vice, simply because they *are* frontiers (Stark et al., 1983; Finke, 1989). And this imbalance will be greatly amplified because of *who* tends to migrate to frontiers.

Who Migrates?

Studies of migration stress two factors: those that *push* people to leave a place and those that *pull* them to somewhere else. Among the major pushes are (1) lack of opportunity, (2) weak attachments, (3) fear of punishment, (4) disgrace, and (5) persecution. Of the five, only the last (and then only when groups are involved) is likely to cause "solid citizens" to migrate. Lack of opportunity can produce desirable migrants too, but the other three will tend to overproduce troubled and troublesome migrants. Those who lack attachments tend to be people who have difficulty forming and maintaining relationships. Those who fear punishment have usually offended, as have those in disgrace.

The major pulls are (1) economic opportunity, (2) anonymity and escape, and (3) greater freedom. Again, the last may attract very desirable migrants—as it did in the case of persecuted religious minorities who came to America. And economic opportunity can draw desirable migrants as well as undesirables.

When the total set of pushes and pulls is examined, however, two typical features of migrants to frontiers emerge. Many of them will be scoundrels, misfits, and others of dubious past and character, who are fleeing their pasts or seeking new opportunities to practice illegal or morally stigmatized activities. And most migrants will be men—some free of attachments, having no wife or family, some fleeing such responsibilities.

Thus we deduce the population of Dodge City, Tombstone, and Deadwood—towns filled with male drifters, gamblers, confidence tricksters, whores, and saloon keepers, and without churches, schools, or respectable women. Thus we also deduce many aspects of the American frontier when it was still back east. These deductions can be fleshed out with concrete facts about colonial America.

Male America: Sex Ratios

The single best measure for locating frontiers is the sex ratio, usually calculated as the number of males per 100 females. The higher the ratio—the greater the imbalance of males to females—the more frontierlike the place. This is especially the case for highly imbalanced sex ratios among younger adults.

It is very significant, therefore, that, in his monumental study in progress[5] of people leaving for America from England and Scotland between December 1773 and spring 1776, Bernard Bailyn (1986) has found

TABLE 2.4

Males per 100 Females by Colony or State

	Colonial census	1790 U.S. Census
Maine	103 (1764)	104
New Hampshire	104 (1775)	101
Vermont	117 (1771)	113
Massachusetts	97 (1764)	96
Rhode Island	97 (1774)	97
Connecticut	102 (1774)	98
New York	107 (1771)	107
New Jersey	107 (1745)	105
Pennsylvania	n.a.	106
Delaware	n.a.	109
Maryland	111 (1755)	106
Virginia	n.a.	106
North Carolina	n.a.	104
South Carolina	n.a.	109
Georgia	n.a.	104

SOURCE: Calculated from population totals reported by the Bureau of the Census (1975, vol. 1, pp. 24–37; vol. 2, pp. 1169–71).

that almost four out of five (77.8 percent) were males; and they were mostly younger males. At a time when only 18 percent of the English and Scottish populations were in the 15–24 age group, half of those leaving for America were in this category. Bailyn's records of these people after their arrival here show that they typically did not linger in the settled areas along the coast, but headed to the frontier areas.

Given these patterns, it is no surprise that in the nation as a whole there were substantially more men than women in the eighteenth century. But it is the variation across colonies that is most instructive (see Table 2.4). On the eve of the Revolution, while in the other colonies men outnumbered women, in Massachusetts and Rhode Island, the women had already come to outnumber the men, a sure sign that the frontier had moved inland. Indeed, these data indicate that the nation was already beginning to split into male and female sections: a settled East, lacking men (especially men in the most marriageable age groups), and a western frontier, lacking women. This regionalization of gender became extremely pronounced in the nineteenth century, as we shall see in later chapters.

The second column of sex ratios in Table 2.4 comes from the first U.S. Census, conducted in 1790. The westward drift of males and of the frontier comes into even, sharper focus. Aside from Maine, New York was the only state for which earlier data exist in which the sex ratio had not declined. By 1790 Connecticut had joined Rhode Island and Massachusetts as states in which the women outnumbered the men. Where were the men of New England going? A glance at a map will provide an answer and will also explain why New York's ratio did not fall.

Because New England is north of New York City, many Americans have the impression it is also north of New York State. But New Englanders heading due west are soon in New York. And by 1790 that is where the western frontier was located, and where the young, migrating males from Massachusetts, Rhode Island, and Connecticut were to be found.

It was long a favorite theme of western movies that when the "nice" women arrived, it was time to build a church, a school, and a good jail. The part about churches was most certainly true. The higher the male to female sex ratio, the lower the rate of religious adherence. In fact, in colonial America an extremely high negative correlation of –.95 exists (–1.0 is a perfect negative correlation) between the sex ratios and rates of religious adherence.

The immense importance of women for church life shows up very strongly when actual membership roles are scrutinized. In a study based on 97 Congregational churches in Massachusetts and Connecticut, Richard D. Shiels (1981) found that 64 percent of all new members were women—a fact he described as the "feminization of American Congregationalism" (p. 46). Recall from chapter 1 that the 1926 census of religious bodies showed the national Methodist membership included but 66.8 males per 100 female members. Similar sex imbalances in church membership, both here and abroad, turn up in study after study (Shiels, 1981; Stark and Bainbridge, 1985; Butler, 1990), thus confirming Cotton Mather's observation in 1691 that "there are far more Godly Women in the World than there are Godly Men" (in Cott, 1977, p. 127). One barrier to the churching of colonial America, and especially the frontier areas, was the lack of women.

Scoundrels and Knaves

Substantial numbers of those who embarked for colonial America were of solid farmer and merchant stock, coming in hopes of greatly improving their lot through honest means. But it is also true, as Bailyn has described, that among them were "many hardened criminals—thieves, black-mailers, pimps, rapists, embezzlers, and thugs available for hire" (1986, p. 295). It is estimated that from 1718 to 1775 at least 50,000 persons, most of them convicted of capital crimes, were forcibly transported to America by order of English courts. Another 16,000 or so were sent over by the courts in Ireland (Bailyn, 1986).

Transported convicts were not the only source of scoundrels and knaves in the colonies. Many immigrants of seemingly highly respectable back-grounds were nothing of the sort. This seems to have been especially true of the clergy. Unlike the Congregationalists, who were soon pro-ducing their own clergy at Harvard and Yale, many of the denomina-tions active in colonial America were dependent on clergy sent from overseas. The Episcopal Church, as the American branch of the Church of England, was served by clergy from the mother country. Many of the Presbyterian clergy were supplied by the Church of Scotland. And the Lutherans, German and Dutch Reformed, and the Roman Catholics de-pended on Europe for their pastors.

But who would come? Few were willing, and so these denominations always were short of clergy—a fact that hindered the churching of the colonies. Worse yet, in light of the constant complaints from their pa-rishioners, we must suspect that many if not most who did come seemed lacking in energy, morals, or even authentic credentials.

Edwin S. Gaustad (1987, p. 15) has reported frequent grumbling by Anglican vestrymen "about clergy that left England to escape debts or wives or onerous duties, seeing Virginia as a place of retirement or ref-uge." In 1724 Giles Rainsford, an Anglican clergyman in Maryland, sent this dispatch concerning three of his colleagues to the Bishop of Lon-don: "Mr. Williamson is grown notorious and consumate in villainy. He really is an original for drinking and swearing. Mr. Donaldson is so vile that the other day, being sent for to a dying person, came drunk, and the poor expiring soul, seeing his hopeful parson in that condition, re-fused the Sacrament at his hands and died without it. Mr. Maconchie is a mere nuisance, and makes ye church stink. He fights, and drinks on all occasions, and as I am told *alienas permolet uxores* [forces his atten-tions on the wives of others]" (in Ritchie, 1976, p. 145).

Later in the century George Whitefield ([1756] 1969) noted in his journal that the Church of England might "flourish" in the colonies "were her ministers found faithful" (p. 386). Having heard of plans by the Society for the Propagation of the Gospel in Foreign Parts to send more mission-aries to America, Whitefield noted in his journal that it would be better "that people had no minister than such as are generally sent over" (p. 387). In response to his own rhetorical question regarding why the Church of England was doing so poorly in America, he blamed the missionaries "who, for the most part, lead very bad examples" (p. 387).

Rainsford's and Whitefield's accusations were echoed later in the century by Thomas Coke (1793), the first Methodist bishop in America. After kind words for the Quakers and praise for the zeal of the Baptist clergy, Coke wrote: "But what shall we say for the Clergy of the Church of *England* in these states . . . . We would fain draw a veil over them, if the truth of history would permit it . . . they were, with a few exceptions to the contrary, as bad a set of men as perhaps ever disgraced the Church of God . . ." (in Powell, 1967, p. 37).

There also seem to have been frequent instances of people pretending to be clergy or falsely confessing to faiths they did not hold. In 1742, when Henry Melchior Muhlenberg arrived in Pennsylvania, having been sent from Germany to take charge of the Lutherans, his worst initial problem was with self-appointed and venal clergymen. Muhlenberg's *Notebook* (1959) is filled with complaints against greedy scoundrels posing as legitimate Lutheran clergy, many of them ordained by Valentine Kraft, whose claims to official standing were fraudulent.[6]

> December 1, 1742. I learned forthwith that Mr. Kraft had traveled through the whole province of Pennsylvania, appointed deacons and elders here and there, and established a general presbytery in the whole country . . . . And besides all this, he had organized a consistory of which he was the president . . . . The purpose of the presbytery was to make it possible for Valentine Kraft and his assessor to travel around the country and carry on their trade with the holy sacraments. The consistory served the purpose of letting him ordain a few more lazy and drunken schoolmasters and place them as preachers in vacant places.

> January 4, 1743. Mr. Kraft now took off his hypocritical mask . . . . He became the boon companion of some worthless, drunken schoolmasters who wander about the country as preachers and make money with the Lord's Supper, baptism, and weddings. He got drunk with these fellows and carried on high.

When Henry Muhlenberg (1711–1787) first arrived in 1742 he found his pastorate occupied by a vagabond preacher, Valentine Kraft, and his pulpit was located in barns (top) and private homes. By 1745, however, Kraft was gone and the Augustus Lutheran Church at Trappe, Pennsylvania, was dedicated (bottom). (Courtesy of the Concordia Historical Institute, St. Louis, Missouri.)

> January 9, 1743. . . . Because the schoolmasters, already described, intended to establish opposition congregations in various places and thus vex me, I made two announcements to the congregation: (1) They were not to pay anything when they had their children baptized, and (2) at the Lord's Supper there was to be no offering of money at the altar for the pastor. Since these vagabonds are concerned only to get a few shillings for a baptism and the offerings at the Lord's Supper . . . I have abolished this abominable custom. (pp. 10–14)

Perhaps the most notorious case of all involved the Catholics. Antonio de Sedella claimed to be a Capuchin friar when he appeared in New Orleans in 1781, and he may have been. Whatever the case, Sedella rapidly became superior of the Capuchins in New Orleans and vicar-general and pastor of St. Louis Cathedral. Père Antoine, as he soon came to be called, was popular in the city because of his reputation for being indulgent of moral weakness. But even the most lukewarm Catholics in New Orleans were humiliated and shocked when Père Antoine died in 1829 and, in accord with his will, was buried with Masonic rites (Hennesey, 1981).

Establishment

Thus major impediments to the churching of colonial America are common features of all frontier settings: transience, disorder, too many men, too many scoundrels, and too few effective and committed clergy. But there were other important factors as well. Writing in 1776, Adam Smith noted how legal establishment of the church saps the clergy of their "exertion, their zeal and industry." He concluded, in a passage quoted at the end of this chapter, that when clergy do not need to depend upon their parishioners for their employment and pay, they neglect their duties and do not develop the skills required to stir up commitment. Taking a similar position, Colonel Lewis Morris, former governor of the New Jersey Colony, wrote from New York to a friend about the impact of establishment upon the Episcopal Church: "If by force the salary is taken from [the people] and paid to the ministers of The Church, it may be a means of subsisting those Ministers, but they wont make many converts . . . . Whereas [without establishment] the Church will in all probability flourish, and I believe had at this day been in a much better position, had there been no act [of legal establishment] in her favor; for in the Jersies and Pennsylvania, where there is no act, there are four times the number of church men than there are in this province of N. York; and they are soe, most of them, upon principle, whereas nine parts in ten, of ours, will add no great credit to whatever church they are of; nor can it well be expected otherwise" (in O'Callaghan, 1855, pp. 322–323). Morris may have slightly exaggerated the statistics, but New York did have an unusually low adherence rate, 15 percent, compared with New Jersey's rate of 26 percent and Pennsylvania's 24 percent (see Table 2.2).

In any event, it must be noted that the two potentially most powerful religious bodies in colonial America, the Congregationalists and the Episcopalians, rested upon legal establishment. The Episcopalians enjoyed legal establishment in New York, Virginia, Maryland, North and South Carolina, and Georgia; the Congregationalists were established in New England.

In Chapter 3 we will trace the slow process of disestablishment during the first part of the nineteenth century and examine how having been established helped to block the growth and westward expansion of both denominations. But even in 1776 the effects of establishment show up strongly in the geography of Congregationalism. Where it could rely on taxpayer support, the Congregationalist Church dominated the religious landscape, albeit this feat is made much less impressive by its very low rate of market penetration (see Table 2.5). In Massachusetts, Congregationalists made up 71.6 percent of adherents, in Vermont 65 percent, in Connecticut 64.2 percent, and in Maine 60.9 percent. But aside from a weak 17.2 percent in Rhode Island, Congregationalism was effectively nonexistent in the rest of the colonies, having not even one congregation in five colonies. Neither the Congregationalists nor the Episcopalians were long on clergy strongly motivated to pursue church growth.

The Sect-Church Process

At this point in our examination of colonial religion, it is necessary to distinguish two primary forms of religious organizations—*churches* and *sects*. These are best conceptualized as the end points of a continuum made up of the *degree of tension* between religious organizations and their sociocultural environments (B. Johnson, 1963). To the degree that a religious body sustains beliefs and practices at variance with the surrounding environment, tension will exist between its members and outsiders. In the extreme case, well illustrated by the sad tales of Quakers persecuted in the Massachusetts Bay Colony, tension is so high that the group is

TABLE 2.5

Percentage Congregationalist by Colony, 1776

Colony	Percentage Congregationalist
Massachusetts	71.6
Vermont	65.0
Connecticut	64.2
New Hampshire	63.2
Maine	60.9
Rhode Island	17.2
Georgia	4.3
New York	1.8
South Carolina	1.2
New Jersey	0.4
Pennsylvania	0.0
Delaware	0.0
Maryland	0.0
Virginia	0.0
North Carolina	0.0

SOURCE: See Table 2.2.

hunted down by outsiders. When a religious body has no beliefs or practices setting it apart from its environment, no tension will exist. *Churches are religious bodies in a relatively low state of tension with their environments. Sects are religious bodies in a relatively high state of tension with their environments.*

There are intimate connections between churches and sects within any given religious economy. These were first noted by H. Richard Niebuhr in his celebrated book *The Social Sources of Denominationalism*, published in 1929. He sought to explain why Christianity was fractured into so many competing denominations. Why weren't Christians content with one church? Why did they constantly form new ones? Niebuhr might as well have asked why *all* religious groups are subject to constant schism, for all the world's faiths come in endless and disputatious variety and the answer he proposed can be generally applied.

In any event, Niebuhr's explanation of religious schism is elegantly simple. Churches and sects differ greatly in their ability to satisfy different human needs, needs that are always reflected in distinct segments of the religious market. As noted in the discussion of pluralism in Chapter 1, it is very difficult for any single religious organization to be at once very worldly and very otherworldly or both strict and permissive. Churches serve the segment of the market with less need for a strict and otherworldly faith; sects serve the segment seeking those features.

The sect-church process concerns the fact that new religious bodies nearly always begin as sects and that, if they are successful in attracting a substantial following, they will, over time, almost inevitably be gradually transformed into churches. That is, successful religious movements nearly always shift their emphasis toward this world and away from the next, moving from high tension with the environment toward increasingly lower levels of tension. As this occurs, a religious body will become increasingly less able to satisfy members who desire a high-tension version of faith. As discontent grows, these people will begin to complain that the group is abandoning its original positions and practices, as indeed it has. At some point this growing conflict within the group will erupt into a split, and the faction desiring a return to higher tension will leave to found a new sect.[7] If this movement proves successful, over time it too will be transformed into a church and once again a split will occur. The result is an endless cycle of sect formation, transformation, schism, and rebirth. The many workings of this cycle account for the countless varieties of each of the major faiths.

More recently, the process by which sects are transformed into churches has been equated with the process of secularization. Social scientists have long used the term "secularization" to identify what was regarded as the master religious trend in modern times: a decline in the plausibility of supernatural beliefs that would culminate in the disappearance of religion. For years, every retreat from a vivid, active conception of the supernatural by major Christian bodies was greeted as another confirmation of the secularization thesis. All contrary signs of continued religious vigor were dismissed as one last flare-up from a dying star.

Eventually, however, the pile of contrary evidence became so immense that even most social scientists could no longer believe that religion was on the wane. At that point it was noticed that the idea that secularization would wipe out religion rested on a very narrow grasp of the sect-church process, one limited to the transformation of sects into churches. Social scientists had correctly observed the movement away from traditional Christian teachings by some of the most prominent denominations. But they had failed to observe the response to these changes elsewhere in the religious economy. Secularization *is a self-limiting process that leads not to irreligion, but to revival* (Stark and Bainbridge, 1985, 1987). As religious bodies become increasingly churchlike they not only lose their vigor but give rise to sects that revitalize the religious tradition in new organizations. As we shall see, the result is not a decline in religion, but only a decline in the fortunes of specific religious organizations, as they give way to new ones.

It is clear that, as products of the Reformation, the primary faiths of colonial America began as sect movements. By the Revolution, many of them had become much more churchlike than sectlike. A fuller understanding of the state of religion in colonial times, therefore, requires an assessment of the secularization process and a search for signs of its self-limiting consequences—revival.

Secularization in Colonial America

What transforms sects into churches? Cotton Mather put it succinctly: "*Religion* brought forth *prosperity*, and the *daughter* destroyed the *mother*." He went on to explain that prosperity was a major threat to piety among Congregationalists, for the "*enchantments* of this world make them forget *their errand into the wilderness*" (in Ahlstrom, 1975, vol. 1, p. 215).

Two centuries later, Niebuhr (1929) gave the same answer. Sects arise to satisfy the needs of those less fortunate in pursuit of the world's goods: "In Protestant history the sect has ever been the child of an outcast minority, taking its rise in the religious revolts of the poor" (p. 19). That religion can make life bearable, even for those in extreme misery, is a central theme of traditional Christian doctrine, including the promise that faith will be rewarded in the world to come, where "the first shall be last, and the last, first." But to offer solace to the poor and downhearted, a religious body must resist many of life's "temptations." An organization filled with members or leaders who have unrestricted access to the "enchantments of this world" is severely handicapped in its capacity to serve the religious needs of the less successful.

In time, however, successful sects come to be dominated by the more successful[8]—those for whom life's pleasures are options. And thus begins the gradual accommodation to the world. Niebuhr explained, "Rarely does a second generation hold the convictions it has inherited with fervor equal to that of its fathers. . . . As generation succeeds generation, the isolation of the [sect] from the world becomes more difficult" (1929,

p. 20). With growing colonial affluence, more worldly versions of Quakerism soon emerged (Doherty, 1967) and the descendents of Mayflower voyagers and many other Puritan immigrants sought less demanding standards for membership.[9]

Yet, it was more than affluence that was eroding the fervor of the once vibrant sects. Clergy trained at Harvard and Yale, nurtured on the flowering intellectual life in New England, soon gave added impetus to secularization. In his volume on the colonial clergy of New England, Weis (1936) reported that of the 1,586 men who had ever served as pastor of a Congregational church, 1,507, or 95 percent, were college graduates. Of these more than 60 percent went to Harvard and 29 percent went to Yale.

It may be that secularization ensues whenever religion is placed within a formal academic setting, for scholars seem unable to resist attempting to explain mysteries and miracles and, failing that, to exclude them. Rather than celebrate mysteries and be thankful for miracles, religious scholars too often seek a purely rational faith. Unable to explain such things as God's origin or His purposes, they fall back on a God whose inexplicability is a function of His lack of consciousness, as in the Tao of eastern philosophers and the "ground of being" as formulated by Paul Tillich and his divinity school disciples. That is, by creating a God incapable of having purposes or of doing anything, all mysteries are solved by exclusion and all miracles are dismissed as illusions. Whether or not this corrosive effect of scholarship on religion is inevitable, this is what went on at Harvard and Yale, starting well before the Revolution. Ahlstrom (1975, vol. 1, p. 483) characterized Harvard late in the eighteenth century as "essentially and conscientiously Unitarian." And as Harvard's divinity school took shape "its faculty and students were Unitarian and remained so with few exceptions during the entire nineteenth century" (p. 483). As for Yale, in 1778 it appointed as its new president Ezra Stiles, who was of the opinion that revivals such as those led by George Whitefield depended upon driving people "seriously, soberly, and solemnly out of their wits" (p. 490).

Given the virtual monopoly on the "manufacture of ministers" enjoyed by Harvard and Yale, it is hardly surprising that the views of their faculty were shared by the Congregational clergy. The liberal faction dominated the desirable Congregationalist pulpits, from which they expressed their agreement with Stiles's views about revival and religious emotionalism. As Ahlstrom reported, "A firm opposition to revivalism and the whole pietistic emphasis on a religion of the heart was a settled conviction with the liberals" (1975, vol. 1, p. 474). Moreover, as the efforts by these

That George Whitefield (1714–1770) was cross-eyed, as shown in this 1742 engraving, can hardly have detracted from his extraordinary rhetorical skills. Benjamin Franklin, who reported so fully on Whitefield's visit to Philadelphia, did not think this worth noting. Instead, he stressed how Whitefield changed the city: "In 1739 arrived among us . . . the Rev. Mr. Whitefield. . . . The multitudes of all sects and denominations that attended his sermons were enormous . . . . It was wonderful to see the change soon made in the manners of our inhabitants; from being thoughtless or indifferent about religion, it seemed as if all the world were growing religious, so that one could not walk through the town in an evening without hearing psalms sung in different families of every street" ([1868] 1916, pp. 191–192). (Courtesy of the Massachusetts Historical Society, Boston.)

liberals to adjust doctrine to reason led rapidly to Unitarianism and deism, their opposition to emotionalism transformed their preaching style. Exhortations to repent and to be saved gave way, as Ahlstrom put it, to "a well-styled lecture, in which the truths of religion and the moral duties of man were expounded in as reasonable a manner as possible. Sermons thus became a species of polite, literature . . . Reviews of published sermons frequently were critiques of syntax and style rather than content" (pp. 474–475). The Puritan sect had given way to the Congregationalist Church.

Sect Formation and Revival

If the leading religious bodies of colonial America were eroded by secularization, and if secularization is self-limiting, where were the revivals? In several places. First of all, in the so-called Great Awakening and the revivals of George Whitefield. Second, and more significant, in the explosive successes of two classic sect movements: the Baptists and the Methodists. How these two upstart sects took center stage soon after the Revolution will be the subject of Chapter 3. But it is useful here to reflect very briefly on George Whitefield's well-planned, well-publicized, and well-financed revival campaigns. In Chapter 3 we will look more closely at the issue of "Great Awakenings" and examine the methods used by Whitefield and other revivalists. But for now we will simply focus on the story itself.

America's First Great Revivalist *George whitefield*

As the Congregational clergy began to substitute lectures on theology for heartfelt sermons of conviction, their flocks began to shrink. Some drifted away to the Baptists, where they could hear preachers who still preached; others probably just drifted. Into this inviting vacuum came the Grand Itinerant, George Whitefield.

Whitefield was an Englishman and belonged to the Holy Club at Oxford along with John and Charles Wesley, the eventual founders of Methodism. After Oxford, Whitefield did some preaching in England and then felt called to Georgia. There he met with considerable success before having to return to England in order to be ordained a priest in the Church of England. In England, like the Wesleys, Whitefield was barred from many pulpits because of his enthusiastic revivalist approach. And like

George Whitefield's Journal: Visit to Boston, October 1740

Sunday, October 2: Spoke to as many as could, who came for spiritual advice. Preached, with great power, at Dr. Sewals meeting-house, which was so exceedingly thronged, that I was obliged to get in at one of the windows . . . . Went with the Governor, in his coach, to the common, where I preached my farewell sermon to near twenty thousand people—a sight I have not seen since I left Blackheath—and a sight, perhaps never seen before in America. It being nearly dusk before I had done, the sight was more solemn. Numbers, great numbers, melted into tears, when I talked of leaving them. I was very particular in my application both to rulers, ministers, and people, and exhorted my hearers steadily to imitate the piety of their forefathers; so that I might hear, that with one heart and mind, they were striving together for the faith of the Gospel . . . .

Boston is a large, populous place, and very wealthy. It has the form of religion kept up, but has lost much of its power. I have not heard of any remarkable stir for many years. Ministers and people are obliged to confess, that the love of many is waxed cold. Both seem to be too much conformed to the world. There is much of the pride of life to be seen in their assemblies. Jewels, patches, and gay apparel are commonly worn by the female sex. The little infants who were brought to baptism, were wrapped up in such fine things, and so much pains taken to dress them, that one would think they were brought thither to be initiated into, rather than to renounce, the pomps and vanities of this wicked world. There are nine meeting-houses of the Congregational persuasion, one Baptist, one French, and one belonging to the Scots-Irish. There are two monthly, and one weekly lectures; and those, too, but poorly attended. I mentioned it in my sermons, and I trust God will stir up the people to thread more frequently the courts of His house. One thing Boston is very remarkable for, viz., the external observance of the Sabbath. Men in civil offices have a regard for religion. The Governor encourages them; and the ministers and magistrates seem to be more united than in any other place where I have been. Both were exceedingly civil during my stay. I never saw so little scoffing, and never had so little opposition. Still I fear, many rest in a head-knowledge, are close Pharisees, and have only a name to live.

the Wesleys, he often preached in open fields or from the steps of buildings fronting on public squares. Soon he returned to America.

Whitefield was quite simply one of the most powerful and moving preachers ever to hold forth. His voice and style were so potent that David Garrick, the most famous English actor of the time, claimed that Whitefield could seize the attention of any crowd merely by pronouncing "Mesopotamia," (W. W. Sweet, 1944). He could be heard and understood by very large crowds, even outdoors. In his *Autobiography*, Benjamin Franklin reported that Whitefield:

> had a loud and clear voice, and articulated his words and sentences so perfectly that he might be heard and understood at a great distance. . . . He preached one evening from the top of the courthouse steps, which are in the middle of Market Street and on the west side of Second Street, which crosses it at right angles. Both streets were filled to a considerable distance. Being among the hindmost in Market Street, I had the curiosity to learn how far back he could be heard by retiring backwards down the street toward the river, and I found his voice distinct till I came near front street . . . . This reconciled me to the newspaper accounts of his having preached to twenty-five thousand people in the field . . . . By hearing him often I came to distinguish easily between sermons newly composed and those which he had often preached in the course of his travels. His delivery of the latter was so improved by frequent repetition that every accent, every emphasis, every modulation of voice was so perfectly well turned and well placed that, without being interested in the subject, one could not help being pleased with the discourse, a pleasure of much the same kind with that received from an excellent piece of music. This is an advantage itinerant preachers have over those who are stationary, as the latter cannot well improve their delivery of a sermon by so many rehearsals. ([1868] 1916, pp. 196–198)

Wherever Whitefield preached, whether in the Middle Colonies or in New England, pandemonium broke loose. Whitefield's crusade for Christ, as it no doubt would be called today, had been preceded by some effective local revivals, especially those led by Jonathan Edwards. But these were sideshows compared with the outburst generated by Whitefield. In Philadelphia, huge crowds gathered—attracting even skeptics like Franklin. In Boston, large numbers were turned away every time Whitefield preached, so he moved outdoors—especially after the tragedy in Reverend Checkley's Meeting House. And when Whitefield finally departed Boston by ship, after a whirlwind visit up the coast, a crowd perhaps as large as 30,000 turned out on the Common to bid him

Among Benjamin Franklin's most famous aphorisms is "A fool and his money are soon parted." These views give added zest to Franklin's confession of how Whitefield's preaching in behalf of funds for the orphanage he founded in Georgia opened his purse: "I happened soon after to attend one of his sermons, in the course of which I perceived he intended to finish with a collection, and I silently resolved he should get nothing from me. I had in my pocket a handful of copper money, three or four silver dollars, and five pistoles in gold. As he proceeded, I began to soften and concluded to give him the coppers. Another stroke of his oratory made me ashamed of that and determined me to give the silver; and he finished so admirably that I emptied my pocket wholly into the collectors dish, gold and all" ([1868] 1916, p. 194). (Courtesy of the National Portrait Gallery, Smithsonian Institution, Washington, D.C.)

farewell. The magnitude of Whitefield's reception can be more fully appreciated by noting that in 1740 the total population of Boston was only about 20,000 (Chandler and Fox, 1974).

Crowds didn't just come to listen to Whitefield. Moved by his extraordinary power, thousands fell to the ground and cried out to God

when Whitefield thundered, "Are you saved?"—and then explained why the answer was "No!" Whitefield was not satisfied to indict only his crowds for their sins. He attacked the local clergy for the predicament of their flocks: "I am persuaded, the generality of preachers [in New England] talk of an unknown and unfelt Christ. The reason why congregations have been so dead, is because they have had dead men preach to them" (Oct. 9, 1740; [1756] 1969, p. 471).

Visits to Harvard and Yale convinced him that they were places where "Light is become darkness." Thousands wept at each place Whitefield departed, but most of the local clergy remained dry-eyed.

With Whitefield gone, the fires soon died down. But several primary results lived on to shape American religion. First, Whitefield demonstrated the immense market opportunity for more robust, less secularized religion. In doing so he provided the model for itinerancy. If you have no pulpit, what does it matter? Preach anywhere people will gather. Soon scores, then hundreds, and eventually thousands followed in his footsteps, ministering to the nation. Second, it was not the "mainline" denominations of the colonies that gathered the primary fruits of Whitefield's awakening of religious sentiments. After all, many of their clergy agreed with Ezra Stiles that Whitefield's results were gained by driving his crowds into madness. Many of those brought shivering and trembling to salvation by Whitefield ended up in Baptist congregations, causing a sudden spurt of growth that carried them past the Episcopalians to become the third largest American denomination by 1776. Not only did many of Whitefield's converts end up Baptists, but his revival methods also took root among the Baptists and subsequently were adopted by the sect movement developing within the Church of England, nourished by Whitefield's old friends, the Wesley brothers. Although Whitefield himself steadfastly refused to become a Methodist, he was in many ways the man who did most to launch the Methodist movement in America.

To conclude this chapter and to set the appropriate stage for the next, let us return to Adam Smith and his analysis in *The Wealth of Nations* of why denominations that have been established faiths are so weakened as to be swept away when and where an unregulated religious economy comes into being.

> [Clergy] may either depend altogether for their subsistence upon the voluntary contributions of their hearers; or they may derive it from some other

fund to which the law of their country may entitle them; such as a landed estate, a tythe or land tax, an established salary or stipend. Their exertion, their zeal and industry are likely to be much greater in the former situation than in the latter. In this respect the teachers of new religions have always had a considerable advantage in attacking those ancient and established systems of which the clergy, reposing themselves upon their benefices, had neglected to keep up the fervour of faith and devotion in the great body of the people; and having given themselves up to indolence, were altogether incapable of making vigorous exertion in defence even of their own establishment. The clergy of an established and well-endowed religion frequently become men of learning and elegance, who possess all the virtues of gentlemen; but they are apt gradually to lose the qualities, both good and bad, which gave them authority and influence with the inferior ranks of people, and which had been the original causes of the success and establishment of their religion. . . . in general every religious sect, when it has once enjoyed for a century or two the security of a legal establishment, has found itself incapable of making any vigorous defence against any new sect which chose to attack its doctrine or discipline. Upon such occasions the advantage in point of learning and good writing may sometimes be on the side of the established church. But the arts of popularity, all the arts of gaining proselytes, are constantly on the side of its adversaries. In England those arts have been long neglected by the well-endowed clergy of the established church, and are at present chiefly cultivated by the dissenters and by the methodists. The independent provisions, however, which in many places have been made for dissenting teachers, by means of voluntary subscriptions, of trust rights, and other evasions of the law, seem very much to have abated the zeal and activity of these teachers. They have many of them become very learned, ingenious, and respectable men; but they have in general ceased to be very popular preachers. The methodists, without half the learning of the dissenters, are much more in vogue. ([1776] 1937, pp. 740–741)

Thus Smith noted in 1776 that in England the Anglican establishment slept, the Calvinist dissenters dozed, and only the "methodists" had fire in their bellies and brimstone on their minds. On this side of the Atlantic it was much the same. Established faiths had drawn such a tepid response from the population that few Americans were churched. Many of their clergy had indeed become "men of learning and elegance," who flocked to Harvard and Yale, scorning the "arts of gaining proselytes."

But upstart forces stirred. Rough and ready itinerants were on the prowl, men who firmly believed that the whole world was to be saved.

FIGURE 3.1 Religious Adherents by Denomination, 1776 and 1850 (as percentage of total adherents)

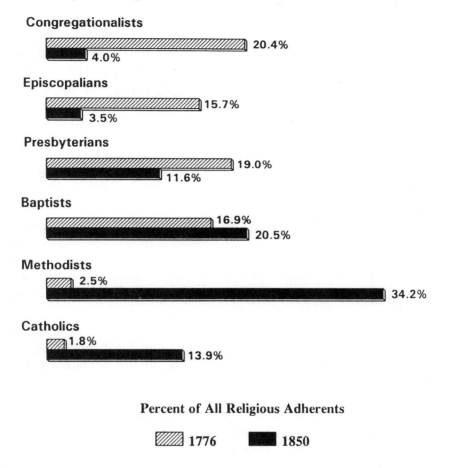

Congregationalists
20.4%
4.0%

Episcopalians
15.7%
3.5%

Presbyterians
19.0%
11.6%

Baptists
16.9%
20.5%

Methodists
2.5%
34.2%

Catholics
1.8%
13.9%

Percent of All Religious Adherents

1776   1850

denomination in 1776, it can only be described as a minor body less than eight decades later—falling from more than 20 percent of total adherents to but 4 percent. Despite this extraordinary shift in their fortunes, Congregationalist leaders during this era expressed surprisingly little concern, aside from complaints about a general decline in religion during the late eighteenth century. Perhaps they didn't think in terms of rates, and instead took pride in the fact that their number of members had more than tripled. It was not until the 1960s, when the failures of the Congre-

Chapter 3

The Upstart Sects Win America, 1776–1850

In 1776 the Congregationalists, Episcopalians, and Presbyterians seemed to be the colonial denominations. Of Americans active in a religious body, 55 percent belonged to one of the three. And at the time it seemed certain that these groups would continue to be the "mainline" for the foreseeable future. Indeed, in 1761 Ezra Stiles using a demographic projection technique taught him by Benjamin Franklin, proclaimed that one hundred years hence there would be seven million Congregationalists in the colonies and fewer than four hundred thousand Baptists. But by 1860 there were actually fewer than five hundred thousand Congregationalists in America, while the Baptists numbered nearly two million. What happened?

In this chapter we argue that, perhaps ironically, the decline of the old mainline denominations was caused by their inability to cope with the consequences of religious freedom and the rise of a free market religious economy. But before taking up these matters, it will be helpful to examine the great shift in religious fortunes that occurred between 1776 and 1850.

If we compare the "market share" of major bodies in 1776 and 1850 (see Figure 3.1), we see that in 1776 the Congregationalists, Episcopalians, and Presbyterians dominated—although their overall market penetration was very poor. Then, in just seventy-four years, the combined market total of these three bodies shrank to only 19.1 percent of religious adherents, even though the proportion belonging to churches had about doubled, to 34 percent.

For Congregationalism, the shift approached total collapse. The major gationalists first turned into losses in actual numbers rather than just in market share, that serious expressions of alarm were heard.[1]

The Episcopalians also fared badly in terms of their share of the religious market, falling from a strong second to last place among leading denominations—from 15.7 percent to 3.5 percent of all church adherents.

The Presbyterians' share of the religious market also declined, from 19 percent to 11.6 percent. But the Presbyterians' growth in actual numbers, unlike that of the Congregationalists and the Episcopalians, did keep pace with the growth of the population. The Presbyterians fared better because they were able to achieve some growth on the new American frontiers. Their share declined, however, because their growth failed to match the expansion of the proportion who were churched.

During this same period the Baptists achieved very substantial growth, primarily through conversion, and the Catholics grew rapidly, through immigration. But the major shift in the American religious market in this period was the meteoric rise of Methodism. In 1776 the Methodists were a tiny religious society with only 65 churches scattered through the colonies. Seven decades later they towered over the nation. In 1850 there were 13,302 Methodist congregations, enrolling more than 2.6 million members—the largest single denomination, accounting for more than a third of all American church members. For such growth to occur in eighty years seems nearly miraculous. But the general histories of American religion would make it even more of a miracle. Because all agree that religion fell into a state of sad neglect in the wake of the American Revolution, they would confine the rise of Methodism to less than fifty years.

Ebb Tide or Torrent?

We noted in Chapter 1 that, for over a century, general historians used nearly uniform language to claim that American religion collapsed during and immediately after the Revolution, a period that Williston Walker (1894, p. 319) described as "the epoch of the lowest spiritual vitality that our churches have ever experienced." Or, to quote Leonard Woolsey Bacon (1897, p. 230): "The closing years of the eighteenth century show the lowest low-water mark of the lowest ebb-tide of spiritual life in the history of the American church." William Warren Sweet ([1930] 1950, p. 223) called the last fifteen years of the eighteenth century "the period of the lowest ebb-tide of vitality in the history of American Christianity." Winthrop S. Hudson (1965, pp. 115–116) agreed that this same period "witnessed

Lyman Beecher (1775–1863). (Courtesy of the Billy Graham Center Museum, Wheaton, Ill.)

that ebb tide of religious life which often characterizes post-war eras." Sydney Ahlstrom (1975, vol. 1, p. 442) reported, "The churches reached a lower ebb of vitality during the two decades after the end of hostilities than at any other time in the country's religious history."

Douglas H. Sweet (1976, pp. 346–347) noted that this belief about an ebb tide seems to have derived from the singular dependence of general religious historians on the accounts of Lyman Beecher and some of his colleagues: "The writings of Lyman Beecher may have exerted a greater influence over twentieth-century historiography than those of almost any other early commentator. As evidence of this, one need consider no more than the frequency with which Beecher's description of Yale in the 1790s is quoted in text upon text. In their search to find an explanation, and perhaps, even a narrative filler, for the period between the American Revolution and the Second Great Awakening, modern church scholars have written an account based largely on the hyperbolized observations and conclusions of clergymen and clerical historians [belonging to] . . . the established order."[2]

We shall have occasion toward the end of the chapter to discuss Lyman Beecher's views on many matters. Here it suffices to note that Beecher's claims about religious decline were as much a reflection of his contempt for Methodists and Baptists and their style of worship as they were a reflection of his awareness of the problems besetting Congregationalists and Episcopalians in this era, including attacks upon their legal establishment. In an 1814 address to a charitable group that funded seminary scholarships, Beecher, a prominent Congregational minister and later the president of Lane Theological Seminary, condemned the preaching of "ignorant and unlettered men." Such men are "utterly unacquainted with theology" and do far more harm than good as far as Christian faith is concerned: "Illiterate men have never been the chosen instruments of God to build up his cause" (in Hatch, 1989, p. 18). Having delivered this line, Beecher seems to have had a jarring second thought—as Nathan O. Hatch has so perceptively noted—for he was prompted to add that the twelve disciples were tutored by Jesus for three years "to supply the deficiency of an education." In any event, Beecher felt entirely justified in calling an area religiously "destitute" as long as it was without educated, mainline clergy, no matter how many Methodist and Baptist churches it might sustain; he regarded the latter two as "worse than nothing."

For better or worse, any accurate characterization of religion in this era must confront statistics on rapid Baptist and Methodist growth, and these are far more compatible with the image of a torrent than with that of a low ebb. The Methodists reported 4,921 members in 1776. By 1800, at the end of the period that Marty (1975, p. 82) has called the "big sleep" in American religious life, the Methodists had grown to 64,894, and by 1806 they numbered 130,570—hardly a "sleepy" performance, given that the nation's population did not even double during this interval.[3] As for the Baptists, they claimed to have numbered 35,101 in 1784, to have grown to 65,345 by 1790, and then to 172,972 by 1810.

The sources of these statistics are neither obscure nor recent. The Methodist data come from the *Minutes* of their annual conferences, which were published yearly. They can also be found in the *Methodist Centennial Yearbook* (1884), which is widely available. The Baptist data were also published in church reports, but we found them in the *American Quarterly Register*

No obs, just a rise in baptists/methodists who were not deemed worthy of counting

(1841), which may still be found in virtually any major university library. Had the "ebb tide" writers made use of the available sources and determined the true state of affairs, the received wisdom concerning this period would be that the colonial mainline bodies began their long slide toward obscurity by the end of the eighteenth century, but that at the same time those feisty upstart sects, the Baptists and the Methodists, had begun a period of torrential growth. Thus the central questions come into clear focus. *Why* did the leading denominations of 1776 crumble in a free market religious economy? What did they do wrong? Or what did the Methodists and the Baptists do right?

The Rise of a Free Market Religious Economy

By the start of the Revolution, the era of harsh religious persecution in the colonies had ended. Religious toleration prevailed in fact, if not yet in statute. And in the immediate post-war period, toleration slowly gave way to religious freedom. In the eyes of the newly established federal government, not only would all faiths be permitted to worship, all would be given equal opportunity. There would be no established church, and the state would be separated from all religious entanglements.

But the religious situation looked quite different when examined at a more local level. The Congregationalists were established in New England, while the Episcopalians, as the Church of England, were established in some of the Middle and Southern colonies. The Episcopal establishments fell quickly after the British defeat. But in New England, the Congregationalists (including their emergent Unitarian division) clung to taxpayer support. Eventually they were beaten by a rather unlikely alliance: the rationalists and freethinkers, on the one hand, and the upstart, aggressive, evangelical Protestant sects, on the other. The freethinkers resented having their taxes go to any religion; the sectarians resented their taxes going to false religions. Given that each of the religious groups wanted religious freedom for itself, even if few of them really wanted religious freedom for all, there was no other safe way to proceed but to create an unregulated, free market, religious economy.[4]

But disestablishment didn't happen overnight, and even then de facto establishment persisted long after the official sanctions had been withdrawn. Connecticut disestablished the Congregationalist Church only in 1818, followed by New Hampshire in 1819. And it was not until 1833 that Massachusetts ceased to collect "church taxes" on behalf of the Congregationalists.

After the battle to disestablish Congregationalism was won, it turned out that the other "mainline" bodies only opposed favoritism that was exclusively for the Congregationalists. They welcomed favoritism as long as it included themselves. And so it came to be that the Congregationalists, Episcopalians, and Presbyterians frequently engaged in collective efforts to benefit from many forms of official support at the local level and formed cartels aimed at preventing free market forces from developing.

The efforts to impose de facto establishment were vigorous, but they failed dismally. Similar efforts to use "nondenominational" front organizations to channel public donations for home missions into narrowly denominational benefits eventually failed too. But we must pause to examine these maneuvers, for in and of themselves they reveal many aspects of the fatal flaws of the old "mainline."

Cartel Agreements and Local Privilege

When George Whitefield brought his itinerant ministry to town, many local ministers found him a dangerous challenge to their privileged position and denied him their pulpits. Whitefield was not forestalled; thousands flocked into fields and public squares to hear him, as we have seen. But when many others began to take up itinerancy in the aftermath of Whitefield's tours, the local clergy and political elites moved against them, especially in New England.

Late in 1743, only three years after Whitefield had captivated the city, the president and faculty of Harvard gathered to issue a unanimous *Testimony against the Reverend Mr. George Whitefield and His Conduct*. Published in 1744, the Testimony began: "In regard of the Danger which we apprehend the People and Churches of this Land are in, on the Account of the Rev. Mr. George Whitefield, we have tho't ourselves oblig'd to bear our Testimony in this public Manner, against him and his Way of Preaching. . . . And we do therefore and hereby declare, That we look upon his going about, in an Itinerant Way, especially as he hath so much of an enthusiastic Turn, utterly inconsistent with the Peace and Order, if not the very Being of the Churches of Christ" (p. 3). Next, the Harvard faculty complained:

> the People, many of them, are strongly attach'd to him (tho' it is most evident that he hath not any superior Talent at instructing the Mind, or shewing

the Force and Energy of those Arguments for a religious Life which are directed to in the everlasting Gospel). . . .

First then, we charge him, with *Enthusiasm*. . . . we mean by an Enthusiast, one that acts, either according to Dreams, or from sudden Impulses and Impressions upon his Mind, which he fondly imagines to be from the Spirit of God, persuading and inclining him thereby to such and such Actions, tho' he hath no Proof that such Perswasions or Impressions are from the holy Spirit. . . . (pp. 3–4)

Shortly thereafter, on January 22, 1744, the Congregational clergy of Boston and of Bristol County gathered in Boston to see what could be done to stop itinerant preachers. "Ministers do not invade the Province of others," they proclaimed, in the familiar tones of those who want regulated, not free, markets. The group subsequently published *The Testimony of the Association of Ministers against the Reverend Mr. George Whitefield and His Conduct*, in which they recorded their "most solemn Testimony against . . . Mr. Whitefield in Person" and "against Itinerant Preaching, as practiced of late among us."

What were Whitefield's sins? That he had traveled "from Town to Town preaching," although God has "no where in the Gospel appointed any such Officer in his Church, where the Officers are already settled in it, and the Gospel fully and faithfully preached; as also directly tending to destroy the Peace and Order of these Churches, and to throw them off from the good Foundation upon which they were settled by our wise and pious *Ancestors*" (1745, p. 4). Worse yet, Whitefield had "used his utmost Craft and Cunning, to strike the Passions and engage the Affections of the People." And finally these angry clergymen cited scripture to prove that God "hath enjoined our Ministers, that they be not Busy-Bodies in other Men's Matters; i.e., don't play the Bishop in another's Charge" (1745, pp. 6–7).

Meanwhile, clergy in Connecticut appealed to the Assembly for protection against the "disorderly intruding" of clergy into "other men's parishes." They were rewarded with three new statutes in 1742: the first prohibited itinerants "from preaching in any parish without the approval of the minister of that parish," the second prevented parishes from "choosing a minister who lacked a college degree," and the third statute required Yale students and faculty to take an "oath affirming their orthodoxy." Clergy protesting the new laws against itinerancy were "called before the legislature, publicly rebuked, and deprived of their offices" (McLoughlin, 1971, p. 363). Whitefield and the new itinerants provoked a similar response from the Anglican establishment of the Southern Colo-

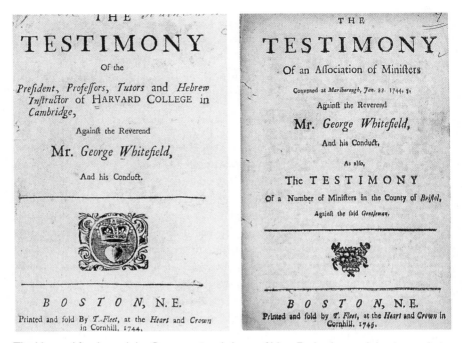

The Harvard faculty and the Congregational clergy of New England argued that it was their "duty" and "obligation" to provide testimony against the "enthusiasm" and "Itinerant Way" of George Whitefield. In other words, they were protesting his emotional message of salvation for the masses and his complete disregard for the cartel agreements of local clergy. (Courtesy of the Billy Graham Center Museum, Wheaton, Ill.)

nies. Writing in the *South Carolina Gazette* in 1740, an Anglican described Whitefield as a "wandering disorderly Comet" whose itinerant preaching threatened the natural order (in Hall, 1994, p. 45). The established churches argued that the itinerants were not only a threat to the ecclesiastical order, they threatened the social order of the entire community. The result was that itinerants faced the constant threat of persecution, or the loss of their "privilege" to preach, even when colonies didn't have laws against itinerancy.

Nearly a century later and far to the west, efforts persisted to maintain "gentlemen's agreements" whereby pastors would not poach on one another's flocks. In his autobiography (1856), the great Methodist itinerant Peter Cartwright offered this example of a phenomenon he often encountered. Arriving in a new community, he was approached by the local Presbyterian minister, who did not object to his preaching, but requested that he make no effort to form a church in this neighborhood because it was within the "bounds of his congregation." Cartwright responded: "I told him that was not our way of doing business; that we seldom ever preached long at any place without trying to raise a society. He said I must not do it. I told him the people were a free people and lived in a free country, and must be allowed to do as they pleased. . . . He said that was true; but if we raised a society it would diminish his membership, and cut off his support" (p. 123). Cartwright explained that he had no option but to continue and that if any cared "to join our Church I shall take them in." He then announced that when he returned in a month he would organize a class, because several local people had requested that he do so. The Presbyterian clergyman responded that he would "openly oppose" Cartwright.

Over the next three Sundays the local minister preached against Methodism and itinerancy. According to Cartwright, these attacks simply produced "a vast crowd" for his return visit, and twenty-seven people joined the Methodists that day. This was only the beginning: "Public opinion was in my favor, and many more of this preacher's members came and joined us, and the minister sold out and moved to Missouri, and before the year was out I had peaceable possession of his brick church" (1856, p. 125).

The most ambitious effort to create a religious cartel was no doubt the 1801 Plan of Union between the Presbyterians and the Congregationalists. Recognizing their mutual Calvinism, the plan called for unified, noncompeting missionary efforts to the western frontier, meanwhile dividing the settled areas into exclusive "markets," the Presbyterians to stay south of New England, the Congregationalists to stay north of the old Middle Colonies. In the end the plan harmed them both, in large part because it reduced their competitive capacities without restricting the efforts of their most serious challengers. The Methodists and Baptists were not in the Union.

An additional source of efforts at de facto establishment came from the fact that local political and economic elites were usually aligned with the colonial mainline bodies. Thus in many communities, especially toward the frontier, the mainline bodies received "use" subsidies in the form of being allowed to hold their services in schools and other public buildings without charge. Whitney R. Cross ([1950] 1982, p. 45) reported: "In Buffalo during 1818, Presbyterians monopolized the court house and Episcopalians, the school house. Methodists could only meet in the latter place at sunrise or sunset."

Peter Cartwright (1785–1872) described his younger self as a "wild, wicked boy [who] delighted in horse-racing, card-playing, and dancing" and "made but small progress" with his formal education (1856, pp. 27–28). Yet he went on to become one of the most famous and respected Methodist itinerants. Twice a member of the Illinois legislature, he lost in his bid for Congress to another famous frontiersman—Abraham Lincoln. (Courtesy of the Billy Graham Center Museum, Wheaton, Ill.)

"Nondenominational" Front Groups

In 1798 the General Association of Connecticut voted to become an agency "to Christianize the Heathen in North America, and to support and promote Christian knowledge in the new settlements, within the United States" (in Ahlstrom, 1975, vol. 1, p. 513). Soon other such groups appeared—voluntary associations of private citizens devoted to "interdenominational" efforts to sustain home missions. In 1826 many of these groups were consolidated by the founding in New York of the American Home Missionary Society (AHMS). For many decades this organization appeared to dominate efforts to convert the godless frontier; it collected and spent large sums annually to support clergy and build churches in the "wilderness," where other means to sustain organized religion were lacking.

The AHMS journal was widely distributed in the cities of the eastern seaboard, and its appeals for funds were carefully nondenominational. For example, in 1827 the journal asked for funds to support a mission to Niagara County in the far western corner of New York State on grounds that the area was almost entirely "destitute of the stated ministry of the gospel of every denomination." At the same time nearby Monroe County was classified as a "moral waste," and "destitute of both religious and moral principles" (in Cross, [1950] 1982, p. 48).

In truth, there were many churches and many ministers of the gospel active in both these counties at the time—but they all were Baptists or Methodists.[5] And that was precisely the rub. The Congregationalists, Presbyterians, and Episcopalians could not sustain churches in these areas without home mission subsidies, if for no other reason than that they depended on a well-educated and well-paid clergy. But as Horace Galpin wrote to Miles Squier at AHMS headquarters, in the West the people could "have the preaching of . . . the Methodists for nothing, to the subversion of the regular ministry" (in Cross [1950] 1982, pp. 45–46). To raise the money needed to offer "free" religion out west, the mainline denominations conspired for decades to deceive the public about why funds were needed and who received them. Clergymen who were willing to claim that places abounding in Baptists and Methodists were unchurched could have no qualms about not sharing "nondenominational" contributions with such outsiders and upstarts.

Indeed, an AHMS missionary to Arkansas wrote back to his superiors in 1846 that the Baptists, Methodists, and other sects were "standing in the way" of the work of the society: "After a minute examination and mature and prayerful deliberation I have come to the settled conviction that it would be decidedly for the religious interests of Arkansas if every minister and preacher of the above denominations were out of the State" (in W. W. Sweet, 1964b, p. 698).

But wishing couldn't make it so. The Methodists and the Baptists were there to stay. And if the Methodists were excluded from using the court house or the school house in Buffalo to hold their services, they were not prevented from building a church. Several years later, after a very successful "revival" led by a circuit rider, they did just that. The same pattern occurred again and again. Even with their AHMS subsidies, the colonial mainline could make only feeble efforts at moving west. Yet somehow sufficient local funds could always be found to build churches out west, if they were Methodist and Baptist churches. But the outcomes would have been very different if Peter Cartwright had been denied the freedom to preach and the Methodists and Baptists had not been granted the privilege of starting new congregations wherever they pleased. Had religious establishments retained their regulatory powers, the story of American religion would read very differently.

The Road Not Traveled

To view history as it might have been, we need only compare the paths of American and English Methodism. British historian David Hempton notes that "how far Methodism should be allowed to shelter under the umbrella of the Church of England . . . became one of the most controversial legal problems of the period between 1740 and 1820" (Hempton, 1988, p. 94). Having begun as a society within the Church of England, the Methodists' rigorous behavioral standards, their itinerant preachers, and even their use of uneducated lay leadership and female exhorters were initially tolerated by the established Church. By the 1790s, however, the Methodists were denied the right to call themselves the "Church of England at prayer." They were now classified as religious dissenters who faced increasing scrutiny from the state (Hempton, 1984). Attempting to preserve this fragile religious toleration, the Methodists refrained from the very activities that were fueling the growth of American Methodism. Rather than starting new churches wherever a gathering could be assembled, they sought to avoid confrontations with the Church. Whereas, the American Methodists embraced itinerancy and camp meetings, the Methodist hierarchy in England sought to curtail these activities despite their obvious popularity with the people. When the American Methodist itinerant Lorenzo Dow arrived to bring camp meetings to the British Isles in 1805, he found immediate support from the people and strong resistance from Methodist leaders. Fearing reprisals, the Methodist hierarchy quickly moved to block his activities. According to Dow, "they warned the Methodists against me, to starve me out . . . [and] they offered to pay my passage home, if I would quit the country, and promise never to return, which in conscience I could not do" (Dow, 1849, p. 256).

The Methodist Conference ruled against this style of revivalism, stating that "it is our judgment, that even supposing such meetings to be allowable in America, they are highly improper in England, and likely to be productive of considerable mischief: and we disclaim all connections with them" (in Hatch, 1989, p. 50).

The English Methodists knew whereof they spoke. Throughout their history they had faced open ridicule, persecution from mobs, and were frequently charged with legal irregularities and ecclesiastical malpractice (Barr, 1916; Whitney, 1951). In 1738, the Bishop of London, Edmund Gibson, charged that Methodists were dissenters "posing as Anglicans" and accused them of violating ecclesiastical law by supporting itinerant preaching that undermined the local parish and by "encouraging extremism, exclusiveness and religious experience" (Hempton, 1988, p. 96). John Wesley's knowledge of law, his prominent contacts, and his allegiance to the English Church and State helped to counter many of the early critics. But following Wesley's death in 1791, and faced with the increasing popularity of Methodism, the Church of England turned them out. In 1811, a few years after Dow's visit, Lord Sidmouth sought virtually to abolish itinerancy through a bill that limited grants of preaching certificates to ministers attached to specific congregations. Although the bill failed to win approval, the threat of parliamentary regulation forced the Methodists to further curtail the activities of their itinerants, which emboldened British authorities to refuse licenses to clergy not tied to a specific congregation or deemed spiritually unfit for service. According to Hempton, the English "Methodists realized that their preaching privileges depended upon continued loyalty and good order" (1984, p. 104).

Thus Methodism in Great Britain floundered while American Methodism soared. As the Methodists in Great Britain struggled to keep pace with population growth, the percentage of Methodists in America continued to climb. As we will see, the meteoric growth could never have occurred with tighter reins on the itinerants and a refusal by the Methodist hierarchy to support camp meetings. Before we explain why the upstarts grew so rapidly throughout the nation, however, we first look more closely at the religious situation in 1850.

Religion in 1850

In 1850 the West "Coast" was not along the shores of the Pacific. That year there were all of 13,294 people in the Oregon Territory, which in-

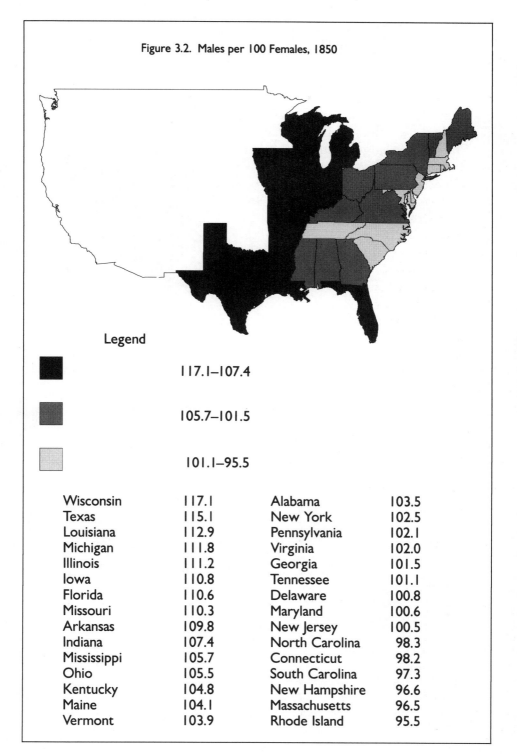

Figure 3.2. Males per 100 Females, 1850

Legend

117.1–107.4

105.7–101.5

101.1–95.5

Wisconsin	117.1	Alabama	103.5
Texas	115.1	New York	102.5
Louisiana	112.9	Pennsylvania	102.1
Michigan	111.8	Virginia	102.0
Illinois	111.2	Georgia	101.5
Iowa	110.8	Tennessee	101.1
Florida	110.6	Delaware	100.8
Missouri	110.3	Maryland	100.6
Arkansas	109.8	New Jersey	100.5
Indiana	107.4	North Carolina	98.3
Mississippi	105.7	Connecticut	98.2
Ohio	105.5	South Carolina	97.3
Kentucky	104.8	New Hampshire	96.6
Maine	104.1	Massachusetts	96.5
Vermont	103.9	Rhode Island	95.5

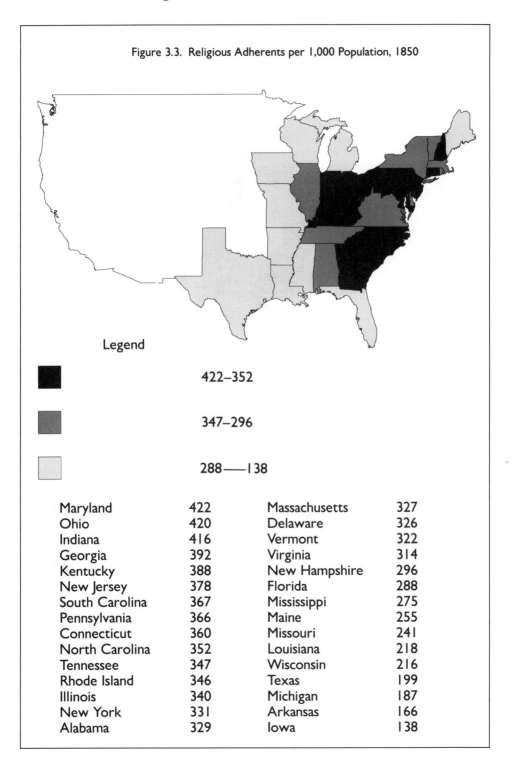

Figure 3.3. Religious Adherents per 1,000 Population, 1850

Legend

■	422–352
▨	347–296
☐	288——138

Maryland	422	Massachusetts	327
Ohio	420	Delaware	326
Indiana	416	Vermont	322
Georgia	392	Virginia	314
Kentucky	388	New Hampshire	296
New Jersey	378	Florida	288
South Carolina	367	Mississippi	275
Pennsylvania	366	Maine	255
Connecticut	360	Missouri	241
North Carolina	352	Louisiana	218
Tennessee	347	Wisconsin	216
Rhode Island	346	Texas	199
Illinois	340	Michigan	187
New York	331	Arkansas	166
Alabama	329	Iowa	138

cluded what was yet to become the Washington Territory, and of the 92,597 residents of California, 85,578 were men—many of whom were forty-niners who had come there during the gold rush that began the previous year. Elsewhere, what is today regarded as the Far West was essentially unsettled. Even in Utah, the Mormon migration had added up to only 11,380 people by the time the 1850 census was taken. In 1850 the west had barely crossed the Mississippi River—Iowa, Arkansas, Missouri, and Texas were the only places across the Mississippi having any substantial population (the Minnesota Territory was still the "North Woods," having but 6,077 residents, two thirds of them men). In effect, the West "Coast" in 1850 was lapped by the waters of the Mississippi.

For this reason we will examine the religious situation of 1850 in an America of thirty states as mapped in Figure 3.2, which shows how well the sex ratio identifies the frontier. The states farthest west had substantially more males than females. In contrast, New England had more females than males.

Recall that in 1776 there was a huge negative correlation between the sex ratio and religious adherence—frontiers always are deficient in churches. Thus Figure 3.3 is no surprise. The frontier states along the Mississippi had noticeably lower rates of religious adherence. Iowa was lowest, with only 138 adherents per 1,000 population. Arkansas, Michigan, and Texas were the other three states below the 200 level. Notice, however, that New England was not the most churched area in 1850: Maryland, Indiana, and Ohio were the states with the highest adherence rates.

Appendix Table A.2, containing the adherence rate per 1,000 population for the three denominations of the old colonial mainline and the two upstart sects, allows us to see in detail where the upstart sects won America. In Maine, for example, of every 1,000 inhabitants, 48 were affiliated with the Congregationalists, 2 with the Episcopalians, 3 with the Presbyterians, 89 with the Baptists and 58 with the Methodists. The "upstart ratio" shows that for every person in Maine affiliated with an old colonial mainline body, 2.8 were affiliated with the Baptists or the Methodists.

Even in New England the mainline denominations had crumbled badly in the face of aggressive Methodist and Baptist activity. Only in Connecticut did the old mainline still outnumber the upstarts. Outside New England, it wasn't even close. Indeed, the bitter fruits of the 1801 Plan of Union between the Presbyterians and Congregationalists come into dramatic focus. For reasons we assess in detail later, the Congregationalists were unable to minister to the West and hence failed to grow with the nation, but the Plan of Union caused them to make no efforts to spread their ministry into the cities and settled areas south of Connecticut, where conditions were much more favorable to their organizational abilities. Moreover, the Plan kept the Presbyterians from mounting efforts to missionize in New England, and because the Presbyterians were the only one of the three mainline faiths that showed any ability to compete with the upstart sects, their absence left the door to New England wide open for the Methodists and the Baptists. If the Presbyterians were left out of the calculations of the upstart ratios for all thirty states, the presence of the colonial mainline could hardly be detected in most of the nation.

The Methodists could function everywhere—on the frontier or in the city. The Congregationalists could function only in "civilized" areas, but even there they could not hold their own against the upstarts. In fact they could not even withstand Methodist and Baptist competition on their home ground of New England.

Why the Upstarts Won

Where there are winners there are losers. Much can be learned from a comparison of the two primary winners in the American religious economy between 1776 and 1850, the Methodists and Baptists, with the two primary losers, the Congregationalists and Episcopalians. There also is much to be gained from examination of the "also-ran" Presbyterians, whose growth kept pace with the population, but not with the increase in the proportions active in churches.

Organizational Structures

Social scientists agree that the structure of an organization can have tremendous impact on its efficiency and success. This has also been stressed in studies of religious organizations (Harrison, 1959; Wood and Zald, 1966; Szafran, 1976; Demerath et al., 1998; Stark and Finke, 2000; Miller, 2000; Finke, 2004). Nevertheless, it would appear at first glance that variations in denominational polity played little or no part in who grew and who did not.

The two most successful denominations, the Baptists and the Methodists, seem to be polar extremes in terms of polity. Historians have often cited the democratic structure of the Baptist church as an attractive feature to the people of the early frontier (W. W. Sweet, 1952; Ahlstrom,

1975; Hudson, 1981), but the Methodist Church was even more success-ful on the frontiers, and everyone knows the Methodists have a hierar-chical structure with strong, centralized authority placing control firmly in the hands of the clergy. Similar variation would seem to exist among the losers. The Protestant Episcopal Church and the Congregational Church seem at opposite extremes, with the Presbyterians falling somewhere in between.

When we look more closely at these denominational organizations, however, we find that the Methodists were about as democratic locally as were the Baptists. The local congregations were divided into small, close-knit groups called classes. Each class met on a weekly basis and was composed of approximately a dozen or more members. Here is where the zeal of camp meetings was maintained, intimate fellowship was achieved, testimonials were offered, new converts were instructed, and the behavior of the faithful was monitored (Hardt, 2000). Known as the "sinews of Methodism," the class meetings were the primary source of spiritual and social support for members (Wigger, 1998, p. 81).

But the class also served as a source for local leaders, where exhort-ers and local preachers for the local congregation were frequently recruited (in Gorrie, 1852, p. 295). And although class leaders, who were deemed responsible for the "moral and Christian conduct" of members, were appointed by the itinerant in newly established missions, the more com-mon practice was for the local (unpaid) preacher to appoint and super-vise their activities. Even the full-time itinerants typically began as lay leaders in the local congregations. In his in-depth study of American Methodism, John H. Wigger (1998, p. 82) concludes that "many, if not most, of the early itinerants began their careers as class leaders." As a result, the denomination remained responsive to the people despite its hierarchical structure, and the average Methodist congregation was a model of "congregationalism," with control residing in the hands of the adult membership.

In this era the actual pastoral functions were performed in most Meth-odist churches by unpaid, local "amateurs" just like those serving the Baptist congregations up the road.[6] A professional clergy had not yet cen-tralized control of the Methodist organization. True, the circuit-riders were full-time professionals vested with substantial authority. But they only visited a congregation from time to time and played the role of visiting bishop[7] and evangelist more than the role of pastor. It was only when the circuit riders dismounted and accepted "settled" pastorates that the "episcopal" structure of Methodism came to the fore. Indeed, it may well be that to the extent that the Methodists were able to create a national organization based on the circuit riders, they had the best of both worlds—centralized direction and local control (Miyakawa, 1964). In any event, despite apparent differences in polity, both the Methodists and the Baptists were surprisingly democratic and thus able to respond to the actual desires of the market.

In contrast, the Congregationalists were not nearly so "congregational" as either of the upstart sects. That Congregationalism was dominated by a highly professional clergy was the result of two interrelated factors. First, as we take up in detail below, the Congregationalists had opted for a highly educated clergy. This led to a chronic shortage of clergy and maximized their bargaining power, both individually and collectively. A second factor was establishment. As the established church of most New England colonies, Congregational churches were organized at town meetings, were supported by the town's "religious taxes," and "the towns played the customary role in concurring in the choice of the minister" (McLoughlin, 1971, p. 795). This system made the clergy influential in local governmental affairs. Moreover, establishment allowed the Congregationalists to depend on secular organizational structures to provide central coordination of their religious affairs within New England and left them with no alternative model for coordination among congregations. Whereas the Baptists would form regional associations whenever four or five Baptist churches were established, Congregational churches established outside of the New England region were often isolated units, lacking any regional support. In fact, to be united with churches beyond the local state line was contrary to the organizational plan of the early Congregational churches (Atkins and Fagley, 1942).

The 1801 Plan of Union with the Presbyterians illustrates the organizational problems of the early Congregationalists. Although the Plan, first supported by the Congregational General Assembly of Connecticut and later approved by the General Associations of Massachusetts, New Hampshire, Vermont, and Maine, was designed to unify the two denominations' frontier missionizing efforts, it resulted in the Congregationalists' being swallowed up by the Presbyterians. This was in large measure because the latter had established presbyteries, in addition to congregations, on the frontier. Because there was no alternative Congregational central structure, the Plan of Union led whatever individual Congregational churches that did arise to end up joining a presbytery and thus effectively to switch denominations (W. W. Sweet, [1930] 1950). Although as Williston Walker (1894) claimed, the Plan of Union was a "wholly honorable arrangement, and designed to be fair to both sides," it inadvertently favored the Presbyterians because only they had a structure sufficient to sustain congregations in less settled areas. As "their Presbyteries were rapidly spread over the missionary districts," Walker continued, "the natural desire for fellowship . . . led Congregational ministers to accept the welcome offered therein" (pp. 317–318). The Congregational associations in the individual New England states were simply not able, or not willing, to support the national expansion of their church. In the end, the Plan slowed the decline of the Presbyterians and confined the Congregationalists to New England.

The Episcopalians and the Presbyterians did have national and regional organizations, but each was beset with organizational problems. The Revolution did great damage to the Episcopalians (Heyrman, 1997). Many members supported the Crown and fled at war's end. Sweet (1952) reported that the majority of Virginia's 100 Anglican parishes were defunct by the end of the war and that the number of active Anglican clergy had dropped from 91 to 28. Sweet also estimated that North Carolina, Georgia, and Pennsylvania each had only one active Anglican priest by the end of the Revolution. In addition to these disasters, the Episcopalians lost their formal connection with the Church of England, thus ending their supervision by the Bishop of London and the substantial flow of subsidies and mission clergy provided by the Society for the Propagation of the Gospel in Foreign Parts. Although the process of national reorganization began in 1783, effective new central authority was lacking for several more decades. Thus in a critical time, when rapid growth was shaping a new nation, the Episcopal Church was struggling to support its remaining churches and to recover from the war. It lacked the resources to expand its share of the religious market.

In contrast, the Presbyterians were well organized and emerged from the Revolution with enhanced prestige. Sweet (1964b, p. 3) suggested that "no church in America, at the close of the War for Independence, was in a better position for immediate expansion than was the Presbyterian." The Presbyterians had established strong presbyteries throughout the nation, and, as we have seen, they fared much better than did the Congregationalists or the Episcopalians during this era. Their growth, however, was constantly plagued by divisions within their organization. Although the Plan of Union contributed to their increases, the new "Presbygational" churches also contributed to doctrinal and polity controversies. Holding camp meetings similarly contributed to Presbyterian growth in rural and frontier areas, but this practice aroused disapproval "back east," leading to sharp regional and doctrinal controversy. The Presbyterians worked tirelessly for unity, which they understood to be rooted in uniformity. Through their efforts to enforce strict national standards on polity and doctrine, they frequently shattered the very unity they sought and prompted regional schisms.

It appears that the situation facing the churches in this period placed very stern demands on denominations to become competitive organizations prepared to seek souls to the ends of civilization and beyond. Polity alone would not achieve this, but organizational structures that prevented a *nationwide* effort were a fatal flaw.

It may be pertinent here to note that though it is convenient to speak of organizations doing this or that, organizations per se never do anything. Only people ever act. Who was representing these denominations in the religious marketplace? What was their background and training and how were they recruited and deployed? And what were their motives?

Ministers

The organizational forms used by the Baptists and the Methodists were quite different, but their clergy were nearly interchangeable. In both denominations, ministers primarily came from the ranks of the common folk and, to a very important extent, remained common folk. Unlike the Congregational, Presbyterian, arid Episcopalian ministers, who typically were of genteel origin and were highly trained and well educated, the Baptist and Methodist clergy were of the people. They had little education, received little if any pay, spoke in the vernacular, and preached from the heart.

The local preacher for either of the upstart sects was a neighbor, friend, or relative of many of the people he served. Although this may have meant that the clergy held the same prejudices as did their flocks—and thus hampered the prophetic role of religion—it fostered a close relationship between the minister and the people in the pews. The minister shared the wants, needs, and desires of the people, and he made every effort possible to share the same religion too.

One of the most striking differences between the clergy of the upstart sects and those of the colonial mainline, and the easiest to document, was in their education. It was no secret that the great majority of Baptist and Methodist ministers had little education. The 1853 *Baptist Almanac* estimated that in 1823 only about 100 of the 2,000 Baptist clergy had been "liberally educated." The famous Methodist itinerant Peter

Cartwright estimated that at the General Conference of 1844 fewer than 50 (of approximately 4,282 traveling ministers) "had anything more than a common English education [grade school], and scores of them not that."

As was true of most Methodist leaders of the time, including Bishop Asbury, Cartwright was opposed not to higher education but, rather, to the use of theological schools for the designing of "man-made" ministers.[8] Nevertheless, the Methodists were in no hurry to found colleges. Between 1780 and 1829, forty colleges and universities were successfully founded in the United States. Of these, 13 were Presbyterian, 6 were Episcopalian, 4 were Congregational, 3 were Baptist, 1 was Catholic, 1 was German Reformed, 1 was a joint effort by the Congregationalists and Presbyterians, and 11 were public (W. W. Sweet, 1964b). None was Methodist.[9] Indeed, just prior to the founding of Indiana Asbury University in 1837, a committee of the Indiana Conference gave reassurance that it would never be a "manufactory in which preachers are to be made." Thus the founders kept faith with the bishop's memory as well as with the spirit of American Methodism as expressed in the *Discipline* of 1784, which advised preachers never to let study interfere with soul-saving: "If you can do but one, let your studies alone. We would throw by all the libraries in the world rather than be guilty of the loss of one soul."

As noted in Chapter 2, Weis (1936), in his invaluable work on the colonial clergy, tabulated data on the educations of all men who held a pulpit in New England from the first settlement through 1776. Of the 1,586 who had ever been pastor of a Congregational church, 1,507, or 95 percent, were college graduates. Of the 127 Anglicans and 51 Presbyterians, all were college graduates. But of the 217 Baptists, only 25 (or 11.5 percent) had a college degree. Weis listed no Methodists. Our data locate only two Methodist congregations in New England as of 1776, and these had probably just appeared.

Somewhat later statistics on seminary enrollments also display the vast educational differences among Protestant clergy. In 1831, according to the *American Almanac* (1833), Congregational seminaries enrolled 234 students, the Presbyterian seminaries 257, Episcopalian 47 (they still drew on men educated in England), and the Baptists 107. The Methodists had none; they were not to found their first seminary until 1847. By 1859, according to the *American Almanac* (1861), the Congregationalists had 275 seminarians, the Presbyterians had 632, the Episcopalians had 130, the Baptists had 210, and the Methodists had 51. The Congregational, Episcopalian, and Presbyterian seminaries had educated over 6,000 ministers before a single student graduated from a Methodist seminary.

The stately seminaries of the colonial mainline were elite educational institutions, but were ill-equipped to prepare clergy for the competition they would face from the upstarts. (Courtesy of the Billy Graham Center Museum, Wheaton, Ill.)

The leaders of the colonial mainline deemed the upstarts' lack of education to be appalling. At the opening of Andover Seminary, Timothy Dwight squared off against anyone who would support such clergy: "While they insist, equally with others, that their property shall be managed by skillful agents, their judicial causes directed by learned advocates, and their children, when sick, attended by able physicians; they were satisfied to place their Religion, their souls, and their salvation, under the guidance of quackery" (in Hatch 1989: 19). Lyman Beecher later echoed Dwight's concerns regarding the "ignorant" and "unlettered" clergy of the sects and further warned that the overly emotional revivalism that they promoted threatened to throw the new nation "back in civilization, science, and religion, at least a whole century" (Beecher and Nettleton 1828, p. 99). The colonial mainline leaders found the sectarian clergy guilty of both dangerous deception and unapologetic ignorance.

The sectarian clergy were not repentant. The Baptists held that "God never called an unprepared man to preach,"[10] and the Methodist *Discipline* of 1784 advised preachers never to let study interfere with soul-saving: "If you can do but one, let your studies alone." Not only did they hold that God called unlettered people to the ministry, they believed that such clergy were superior to those with seminary training. Cartwright boasted that these uneducated clergy "preached the Gospel with more success and had more seals to their ministry than all the sapient, downy D.D.'s in modern times" (Cartwright, 1856). Although the Baptists opened theological schools long before the Methodists, seminary-trained Baptists ministers were always a small minority and largely confined to the urban areas of the Northern states. Thus, even by the middle of the nineteenth century, the Baptists and the Methodists still relied on an uneducated clergy.

But if the Baptist and Methodist ministers lacked education in comparison with the other leading Protestant bodies, they were not less educated than the people they served. In 1870, for example, only 2 percent of seventeen-year-olds graduated from high school (Bureau of the Census, 1975). The Methodist bishop Francis Asbury argued, "a simple man can speak and write for simple, plain people, upon simple truths" (in Miyakawa, 1964, pp. 90–91). On the frontier or even in New England, the Baptist and Methodist clergy held the same level of education as the population in general. Although their lack of education is often viewed with scorn (Sweet was clearly eager to show how his Methodist forebears had made up for this later in the nineteenth century by founding many colleges), it was, in fact, the education of the clergy of the colonial mainline denominations that was truly unusual. These men were recruited from and moved most comfortably within "society"—the social and financial elite. Robert Baird noted in 1844 that many ministers of these denominations "belong to families of the first rank in the country; and as they can at least give their families a good education, with the advantages of such an education, as well as a good character, and the good name of their fathers, their children are almost invariably prosperous and often form alliances with the wealthiest and most distinguished families in the country" (p. 306).

Genteel social origins, combined with advanced levels of education, often increased the social distance between the minister and many of his congregants, to say nothing of the barriers raised between clergy and the vast unchurched population. As democratic convictions grew, many Americans began to detect objectionable attitudes among the highly educated, often regarding them as snobs who thought they were better than ordinary folks. This was particularly true in the growing frontier areas and in the South, where many people retained bitter memories of having been looked down upon by the educated and salaried clergy of the established churches of the past. And in New England, where battles were being waged over religious taxes and disestablishment, the privileges of the highly educated and well-paid clergy were widely questioned. One Connecticut dissenter provided this succinct critique: "Preachers that will not preach without a salary found for them by law are hirelings who seek the fleece and not the flock" (in McLoughlin, 1971, p. 927). The highly educated minister might have enhanced the "respectability" of religion, but he did little to gather the flock.

In addition to influencing patterns of interaction between minister and flock, an educated clergyman had expanded career opportunities. For many, teaching at a seminary or college, rather than being a famous preacher or serving as a leader in the local association or conference, represented the pinnacle of success. Once again, Cartwright provided a pithy summary: "Multiply colleges, universities, seminaries and academies; multiply our agencies, and editorships, and fill them all with our best and most efficient preachers and you localize the ministry and secularize them, too; then farewell to itineracy" (1856, p. 81). In short, well-educated clergy entered a prestigious full-time profession with a variety of career opportunities, whereas the uneducated clergy answered a call from God and the people to serve the local church in saving souls.

Reliance on well-educated clergy also created a serious practical problem for the colonial mainline: a constant shortage of clergy. The 1789 *Minutes of the General Assembly* reported that of the 419 Presbyterian congregations submitting data, only 215 were supplied with ministers and the remaining 204 positions were vacant. In 1804, the last year the *Minutes* reported on vacancies, over one half of all Presbyterian churches submitting data had vacant positions.[11] During that same year, Reverend David Rice from the Presbytery of Transylvania requested permission to license and ordain men without a "liberal education." The Assembly, fearing more revivals like Cane Ridge, denied his request and offered the following explanation.

> An ardent zeal, too often united with a certain spiritual pride, and strong self-love, is apt to inspire some weak persons of an enthusiastic temperament, with vehement impulses to preach the gospel, which they flatter themselves are calls from heaven; but experience has repeatedly shown us, that these inward impulses most commonly affect men of great imbecility of mind, or of strong vanity. (*Minutes of the General Assembly of the Presbyterian Church, 1789–1820*, p. 300)

The Assembly went on to add that a liberal education was not "absolutely essential . . . but reason and experience both demonstrate its high importance and utility." Thus, the shortage remained, allowing clergy

What? Have You Found Me Already?

In a feature article on the "Circuit Preacher" in the October 12, 1867, edition of Harper's Weekly, *the following story was offered to illustrate the persistence and determination of circuit riders in the early nineteenth century.*

Richard Nolley was one of the most famous circuit heroes of the South, and is now venerated as a martyr. He labored sturdily against fierce persecution. Fire-crackers were often thrown upon him in the pulpit, and while he was upon his knees praying. . . . His voice was a trumpet, and no man of the Southwest proclaimed the Gospel with greater energy. He penetrated to the newest settlements on the Tombigbee, Alabama, where he was beset with Indian perils. . . . It was in this wild region that happened the fact often cited as an illustration of the energy of the primitive circuit preacher. Nolley came to a fresh wagon track in the woods and soon found an emigrant family, which had just pitched on the ground of its new home. The man was unlimbering his team and the wife was busy about the fire. "What," exclaimed the settler, on hearing the salutation of the preacher and glancing at his unmistakable appearance, "have you found me already? Another Methodist preacher. I left Virginia to get out of their reach; I went to Georgia and thought to have got a long whet, but they got my wife and daughter into the church; then in this purchase (Choctaw Corner) I found a piece of land and was sure I should have some peace of the preachers, and here is one before my wagon is unloaded!" Nolley gave him small comfort. "My friend," he said, "if you go to heaven you will find Methodist preachers there; if you go to hell you will find some there, I fear; and you see how it is in this world, so you had better make terms with us and be at peace."

to be very selective in their placement, and nearly all chose to serve a well-established congregation rather than to pioneer a new one. In contrast, the Baptists and the Methodists had a surplus of available clergy and thus could find plenty of pastors to move west with the people. As a result, the Baptists and the Methodists were usually the only churches operating in the newer market areas.

But why did the Baptists and the Methodists have an abundance of clergy? Both denominations developed systems that made it easy for gifted laymen to enter the ministry. Among the Baptists the local preacher, or farmer-preacher, was often a man of local origins whose call was ratified by his fellow congregants. It was not uncommon for more than one member of a congregation to receive "God's call." Those not selected to fill the local pulpit had to seek one elsewhere, typically by starting a new congregation. The result was free market competition among Baptist preachers and a generous supply of clergy to fill any available slot. The Baptist farmer-preachers came with the people because they *were* the people.

Although the Methodist literature is filled with concerns over a shortage of itinerant clergy, the circuit rider was only the most visible and romantic element of the Methodist system for serving sparsely settled areas. The itinerants would organize and coordinate the activities of the local churches, and their visits provided variety, excitement, and supervision. But much of the responsibility was delegated to the locals. Class-leaders, for example, were charged with the "duty" of inquiring into the "spiritual state of each member . . . to reprove, comfort, or exhort them as occasion may require" (in Gorrie, 1852, p. 206). And it was the exhorters, stewards, and local preachers who carried on the day-to-day functions of the local church.

Not only could the Baptists and the Methodists generate surplus clergy, both denominations operated with incredibly low overhead. The Baptists typically paid their preachers nothing at all; most earned their living with a plow just like other members of the congregation. Local Methodist church leaders also received little, if any, pay. Even the circuit riders, who faced constant danger from the elements and spent most of their days in the saddle, received only the most meager wages. Their official salary was $100 per year in 1834, but the western circuit riders were often granted only a small percentage of this sum (Miyakawa, 1964). If itinerant ministers were married, which was strongly discouraged,[12] the official policy was to grant an additional $100 for the wife, $16 for each child under seven, and $24 for each child from seven to fourteen years of age. These additional stipends, however, were almost never granted to the western circuit riders. The report of the *Methodist Western Conference Committee of Claims* for 1803, considering the circuit rider Jesse Walker's claim for back pay, noted: "It appears to us that $76 are

Francis Asbury (1745–1816). (Courtesy of the Billy Graham Center Museum, Wheaton, Ill.)

for children. It is our judgment that the demand for children be deducted, and then he is deficient [owed] $89.37." In similar fashion the board noted that of Benjamin Young's claim of $28.95, "$4.75 is for Doctor's bills, which we judge an improper charge and therefore allow him but $24.14" (in W. W. Sweet, 1920, p. 87).

Even after applying such rules of frugality, the committee could only make partial payments. In the end Walker got $61.56 and Young received $10.14. And Francis Asbury, the famous Methodist bishop in America, was owed $20.36 and was actually paid $10.00. The 1808 report shows that Peter Cartwright received $65 from the committee, of which he donated $25 back to the church. That same year Asbury was paid $25 and donated $5 of it to the church. Little wonder that Asbury, despite his power and fame,[13] hardly ever had more than a dollar and was utterly dependent upon small donations from those he encountered along the road to sustain him. When a friend once asked to borrow $50, Asbury reflected, "He might as well have asked me for Peru" (in Marty, 1984, p. 172).

Like the Methodists, Baptist clergy received little, if any, pay outside the settled areas of the East. The Long Run Association *Circular Letter* of

1838 reported that only 6 of nearly 600 Baptist churches in Kentucky attempted "to support their ministry; and of those, only two could be said to do it" (in Shurden, 1980, p. 53). And even in the settled areas, salaries of only $60 to $100 a year are frequently reported in biographical accounts (W. W. Sweet, 1964a).

In comparison, the average yearly income for Presbyterian and Congregational ministers at this time was estimated at between $1,000 and $3,000 in large towns and between $400 and $1,000 in small country towns (Hayward, 1836, p. 155). Indeed, in his *Autobiography* (1910), Barton W. Stone, the young organizer of the Cane Ridge camp meeting, reported that when he gave up his Presbyterian congregation in rural Kentucky "I sacrificed . . . an abundant salary for the support of myself and family" (1910, p. 171). The mainline clergy also enjoyed "job" security that was unknown to the Methodist and Baptists. Whereas Baptist clergy were routinely dismissed by their congregations and the Methodist itinerants were typically assigned to a new circuit each year (Heyrman, 1997), the shortage of educated mainline clergy and the local appointment process of the Congregationalists gave these clergy far more stability. Wigger (2001, p. 91) reports that "of the 550 graduates of Yale College who entered the Congregationalist ministry between 1702 and 1794, a remarkable 71 percent ministered for their entire career at only one church. Only 4 percent served more than three pastorates."

The uneducated and often unpaid clergy of the Baptists and Methodists made it possible for these denominations to sustain congregations anywhere a few people could gather, for it was the pursuit of souls, not material comfort, that drove their clergy forth. Indeed, it would be hard to imagine that any sum of money could have motivated Bishop Asbury to travel nearly 300,000 miles on horseback, disregarding weather and chronic ill-health, to supervise his far-flung network of itinerants and circuit riders. It was thus that the upstarts swept over the nation. Just like the Confederate general Nathan Bedford Forrest, they always got there "fustest with the mostest." Moreover, they knew what to do when they got there: preach!

The Message

The education and background of the ministers influenced the message they brought and how they delivered it. Perhaps the contrast between faith and theology best conveys the vivid differences between "called" and educated clergy. Does the religious message address matters of faith

How the West was won: a Methodist circuit-rider, determined to reach the next congregation in time for services, pushes on through a stormy night. (Courtesy of the Billy Graham Center Museum, Wheaton, Ill.)

that are directly relevant to the experience and concerns of the laity, or is it a discourse on abstruse theological matters? Put another way, is it a message of conversion or a message of erudition?

We should point out, however, that it is not education in general that leads to secularization. Clearly, religious participation did not decline as the education of the population increased. Instead, we are suggesting that the message becomes more worldly, and is held with less certainty, as religion becomes the focus of scholarly critique and attention.

Neither the Baptists nor the Methodists set forth their confessions in complex theological writing that required extensive instruction or teaching. The Baptists had traditional ties with Calvinism, whereas the Methodists emphasized Arminian views, but both denominations stressed spiritual conversion and a strong individual responsibility to God. For both denominations the power of God was experienced as well as taught, and their message seldom excluded the topics of sin and salvation, or hellfire and redemption. Their emotion-packed messages centered on experience with the sacred and warned of the evils of the secular. Writing in 1792, Jedidiah Morse, the "father of American Geography," described Methodist preachers thus: "Their mode of preaching is entirely extemporaneous, very loud and animated. . . . They appear studiously to avoid connection in their discourses, and are fond of introducing pathetic stories, which are calculated to affect the tender passions. Their manner is very solemn, and their preaching is frequently attended with surprising effect upon their audiences" (in Gaustad, 1982, p. 308). Although appearing entirely unpremeditated, the clergy made careful use of vernacular imagery, metaphors, and stories that applied to the everyday life of their audience (Bilhartz, 1986; Williams, 2000). Like Whitefield, the Methodist itinerants and traveling Baptist preachers had the additional advantage of repeating their sermons and stories until they could elicit the desired effect.

It is not only content that is involved here, but the style of delivery—Marshall McLuhan might have suggested that in some ways the minister was the message. The Baptist and Methodist preachers looked like ordinary people because they were, and their sermons could convert and convince ordinary people because the message was direct and clear and the words were not read from notes, but seemed (to both speakers and hearers) to issue directly from divine inspiration. No wonder that Baptist and Methodist services could so often become outbursts of emotional participation.[14] Peter Cartwright recalled, "while I was preaching the power of God fell on the assembly, and there was an awful shaking among the dry bones. Several fell on the floor and cried for mercy" (1856, p. 65). We must never underestimate the impact of humble and ardent preachers on the spread of faith.

In contrast, the denominations of the colonial mainline offered a message that was literate and intellectual, but one that increasingly said less about salvation, hellfire, or other principal themes of the Baptist and Methodist sermons. The carefully drafted and theologically rich sermons generated neither the emotion nor the urgency of their counterparts. If the goal was to arouse faith, the scholarly and often dry sermons of the learned clergy were no match for the emotional pleas of the uneducated preacher. Theology has its place, but it does not save souls in the way that the Methodists and Baptists understood the task at the turn of the nineteenth century.[15] What saved souls, they had discovered, was a heartfelt message of conversion.

The Presbyterians of Kentucky, Tennessee, and other frontier areas, where they placed more emphasis on religious experience, are somewhat of an exception; but even there an introduction to Presbyterianism often required an instructional approach that was attractive to the well-educated but was often viewed as overly formal by the average farmer.

The Harvard and Yale divinity schools did not train their students to earn their own livings behind a horse and plow or prepare them to spend half their days in the saddle going from one rural hamlet to another. As George Whitefield charged, the primary impact of these schools on many of their students, then as now, may have been to replace faith with theology and belief with unbelief. For seminaries, a desire for intellectual integrity and academic acceptance soon takes precedence over developing the skills desired and the piety admired by those in the pew.[16] Indeed, it was in the religion departments and divinity schools, not in the science departments, that unbelief was formulated and promulgated in American intellectual life. As James Turner (1985, p. xiii) concluded, "In trying to adapt their religious beliefs to socioeconomic change, to new moral challenges, to novel problems of knowledge, to the tightening standards of science, the defenders of God slowly strangled Him. If anyone is to be arraigned for deicide, it is . . . not the godless Robert Ingersoll but the Godly Beecher family."

As we shall see, the opposition by Lyman Beecher and other pillars of the Congregationalist establishment to their co-religionist Charles Finney's immensely successful revival campaigns along the frontier displayed their strong preferences for intellectualized and "reasonable" religion, whatever the cost in terms of the failure to convert or mobilize support. Had they been able to embrace Finney and use his methods, it might have been the Congregationalists who towered over the nation in 1850. But as described in Chapter 2, they were already too far down the path of secularization—the faith of the Puritans had been so accommodated that it no longer could inspire or sanctify.

Awakenings and Routine Revivalism

Great Awakenings are perhaps the most dominant theme in general histories of American religion. The underlying thesis is that the nation has been subject to periodic paroxysms of public piety. There has been near unanimity across the theological spectrum that something extraordinary happened during the period approximately from 1739 through 1742 that is worthy of the name Great Awakening. From the early 1800s through the early 1830s there was apparently a second outbreak of religious excitement, especially along the western frontier, that eventually became known as the Second Great Awakening. Many historians have identified several later awakenings and argue in favor of a cyclical theory of American religious expression.

The distinguished historian William G. McLoughlin (1978, 1983) explains that great awakenings are "cultural transformations affecting all Americans," and that they "begin in periods of cultural distortion and grave personal stress, when we lose faith in the legitimacy of our norms, the viability of our institutions, and the authority of our leaders in church and state" (McLoughlin, 1978, p. 2). Many social scientists have been equally certain that revivals are caused by such things as social turmoil or financial crises (Gordon-McCutchan, 1983; Barkun, 1986) and some have echoed the charges by Ezra Stiles that awakenings are interludes of widespread hysteria and attribute them to various psychic insecurities (Gordon-McCutchan, 1981).[17] For McLoughlin (1978, p. 59) and many historians, awakenings represented a "breaking out of the dead skin of the past" and the dawn of a new era.[18]

But a growing number of scholars now suggest that there *never were any awakenings*, or at least none that took the form of huge spontaneous outbursts. Jon Butler (1982, 1990) labeled the First Great Awakening as "Interpretive Fiction" and proposed that use of the term should be abandoned. This suggestion generated the academic equivalent of shouts of "heresy." Frank Lambert (1999) traced the revivalists and anti-revivalist activity throughout the colonies and concluded that the revivalists themselves "invented" the idea of an intercolonial revival. What he found was a series of local revivals and the highly successful campaigns of George Whitefield, but there was no sudden outburst of revival due to social turmoil or other cultural distortions. Instead, he found carefully organized revivals promoted with skill and enthusiasm.

The revivals of Whitefield have been especially instructive. In his extraordinary study based on Whitefield's records, Lambert remarked: "What was new about Whitefield was the skill as an entrepreneur, an impresario, that made him a full-fledged forerunner of evangelists like Charles Grandison Finney and Billy Graham." (1990, p. 813). Lambert noted that Whitefield was a master of advance publicity who sent out a constant stream of press releases, extolling the success of his revivals elsewhere, to cities he intended to visit. These advance campaigns often began two years ahead of time. In addition, Whitefield had thousands of copies of his sermons printed and distributed to stir up interest. He even ran newspaper advertisements announcing his impending arrival. When Benjamin Franklin became Whitefield's publisher, sales of the Great Itinerant's journals and sermons soon amounted to a very large proportion of Franklin's gross receipts. In some cities, according to Lambert, Franklin sold more copies of Whitefield's works than he did of his own popular *Poor Richards Almanac*. It was from these efforts that the crowds "materialized."

As for the Second Great Awakening, it was no more (or less) than a series of local revival meetings, organized and led by evangelists. It is true that these revival meetings were frequent and that church membership was rising. But the revivals were not spontaneous or dependent on a sudden shift in the culture or the economy. Terry D. Bilhartz reports that there was nothing mysterious about religious awakenings in early national Baltimore. In his words the revival of religion was "not clearly related to economic activity, class, or city growth . . . Revival erupted among those who wanted it, and who labored diligently to promote it" (1986, p. 99). Bilhartz concludes that there was no sudden upsurge in the demand for religion. Instead, the most dramatic changes were in the increasing supply of new religions and churches in the city.

Timothy L. Smith (1957; 1983) found that this "routine revivalism" was equally important in explaining the religious activity of the so-called Burned-Over District of western New York and Ohio in the 1820s. When he claimed that nothing really unusual was going on in this area, he was well aware that hundreds of local revivals occurred at that time. Smith's point is that they were neither spontaneous outbreaks nor unusual. Rather, they were planned well ahead and conducted according to the routine methods by which clergy of many denominations sought periodically to energize commitment within their congregations and also to draw in the unchurched. Smith found that the revivals "persisted, year in and year out" and that any evidence of a cyclical pattern was due more to the "attention of the secular writers" than the "actual religious excitement" (1983, p. 98).

It is perhaps even more telling that Charles Finney, who was the moving force behind much of the revival activity that caused outsiders to perceive western New York as the Burned-Over District, stressed that revivals did not simply happen, but had to be carefully staged. Although Finney ([1835] 1960, p. 13) often felt the Holy Spirit within him when he preached, he flatly denied there was anything miraculous about revivals: "[A revival of religion] is not a miracle. . . . It is a purely philosophical result of the right use of the constituted means." As for the "constituted means," Finney published lengthy instructions explaining just what to do and how to do it, if one wanted to hold a successful revival meeting. A key passage makes the point:

> Ministers ought to know *what measures* are best calculated to aid in accomplishing . . . the salvation of souls. Some measures are plainly necessary. By measures I mean what things ought to be done to get the attention of the people, and bring them to listen to the truth. Building houses for worship, and visiting from house to house, are all "measures," the object of which is to get the attention of the people to the gospel. . . .
>
>   What do the politicians do? They get up meetings, circulate handbills and pamphlets, blaze away in the newspapers, send their ships about the streets on wheels with flags and sailors, send coaches all over town, with handbills, to bring people up to the polls, all to gain attention to their cause and elect their candidate. All these are their "measures," and for their end they are wisely calculated. The object is to get up an excitement, and bring the people out. They know that unless there can be an excitement it is in vain to push their end. I do not mean to say that their measures are pious, or right, but only that they are wise, in the sense that they are the appropriate application of means to the end.
>
>   The object of the ministry is to get all the people to feel that the devil has no right to rule this world, but that they ought all to give themselves to God, and vote in the Lord Jesus Christ as governor of the universe. Now what shall be done? What measures shall we take? Says one, "Be sure and have nothing that is new." Strange! The object of our measures is to gain attention, and you *must have* something new. (Finney, [1835] 1960, p. 181)

Finney went on at length to advise that good ventilation was important, that too much singing could be a distraction, that prayers should be intense but short, that dogs and young children should be left at home, that ministers should not be reluctant to confront sinners and reprobates in the audience by name, and that conversions made while the convert was under the influence of liquor seldom took.

Finney's actions were as direct and rational as his advice. He mounted his revivals with careful plans and preparations. Large numbers of lay workers were recruited ahead to make preparations, and both local clergy and laity were trained to minister to sinners as they came forward: "The whole process was carefully planned and organized to reach out as widely as possible. Urban revivalism required extensive financing from well-to-do lay leaders. In later years professional urban evangelists improved

Charles Grandison Finney (1792–1875) and his second wife, Elizabeth Atkinson, posed for this daguerreotype during an evangelistic tour of Britain in 1850. (Courtesy of the Oberlin College Library, Oberlin, Ohio.)

on Finney's techniques, but they did not fundamentally alter his approach" (McLoughlin, 1978, p. 128).

Finney well knew that to remain healthy, all organizations, be they churches, fraternal lodges, or corporations, must have some means for periodically renewing commitment and that the key to such renewal lies in a sudden intensification of the perceived benefits of belonging. The primary benefits of religious membership come in both worldly and otherworldly forms. Hence, Christian evangelists seek to revive among their listeners gratitude for the benefits of salvation. The primary worldly benefits of religion derive from human relations, from the attention, respect, and affection members bestow on one another. And there is nothing like taking part in a revival to strengthen the flow of affect among members. Finney explained that a primary purpose of a prayer meeting is to let everyone take part in order to "diffuse union, confidence, and brotherly love through the whole."

Application of the right methods produces a great sense of rededication and strengthened interpersonal ties among participants in revival meetings, feelings they perceive as true blessings. Usually the meetings have been scheduled for months or even years. Most people have done it before. No one was shocked when Finney ([1835] 1960, pp. 9–10) told his listeners: "Religion is the work of man. It is something for man to do. . . . [But] Men are so spiritually sluggish, there are so many things to lead their minds off from religion, and to oppose the influence of the gospel, that it is necessary to raise an excitement among them, till the tide rises so high as to sweep away the opposing obstacles."

However, although all organizations need renewals or revivals of member commitment, it also is true that these must be episodic. People can't stay excited indefinitely. Here too the itinerant revivalist offers the perfect solution. When he or she leaves, the revival is concluded, leaving local pastors to consolidate the gains made during the revival.[19]

Camp Meetings: Revival and Recreation

Both Whitefield and Finney held their revivals in towns and cities, and revivals remain primarily an urban phenomenon. But at the turn of the nineteenth century, rural America developed an equally potent counterpart, the camp meeting.

It is uncertain just where or when camp meetings originated. One of the first camp meetings took place at the Gasper River Church in Kentucky during July 1800. There James McGready, a Presbyterian, aided by several other ministers, scheduled several days of religious services to be held outdoors and suggested that people come prepared to camp over. This "camp meeting" drew farm families from substantial distances and was a huge success. A year later, a similar meeting was held in the spring in Logan County Kentucky. Barton W. Stone, a newly ordained Presbyterian minister from Concord, Kentucky, attended this meeting in order to see for himself how these open air revivals were conducted:

> Having heard of a remarkable religious excitement in the South of Kentucky . . . I was very anxious to be among them, and early in the spring of 1801 went there to attend a camp-meeting. There, on the edge of a prairie in Logan County, Kentucky, the multitudes came together, and continued a number of days and nights encamped on the ground, during which time worship was carried on . . . . The scene to me was new and passing strange. It baffled description. Many, very many, fell down, as men slain in battle, and continued for hours together in apparently breathless and motionless state—sometimes for a few moments reviving, and exhibiting symptoms of life by a deep groan, or piercing shriek, or by a prayer for mercy most fervently uttered. After lying thus for hours, they obtained deliverance. The gloomy cloud, which had covered their faces, seemed gradually and visibly to disappear, and hope in smiles brightened into joy—they would arise shouting deliverance, and then would address the surrounding multitude. (in Rogers, 1910, pp. 153–154)

Upon his return, Stone stopped at the Cane Ridge Meeting House, where he gave an enthusiastic account of the Logan County meeting: "The whole country appeared to be in motion to the place, and multitudes of all denominations attended. All seemed heartily to unite in the work and in Christian love. Party spirit, abashed, shrunk back. To give a true description of this meeting can not be done; it would border on the marvelous. It continued through five days and nights without ceasing. Many, very many, will through eternity remember it with thanksgiving and praise" (in Rogers, 1910, p. 157).

Stone immediately began to prepare for a similar meeting scheduled to begin on August 6, 1801, at Cane Ridge, in Bourbon County, Kentucky. He saw to it that the Cane Ridge meeting was "given full publicity at the first great meeting in Logan County" and also was "proclaimed from the pulpits throughout Kentucky" (Rogers, 1910, p. 55). When the day arrived a very large crowd gathered—at least 10,000 and perhaps as many as 20,000. Considering that at this time, nearby Lexington, then the state's largest city, had barely 2,000 inhabitants, this was a huge turnout. During the course of the next week an estimated 3,000 were converted. The camp meeting was marked by multitudes writhing on the ground—a form of worship then referred to as "muscular"—in response to nonstop preaching by scores of ministers. Stone (1910) describes the scene:

> Four of five preachers were frequently speaking at the same time, in different parts of the encampment, without confusion. The Methodist and Baptist preachers aided in the work, and all appeared cordially united in it—of one mind and one soul, and the salvation of sinners seemed to be the great object of all. We all engaged in singing the same songs of praise— all united in prayer—all preached the same things—free salvation urged upon all by faith and repentance.
> . . . Many things transpired there which were so much like miracles that, if they were not, they had the same effect as miracles on infidels and unbelievers; for many of them were convinced that Jesus was Christ, and bowed in submission to him. This meeting continued six or seven days and nights, and would have continued longer, but provisions for such a multitude failed in the neighborhood. (in Rogers, 1910, pp. 157–158)

Cane Ridge holds such a central place in histories of American religion because it, unlike previous meetings that may have been as large and that certainly produced as much emotional response, came to the attention of the eastern press. These press reports about Cane Ridge seem initially to have caused a joyful response from mainline church leaders, for the meeting was everywhere hailed as a miracle and the "greatest outpouring of the Spirit since Pentecost" (Ahlstrom, 1975, p. 525), though ultimately the methods were condemned.

Unfortunately, most of the writing about Cane Ridge fails to penetrate beneath the surface of the crowd's emotional involvement and the apparent spontaneity of the affair. But as in the case of urban awakenings, the facts support a much more reasonable interpretation of what people were really doing and why.

Like Whitefield and Finney's urban meetings, the meeting at Cane Ridge was carefully planned: "The grounds were prepared for the vast throng. For several hundred yards an oblong square with [a] temporary pulpit in the center made of split boards with [a] handrail for its protection, and rough hewn logs at regular intervals for seats. The surrounding grounds were filled with tents in regular street order. From five to seven ministers were speaking at one time. The church-building was set apart as a lodging place for the preachers. Every obstacle seems to have been surmounted, that all might be present" (Rogers, 1910, p. 56). As already noted, vigorous efforts were made to attract a crowd. Moreover, those

Barton Stone Explains Religious Exercises

The old colonial mainline issued many objections to the uncontrolled religious fervor of revival meetings such as Cane Ridge, especially the unexplainable "bodily agitations." In contrast, the upstart sects viewed these bodily agitations as proof of "spiritual outpouring." Barton Stone gives the following account of these "bodily agitations" known as "religious exercises" (in Rogers, 1910, pp. 159–162).

The falling exercise was very common among all classes, . . . The subject of this exercise would, generally, with a piercing scream, fall like a log on the floor, earth or mud, and appear as dead. I have seen very many pious persons fall in the same way from a sense of the danger of their unconverted children, brothers or sisters. . . . I have heard them agonizing . . . and speaking like angels to all around.

The jerks can not be so easily described. Sometimes the subject of the jerks would be affected in some one member of the body, and sometimes in the whole system. When the head alone was affected, it would be jerked backward and forward, or from side to side, ... When the whole system was affected, I have seen the person stand in one place and jerk backward and forward in quick succession, ... I have inquired of those thus affected. They could not account for it; but some have told me that those were among the happiest seasons of their lives.

The dancing exercise. This generally began with the jerks. . . . The subject, after jerking awhile, began to dance, and then the jerks would cease. Such dancing was indeed heavenly to spectators; . . . While thus exercised, I have heard their solemn praises and prayers ascending to God.

The barking exercise (as opposers contemptuously called it) was nothing but the jerks. A person affected with the jerks, especially in this head, would often make a grunt, or bark, if you please, from the suddenness of the jerk.

The laughing exercise . . . was a loud, hearty laughter, but one *sui generis*; it excited laughter in none else . . . and his laughter excited solemnity in saints and sinners. It is truly indescribable. . . .

I shall close this chapter with the singing exercise. . . . The subject in a very happy state of mind would sing most melodiously, not from the mouth or nose, but entirely in the breast, the sounds issuing thence. . . . It was most heavenly. None could ever be tired of hearing it.

in charge intended to stir up intense, emotional outbursts during the services. Those who came knew what to expect (many had been to camp meetings before) and if they responded with unusual enthusiasm this could be explained by their lack of regular access to worship services and by the duration of the event. Finally, if the size of the crowd that showed up amazed the eastern press, city folks failed to grasp that camp meetings provided the ideal religious and social solution to the isolated circumstances of American farmers.

Unlike European peasants who huddled together in villages from which they went out to the fields each morning, American farmers lived on their individual farmsteads. Even in the more densely settled areas, the next farm was a goodly distance away. It was hard to sustain rural churches because so few families lived within reasonable travel distance of one another. Indeed, this is one reason why the Methodist circuit riders and the Baptist farmer-preachers so dominated these areas. Similarly, many farm families suffered greatly from loneliness. Wives often went months without seeing another adult woman and their husbands seldom saw other adult men.

But if Cane Ridge demonstrated the capacity of revivals for stirring religious interest in rural areas, it was Francis Asbury who harnessed the new methods for use in the young Methodist Episcopal Church.[20] Only several months after attending his first camp meeting in 1800, Asbury ([1852] 1958) notified his itinerants of the "pleasing, growing prospect" of this new method. By January 1801 he proudly reported: "I have received great news from Vermont, of a work of God equal to that in Cumberland. Good appearances in Massachusetts, and in the State of [New] York, in Philadelphia and Baltimore, Maryland, Delaware and some places in poor, rich, dry, barren, formal, Pennsylvania. . . . God hath given us hundreds in 1800, why not thousands in 1801, yea, why not a million if we had faith. 'Lord increase our faith'" (vol. 3, p. 196). He followed this with letters to circuit riders who had yet to organize a camp meeting. Asbury's letter to Thornton Fleming in South Carolina in 1802 is characteristic: "I have heard of two men that preached against the work [holding camp meetings], one in particular, that was suddenly called away by death. If a man should thus sin against God by opposing his work, who shall entreat for him? . . . I wish you would also hold camp meetings; they have never been tried without success. To collect such a number of God's people together to pray and the ministers to preach, and the longer they stay, generally, the better—this is field fighting, this is fishing with a large net" (vol. 3, p. 251). Nor was Asbury's letter without

Even the shape of the camp meeting grounds was carefully planned. To the left are three of the most common encampment shapes, and to the right is a more detailed outline of the "oblong square" encampment shape. Regardless of the shape used, the "Speaker's Stand" and "Mourner's Bench" held center stage. (From C. A. Johnson, 1955, pp. 43, 47.)

success. Less than a year later, Asbury and Fleming jointly conducted a camp meeting attended by several thousand.

Through the years, Asbury's enthusiasm for camp meetings continued to grow. But it wasn't just enthusiasm and dedication that made Methodists the masters of the camp meeting. Their system of circuit riders was ideal for organizing and promoting camp meetings. Although early historical accounts stressed the rural camp meetings, Methodists circuit riders were soon promoting camp meetings everywhere, from the remote areas of the frontier to the major urban centers of the East. Two decades before Finney was introducing the "new measures" to major urban areas, Methodists were attracting urbanites to camp meetings on the outskirts of major cities (Bilhartz, 1986; Richey, 1991). Asbury also encouraged his itinerants to hold camp meetings on a regular basis by converting their quarterly district meetings into camp meetings. In 1806 he boldly predicted that "when all our quarterly meetings become campmeetings, . . . our American millennium will begin" (vol. 3, p. 357).

Camp Meeting Schedule

The Reverend B. W. Gorham's Camp Meeting Manual *(1854, pp. 155–156) offered the following schedule as one that "worked well."*

1. Rise at five, or half-past five in the morning.
2. Family prayer and breakfast from half-past six to half-past seven.
3. General prayer meeting at the altar, led by several ministers appointed by the Presiding Elder, at half-past eight, A.M.
4. Preaching at half-past ten, followed by prayer meeting to twelve, P.M.
5. Dine at half-past twelve, P.M.
6. Preaching at two, or half-past two, P.M., followed by prayer at the altar till five.
7. Tea at six, P.M.
8. Preaching at half-past seven, followed by prayer meeting at the altar till nine or ten.
9. All strangers to leave the ground and the people to retire at ten, or immediately thereafter.

In 1854 Rev. B. W. Gorham distilled fifty years of Methodist experience with camp meetings into a massive *Camp Meeting Manual* containing "practical observations and directions" on running a camp meeting. He explained how to select and prepare a site for the meeting and provided detailed plans for building the preaching stand, the altar, and the benches. He also explained how to make and set up the tents. He advised that the meeting should last from five to eight days, stressed the importance of proper policing, and suggested a schedule that "worked well." Finally, Gorham noted that no matter how well planned, the success of a camp meeting depended on effective preaching: "Preaching; not dry, dogmatic theorizing; not metaphysical hair splitting; not pulpit bombast; but plain, clear, evangelical Bible truth, uttered with faithful, solemn, earnestness, and with the Holy Ghost sent down from heaven" (1854, p. 63).

Camp meetings, whether promoted by Methodists or others, were quickly recognized as major social events. A persistent problem for camp meeting organizers was intrusive outsiders who came only for the "mammoth picnic" or social holiday, and not for religion. Cartwright's (1856) autobiography is filled with scenes of confrontations with "drunken rowdies" who sought to disturb the camp meetings. He proudly recounted the time he took whips away from some young men sitting with the ladies, and the time he knocked down drunken "Philistines" who attempted to ride through a Tennessee campground. Drunks and vendors of various vices became so common on the periphery of camp meetings that several states passed laws against the sale of liquor within a mile or two of a camp meeting (C. A. Johnson, 1955, p. 224).

A friendly critic of the camp meeting noted, "Take away the worship, and there would remain sufficient gratifications to allure most young people" (in C. Johnson, 1955, p. 208). Camp meetings not only satisfied the soul, they were fun. It was widely said along the frontier that during camp meetings as many souls were conceived as were saved.

Reaching Slave and Free

Just as the upstarts proved effective in challenging the strongholds of the old colonial mainline, appealing to the growing urban populations, and reaching even the most desolate frontiers, they were also proving effective in appealing to the millions of Americans of African descent. Although the importation of African slaves was not prohibited until 1808, many of the slaves and freed blacks had been in North America for several generations by the end of the eighteenth century. The number of native-born slaves first exceeded 50 percent in the 1740s and was about 80 percent by 1780 (Stark, 2003). Many of the initial linguistic and cultural barriers to missionary work were gone, yet only the Baptists and Methodists generated clergy and a message that readily appealed to the African-American population.

The Church of England's Society for the Propagation of the Gospel (SPG) was established in 1701 for "the conversion of the Indian savages, and the conversion of the Negroes" to Christianity (in Richardson, 1976, p. 24). By their own admission, however, the results were meager. An early SPG missionary complained that even when he had baptismal converts, "all other slaves do laugh at them" (in Campbell, 1995, p. 4). The SPG's dry religious instruction and formal organizational structure—both requiring the leadership of educated white missionaries—found little support from the slaves. Baptists and Methodists, however, found that the techniques that worked so effectively with whites, also worked with blacks.

FIGURE 3.4 African-American Members in the Methodist Episcopal Church, 1790–1851

SOURCE: Minutes of the annual Conferences of the Methodist Episcopal Church.

Figure 3.4 charts the rapid ascent of the Methodists. The membership totals for black Methodists were reported annually in the *Minutes of the Annual Conferences* for each circuit, district, and conference, and appear to be quite accurate. When we converted the Methodist data to rates of growth, we found the growth of black membership mirrored the growth of white membership. In 1790, 2.7 percent of adult blacks and 2.6 percent of adult whites were members of the Methodist Episcopal Church. By 1851 the percentages increased to 7.8 for blacks and 8.1 for whites.[21] Although the Baptist data don't allow us to draw such refined comparisons, the Baptists apparently enrolled far fewer black members. Robert Gardner's (1989) enumeration of all black churches in 1790 located 9,011 black members. Given the slower growth of the Baptists in the early nineteenth century, their increase in black membership most likely continued to fall behind that of the Methodists prior to the Civil War.

Unlike their appeal to the white population, the Baptists and Methodists faced little competition for black membership. Episcopalians, Catholics, and Presbyterians each had missions to the slaves and congregations for freed slaves, but none supported a sizeable membership. Even when other denominations were successful in their appeal to blacks, they could not keep pace with the Methodists and Baptists. Gary Nash's research on the black community of Philadelphia in the late eighteenth and early nineteenth century offers one example.

Shortly after Richard Allen, Absalom Jones, and other recently freed Philadelphian blacks incorporated a "quasi-religious" mutual aid society known as the Free African Society in 1787, they began discussing the formation of an independent congregation for blacks. After several delays and financial shortfalls, the Philadelphia church was nearing completion in early 1794 and members gathered to choose the denominational affiliation of the African Church. But when they voted to affiliate with the Episcopalians and asked Richard Allen to serve as their minister, Allen withdrew from the congregation and informed them that he "could not be anything else but a Methodist" (in Nash 1988, pp. 126–127). Absalom Jones went on to become pastor of the new church, quickly formalized ties with the Episcopal Church, and changed the church's name from African Church to St. Thomas. But Allen didn't give up his hope of starting a Methodist church for blacks. After convening a group of ten black Methodists interested in forming their own church, he used his personal funds to purchase a building that had housed an old blacksmith shop. Allen moved it to a site within a few blocks of St. Thomas, renovated the blacksmith shop into a modest church, and founded Bethel Methodist Church,

TABLE 3.1

African-American Church Membership in Philadelphia, 1795, 1813, and 1837

	1795	1813	1837
Methodist	121	1,426	2,860
	(22%)	(60%)	(69%)
Episcopalian	427	560	250
	(78%)	(24%)	(6%)
Presbyterian		300	325
		(13%)	(8%)
Baptist		89	700
		(4%)	(17%)
Lutheran			10
			(0.2%)

SOURCE: Nash (1988, pp. 132, 260).

a congregation that would later serve as the mother church of the African Methodist Episcopal denomination. Perhaps the most amazing part of the founding of Allen's new church was that he purchased, moved, and renovated the blacksmith shop in a mere seven weeks. Bethel Methodist Church and St. Thomas Episcopal opened their doors for worship in mid-1794 (Nash, 1988; Campbell, 1995).

Supporting a new building and holding a large membership, St. Thomas Episcopal was the pride of Philadelphia's black community. One year after opening, St. Thomas's membership was over three times larger than Bethel Methodist (see Table 3.1). Eighteen years later, however, their fortunes were reversed. The Methodists had started a second church, their membership increased by over tenfold, and they exceeded the Episcopalians by 866 members. During the next twenty-four years the Methodists continued to soar and the Baptists surged, as the Presbyterians showed only modest gains and the Episcopalians began to slide. By 1837 the Methodists and Baptists supported twelve independent black churches in Philadelphia, representing 86 percent of the membership.

When we look closer at the rapid growth of black membership in Baptist and Methodist churches, we find that black membership grew for many of the same reasons as white membership. Like white congregations, the

Methodist classes and small Baptist congregations provided a rich source of intimate fellowship, social support, and spiritual experience. The local churches also allowed members to quickly enter into leadership positions. The black Methodists could serve as class leaders, exhorters, and even itinerants, and the black Baptists gave public testimonies of faith, served as deacons, and the most gifted were invited to preach. These leaders not only provided leadership for other black members during worship and prayer meetings in the church, they provided leadership and support for members outside the church.

The flexibility of the organization also allowed Baptists and Methodists to provide a message and a messenger that appealed to the people. Despite facing restrictions on their relationships with whites, especially for the slaves, talented black preachers quickly emerged. Like their white counterparts, they faced few educational requirements and this resulted in an abundance of clergy. The most famous black preacher was the Methodist itinerant Harry Hosier, known as Black Harry. He often traveled and preached with the Methodist bishops in the 1780s and 1790s and the crowd sizes he drew frequently surpassed those of the bishops (Richardson, 1976; Wigger, 1998). Although he was typically scheduled to preach for the blacks, Bishop Coke soon learned that the "whites always stay to hear him." Coke described Hosier as "one of the best preachers in the world, . . . though he cannot read" (in Richey, Rowe, and Schmidt, 2000, p. 79). But it wasn't just a few black itinerants who captured the attention of the larger community, local preachers, exhorters, and prayer leaders amazed their white audiences with the power of their message (Heyrman, 1997).

Historical attention typically focuses on how slaves were shaped by the "white" church, but the slaves and freed blacks clearly helped to form the distinctive religious culture of the South.[22] Perhaps the most obvious influences were in the area of worship. The emotional and informal worship of the upstarts, combined with their open expression of visions and spiritual experiences, allowed African Americans to experience their religion and express the message using distinctive and meaningful cultural forms (Sobel, 1979). Although, when compared to slaves on Caribbean or Brazilian plantations, there was little synergism between Christianity and African religions, native-born American blacks quickly developed their own style for practicing and professing the faith. Historian Sylvia R. Frey notes that "Africans had a distinct musical system, characterized by idiosyncratic use of pitch, of chords, counterpoint, harmony, tempo, and rhythm and incremental leading lines with choral repetitions"

FAMILY WORSHIP IN A PLANTATION IN SOUTH CAROLINA.—SEE PAGE 574

Family worship at a plantation in South Carolina. (Courtesy of the Billy Graham Center Museum, Wheaton, Ill.)

(1991, p. 299). Even without instruments, the rhythms could be achieved by clapping hands, tapping feet, and swaying bodies. This worship style may have been ridiculed by some whites, but it soon strongly influenced worship in white southern churches.

The simplicity of the message, filled with the familiar themes of redemption and rebirth and requiring no formal training, was also attractive. But the message offered more than a spiritual rebirth, or a promise for the life hereafter; the message offered values, principles, and guidelines for the here and now. When Richard Allen refused to become an Episcopalian, he did so in part because he thought that Methodism provided the personal discipline and reform needed for people being held in bondage. As Nash explained, "to Allen and other black Methodist leaders it seemed a perfect system for lifting up an oppressed people" (1988, p. 193).

Finally, we should acknowledge that at the close of the eighteenth century, the Methodists, and to a lesser extent the Baptists, were advocates for granting more rights and even complete freedom to the African slaves. Not only were they bold enough to bring blacks and whites together for worship and revivals in the South and invite them to pray and preach in public, they took formal stances against slavery (Frey and Wood, 1998; Wigger, 2001). Each of their efforts would ultimately prove ineffective, yet a few examples illustrate the initial position of the two churches. Following the lead of Wesley, Coke, Asbury, and other Methodist leaders, the 1784 Methodist Conference ruled that slavery was "contrary to the laws of God, of men, and of nature" and called upon all members to free their slaves. Six months later, however, they suspended the rule due to pressure from Methodist leaders in the South. Sixteen years later, in 1800, they made another effort. This time the General Conference commanded all circuit preachers to free their slaves or face expulsion and called for all state conferences to petition their state to develop laws leading to emancipation. Coinciding with the first major slave revolt, the resolution faced immediate resistance. Baptist efforts followed a similar path. Supporting no centralized national hierarchy for making pronouncements, representatives of Virginia's churches and associations approved a resolution declaring "heredit[ar]y slavery to be contrary to the word of God." Initially a committee was appointed to develop a plan for emancipation, but the objections soon became too great and the efforts were abandoned. Although additional pronouncements would be made by the Baptist clergy, public sentiment in the South soon came to favor slavery and gradually the clergy of the South increased their support as well. By 1812 the Methodist General Conference gave in to political expediency and allowed the local Annual Conferences to form their own regulations on slavery (Frey, 1988, pp. 245, 247).

Over time, a segregation of the races during worship increasingly became the practice and the law in the South, and the views of the early evangelicals began to fade. Frey explains that "by 1815 the pioneering first generation of evangelicals, whose rejection of slavery had branded them as antisocial revolutionaries, was passing from the scene" (1988, p. 264). Randy J. Sparks reports that in Mississippi "until the 1830s, most churches were remarkably egalitarian when compared to the larger society" and that "black preachers benefited from the ideal of the equality of all believers" (1994, p. 132). By the 1830s, however, slaves were facing increasingly strict laws on where and when they could gather for worship, most churches in the South were now building galleries or

A Methodist camp meeting, where men and women in front of the covered speaker's platform gesticulate, shout, dance, and swoon in response to the preacher's exhortations, while many others look on and four more preachers await their turn. Notice the large number of women in the crowd. Notice too that everyone is dressed up. Besides their obvious religious function, camp meetings had social and recreational aspects as well. (Courtesy of the New-York Historical Society, New York City.)

balconies for black members, segregated seating was fully enforced, and by the end of the antebellum era a growing number of states required whites to supervise the worship of slaves (James, 1988; Harvey, 1997; Frey and Wood, 1998; Sparks, 2001). Despite these increasing social controls, talented black clergy and leaders continued to emerge in Baptist and Methodist congregations; leaders who preached the early evangelicals' message of equality under Christ (in the slave quarters and brush arbors, if necessary) and were prepared to lead a church that would soon have new social and religious freedoms.

Choosing to Lose

It was abundantly clear to all parties that enthusiastic preaching, revival campaigns, and camp meetings were potent methods for mobilizing religious participation. Thus it was well known, even among professors at Harvard and Yale, that the Baptists had benefited greatly from Whitefield's crusade, and even the popular press recognized the rapid growth of Methodism following the Revolution. Moreover, because 94 percent of Americans lived on farms in 1800, the camp meeting was even more important for church growth than were urban revivals. None of this, however, prompted the colonial mainline denominations to adopt similar "marketing" tactics. To the contrary, their leading lights condemned all such methods while ridiculing Methodist and Baptist preachers as ignorant, and even dangerous, fools.

Indeed, when Finney began setting revival fires in western New York, as a Congregationalist minister operating under the 1801 Plan of Union, he was quickly condemned by Congregationalist and Presbyterian leaders. Asahel Nettleton thundered that Finney and his revivalists are doing the "cause of Christ great mischief" (Beecher and Nettleton, 1828, p. 11). How? First, by invading towns without invitations from local pastors. Nettleton explained: the settled pastor "has a right to pursue his own measures, within his own limits . . . no itinerant has any business to interfere" (p. 20). Second, by "the practice of females praying with males," in public assemblies—"some of my brethren have been absolutely insulted by females on this subject" (pp. 10, 15). Third, by preaching in the vernacular, using excessive informality and "passion." Nettleton cautioned against kindling "fires where there was not some spiritual watchman near, to guard and watch against wildness" (p. 16). Worst of all, Nettleton charged, Finney's revivals aroused the riffraff against their betters—referring to Finney's followers as "the *ignobile vulgus*" (p. 15).

Soon the most famous religious intellectual of the time also came down against Finney. Lyman Beecher boldly predicted that this "mode" of revivalism "threatens to become one of the greatest evils which is likely to befall the cause of Christ" and threatens the new nation by throwing it "back in civilization, science, and religion, at least a whole century" (Beecher and Nettleton, 1828, pp. 80, 99). Beecher was appalled that Finney and his followers displayed little respect for the settled and learned ministry, allowed "female prayer" in mixed assemblies, and used a "language of unbecoming familiarity with God" (p. 91). Moreover, Beecher too was greatly concerned that Finney's message would cause common people to lose proper respect for their betters. If Finney followed the belief that "all men, because sinners, are therefore to be treated alike by the ministers of the gospel, without respect to . . . station in society," the result would be "anarchy and absolute destruction" (p. 89).

Ironically, Beecher was one of the few Congregationalist leaders who recognized the competitive threat posed by the Baptists and Methodists, even in New England, and he proposed Congregationalist revivals as the best defense against them. But these revivals must not use vulgar methods, must not cause "muscular" reactions, must not infringe on local cartel arrangements, and must not give the lower classes the idea that all are equal in the eyes of God. That is, revivals were fine as long as they weren't very successful.

Finney defended himself against Beecher and Nettleton's charges, meanwhile continuing his campaigns. But the opposition made local mainline clergy less willing to be linked to his efforts. Hence it was the Baptists and Methodists who gained most from the fires that Finney set. Some years later, Finney and Beecher came to an understanding, but only after Finney had adopted a much more cautious approach to revival preaching and had ceased his campaigns in western New York. By then revival meetings were virtually monopolized by the Baptists and Methodists.

The same thing had happened to camp meetings. Originated by Presbyterians in Kentucky, concern was soon expressed that these meetings would lead to excesses and to disregard for ministerial authority. That Methodist and Baptist preachers were usually given time in the pulpit during the many days of services also raised serious objections. According to Barton Stone (1910, pp. 166–167): "At first they were pleased to see the Methodists and Baptists so cordially uniting with us in worship, no doubt hoping that they would become Presbyterians. But as soon as they saw these sects drawing away disciples after them, they raised the tocsin of alarm—the Confession is in danger!—the church is in danger!"

Several years after the Cane Ridge meeting, the Presbyterian Synod of Lexington, Kentucky, suspended Barton Stone and four of his friends for "insubordination" because they refused to affirm their commitment to strict Calvinist doctrines. For Stone and his associates, these doctrines were at odds with the fundamental theological basis of camp meeting revivals: that all could be saved. He later complained: "Calvinism is among the heaviest clogs on Christianity . . . discouraging. . . sinners from seeking the kingdom of God" (1910, p. 153). Stone observed that the strict Calvinist doctrines (reserving salvation for the elect few) could not cause the kind of fervent faith and changed life that Methodists and Baptists sought from their hearers. Hence, Stone offered pragmatic as well as theological grounds for preaching that all could be saved, and that salvation goes to all who "believe in Jesus and come to him." As he put it:

> When we began first to preach these things, the people appeared as awakened from the sleep of ages—they seemed to see for the first time that they

Presbyterian Leaders Respond to the Western Revivals

Despite some "irregularities," Presbyterian leaders initially celebrated the western revivals as a "dispensation of the grace of God." By 1804, however, they sought to curb what they saw as the "excesses" of the revivals. The following excerpts are taken from the Minutes of the General Assembly of the Presbyterian Church, 1789–1820.

May 28, 1801:
On of the borders of Kentucky and Tennessee, the influences of the Spirit of God seem to have been manifested in a very extraordinary manner. . . . it is probable that some irregularities may have taken place, yet from the information which the Assembly [has] received, they cannot but exceedingly rejoice in the abundant evidence given them that God has visited that people, and poured out his Spirit remarkably upon them. (p. 223)

May 26, 1803:
In many of the southern and western Presbyteries, revivals more extensive, and of a more extraordinary nature, have taken place. . . . There have been multitudes of instances in which great bodily agitations, and other circumstances out of the usual course of religious exercise, have attended the work. . . . The Assembly cannot believe that a dispensation by means of which the ignorant are enlightened, the vicious reclaimed, the erroneous made to acknowledge and obey the truth as it is in Jesus, the haughty infidel humbled, and brought to bow, penitent and believing, before the cross of Christ, and the general aspect of society, changed from dissoluteness and profanity, to sobriety, order, and comparative purity, can be any other than a dispensation of the grace of God. (p. 274)

May 29, 1804:
We strongly bear our testimony against those persons who pretend to immediate impulses and revelations from heaven; those divine communications which were given only to the prophets and apostles, who were appointed by God to reveal to mankind the way of eternal life. When men presume that the Holy Spirit, contrary to the established order of providence, interferes by particular impulse

(continued)

to direct them in all the common affairs of life; when they deem themselves to be impelled by him to particular acts of particular religious exercises, contrary to the established order of the gospel, and the obvious duties of the moment; when finally they pretend to miraculous powers or prophetic influences, and the foretelling of future events, all these are evidences of a wild enthusiastic spirit, and tend eventually to destroy the authority of the word of God, as the sole rule of faith and practice. . . . Dear brethren, and fellow labourers in the gospel of our common Lord, study to prevent excesses so dishonorable, and contrary to the beautiful order of the church of Christ, or zealously endeavour to repress them wherever they begin to appear. (pp. 315–316)

May 25, 1808:
It is observable that the work, though powerful, has progressed with great silence, uncommon solemnity, and free from all appearances of extravagance. . . . In the southern parts of our bounds, the extraordinary revivals of religion have considerably declined; bodily agitations are gradually disappearing; in one instance, where extravagance and wild enthusiasm had been avowed and defended, in opposition to the pastoral advice of this body, we are happy to learn that the abettors have acknowledged their error, and returned to the good order of our Church. (pp. 401–402)

were responsible beings, and that a refusal to use the means appointed was a damning sin.

The sticklers for orthodoxy amongst us writhed under these doctrines, but, seeing their mighty effects on the people, they winked at the supposed errors, and through fear, or other motives, they did not at first publicly oppose us. (1910, p. 166)

If the Presbyterians thought they could silence Stone and his four associates through suspension, they had misread them. Upon notification of their suspension all five young preachers "forever dissevered the ties which bound them to the mother church" (Rogers, 1910, p. 64). But they kept

FRANK LESLIE'S
ILLUSTRATED
NEWSPAPER

No. 1,406—Vol. LV] NEW YORK—FOR THE WEEK ENDING SEPTEMBER 2, 1882. [Price 10 Cents.

AN OLD-FASHIONED CAMP-MEETING—AN EXHORTER PRAYING FOR THE FAMILY OF A CONVERT.
FROM A SKETCH BY A STAFF ARTIST.—SEE PAGE 23.

One of the objections to revivals and camp meetings was that women were allowed to pray with men. These charges were often directed against the Methodists, because women took an active role in their prayer meetings and served as exhorters at camp meetings, as here. By the 1850s, however, Cartwright (1856, p. 517) reports that there were "fashionable objections to females praying in public." (Courtesy of the Billy Graham Center Museum, Wheaton, Ill.)

right on preaching and eventually joined with the Campbellites to form the Christian Church.

Thus did the old mainline cease participating in the camp meetings, thereby surrendering all of the pulpit time to the Baptists and the Methodists. But if the old mainline denominations would not take part in camp meetings or hold their own, they were not unaware of the immense gains that the Methodists and the Baptists were making through these means. In keeping with their monopolistic thinking, mainline clergy began to inspire local officials to define camp meetings as disturbances of the peace or as violations of other statutes. This subject seems to have been ignored by church historians, but turns up in sources such as Asbury's letters and journals. For example, Asbury wrote to Stith Mead, presiding elder of the Richmond Virginia District: "A spirit of persecution is waked up over the whole continent. All earth and hell is roused against field meetings, but we will endure fines, imprisonment, and death sooner than we will give them up. We have 25.00 dollars [a fine] to pay, on the Eastern shore of Virginia, no law, or justice for Methodists" (Asbury, [1852] 1958, vol. 3, pp. 380–381).

How did the upstart sects win America? Partly by default. As free market conditions increasingly prevailed in the religious economy, the old mainline denominations failed to meet the competitive challenges and eventually abandoned the marketplace to the upstarts.

Comfortable, well-paid mainline clergy rarely desired to go West and had no taste for ministering to the *ignobile vulgus*. They earned more esteem from publishing their sermons in books than from bellowing them to multitudes in open fields. In any case, clergy flirting with Unitarianism or who thought Methodists and Baptists were literally "out of their wits" would have been of little worth out where the great harvest of souls was under way, even had they been willing to venture forth. It is impossible to imagine Lyman Beecher exhorting the "muscular" sinners at Cane Ridge.

Moreover, clergy accustomed to gentlemen's agreements limiting competition and who thought good manners forbade recruiting from a colleague's flock were ill-equipped to hold their own in a free market. In contrast, when Baptists and Methodists collided in pursuit of flocks no holds were barred and no quarter was asked or given. For example, no sooner had the Methodist Peter Cartwright left a stop on his circuit after having made twenty-three converts, when nearby Baptists responded by sending three preachers to recruit them. Word was sent to Cartwright

(1856, p. 66) "for fear these preachers would run my converts into the water before I could come round." Arriving in the nick of time, with his converts standing on the bank of the creek, Cartwright managed to recover them to the fold of those who believed in "infant sprinkling."

The Design of Victory

The victory of the upstarts was a matter not only of what the mainline did wrong, but of what the Methodists and the Baptists did right. Just as revivals aren't simply spontaneous, happenstance events, but require careful planning and the application of appropriate methods, so too with church growth—the Methodist "miracle" of growth between 1776 and 1850 didn't just happen, either. The Methodists knew perfectly well what they were up to, what worked and didn't work in gaining and holding members, and why. It therefore is instructive to consult a remarkable book, published on the occasion of the "first century of American Methodism," by the Reverend C. C. Goss (1866). In it, the design for the Methodist "miracle" is presented in detail. There could be no better summary of the arguments we have developed in this chapter than these excerpts from Goss's neglected analysis.

> This poor despised people, called Methodists, celebrating their first centennial, head and shoulders above the older denominations of the country, the question naturally arises, What has conduced to such a rapid growth? . . .
>
> ITS MODE OF PREACHING
>
> When compared with most of the leading denominations, the style of the Methodist preacher is peculiar, both as to matter and manner. Although it is not quite as marked as in days gone by, yet it is sufficiently discernable at the present. . . . As a rule, a Methodist addresses himself directly to the heart, while many others appeal to the intellect. . . . Methodist preachers never converted the pulpit into a professor's chair; but with earnestness have urged and beseeched men to flee the wrath to come. . . . To [the Methodist preacher] the mathematical, or dry Scotch mode of working out the problem of salvation, is too slow a process.
>
> As a general rule, a Methodist preacher comes directly from the people. His former life was spent in the workshop, or in some other way where he was called to mingle with his fellow-man. . . .
>
> The sermons, too, of these men have been mostly extemporaneous. . . .

A subdued and orderly camp meeting, pictured on the front page of the Reverend B. W. Gorham's *Camp Meeting Manual*. Writing in 1854, when camp meetings were in decline, Gorham was trying to promote their use and to disarm critics, who charged they were a source of "wickedness" and "undue excitement." (Courtesy of the Billy Graham Center Museum, Wheaton, Ill.)

These sermons also have been delivered in plain, simple language—the language of the people. . . . Book language has not been so much used as the common language, hence the people have known where to say Amen. . . .

SELF-SACRIFICING SPIRIT OF ITS MINISTRY

. . . As no class is more identified with Christ in effort for the salvation of the lost than the ministry, so no class are called upon to make greater sacrifices. The Methodist ministry are perhaps sharers with Christ in this respect to a greater degree than others. It is a part of the system with which they are identified. As they have no certain dwelling-place, they are rightfully styled itinerants. . . .

SYSTEM OF FREE CHURCHES

This system was not only necessary in the outset, in order to secure an attendance, but it was as providential as it was necessary. As Methodism was raised up to meet the spiritual wants of a large class, not blessed with an abundance of this world's goods, it was important that they not be debarred by any financial considerations. Beside there is somewhat of a connection between a "free gospel" and "free seats." . . .

The system of renting pews in the house of God, or of selling them, is very deleterious to the spread of the gospel. . . .

ITS FREQUENT REVIVALS

Methodism originated with revivals; its lifepower has been drawn from them, it can only exist by their continued use. Scarcely a Methodist minister passes a winter without a revival. Camp-meetings also tend to keep the revival spirit alive during the summer. . . .

ITS LAY EFFORTS

That every member of the Methodist Episcopal Church is a working member we do not pretend; that there are many such also in other Churches we admit; but what is asserted is, that the growth of the denomination has been in proportion to its activity, and, in a special sense, may be attributed to its efficient system of lay operations.

When a person unites with the Church he is immediately placed in one of the classes, under the care of a person of experience and discrimination. . . . The Methodist Episcopal Church is not a spiritual lounging place, in which members can simply take comfort, it is not a spiritual restaurant, where persons enter to feast upon the good things of the kingdom; but it is a spiritual workshop, where persons who enter are expected to work for Christ. It would be a fatal day for Methodism if its members ever get too proud or too indolent to work for Christ. Its activity has been its life, the law of its growth, and it can only exist and prosper by its continued operation.

ITS MISSIONARY SPIRIT

. . . Methodist preachers have always acted on the presumption that they were included in the call, to "go and preach the Gospel to every creature," hence they have gone whether invited or not; and sometimes have gone when they were invited in a very emphatic manner to leave. This missionary spirit has given to the Church the epithet, "the pioneer Church," and to its ministry, "the circuit-riders."

While the mission of some other churches may be to settle, the peculiar prerogative of the Methodist Episcopal Church is to push out into destitute regions, to break new ground, to urge upon the masses generally the saving truths of the Gospel.

DOCTRINE OF SANCTIFICATION

> In Methodism this doctrine has occupied a prominent place. . . . No matter what the terms used, whether sanctification, perfection, consecration, resignation, or any other, the meaning was "holiness of heart, without which no man shall see the Lord.". . . This is not needed simply as a doctrine believed and preached, but inwardly experienced; then it will be preached both in the pulpit and in the life.
> . . . It is this spiritual essence that satisfied the spiritual nature, for which thousands are hungering and thirsting. And with inward spiritual power and outward aggressive effort to meet this felt want, Methodism may be the means under God, during this second century, of lifting this wicked disquieted world into a purer, serener, and diviner region. (Goss, 1866, pp. 162–186)

By the time Goss wrote these insightful lines, however, they no longer applied. Most congregations were no longer the province of local class-leaders and exhorters—the amateurs had been replaced as the circuit riders dismounted and settled into comfortable parsonages. The professional clergy now ran the Methodist Church in a fully realized episcopal fashion. Many Methodist clergy had begun to *read* their sermons, and many of the younger ministers now came to the pulpit from Methodist seminaries. In an astonishing reversal of their original principles, some Methodist congregations had begun to rent their pews, and the word "sanctification" was appearing far less frequently in Methodist publications. Gorham devoted the entire first half of his *Camp Meeting Manual* to a defense of the camp meeting and to an expression of deep regret that each year fewer Methodist camp meetings were being held. We shall return to the Methodist story in Chapter 5.

Chapter 4

The Coming of the Catholics, 1850–1926

Too often the growth and vigor of American Catholicism are simply explained as a matter of immigration. All the priests had to do was stand at the gangplanks and enroll the faithful as they disembarked—a task made all the easier because these newcomers were people accustomed to "blind obedience."

In truth, most of the millions of immigrants from "Catholic" nations who flowed into the United States in the latter part of the nineteenth century were at best *potential* American Catholic parishioners. To tap this potential, the Roman Catholic Church had to counteract the vigorous efforts of Protestant sects to recruit these immigrants, and it had to inspire them to entirely new levels of commitment and participation. For the fact is that the great majority of people in "Catholic" nations are not very good Catholics, in that they seldom attend mass, rarely participate in the sacraments, and do not contribute money to the church (Martin, 1990; Stark, 1992c; Gill, 1998). Ironically, it is only where the Catholic Church is in the minority and is somewhat embattled that it can generate the vigorous participation we have come to associate with American Catholicism (Stark and McCann, 1993). In the United States, the Roman Catholic Church became an extremely effective and competitive religious firm when forced to confront a free market religious economy.

Catholic Membership Statistics

Estimates of the Catholic population in the United States during the nineteenth century were incredibly inflated. *The American Almanac* for 1826 stated that there were 1,071,000 Roman Catholics in the nation. Hayward (1836) estimated that there were from 800,000 to 1.2 million American Catholics in 1835, and 1.2 million is the number given by Bishop John England in 1836 when asked the number of Catholic church members. These totals rose rapidly. In the 1856 revised version of his book *Religion in America*, Robert Baird set Catholic membership at 3.3 million for 1855. The report of the 1906 census of religious bodies cites A. J. Schemm as having established that there were a total of 4.5 million American Catholics in 1860.

To the extent that these numbers were based on anything but pure guesswork (and Bishop England said he was only guessing), they were the result of a great fallacy. People simply added all immigrants from all "Catholic" countries to the previous Catholic total and then factored in a high rate of natural increase. Ford claimed that Irish immigration and fertility alone should have produced 24 million Catholics by 1870, to say nothing of the millions more that should have been produced by immigrants from elsewhere. A more cautious estimate was offered by Abbé Villeneuve, who added together the Irish, German, French, Belgian, and Italian immigrants and claimed there ought to have been at least 20 million American Catholics by 1890 (Shaughnessy, 1925).

Because these overcounts were taken for fact, the results of the religious census of 1890 seemed to ratify the proposition (long advocated by both Protestants and Catholics) that, when presented with the opportunity to choose, millions of immigrants had deserted the faith. This census, the first to ask each congregation for its membership totals, reported only slightly more than 7 million Catholics. If millions more "Catholics" had entered the nation, where were they? Defection seemed the only possible conclusion. Bishop England estimated that more than 3 million Catholic immigrants had defected by 1836, and throughout the rest of the century the American Catholic hierarchy grew increasingly upset about the church's terrible losses. In a memorial presented to the Pope in 1910, the loss of members was estimated to be 10 million. Others placed it at 20 million. "What, then, has become of the other twenty millions?" Villeneuve asked. "They have turned Protestant or have become indifferent," he answered (in Shaughnessy, 1925, p. 233).

But it wasn't true. In 1925 Gerald Shaughnessy published a quantitative study, notable for its sophistication and careful scholarship, entitled *Has the Immigrant Kept the Faith: A Study of Immigration and Catholic Growth in the United States, 1790–1920*. What Shaughnessy demonstrated should have been obvious all along. The "missing" millions had never existed, because the millions of immigrants from "Catholic" nations weren't Catholics. Consider the Irish. Weren't nearly all Irish immigrants at least nominally Catholic? Of course not. Very substantial proportions of Irish immigrants were ardent Protestants from the North. As Andrew Greeley (1979) has shown, even today the majority of Americans of Irish descent are Protestants, and the same is true for those of French descent.

By factoring all the immigration statistics to reflect the actual Catholic composition of the nations from which immigrants came, Shaughnessy estimated the Catholic population in 1850 as 1.6 million, not 3.5 million. Even this figure is high. For one thing, Shaughnessy assumed that immigrants accurately reflected the religious composition of their homeland. But that often was not true—French immigrants, for example, seem to have been disproportionately Protestant. For another, Shaughnessy knew that there would be vigorous efforts to refute his findings and so he was always careful to select the most conservative assumptions. Nevertheless, his estimates for 1850–1880 are far closer to our estimates than they are to the figures used by earlier writers.

Many leading Protestant historians have ignored Shaughnessy's statistics. Even though he favorably cited Shaughnessy's statistics for 1880–1910, Sweet ([1930] 1950, p. 273) repeated errant estimates of 600,000 Catholics in 1830, 3.5 million in 1850, and 4.5 million in 1860. Olmstead (1961, p. 83) set the 1860 Catholic total at only 3.1 million, but still claimed that they "constituted the largest single denomination in the United States." Ahlstrom (1975, vol. 1, p. 633) wrote: "So incredibly large was the flow of immigrants that by 1850 Roman Catholics, once a tiny and ignored minority, had become the country's largest religious communion." He placed Catholic membership at 3.5 million in 1860, a million fewer than Sweet had claimed, but still far too high. Neither Hudson (1981) nor Marty (1984) offers sources for his statistics, but each accepts Ahlstrom's conclusion. Hudson wrote that "by 1852 . . . the Roman Catholic Church had become the largest ecclesiastical body in the nation" (p. 128), and Marty offered Catholic membership figures for 1800 to highlight the growth by 1850: "In 1800 only 50,000 Catholics lived in the United States; by 1850 theirs was the largest church in America" (p. 272).

Even those few historians who accepted Shaughnessy's greatly reduced statistics mistakenly concluded that by 1850 the Catholics had surpassed all other Christian denominations (Dolan, 1978). The error lay in failing either to deflate the Catholic totals for members under age thirteen (Catholics count all baptized persons as members) or to inflate the figures for groups, such as the Methodists and the Baptists, who do not count children.

Given that 39 percent of the nation's population in 1850 was age thirteen or under, failure to standardize produces very distorted comparisons—which is why we rely here on adherence rates that standardize definitions of membership.

When we use estimates based on census data (Finke and Stark, 1986) and standardize for denominations not counting children, the statistics reveal a very different profile (see Figure 4.1). In 1850, the year by which religious historians say Roman Catholicism had become the largest denomination in the country, Catholic totals are only slightly higher than those of the Presbyterians and fall far below those of the Baptists and the Methodists. It was another generation before Roman Catholics became the largest denomination in America.

But can it really matter that much just when the Catholics became number one? We think it does. As already noted, exaggerations of Catholic membership led to subsequent misapprehensions about huge rates of Catholic defection. In addition, as we see in Chapter 5, Catholic membership gains were incorrectly used to excuse the relative decline in many major Protestant bodies in the latter part of the nineteenth century.

In any event, Table 4.1 allows us to examine Catholic growth from 1850 through 1926. According to our calculations, in 1850 there were only slightly more than a million American Catholics, or 5 percent of the total population (14 percent of all church adherents). The massive waves of immigration during the 1850s more than doubled the Catholic total by 1860, to nearly 2.5 million adherents. But the substantial non-Catholic component of immigration in this decade limited the increase in the proportion of Americans who were Catholic to only 8 percent. Indeed, the largest increase in the proportion who were Catholic occurred between 1890, when the census recorded more than 7 million Catholics (making up 12 percent of the population), and 1906, when the census found more than 14 million Catholics (making up 17 percent of the population). From 1906 through 1926 the Catholic "market share" remained constant at 16 percent of the population.

If we examine the regional and ethnic dispersion of American Catholics in 1860, we find that Rhode Island was the most Catholic state. The Irish and the Italians were no doubt a major component of the 21.4 percent of Rhode Islanders who were Catholic. But Hispanics put California in second place with 19 percent Catholic. French Cajuns made up the bulk of Louisiana's 16.6 percent Catholic population; Germans (many of them living in St. Paul) were a major reason Minnesota was fourth, with 14.8 percent of its population enrolled in the Catholic faith.

FIGURE 4.1 Total Adherents by Denomination, 1850–1890 (in thousands; adherents include children and adults)

Year

Total Adherents

- ■ Catholic
- ▨ Methodist
- ☐ Baptist
- ▧ Presbyterian

In 1890, the impact of Hispanics on Catholic membership showed up clearly in New Mexico, where 77 percent were Catholic, and Arizona, where 37.5 percent were Catholic. Then came Rhode Island (33 percent), Massachusetts (32.3 percent), and Minnesota (24.5).

Notable is the tiny Catholic population in the South, where few immigrants settled. Even today, Catholics make up only a tiny proportion of the populations of southern states, other than Louisiana.

These statistics make it clear that the major growth in the proportion

TABLE 4.1

Catholics as Percentage of Total Population and Church
Adherents, 1850–1926

	1850	1860	1870	1890	1906	1916	1926
Catholic adherents	1,088	2,439	3,555	7,343	14,211	15,722	18,605
% of total population	5	8	9	12	17	16	16
% of total adherents	14	21	26	26	32	30	28

SOURCE: The years 1850, 1860, 1870 are based on membership estimates (Finke and Stark, 1986). Other years from Bureau of the Census.

of Catholics in the United States took place much later than previous writers have claimed and that, when they finally did arrive by the millions, the immigrants kept the faith. Shaughnessy concluded: "There is no evidence of even an appreciable or measurable loss [of immigrant Catholics]. . . . It is very probable that there has been no loss at all, beyond that defection of Catholics which ordinarily takes place" (p. 221).

Faced with a free market religious economy with a full spectrum of denominational options, "Catholics" from Germany, Italy, and Poland, like Irish Catholics before them, chose Roman Catholicism. Indeed, to a substantial degree these immigrants chose to *become* Catholics, because their prior Catholicism often had been quite nominal. How did the Catholic Church become such an effective competitor when faced with a free market?

The basis of Catholic success is remarkably similar to that of the upstart Protestants—the Baptists and the Methodists. The Catholics aggressively marketed a relatively intense, otherworldly religious faith to a growing segment of the population. Besides offering familiar liturgy, symbols, and saints, the Catholic Church also emphasized personal renewal through devotional activities and in effect produced its own brand of revivalism. In terms of clergy, too, the Catholics were more like the upstarts than like the old mainline Protestant bodies. Whether they were sent from abroad or recruited locally, the Catholic clergy were not of genteel social origin, nor did they aspire to a comfortable salary. Priests, nuns, and brothers were ready to go wherever they were sent and to do what needed to be done. Locally, the parish church provided a secure haven for ethnic subcultures in which immigrant groups could retain aspects of their native culture—especially language, food, child-rearing practices, and styles of worship—while adapting to their new nation. A major achievement of the American Catholic Church was its ability, despite its overwhelmingly Irish hierarchy, to appeal to a broad spectrum of ethnic backgrounds and to prevent ethnic differences from producing major schisms. In addition, above the parish level the church created an encapsulated social structure—a kind of parallel Catholic America—that protected Catholics from the dominant and often hostile Protestant environment.

Making American Catholics

At the end of the nineteenth century, the German sociologist Max Weber expressed amazement at the levels of voluntary financial support that Americans freely gave their churches: "church affiliation in the U.S.A. brings with it incomparably higher financial burdens, especially for the poor, than anywhere in Germany. . . . I have personally known of many burdened cases in a congregation in a city on Lake Erie, which was almost entirely composed of German immigrant lumberjacks. Their regular contributions for religious purposes amounted to almost $80 annually, being paid out of an average annual income of about $1,000. Everyone knows that even a small fraction of this financial burden in Germany would lead to a mass exodus from the church" (1946, p. 342).[1]

This situation was precisely what confronted the American Catholic Church. How could pastors convince European immigrants, accustomed to inexpensive religion from a church supported by lands, endowments, or government subsidy, to provide funding at a level that Weber thought would empty the churches of Europe? This task would have been impossible with parishioners who displayed the relatively low levels of commitment and participation typical in Europe. Indeed, to get immigrant Catholics to give as Methodists and Baptists did, it was first necessary to get them fired up with religious conviction in the same way that the Methodists and Baptists were.

Moreover, the local Catholic parish had to gather and motivate the faithful while fending off mission efforts by Protestant sects. Some went to amazing lengths in their efforts to gain Catholic adherents. Shaughnessy (1925, p. 221) reported: "Statues, altars, candles and similar appurtenances are used by certain sects, in their 'Italian missions,' to entrap the unwary and the ignorant." Here Shaughnessy raised a very sensitive matter. Over the decades many American Catholic leaders had complained of the religious ignorance and indifference of Italian immigrants. In 1888 Archbishop Corrigan of New York wrote to Cardinal Manning: "There are 80,000 Italians in this city, of whom only two percent have been in the habit of hearing Mass" (in Ellis, 1956, p. 483). In a similar vein, Bishop Thomas A. Becker of Wilmington wrote in 1883: "It is a very delicate matter to tell the Sovereign Pontiff how utterly faithless the specimens of his country coming here really are. Ignorance of their religion and a depth of vice little known to us yet, are the prominent characteristics. The fault lies higher up than the poor people. The clergy are sadly remiss in their duty" (in Hennesey, 1981, p. 174). Apparently someone was finally willing to mention this matter to the Pope, for on December 10, 1888, Pope Leo XIII wrote a special plea to the American hierarchy on behalf of Italian immigrants (as translated in Ellis, 1956, pp. 482–485). The Pope urged American priests to guard their flocks from the "ever present excitement of the passions, and the deceits practiced by the sects that flourish widely [in the United States]." The Pope's message also mourned the "wretched lot of so many whom we perceive to be wandering like sheep without a shepherd."[2] But the Pope took no notice of any shortages or shortcomings of shepherds back in Italy. The American hierarchy, however, continued to grumble about the problem. In 1913 Archbishop James Quigley of Chicago remarked: "the Italians who come from Southern Italy and Sicily are unexcelled in their ignorance of religion" (in Hennesey, 1981, p. 174).

Similar complaints were being made about French-Canadian immigrants. The Bishop of Burlington, Vermont, complained in 1886 of their "complete ignorance of religion . . . [and that they] knew not either confession or communion and many . . . have been invalidly married before Protestant ministers" (in Hennesey, 1981, p. 175).

To survive in America the Catholic Church had to overcome ignorance and apathy. Of course, this was precisely the task that had faced the Baptists and the Methodists as they confronted an overwhelmingly unchurched population following the Revolution. Even as the first large waves of Catholic immigrants began to arrive, American Protestantism had not yet enlisted the majority of the population in a local church. Given the similarity in the situations they faced, it is not surprising that Catholics and evangelical Protestants employed similar tactics.

Revivalism and Personal Renewal

Revivals, miraculous cures, heartfelt religious experiences, and emotional spiritual renewal are activities usually associated with various sects of evangelical Protestantism. But each of these was also an important part of parish life in the immigrant Catholic church. By the middle of the nineteenth century, evangelism had come to the fore of parish life. In Dolan's (1978, p. 186) words, "the widespread neglect of religion [to which European immigrants had been accustomed] and the competitive spirit of the American religious environment demanded something more than ritual and ceremony." Led by the religious orders, especially the Redemptorists, Paulists, Jesuits, and Passionists, Catholic revivalism and devotionalism spread to every region of the nation.[3]

At the center of this new evangelical surge was the Catholic revival campaign. American Catholics didn't call these revivals, nor did they label those who led them evangelists. But revival meetings are what they were and they occurred about as frequently and regularly in Catholic parishes as in Baptist and Methodist congregations.

Their origins can be traced to sixteenth century Europe when the Jesuits, Vincentians, Redemptorists, and other religious orders were conducting missions in the European countryside as part of the Counter-Reformation (Chadwick, 1981; O'Malley, 1993; McBrien, 1995). By the late sixteenth century, "elaborate instructions outlined the method and program of the mission" and its practice continued to expand throughout Europe (in Dolan, 1978, p. 13). Missions were described as times of intense preaching, where the sacraments of penance and the Eucharist were made available, and all were exhorted to accept the traditional teachings of the church and spare themselves eternal damnation. Whether they were conducted in sixteenth-century Europe or nineteenth-century America, the goal was the same: to revive the faithful and recapture the lost (Finke and Wittberg, 2000).

In his authoritative study of Catholic revivalism from 1830 to 1900, Jay Dolan (1978, p. 44) reported that "as many as thirteen [religious orders] were conducting missions at any one time"—the Redemptorist Order alone conducted 3,955 local revivals from 1860 to 1890.[4] The Jesuit revivalists Father Arnold Damen and Father John Coghlan reported that during the mission season of 1876–77 they had given communion to 116,265 church members in various parishes scattered across the nation, received 484 Protestant converts in the faith, and had conducted 1,464 first communions and 2,056 confirmations (Garraghan, 1984, pp. 95–96). Despite these Herculean efforts, the orders could not meet the demand for parish missions. Father Damen wrote: "If I could double myself and give four missions at one and the same time, I could not satisfy all the requests with which they press me to come to their assistance" (in Garraghan, 1984, p. 101). During the late 1870s Damen's mission schedule was always filled at least two years in advance.

Even in 1906, when religious orders such as the Jesuits and the Passionists were beginning to shift their attention to retreats for the laity, the Census of Religious Bodies reported: "The home missionary work of the church, . . . is less an organized work for church extension than a series of evangelistic or revival services, which are called missions" (1910, p. 606). Though the census report was unable to offer statistics on the number of revivals conducted by five of the orders active in parish missions, including three of the most active orders (the Redemptorists, the Paulists, and the Passionists), it tallied 672 missions conducted by the remaining six orders in 1906. If the five uncounted orders conducted even another 600 parish missions in 1906, there would have been one mission for every ten parishes in existence that year, and there is good reason to suppose that these five orders actually conducted far more than 600 missions. The recommended interval between parish missions was no oftener than every three years and no less often than every ten years. It seems clear that most parishes conformed to this recommendation and that missions were a common feature in the parishes of the immigrant church.

Like Protestant revivals, the Catholic parish mission was not a spontaneous outburst of renewal. Dolan (1978, p. 60) noted: "Handbooks spelled out in detail the sermons that should be preached, the ceremonies that should be conducted and the atmosphere to be created." The famous Jesuit revivalist Francis X. Weninger published three books in which he attempted to share with other priests his insights about holding effective missions, and to explain "the matter of sermons, the instructions to the various classes of exercitants, the address, the solemnities to be observed, together with the whole conduct of the mission" (in Garraghan, 1984, p. 58).

Like the revivals of Whitefield and Finney, the parish missions of the religious orders were planned far in advance and required weeks or even months of preparation. At the appointed date one or more full-time traveling evangelists from one of the religious orders would arrive to conduct a series of services based on the same emotional dynamics as those held by their Baptist and Methodist counterparts—albeit the key symbols and rhetorical devices had a distinctively Catholic flavor. Beneath the references to saints and apart from the incense and the votive candles, the evangelistic concerns were the same: to stir the spirit and save the soul. Moreover, the fundamental message was the same: that the gates of hell are gaping and eternal fires await.

A popular manual on conducting parish missions suggested that one sermon should be devoted to death and advised that a catafalque be placed at the front of the church. Following a mournful hymn, the preacher should ask the people where their souls would be if they were today lying in state ready for burial. The manual noted: "This ceremony never fails to make a very deep impression" (Wissel, 1886, p. 115).

And just as Protestant evangelists often exhorted their audiences to tears and physical reactions, so too did Catholic preachers. Father Burtsell reported in his diary that during a revival preached by the famous Joseph Wissel in New York City in 1867, "one woman began to cry aloud; twenty others joined in as a chorus; and the whole congregation showed similar symptoms when the preacher said: 'Don't cry now but cry at your confession: then bewail your sins" (in Dolan, 1975, p. 156). In 1848, as Charles Finney was preparing to take his evangelistic campaign to England, Francis X. Weninger conducted his first parish mission not far from Finney's home. The Cincinnati *Wahrheits freund* described Weninger's success: "Not a single Catholic who attended the mission failed to go to confession. . . . [Father Weninger] all along drew tears of repentance and consolation from the eyes of his hearers. Often there was general sobbing and weeping throughout the church" (translated in Garraghan, 1984, p. 54). The results of a parish mission in New York City in 1863 were quantified in the local Catholic paper: "fifteen to thirty priests were occupied without interruption from morning to night in hearing confessions [and] twenty-thousand persons approached the tribunal of penance" (Garraghan, 1984, p. 92).

A typical Catholic revival lasted for eight days, but many went on for two weeks, Jesuits such as Father Weninger preferred a two-week revival, because this allowed them to devote the first week to women and the second week to men—the idea being that initially it was easier to draw women to the services. Once the proper spirit had been established among them, they would "urge their husbands, sons, or brothers to avail themselves of its graces" (Garraghan, 1984, p. 96).

Gilbert J. Garraghan (1984, p. 96) has recorded a typical daily schedule for a parish mission:

5 A.M.	Mass and sermon
8:30 A.M.	Mass and sermon
3 P.M.	Way of the Cross
7:30 P.M.	Rosary, sermon and Benediction of the Blessed Sacrament

Despite the many daytime activities offered, the main event was the evening service. As the audience gathered, songs and prayers were used to "warm up the audience" and then the preacher held sway for about an hour (Dolan, 1975).

A leaflet distributed to members of St. Paul's Parish in New York City in 1895 illustrates the similarities between the Protestant revival and the Catholic mission.

> A mission is a time when God calls with a more earnest voice than at other times all persons, but sinners especially, to work out their salvation with fear and trembling. It is an extraordinary time to make your friendship with God. It is a time when the greatest truths of religion—heaven, hell, the evil of mortal sin, the justice of God, his tender mercy—are preached to you. It is a time when priests from early morning till night wait in the confessionals for you, to absolve you from your sins, and restore you to God's favor. . . . It is a time when you are exhorted, by the cross and blood of Christ, if indeed you have a spark of gratitude or love towards God, to turn your face to him with contrition. (in Dolan, 1978, p. 58)

But this passage also makes it clear that the parish mission was embedded in a distinctively Catholic culture. The revivalists relied on Catholic rituals and sacraments. Spiritual renewal was completed with the sacraments of confession and communion. The revivalists used these sacraments, and others such as reciting the rosary, because their aim was to renew and reactivate the faith of parish members, not to convert Protestants. Although Catholic revivalists took pride in any Protestant converts they gained, attempts to increase the number of missions to non-Catholics seldom received strong support and often faced resistance or open hostility (Jonas, 1988). This no doubt reflected concern that such efforts played into the hands of those who stirred up public fears concerning Catholic intentions.

In any event, just as the aim of Methodist evangelists was to strengthen commitment to the local congregation, the aim of the Catholic evangelist was to animate the religious life of the parish. One of our colleagues, recalling several revivals held in his suburban Boston parish during the 1950s, reported: "Those guys [the visiting evangelists] said things to us that our local pastor couldn't ever say because he was a sweet man and

Francis Xavier Weninger (1805–1888). "I continually am giving Missions in the woods as well as in the metropolis going to every chapel, no matter how many families there are. In the course of the year I am preaching over 1,000 times every year" (in Garraghan, 1984, p. 57). (Courtesy of the Archives of the University of Notre Dame.)

besides it was his job to forgive us. They told us we were all sure to go to hell unless we went to confession and told the truth for a change." Dolan (1978, p. 181) summarized the benefits to the parish: "Personal conversion was completed through the sacraments of the church; parish schisms were healed; pastors were invested with godlike authority; orthodox religious behavior, centered around a new devotional piety, was promoted; and the organization of parish confraternities took place."

Confraternities are organized lay groups within a parish that meet regularly and pursue a special program of devotions. One of the oldest is the Archconfraternity of the Holy Rosary, whose specific purpose is to foster praying of the rosary. Confraternities are the Catholic analogue of prayer groups within evangelical Protestant congregations. Just as prayer groups were used to consolidate and sustain the religious enthusiasms stirred up by revivalists, Catholic confraternities were assigned that role in Catholic parish life. Father Weninger claimed that confraternities were necessary for "the continuance of the fruit of the mission after it has closed" (in Garraghan, 1984, p. 59). Moreover, just like Protestant prayer groups, the special devotional gatherings of the confraternities were the primary setting for unusually intense religious experiences such as "communion with the saints" and the reception of gifts and favors from God. According to Taves (1986, p. 62): "miraculous cures were usually associated both with devotional acts, such as novenas, confession, communion, or prayers to Mary and the saints, and with devotional objects that were believed to have or transmit supernatural power, such as eucharistic wafers, scapulars, or relics."

Thus we can begin to grasp how American Catholicism met the challenges of an unregulated religious economy. The parish pastors did not wait for immigrants to come to mass: they went out and rounded them up, often making effective use of revivalism and emotional worship services. During a parish mission held in St. Paul's Parish in New York City in 1859, a substantial number of young men received communion for the first time, many years past the normal age—and nearly all of them were immigrants of "Catholic" backgrounds. Nor was this limited to New York City. In his insightful history of American Jesuits in middle America, Garraghan (1984, p. 97) noted "a curious feature of these early parish-missions was the large number of adults who made their first holy communion on such occasions. This delay in receiving the sacrament was due in most cases to neglect on the part of the parents." And we have ample testimony that this neglect was the common "Catholic heritage" of the vast majority of immigrants as they came down the gangplanks.

Thus, entirely dependent upon voluntary contributions from members for the support of the church, and facing vigorous competition from highly skilled, itinerant Baptist and Methodist evangelists who were ready to travel the nation exhorting the faithful, the Catholic religious orders quickly responded by sending forth equally skilled evangelists to ride many of the same trails.

American Priests

Just as Francis Asbury was willing to ride nearly 300,000 miles up and down America to build Methodism, later in the century the Jesuit revivalist Francis X. Weninger was equally willing to travel more than 200,000 miles to preach more than eight hundred Catholic parish missions.[5] In similar fashion, no sooner had the Baptists put six railroad "chapel cars" into service to missionize in the western states,[6] than the Catholics responded by commissioning three of their own (Hooker, 1931; Mondello, 1987). Let us therefore look more closely at those primarily responsible for creating a church capable of meeting all these challenges—the clergy.

After an early period of "trusteeship," during which lay members asserted control over local congregations, the Roman Catholic Church emerged in America with a fully episcopal structure in which bishops presided over their dioceses and pastors ruled their parishes. Moreover, the American Catholic Church was (and is) far more directly responsible to the Pope than is typical of national Catholic churches in Europe. Ironically, the reason for direct Roman control of the American church lies in the principle of the separation of church and state. The U.S. government has never negotiated any conditions for the appointment of bishops. Thus papal appointments within the American hierarchy are subject to no other authority; whereas in many parts of Europe the head of state holds veto power over such appointments.

Despite the strict authority held by a trained and professional clergy, however, American Catholicism has always been in very close touch with its laity (at least until recently). A major reason for this involves the recruitment, training, and placement of parish clergy.

There are two kinds of Catholic priests. The "religious" priests are members of religious orders, such as the Jesuits and the Paulists. "Secular" priests are those who serve the local parishes and staff the diocese. "Religious" priests typically take vows that are considerably more restrictive than those taken by secular priests—for example, secular priests

CHAPEL CAR "ST. ANTHONY"

The Catholic Extension Society of the U. S. A.   General Offices: The Rookery, Chicago.

SOLEMN HIGH MASS ON MOTOR CHAPEL "ST. PETER"
ON A RANCH NEAR BROWNSVILLE, TEXAS.

EXTERIOR VIEW OF MOTOR CHAPEL "ST. PETER" OWNED BY
THE CATHOLIC CHURCH EXTENSION SOCIETY OF THE U. S. A.
GENERAL OFFICES, McCORMICK BLDG., CHICAGO.

do not take vows of poverty. Because the religious orders are of national and international scope, religious priests are trained in a few central seminaries and placed wherever they are needed, often far from home. Secular priests, however, are typically local Catholics, recruited from, trained by, and assigned to their home diocese. Most priests in Chicago are natives of the Chicago area. The secular priest usually works amid his relatives and life-long friends and serves a community with which he is utterly familiar and sympathetic. Although it is true that most priests do not come from lower-class backgrounds, neither do they tend to come from upper-status families. Most priests come from families typical of the parish in which they reside (Fichter, 1961). Hence, like Baptist and Methodist clergy during the nineteenth century, Catholic priests are "of the people."

As graduates of local seminaries secular priests are trained by other local secular priests, not by "learned professors," and their interpretations of Catholic doctrine will tend, therefore, to be quite orthodox and in keeping with local practices. Because all priests take vows of celibacy, moreover, the priesthood does not become a family occupation passed from father to son, as it so typically did among clergy in the old Protestant mainline denominations. Rather, priests are recruited in each generation from among young men with more intense personal religious convictions. The doctrine that a clergyman must be "called" by God has long been a central Catholic teaching.

The ordinary social origins and local training of secular priests were clearly displayed in the sermons given by nineteenth-century parish pastors. Dolan (1975) examined many surviving manuscripts of sermons given by parish priests in New York City during the nineteenth century and found them to be plain spoken and without literary pretensions. Even the sermons of Bishop John Hughes, whose preaching was widely admired, were phrased in colloquial language and aimed primarily to "attract the attention of his audience and awaken their emotions" (Dolan, 1975, pp. 147–148): "His style was simple and his argument plain, not theologically complicated . . . [his sermons] included doctrinal instruction as well as moral exhortation; one cannot escape the impression that Hughes always sought to instruct his listeners as well as move their wills."

Train and motor chapel cars, supported by the Catholic Extension Society in the early twentieth century, were used to initiate and support missions to the pastorless people of rural America. The mobile chapels would hold mass wherever Catholics could be found— or converted. (Courtesy of the Lake County, Ill., Museum, Curt Teich Postcard Archives.)

Thus did local Catholic pastors hold their own against the powerful sermonizing of the Baptists and the Methodists. The Catholic clergy also understood that sermons were for saving souls and energizing the faithful. They exhorted sinners to confess and be saved, and they did so in the most direct and forceful language they could summon. But they did something more. Typically they preached to their immigrant parishioners in their native tongue and did so within the security of a familiar ethnic as well as religious community—a community that helped both to gain and to retain the active participation of the immigrants and their children.

Ethnic Parishes

Because Catholic parishes are geographical units, they are often very homogeneous in terms of class or ethnicity. To the extent that a city has distinct rich and poor neighborhoods, this will be reflected in the makeup of parishes serving those neighborhoods. Similarly, cities having solidly ethnic neighborhoods will also tend to have parishes that are each dominated by one ethnic group. American Catholicism in the nineteenth century was a mosaic of ethnic parishes. It would be hard to overstate their variety (Olson, 1987; Liptak, 1989).

Consider that the 1916 census of religious bodies found that approximately half (49 percent) of all Catholics attended a parish where a language other than English was used in religious services. In those days, of course, the Mass was said in Latin in all Catholic parishes around the world. But the sermon was in the local language. In the United States the "local" language was what the people in a parish spoke. If we consider that the sermons in Irish-American parishes were given in English, it is even more powerful testimony to the recent immigrant status of Catholics that half of the parishes in 1916 had non-English services. In fact, 21 percent of Catholics in 1916 attended a parish where only foreign languages were used, and the remaining 28 percent attended parishes where religious services were conducted in both English and a foreign language.

Foreign language services included a very broad range of languages (see Table 4.2). The five largest groups were the Germans, Italians, Poles, French (many of them Canadian immigrants), and Hispanics (in those days primarily persons of Mexican origin). The census listed twenty-four other languages being used for religious services in Catholic parishes. Despite the fact that the Irish dominated the ecclesiastical hierarchy of the American Catholic Church, sufficient non-Irish priests were available to staff an immense number of foreign-language parishes. It was not simply language, however, that told visitors that they were in an Italian or German parish. The Catholic Church may have presented itself as the guardian of the "one true and holy, Roman apostolic faith," but the character of that faith differed greatly across the nations of Europe and therefore across the parishes of America. Members of a German parish might have been shocked to observe "tongue dragging" by women in Italian parishes, a feast day practice in which especially pious women dragged their tongues on the floor as they crawled or were carried down the aisle to the statue of the Madonna (Orsi, 1985). Italians, in turn, might have been puzzled as to the religious significance of the huge, quasi-military pageants and processions held in German parishes to mark each of the major holy days. But a woman newly arrived from Germany commented happily, "Oh, so we find ourselves again in a new, holy Germany" (Dolan, 1975, p. 77).

For many American Catholics, preferences for versions of the faith based on ethnicity persisted far beyond the first generation. When with the passage of time it proved impossible to continue to serve these desires through neighborhood parishes, the traditional territorial design was altered to allow the formation of "national parishes" that could be attended by members of a specific "nationality" from all across the city. These parishes, organized by nationality or language, became increasingly popular as the diversity and the number of non-English speaking immigrants increased. Joseph Casino (1987, p. 40) reported: "Whereas between 1850 and 1880 only 9% of the new parishes established in the Northeast were national parishes, between 1880 and 1930, 30% were national." He noted that in Manhattan and Philadelphia as much as 50 percent of all new parishes were national during the years 1902–1918 for Manhattan and 1897–1908 for Philadelphia. The number of national parishes in the United States would eventually rise to over 2,000 in 1940, representing twenty-eight different ethnic groups (Olson, 1987, p. 122).

As a result of such growth, an urban neighborhood might have two or more Catholic parishes, one based on the neighborhood and others on ethnicity (Gleason, 1987). In the Back of the Yards neighborhood of Chicago, Robert A. Slayton (1986, pp. 18–19) found nine Roman Catholic parishes in the early twentieth century: three Polish, one Slovak, one Bohemian, one Lithuanian, one German, one Irish, and one Mexican. Eight of the nine parishes fell within a five block radius and Holy Cross (Lithuanian) was nearly across the street from Sacred Heart (Polish). Yet, there was very little interaction among these parishes. Slayton found that

TABLE 4.2
Parishes Reporting Use of a Foreign Language for Services, 1916

Language reported	Total using foreign lang.		Use only foreign lang.		Use English and foreign lang.	
	Parishes	Adher.	Parishes	Adher.	Parishes	Adher.
French	699 (11.5%)	1,026,966 (13.4%)	200 (9.0%)	478,255 (14.5%)	499 (13.0%)	548,711 (12.6%)
German	1,890 (31.1%)	1,672,690 (21.8%)	206 (9.2%)	191,347 (5.8%)	1,684 (43.8%)	1,481,343 (33.9%)
Italian	476 (7.8%)	1,515,818 (19.7%)	149 (6.7%)	420,511 (12.7%)	327 (8.5%)	1,095,307 (25.1%)
Polish	735 (12.1%)	1,425,193 (18.6%)	466 (20.9%)	1,165,604 (35.2%)	269 (7.0%)	260,129 (6.0%)
Spanish	841 (13.8%)	552,244 (7.2%)	530 (23.8%)	278,748 (8.4%)	311 (8.1%)	273,496 (6.3%)

Bohemian	178 (2.9%)	133,911 (1.7%)	76 (3.4%)	67,827 (2.1%)	102 (2.7%)	66,084 (1.5%)
Indian	100 (1.6%)	26,402 (0.3%)	39 (1.7%)	5,839 (0.2%)	61 (1.6%)	20,563 (0.5%)
Lithuanian	96 (1.6%)	150,227 (2.0%)	87 (3.9%)	140,144 (4.2%)	9 (0.2%)	10,133 (0.2%)
Slavic	113 (1.9%)	118,264 (1.5%)	98 (4.4%)	106,927 (3.2%)	15 (0.4%)	11,337 (0.3%)
Slovak	109 (1.8%)	125,687 (1.6%)	69 (3.1%)	78,447 (2.4%)	40 (1.0%)	47,240 (1.1%)
Misc.*	839 (13.8%)	929,719 (12.1%)	310 (13.9%)	373,330 (11.3%)	529 (13.8%)	556,389 (12.7%)
TOTALS	6,076 (100%)	7,677,171 (100%)	2,230 (100%)	3,306,439 (100%)	3,846 (100%)	4,370,732 (100%)

SOURCE: Bureau of the Census (1919, vol. 1, pp. 81–82).
*Many of the parishes included in this row reported the use of more than one foreign language for religious services. One parish reported the use of six different languages.

"parents and priests alike tried to prevent 'mixed marriages' between children of different nationalities . . . [and] each priest viewed his parish as a separate national unit, to be ruled as a private domain, a 'kingdom'" (pp. 146, 148). Divisions would even occur across the three Polish parishes. For example, the Poles of Sacred Heart were mountaineers from the Tatra Mountain range who had distinctive accents and customs and were viewed by other Poles as the "equivalent of hillbillies." June Granatir Alexander (1987) found similar regional divisions when she studied five Slovak parishes in Pittsburgh. She reports that in more than 90 percent of 1,316 marriages performed between 1895 and 1913, both bride and groom were from Slovakia, 65 percent from the same county in the old country and 38 percent from the same village.

The ethnic and social class homogeneity of most parishes allowed the Catholic Church to serve the specific needs of special segments of the religious market, while the diversity across the parishes allowed specialized appeals to the broad spectrum of immigrants. The national church (and numerous ethnic churches not established as national churches) gave ethnic groups local autonomy without sacrificing the unity of the larger whole. (In contrast, the Lutherans were fragmented into twenty-one different denominations in 1916—most of them created by rather modest linguistic and cultural differences.) At the very time when Protestants viewed the Catholic Church as a Roman monolith, the Irish hierarchy was painfully aware of the ethnic mosaic that lay within.

Many ethnic parishes were also partly sustained by mutual benefit societies, such as the Sons of Italy, that were brought over from the homeland. These societies provided members with insurance benefits in time of sickness or death, but they also provided the immigrant with a sense of ethnic identity. The mutual benefit society became the ethnic group's representative organization, and the immigrants turned to their society to initiate actions on behalf of their specific ethnic group. For this reason, the societies often served as the catalyst for establishing a parish and remained an active part of parish life once the parish was established (Dolan, 1984; Gleason, 1987). These societies, along with numerous publications and other organizations, helped to cement the bond between ethnicity and religion.

Up until 1880 the mutual benefit societies and the numerous devotional confraternities were the two main types of societies founded in the parish (Shaw, 1987). But Dolan (1985, p. 204) reports that after 1880 the parish "was transformed into a community institution." Suddenly there was a sharp increase in both the number of societies and in the stated purpose of the parish societies established. The societies now included social, recreational, and charitable groups as well as the long-standing devotional and mutual benefit societies. The parish was rapidly becoming the social and cultural center for the parishioners it served.

Perhaps the most visible institution in the Catholic subculture was the parish grammar school (Greeley and Rossi, 1966; Baker, 1999; Walch, 1996). This institution was so prized that in 1884, when approximately four out of every ten parishes had a grammar school, the Third Plenary Council of Baltimore decreed that within two years a parochial school should be erected near each church (Hennesey, 1981). As we shall see when we discuss Catholic schools more fully below, the goal of a school in every parish was never achieved. But even to have announced such an aim is indicative of the strong support of the bishops, as well as the parishes, for parochial school education. Because each school was created and sustained by the parish, Catholic education was greatly decentralized (Baker, 1992). Each school was a reflection of the parish itself (Shaw, 1987; Perko, 1988). If it was an ethnic parish, then the school could transmit the ethnic heritage as part of its curriculum—to say nothing of the informal transmission of ethnicity as part of the daily interaction of students with a common heritage.

The parish subculture as a whole passed on a culture that was different from the dominant culture. The Catholic parish could provide social, religious, and cultural supports that were simply not available from the Protestant churches. Catholicism and ethnicity were intertwined in the local parish to provide the immigrants and their children a community unto themselves.

Nuns

The key to the parochial school system, and, indeed, a central element in the life of the Catholic community, was the American nun (see Fialka, 2003).[7]

The American nun initially made the parish school possible. She was also responsible for the extensive network of Catholic hospitals, which, according to the census report numbered 543, and for many of the 645 Catholic orphanages established by 1916 and providing a home for more than 130,000 children (Bureau of the Census, 1919). But the most frequent assignment given to American nuns was to form and maintain parish schools. Receiving salaries of less than a third of those paid to teachers in the public schools—and even substantially below the pay of Catholic

Postcards designed by Lithuanian (ca. 1919), German (ca. 1915), and Polish (ca. 1916) Catholic parishes in Chicago illustrate the importance of ethnicity. All clearly identify their nationality, but the Lithuanian and Polish parishes signify their Roman Catholic identity with only initials. (Courtesy of the Lake County, Ill., Museum, Curt Teich Postcard Archives.)

	1st Grade	2d Grade	3d Grade	4th Grade	5th Grade	6th Grade	7th Grade	8th Grade
Catechism(Polish)	135	135	135	135	135	135	90	90
Bible History (Polish).......	90	90	90	90	90	90	...	...
Church History (Polish).......	...	...	...	...	...	...	60	60
Reading (Polish) .	315	285	210	150	150	150	135	135
Grammar & Composition (Polish)	...	...	60	90	90	90	90	90
History of Poland (Polish)........	...	30	30	60	60	60	...	...
Literature(Polish)	...	...	...	...	...	...	90	90
Arithmetic (Eng.)	300	300	300	300	300	300	300	300
Reading & Spelling (English)....	360	300	210	150	150	150	150	150
Grammar & Composition (Eng.)..	...	...	60	90	90	90	90	90
History of United States (Eng.) ...	...	...	60	90	90	90	90	90
Geography (Eng.)	...	60	60	60	60	60	60	60
Penmanship.	90	90	90	90	90	90	90	90
Drawing.........	60	60	60	60	60	60	60	60
Vocal Music (Eng. and Polish).....	105	105	90	90	90	90	90	90
Recess..........	150	150	150	150	150	150	150	150
Total no. minutes per week . .	1605	1605	1605	1605	1605	1605	1605	1605

A curriculum said to be "typical" for a Polish Catholic school in the early twentieth century. Approximately 40 percent of the first-grade curriculum was conducted in Polish. This was reduced only slightly, to 35 percent, by the eighth grade. (From J. A. Burns, [1912] 1969, p. 324.)

brothers—nuns made it possible for even poor parishes to sustain parochial schools.

But it wasn't merely or even primarily the nuns' hard work for little pay that made them so central to Catholic life. What was most crucial was their direct role in shaping and passing on Catholic culture (Finke and Wittburg, 2000). "Sister said," became a key phrase in the conversation of Catholic children. The nuns were also frequently a direct link between an ethnic group and its country of origin. Each immigrant group supported religious orders of its own national background, and these orders in turn provided nuns familiar with the language, culture, and religious beliefs of the people. The more common problem was that many sisters coming over from the old country could not speak English (Dolan, 1985, p. 130). Writing in 1912, James A. Burns reported that "most new teaching orders came from abroad. . . . their first members—usually either French or German—were unable to speak English upon their arrival. . . . [when only one of eight nuns in a Cincinnati school could speak English] she went from class to class in order to help, until the teachers had acquired enough English to talk with their pupils."[8]

Despite their lack of official authority, women religious essentially ran the local parish schools. The parish pastor was officially the principal of the parish school, but in practice he was too busy to oversee the day-to-day operations. And in any case, most pastors were fully aware that the sisters knew far more about schooling than they did. Bishops with big-city Catholic school systems to sustain expended great effort to attract communities of teaching nuns from Europe.

Fortunately, the American Catholic Church also proved very productive of nuns during the late nineteenth and early twentieth centuries, and soon nuns far outnumbered male religious. Unfortunately, no good nationwide data on nuns are available for this era. The census took pains, for example, to classify priests as religious and secular, to count churches, church members, seminaries, seminarians, schools, students, hospitals, patients, orphanages, and orphans—but not nuns. This omission probably reflected the state of Catholic statistics per se. The *Catholic Directory* lacks any data on nuns during this era, despite offering a detailed statistical portrait of most things Catholic—including the names of all Catholic players on major league baseball teams.

Catherine Ann Curry (1988) has attempted to reconstruct statistics on nuns from 1820 through 1900, assembling data from the records of the various orders (see Table 4.3). Curry warned that her national totals must be "lower than reality," adding that she was confident that "these statistics are more accurate than anything at hand." We agreed. Even if the numbers are quite underestimated, they reveal that the rate of women religious per 10,000 Catholics hovered around 12 to 16 between 1820 and 1860 and then began a rapid climb to 41 per 10,000 by 1900. Thus women in religious orders outnumbered priests by two to one in the period 1820–1860, and by 1900 the ratio was at least four to one. This was the essential fact making Catholic education possible.

TABLE 4.3
Number of Women Religious in the Immigrant Church,
1820–1900

Year	Women religious	Priests	Women religious per priest	Women religious per 10,000 members
1820	270	150	1.8	13.8
1830	448	232	1.9	14.1
1840	902	482	1.9	13.6
1850	1,941	1,081	1.8	12.1
1860	5,090	2,235	2.3	16.4
1870	11,424	3,780	3.0	25.4
1880	21,835	6,000	3.6	34.9
1890	32,534	9,168	3.6	36.5
1900	49,620	11,987	4.1	41.2

SOURCE: Adapted from Curry (1988). "Women religious per 10,000 members" based on Shaughnessy's (1925) membership estimates.

American Catholicism as an Irish "Sect Movement"

Although the American Catholic Church was an amazing ethnic mosaic, the fundamental characteristics of American Catholicism, as it was taught, preached, and practiced, were Irish. The Irish predominated in the first great wave of Catholic immigration, had the added advantage of being English-speakers, and soon dominated the ecclesiastical hierarchy. In 1886 more than half of the American bishops were of Irish birth or descent, and by 1900 the proportion rose to two thirds (Hennesey, 1981; Dolan, 1985).

The *kind* of Catholic Church the Irish brought with them to America had much more in common with the upstart Protestant sects than it did with the Catholicism of the "Catholic" nations of Europe. This was not a low-tension Catholicism, on comfortable terms with its social environment, its bishops hobnobbing with the rich and powerful. It was a high-tension faith if only because it was the primary vehicle of political resistance by the poor Irish tenants and laborers against their English rulers and landlords. Transferred to the United States, where the Irish immediately encountered substantial prejudice and discrimination on both ethnic and religious grounds, the prickly stance toward the environment was maintained.

The Irish Catholic Church had not always been a model of zeal and commitment. Historians have paid considerable attention to the "devotional revolution" that transformed the church in Ireland beginning in 1850 (Larkin, 1972). During this era there was a very great increase in attendance at Mass, from perhaps 33 percent to more than 90 percent. The number of persons seeking ordination or enrolling in religious orders rose very rapidly—so much so that Ireland was able to export substantial numbers of priests and nuns to America until well into the twentieth century. Without these Irish "imports" it is hard to imagine how churches could have met their staffing needs. A letter penned by Father Eugene O'Connell from San Francisco in 1853 makes it clear how dependent the Catholic Church was on Irish priests to serve on the frontier. As recently as 1963, when a sample of parishes was selected from the Archdiocese of San Francisco, more than a third of the pastors had been born and ordained in Ireland.

Without pausing to explore the causes of the Irish devotional revolution here, we may note that this revolution spread to America with successive waves of Irish immigrants (Larkin, 1972). And in combination with the immense predominance of Irish clergy, the sectlike qualities of Irish Catholicism predominated as well.

Once committed to the zealous conviction of the Irish brand of faith, the average American Catholic held as many moral reservations toward the general secular culture as did the average Baptist or Methodist. Granted, Catholics did not condemn drinking and dancing, for which they were constantly reproved by evangelical Protestants. But Catholics adhered to many moral and behavioral standards that were far stricter than those of secular society. Indeed, millions of evangelical Protestants took their cues about the moral suitability of movies from the ratings issued to guide Catholics by the National Legion of Decency. Like Baptists and Methodists, Catholics also stressed stricter sexual norms, greater modesty in dress, and were strongly opposed to "swearing" (as they defined it). Moreover, the Catholic Church required its members to make quite visible sacrifices, such as not eating meat on Friday and observing special restraints during Lent. Perhaps the most dramatic "sectarian" limits of Catholicism were its prohibitions on divorce and on contraception. These restrictions were the subject of constant comment among Protestants and stood as a very substantial barrier to intermarriage.

Within the context of American culture, the Catholic Church was thus far more sectlike than churchlike during the nineteenth and early twentieth centuries.

A Separate Catholic America

Both authors of this book are members of a scholarly organization known today as the Association for the Sociology of Religion. Until 1970, however, this organization was known as the American Catholic Sociological Society, and because neither of us is Catholic, we would not have belonged back then.

It wasn't just Catholic sociologists who created their own separate organization. There also was an American Catholic Psychological Association, a Catholic Anthropological Conference, a Catholic Economic Association, an American Catholic Philosophical Society, and a United States Catholic Historical Society. The Catholic Actors' Guild of America was founded in New York City in 1914 "for the spiritual and temporal welfare of persons in the theatre" (in Foy, 1965, p. 667). Catholics in most professional and semiprofessional occupations enrolled in local chapters of organizations such as the Catholic Accountants' Guild, the Catholic Lawyers' Guild, the Catholic Newsmen's Association, the Catholic Petroleum Guild, the Catholic Writers' Guild, the Catholic Broadcasters' Association, the Druggist Guild of St. James (founded to "promote high ideals among druggists; combat sale of contraceptive devices and drugs, and of indecent literature in drug stores" [in Foy, 1965, p. 622]), the Guild of Catholic Psychiatrists, and the National Federation of Catholic Physicians' Guilds.

The Catholic War Veterans duplicated the American Legion and the Veterans of Foreign War. From their founding in 1882 the Knights of Columbus provided a Catholic alternative to fraternal lodges such as the Masons, which Catholics were forbidden to join. And the Catholic Daughters of America were modeled on the Daughters of the American Revolution.

In these and countless other ways, American Catholics created a parallel society within which they were protected from Protestant insults as well as from Protestant influences. But the primary structure of a separate Catholic America was an immense system of schools and colleges.

Father O'Connell's Letter Home

Father Eugene O'Connell's letter home (in Ellis, 1956, pp. 312–314) was addressed to Father David Moriarty, president of All Hallows College of Dublin, Ireland, established in 1842. During its first sixty years All Hallows supplied the New World with 1,500 priests (Thernstrom, 1980).

San Francisco
June 15th, 1853

My dear Father Moriarty
. . . How can I express to you my gratitude for your kind invitation to All Hallows after my wanderings in the Far West? I only await the arrival of one of the six missionaries whom Dr. Alemany [the Archbishop of San Francisco] expects from All Hallows previous to my departure. You would really pity the poor Bishop were you to see the fluctuating soldiers he has to fight his battle . . . he was obliged to make the two seminarians he has swear to remain with him.

You must, I'm sure, have received letters from [the Archbishop] which shew you the urgent need he has of Irish clergymen and the provision he is making to secure a constant supply from All Hallows. . . . Since the Bishop transferred me from Santa Ynez to this city about three or four months ago, there has been a fire almost every month and the value of thousands of dollars consumed . . .

The temporal burnings of which I am speaking naturally remind me of the everlasting ones which they presage to thousands of the citizens of San Francisco, unless they stop in their career of iniquity. The rage for duelling, the passion for gambling and barefaced depravity prevail to a frightful degree. . . . Venus has numerous temples erected to herself in this city but, thank God, the Catholic church is not deserted all the while.

Catholic Schools

The 1916 Bureau of the Census report on religious bodies contained the following paragraph on Catholic education: "At the end of 1916 there were under the auspices of the Roman Catholic Church in the United

States 102 ecclesiastical seminaries, with 6,898 seminarians; 216 colleges for boys, with 49,813 students; 676 academies for girls, with 96,194 students; and 5,687 parochial schools, with an attendance of 1,537,644 children" (vol. 2, p. 652). These numbers represented a massive school-building effort begun by the Catholic Church in the 1840s. There was a consensus among American educators during the nineteenth century that it was a primary duty of the schools to give moral instruction. Horace Mann, the famous New York educator, wrote that public education "earnestly inculcates all Christian morals; it founds its morals on the basis of religion" (in Dolan, 1975, p. 101). Every priest in New York City agreed with him. But the trouble was, which Christian religion did Mann mean? The answer to that question was never really in doubt. In most places, the schools were frankly Protestant. As a result, in 1840 John Power, vicar general of the Diocese of New York, wrote in the Catholic newspaper: "How can we even think of sending our children to those schools in which every artifice is resorted to in order to reduce them from their religion?" (in Dolan, 1975, p. 103). His archbishop, John Hughes, said flatly, "the benefits of public education are not for us" (in Dolan, 1975, p. 104).

Thus American Catholics, though repeatedly denied any public funding or relief from public school taxes, set out to create a separate school system. The official aim was to provide a school in every parish, as we have seen. Many parishes found that they didn't really need to maintain a parochial school, however, because their community (or their neighborhood) was so overwhelmingly Catholic that the public school sufficed. In many small rural communities with significant Catholic populations, the school board hired nuns to staff the local public school. Eventually some states responded to this practice by passing "anti-garb" statutes, which prohibited teachers from wearing recognizable religious clothing in the classroom. Nevertheless, the Catholic school system was large. By 1916 more than a third of parishes (5,687) had schools. When the Catholic school system reached its peak in the mid-1960s, two thirds of American parishes did so.

In addition to parish schools, Catholic America created its own institutions of higher education, including such well-known institutions as Notre Dame, Fordham, Boston College, De Paul, Georgetown, Holy Cross, Loyola, Marquette, St. John's, Santa Clara, Seton Hall, and Villanova. The number of these institutions also peaked in the 1960s, at 295, and at the dawn of the twenty-first century there are 238 Catholic colleges and universities in the United States.

Although there is persuasive evidence that attending public rather than parochial schools has not appreciably reduced the commitment of Catholics, it is equally apparent that the Catholic educational system has provided the Catholic community with a social elite unified by "old school ties" as well as by religious affiliation (Greeley and Rossi, 1966).

Westward with the Cross

We have seen that a major factor in the defeat of the colonial mainline denominations was their inability to move west with the nation. Educated clergy able to command well-paying pulpits were unwilling and unsuited to minister to the needs of rough-and-ready frontier communities. Because, by comparison with Protestants, Catholics today are so over-represented in the major cities of the United States, it can easily be overlooked that Catholic priests, monks, and nuns were very active along the frontiers. No one is surprised that in some counties in the Northeast, more than half of the population is enrolled in local Catholic parishes. But it is much less well known that there are many such counties scattered across the agricultural midwest.

It wasn't simply the Catholic capacity to dispatch missionaries westward that built these large Catholic settlements. Midwestern bishops, especially Bishop John Ireland of St. Paul, Minnesota, were effective in working with the railroads to attract Catholic homesteaders (J. P. Shannon, 1957). In this way very substantial Catholic settlements sprang up, not only in Bishop Ireland's Minnesota, but in Iowa, Nebraska, Kansas, and the Dakotas. "Manufactured" homes were purchased by many Catholic settlers in areas such as Greeley County Nebraska, which, in 2000, was over 70 percent Catholic. Such Catholic settlements would have been even more numerous had it not been for the stern opposition to western settlement by Archbishop John Hughes of New York (J. P. Shannon, 1957). His hostility underscores the importance of statistics. Misled by the false numbers we reviewed at the beginning of this chapter, Hughes mistakenly believed that millions of Catholics had already defected from the faith. Hughes could see no signs of such defections in New York and other eastern cities, and therefore he concluded that the scene of most defection was along the western frontier. It seemed to him that to encourage more Catholics to go west was simply to worsen the defection problem.

In addition to the western migration of Catholics, the Louisiana Purchase (1803), the annexation of Texas (1845), and the Treaty of Guadalupe

Hidalgo (1848), which yielded California and the rest of the American Southwest, brought the nation vast areas that were over-whelmingly Catholic. Thus as the first American settlers—and the first Methodist and Baptist preachers—moved west toward the Mississippi, they encountered Catholics and their churches. Although the upstart Protestant sects did very well in these frontier areas, Catholic influence remained very strong as well. For example, Catholics were sufficiently established in Dubuque, Iowa, by 1837—long before substantial Catholic immigration had begun—that a bishop was appointed. He was Mathias Loras, originally from France, who had already served for seven years in Mobile, Alabama. Catholics still make up nearly 65 percent of the population of Dubuque. Similarly, Catholics further west never ceased their efforts to further church growth. Just as Bishop Francis Asbury almost lived on horseback while building Methodism westward from the Atlantic states, Bishop Juan Bautista Lamy ranged far and wide from his cathedral in Santa Fe, New Mexico, building up the church within his diocese. His territory included New Mexico, Arizona, Colorado, and southern Utah. While serving as bishop, Lamy rode as far east as Kansas City, roamed south to Mexico City, and west to Los Angeles (Horgan, 1975). He did not limit his attentions to his Hispanic flock, but sustained vigorous missionary efforts among the miners and ranchers who were drawn to the region.

On the West Coast, it was much the same. Stout missionary efforts helped the Catholic Church hold its own as the gold rush brought a horde of newcomers. Archbishop Alemany may have had to depend on priests imported from Ireland to minister to San Francisco, but he seems to have little trouble raising $100,000 to construct St. Mary's Cathedral. Father O'Connell had to admit in his letter to All Hallows College in 1853 that on Sunday the San Francisco Catholic churches were "full to overflowing." The same is true today; Catholics make up more than 60 percent of the church members in San Francisco, but only about a quarter of the population.

Martyrs for the Faith

In the final analysis, the Catholic Church succeeded in America because it too was an upstart sect. It offered an intense faith with a vivid sense of otherworldliness—Catholic evangelists could depict the fires of hell as graphically as any Baptist or Methodist. Like the Protestant upstart sects, moreover, the Catholic Church made serious emotional, material,

A PORTABLE HOUSE

"Admirable frame houses, 14 x 20, 'rain, wind and waterproof,' having three rooms, can be bought in the colony for about $200. These houses are made in Chicago, without nail or screw, are portable, and do not require a skilled workman to put them together, or take them apart. They do not need plastering inside, a hurricane can make no impression on them, and, if painted regularly, will last for a century."
—*Catholic Colony, Greeley County, Nebraska.*

Prefabricated housing, Catholic Colony, Greeley County, Nebraska. (From J. P. Shannon, 1957, p. 198.)

and social demands on its adherents—to be a Catholic was a far more serious undertaking than to be a Congregationalist or an Episcopalian. And the American Catholic Church was served by ardent clergy and nuns, recruited from the common people and prepared to make great sacrifices to serve their faith. The Catholics too could staff the frontiers and wilderness areas because they were prepared for hardship and for little or no pay.

The "sectlike" nature of the Catholic Church in nineteenth-century America is also demonstrated by the reaction of the prominent members of the old colonial mainline denominations. They were even more contemptuous of "papists" and "Romanism" than they were of Baptists, Methodists, and "muscular" religious responses. Here again the example of Lyman Beecher is instructive. On Sunday, August 10, 1834, this stalwart of the Congregationalist establishment gave three thunderous sermons in Boston during which he repeated the theme of his *Plea for the West* ([1835] 1977), a tract that warned against a plot by the Pope to seize control of the Mississippi Valley: "American travelers at Rome and Vienna, assure us, that in the upper circles the enterprise of reducing our western states to spiritual subserviency to the see of Rome is a subject of avowed expectation, and high hope, and sanguine confidence . . . the correspondence of Catholic bishops and priests in this country . . . are full of the same predictions and high hopes" (1835, p. 110). As a result of these sermons, Beecher received donations of $4,000 to help fight "popery." The next night a mob did its bit against "popery" by burning down Boston's Ursuline Convent while local fire companies refused to respond, a result that even Beecher had not desired.[9]

This helps us recognize a final aspect of Catholic strength and, indeed, of the strength of all sects. Sect movements can be strengthened not only by their opposition to the world but by the pressures the world imposes on them. Protestant prejudice did much to cement solidarity among American Catholics of diverse ethnic backgrounds and to spur them to high levels of commitment.

Competing for the Immigrants

We have limited our attention to Catholics, but when other immigrant faiths faced the unregulated religious market, they too were forced to compete for adherents. A Swedish Lutheran immigrant noted the sharp differences when first arriving: "In America the shepherd seeks the sheep and gathers them to his bosom, and does not conduct himself after the manner of Sweden, where the sheep must seek the shepherd and address him with high-sounding titles." (in Stephenson, 1926, p. 715). Gone were the subsidies that guaranteed support of the churches and gone was the state's suppression of unwanted religious competitors. The Lutheran and Reformed establishments of Europe had to transform the way they promoted religion in America.

The former Protestant establishments felt the immediate effects of competition just as the Catholics did. When Friedrich Wyneken, an ordained Lutheran pastor born in Hanover, went to America in 1838 he was dismayed by the ubiquitous Methodists and Baptists and was appalled at the sectarian clergy's bold appeals to the German immigrants (Gustafson, 1994). When making a "distress call" to his fellow Germans, he explained that the numerous sects (and the Roman Catholics) are "dangerous enemies" and that "there is hardly a Lutheran or Reformed congregation which does not have to suffer from these swarming pests. Many congregations have been completely scattered by them, others are constantly exposed to their attacks and banter, and complaints about these agitators come from all areas" (Wyneken, [1843] 1982, p. 32). He viewed the Methodists as the greatest threat, warning that "unless the Lord sends help very soon, [they] will certainly even wipe out the name of the

THE

PAPAL CONSPIRACY

EXPOSED,

AND

PROTESTANTISM DEFENDED,

IN THE LIGHT OF

REASON, HISTORY, AND SCRIPTURE.

BY

REV. EDWARD BEECHER, D.D.

New York:
PUBLISHED BY M. W. DODD,
CORNER OF SPRUCE ST. AND CITY HALL SQUARE.
1855.

Lyman Beecher's son Edward was well known as an educator and abolitionist, but like his father he warned of a "papal conspiracy." Lyman's daughter Catherine was a champion of higher education for women and his daughter Harriet was renowned for *Uncle Tom's Cabin*.

Lutheran church in the [W]est . . . [and the] flood will soon enough flow across the Atlantic toward our German fatherland" (pp. 30, 50).

Wyneken's fear of the Methodists and other sects was well founded. Although his warnings on the annihilation of Lutheranism in western America were inflated to garner assistance from the fatherland, his detailed descriptions of the sects' revival meetings, the emotional pleas of their clergy, and the open competition they fostered are in complete agreement with other historical accounts. Even his warning about Methodism flowing to the fatherland proved accurate when Methodist missionaries were sent to Bremen, Germany, in 1849 and a mission conference was formed in 1856. In 1835, seven years before Wyneken wrote *The Distress of the German Lutherans in North America*, the Methodists began supporting missions to the German immigrants. Two years later, in 1837, the German missionary William Nast proposed a German language press to provide a periodical that would combat the "invectives against Christianity" in the Roman Catholics' German papers and to publish Methodist books in the German language to replace the "miserable" existing translations" (in Douglass, 1939, p. 57). The 1837 Ohio Conference approved the immediate publication of major Methodist works, such as the *Wesleyian Catechism*, in German, and on January 4, 1839 the first German Methodist periodical was published by the Methodist Book Concern in Cincinnati and edited by Nast. In 1841, the year before Wyneken's distress call, the Methodist Episcopal Church reported eleven German missions in four conferences (Douglass, 1964). One of the conferences, Indiana, was where Wyneken served the Lutherans.

The sectarian groups' outreach to the immigrants eventually proved less effective than the appeals of the Lutheran, Reformed, and Catholic congregations, but their appeals played a significant role in the churching of new immigrants. First, it forced the former establishments to compete for adherents because the sects were perceived as a viable threat. In his expansive review of *The Lutherans in North America*, E. Clifford Nelson reports that "during the last quarter of the nineteenth century, home mission activity took priority over all other forms of church work for Lutherans in America" (1980, p. 258). Without the threat of the Methodists and other sects, Wyneken might have never issued his distress call. At the very least, his appeal would have been far less urgent. Reporting on lax members with no religious fervor would have attracted little concern in a homeland where this was the norm.

Second, the sects attracted enough members to offer a local alternative. For example, in 1906 the Methodist Episcopal Church alone reported 1,400 congregations conducting worship services in a language other than English and 1,228 of these congregations held no English services. Their most successful appeals were to the Germans and Scandinavians, but they also reported 55 Spanish, 26 Italian, 14 Japanese, and 6 or more Bohemian, Chinese, and French congregations. Although their 864 German congregations paled in comparison to the 5,532 German Lutheran and 1,881 German Catholic congregations in 1906, their presence was felt in German settlements throughout the country. When the Methodists began publishing their own German periodical and books in 1839, they were perceived as a potential threat; but when they began founding German Methodist congregations in the 1840s, that potential was transformed into a church next door.

Finally, the sects served as models for mobilizing commitment. Wyneken loathed the emotional revivalist appeals of the sects that included

This picture is taken from the front of a postcard published by the Board of Home Missions and Church Extension of the Methodist Episcopal Church. The back of the postcard explained: "In the mines, at the coke ovens, on the railroads, and in the construction gangs, toilers who speak a foreign tongue live with very little done to teach them English, to interpret Americanism to them, and to give them the blessings of Protestant Christianity. In many of the communities where they labor no provision is made for the worship of God. . . . $25 to $1,000 will help in the process of Christian Americanization." (Courtesy of the Billy Graham Center Museum, Wheaton, Ill.)

"moaning and groaning" and "stirring up the senses and the nerves" (p. 31). Yet, his own emotional pleas to other Lutherans would have made a sectarian revivalist proud. He complained that Methodism has "infected almost all of Christendom" and that "they destroy church life with the help of erected chapels, hired preachers, evangelists, colporteurs, and treatises; they see to win for themselves the faithful who do not recognize the church or despise it" (p. 49). But, by the end of the century Lutherans had followed suit in each of these areas and by the twentieth century they were leading the way in a new form of evangelism: radio broadcasting.

The newly forming churches of the immigrants not only faced the threat of religious competition, they also faced persecution, just as the Catholics did. Indeed, they often became the joint target of nativist attacks, temperance advocates, and those objecting to the use of the German language during World War I. Lutherans and Catholics joined forces for many a battle over attempts to regulate and even banish their parochial schools (Walch, 1996, p. 64). But even their shared status as victims couldn't overcome centuries of antagonism, and their alliances were tenuous and short-lived. After joining Catholics to defeat a Michigan amendment seeking to prohibit all parochial and private elementary education in 1920, the Lutheran Schools Defense Executive Committee issued a letter assuring members that "contrary to an impression which some people might have gained during the course of the campaign, the Lutheran Church is today precisely as aloof from Rome as she ever has been" (in Pies, 1986, p. 229).

Like Catholics, the Lutheran, Reformed, and Jewish denominations built a distinctive subculture that paralleled the dominant culture. The religious freedoms of their new nation allowed churches to become an institutional free space where even oppressed minorities could build a community that was responsive to their needs. The churches soon catered to the unique language, political, social, and religious needs of the new immigrants, providing them with a distinctive religious and ethnic enclave supported by a host of institutions. Educational, recreational, and social service institutions are the most obvious examples, but the mutual benefit societies and professional associations also served to integrate immigrants into the tight-knit enclave (Smith, 1978a; Chiswick, 1999).

The irony is that the distinctive subcultures of the Protestant, Catholic, and Jewish enclaves served the dual role of preservation and assimilation. Despite separating the new immigrants from a foreign world and preserving a distinctive religious and ethnic subculture, the enclaves also assimilated immigrants into the larger culture (Greeley, 1977). As the first generation learned English and the ways of the new world, the second and third generations were instructed in the ways and language of the past. For all generations the ethnic enclave provided education, information, social networks, and training needed for success in the new land. But the immigrant churches would soon face a new challenge: retaining their distinctive religious identity after ethnicity faded.

Chapter 5

Methodists Transformed, Baptists Triumphant

When we left them in 1850, the Methodists had just achieved a virtual miracle of growth, rising from less than 3 percent of the nation's church members in 1776 to more than 34 percent by 1850, making them far and away the largest religious body in the nation. But by 1890 they had been overtaken by the Roman Catholics.

Histories of American religion attribute this shift to the rising tide of Catholic immigrants in the latter half of the nineteenth century. But that's not the whole story. It was not simply a rising tide of Catholics that cut the Methodist market share after 1850; it was an actual decline in the relative capacity of the Methodists to attract and retain members. How can we tell? Because the Baptist market share did not decline in this era, but instead rose sharply even as the total Protestant segment of the market declined.

Consider the growth curves for Methodists and Baptists from 1776 through 1980 (see Figure 5.1). The Methodist "miracle" of 1776–1850 stands out. Holding a far smaller market share than the Baptists in 1776, the Methodists towered over them by 1850—even though the Baptists had displayed an outstanding growth rate. Notice, however, that while the Methodist market share began to decline prior to 1890 (117 to 114) and showed a sharp decline between 1890 and 1926 (114 to 101), the Baptists kept right on growing (70 to 106).[1] By 1906 the Baptists had overtaken the Methodists, and since World War II they have become much more numerous than the Methodists. If the Baptists managed to grow despite the waves of Catholic immigration, then Catholic growth does not account for Methodist decline.

FIGURE 5.1 Adherents per 1,000 Population for Methodist and Baptist Denominational Families, 1776–1980

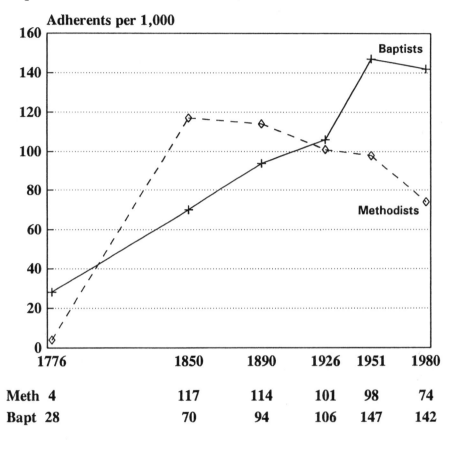

	1776	1850	1890	1926	1951	1980
Meth	4	117	114	101	98	74
Bapt	28	70	94	106	147	142

–◇· **Meth**   —+— **Bapt**

Moreover, the Methodist decline was evident even in areas without Catholic immigration. Because the South had little immigration, and was dominated by the Methodists and Baptists in 1850, it serves as an ideal location to watch the changing fortunes of these two denominations. The pattern in the South is one of Methodist concession and Baptist growth: as the Methodists declined from 42 to 28 percent of all adherents, the Baptists grew from 30 to 43 percent (see Figure 5.2). The Methodists' share of the market declined consistently from 1850 to 1906, with their sharpest

FIGURE 5.2 Methodists and Baptists in the South as Percentage of Total Adherents, 1850–1926

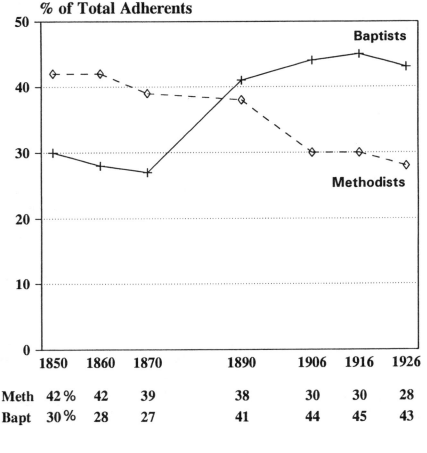

	1850	1860	1870	1890	1906	1916	1926
Meth	42%	42	39	38	30	30	28
Bapt	30%	28	27	41	44	45	43

−◇· **Meth** —+— **Bapt**

decline occurring between 1890 to 1906. It is during this time period, we will argue, that the Methodists made strong efforts to abandon their sectarian origins. Methodist losses, however, were Baptist gains. Despite declines during the Civil War era, the Baptists made rapid gains from 1870 to 1890 and continued to increase their share of all southern adherents on into the twentieth century.[2]

This same pattern of Baptist growth and Methodist decline is evident if we look at specific denominations rather than denominational fami-

FIGURE 5.3 Adherents per 1,000 Population for Methodist Episcopal Church and Southern Baptist Convention, 1890–1986.

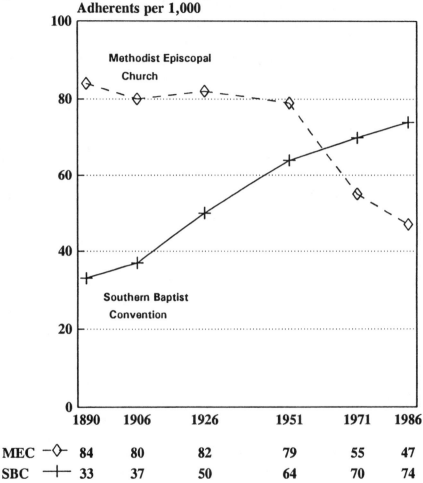

	1890	1906	1926	1951	1971	1986
MEC ─◇─	84	80	82	79	55	47
SBC ─┼─	33	37	50	64	70	74

(The rates for the Methodist Episcopal Church are slightly inflated, after 1926, owing to mergers. The rates for 1890, 1906, and 1926 include only the Methodist Episcopal Church and the Methodist Episcopal Church, South. Later rates include the Methodist Protestant Church, added in 1939, and the Evangelical United Brethren, added in 1968.)

lies. Figures 5.1 and 5.2 are based on all denominations that claim to be Baptists, on the one hand, and Methodists, on the other, in order to keep the modern data comparable with those from earlier times. It is possible, however, that the total adherence rates are made up of a welter of contradictory shifts in membership among the many bodies included in each group. In Figure 5.3, therefore, we compare only two specific groups—the largest Baptist and the largest Methodist denomination. The pattern is the same. In 1890 the Methodist Episcopal Church (including the Methodist Episcopal Church, South) had 84 members per 1,000 Americans, compared with 33 for the Southern Baptist Convention. The Methodist Episcopal Church later merged with the Methodist Protestant Church, in 1939, and the Evangelical United Brethren Church, in 1968. Yet, despite these mergers, the rate for the Methodist Episcopal Church (now the United Methodist Church) has been sliding downward while the Southern Baptists have been growing rapidly.

Thus when the time series is extended only a few years forward from 1850, we see that the Methodist "miracle" became the Methodist roller coaster. What went wrong? How could the confident, even boisterous, church of Francis Asbury and Peter Cartwright have suddenly fallen on such evil times? The same underlying processes that transformed the Puritan sect into the Congregational Church subsequently transformed the upstart Methodists into the Methodist Episcopal Church. When successful sects are transformed into churches, that is, when their tension with the surrounding culture is greatly reduced, they soon cease to grow and eventually begin to decline.

Tracing the forces that rapidly secularized Methodism in the latter half of the nineteenth century offers an opportunity to test our arguments about why the Methodists were initially so successful. That is, if we have correctly identified the sources of the Methodist "miracle," then shifts in these same factors ought to be associated with the Methodists' downward slide. If, for example, the Methodists were strengthened by relying on untrained lay preachers in the local congregations, then (other things being equal) when they changed their policies and began to rely on seminary-trained ministers, they ought to have become less successful. If we are correct about why the upstarts won, then the continued success of the Baptists ought to be associated with retaining these characteristics or finding effective substitutes.

From Sect to Church: The Methodists Transformed

In Chapter 2 we outlined the elements of sect-church theory. Successful sect movements develop strong internal pressures to lower their tension with the surrounding culture. These pressures come from having an increasingly affluent membership and from an increasingly "profession-alized" clergy. Together, the privileged laity and the "well-trained" clergy begin to lift restrictions on behavior and to soften doctrines that had served to set the sect apart from its social environment—a process known as sect transformation or secularization.

Early Signs of Methodist Secularization

In 1850 a number of Methodist ministers in the Genesee Conference, located in the Burned-Over District of western New York, began to issue complaints about the way in which the church was drifting away from its historic teachings and practices. Led by the Reverend Benjamin Titus Roberts, the dissidents were highly critical of trends in Methodist doctrines that they characterized as "liberal to the point of Unitarianism" and of a departure from "nonconformity to the world; simplicity, spirituality, and freedom in worship." They were especially critical of the introduction of "pew rentals" as abandoning the poor and of the growing centralization of "executive power and ecclesiastical machinery" and its use to oppress local congregations and clergy (Bureau of the Census, 1910, vol. 2, p. 487).

By 1857 the complaints of this outspoken minority of Genesee Conference pastors, supported by a substantial lay faction, were given widespread public expression in an article Roberts published that year in the *Northern Independent*, entitled "New School Methodism." In it he charged that Methodism had been split into "New School" and "Old School" factions, and he documented how recent changes in the church introduced by the New School Methodists departed from Wesleyan teachings and practices.

Roberts began by noting that, given the New School's abandonment of "creed," it was appropriate, though symptomatic, that its supporters had changed the name of *The Buffalo Christian Advocate* to *The Advocate*—"We commend the editor for this instance of honesty." But the majority of Robert's article is made up of quotes from articles in *The Advocate* that attacked the doctrines of the Old School as narrow, illogical, and superstitious.

> But their theory of religion is more fully set forth in the leading editorial of *The Advocate* for May 14th, under the title—"Christianity a Religion of Beneficence Rather than Devotion." . . . it was written by a leading New School member of the Genesee Conference. . . . It says, "Christianity is not, characteristically, a system of devotion. It has none of those features which must distinguish a religion grounded on the idea that to adore the

Divine character is the most imperative obligation resting upon human beings. . . ."

The following sneer is not unworthy of Thomas Paine himself. It falls
below the dignity of Voltaire. "Christianity in nowise gives countenance
to the supposition that the Great Jehovah is so affected with the infirmity
of vanity, as to receive with peculiarly grateful emotions, the attentions
and offerings which poor, human creatures may pay directly to Him in
worship."

The above may be sufficient to show what Christianity is not, in the
opinion of these New School divines. Let us now see what it is. "The characteristic idea of this system is benevolence; and its practical realization
is achieved in beneficence. It consecrates the principle of charity, and in-
structs its votaries to regard good works as the holiest sacrifice, and the
most acceptable which they can bring to the Almighty. . . .

"Whatever graces be necessary to constitute the inner Christian life, the
chief and principal one of these is love to man." (in Norwood, 1982, pp.
375–376)

But it was not only a preference for a much more worldly theology
that separated the Old and New School Methodists. Roberts was equally
incensed at the affluent worldliness of the New School congregations,
where even the wives and daughters of the clergy had begun to wear
"gold and costly apparel," and he brought this fully into public view in
his article. He noted that the New School built fancy churches and employed "organs, melodeons, violins, and professional singers, to execute
difficult pieces of music for a fashionable audience." Worse yet, when
they:

desire to raise money for the benefit of the church, they have recourse to
selling pews to the highest bidder; to parties of pleasure, oyster suppers,
fairs, grab-bags, festivals and lotteries. . . . The New School Methodists
appear to depend upon the patronage of the worldly, the favor of the proud
and aspiring; and the various artifices of worldly policy. . . . unmistakable indications show that prosperity is producing upon us, as a denomination, the same intoxicating effect that it too often does upon individuals
and societies. The change, by the General Conference of 1852, in the rule
of Discipline, requiring that all our houses of worship should be built plain,
and with free seats; and that of the last General Conference in the section
respecting dress, show that there are already too many among us who would
take down the barriers that have hitherto separated us from the world.
The fact that the removal is gradual, so as not to excite too much attention and commotion, renders it none the less alarming. (in Norwood, 1982,
p. 379)

Should the New School prevail, Roberts wrote, "it needs no prophet's vision to foresee that Methodism will become a dead and corrupting body" (p. 379). But it was already too late. The transformation of the upstart Methodist sect into the Methodist Episcopal Church was far along.

Roberts's article provoked a vindictive reaction from the New School faction, for indeed they were in control of "executive power." Roberts was hailed before the conference, declared guilty of unchristian and immoral conduct, and sentenced to be reprimanded by the bishop. Shortly thereafter, the article was republished by a layman, which led to the formal expulsion of Roberts from the conference and from the church. The expulsion of all other clergy associated with Roberts soon followed. When a large gathering of laymen was convened to protest these expulsions, they were officially "read out" of the church on charges that by gathering they had withdrawn from the Methodist Episcopal Church. When their appeals for readmission were rejected, Roberts and his followers formed the Free Methodist Church during a convention in Pekin, New York, in 1860.

The most certain sign that a religious group has secularized to a significant degree is, of course, sect formation. And the truth is that Roberts and his Free Methodists were entirely correct that the Methodists in 1850 were no longer the church of the Wesleys or of Bishop Asbury. Leaders of the Genesee Conference did not deny that some congregations had begun to charge rent for pews, for example. Rather, they labeled Roberts unchristian for criticizing this and the many other signs of worldliness, and for publicizing the drift away from traditional standards of "simplicity and spirituality."

The departure of the Free Methodists had no statistical impact on the Methodists (nearly a half century later in 1906 they still numbered only 32,838 members), but it was a valid portent of troubles to come. As the century waned, a much larger and more influential movement emerged in response to increasing Methodist secularity. In the end, many more sects erupted and abandoned the Methodist Episcopal Church. Before we examine this development, however, it will be well to see specifically what was going on within the Methodist Church. What exactly was changing and why did it matter so much?

The Circuit Riders Dismount and Democracy Wanes

By the middle of the nineteenth century the Methodist church was no longer staffed by local amateurs supervised by professional circuit riders—

most of the circuit riders had dismounted and were now "settled" pastors. It is no surprise that clergy would prefer this arrangement. The life of a circuit rider was one of extreme hardship. Of the first 700 Methodist circuit riders, nearly half died before age thirty, 199 of them within their first five years of service (Clark, 1952).

But if dismounting was good for the clergy, it had many harmful organizational consequences. The mobility, low cost, and flexibility of the church's organization were all threatened by a stationed clergy (Nickerson, 1983). In addition, the local congregations were now under the full authority of the centralized clerical hierarchy. When the circuit rider served ten to twenty stations on his frontier circuit, and was moved from one circuit to another every year, the laity (especially the lay preachers) provided leadership and continuity for the local church. By the latter half of the nineteenth century, however, the stationing of clergy resulted in more full-time clergy and fewer lay preachers—commonly referred to as local preachers in the *Methodist Minutes*. Between 1843 and 1882 the number of full-time clergy went from approximately one third to one half of all clergy (41 percent in the South) and the number of clergy per 1,000 members increased from 3.6 to 7.0 (4.6 in the South). Not only were there more full-time clergy, but the clergy could now remain in one location for a longer period of time. The 1804 General Conference had ruled that a bishop should *not* allow full-time clergy to "remain in the same station more than two years successively," but the limit was raised to three years in 1864, to five years in 1888, and was completely removed by 1900 (Cameron, 1961). Rather than serving as a visiting "bishop" who helped to guide the local leadership, the itinerant was now the local "pastor." The esteemed itinerant, Peter Cartwright, offered this blunt evaluation in 1856: "As sure as a leaden ball tends to the earth in obedience to the laws of gravity . . . if this course is pursued a little longer, the Methodist Church will bid a long farewell to her beloved intineracy, to which we, under God, owe almost every thing that is intrinsically valuable in Methodism" (p. 82).

Recall from Chapter 3 that as long as the Methodists relied on a local amateur clergy, they enjoyed nearly as much local autonomy and democracy as did the Baptists. But with a settled clergy, the "Episcopal" structure of the Methodists became the reality—it was a church ruled by bishops who appointed and removed local pastors as they wished. What Roberts and his "reformers" were objecting to when they complained of being oppressed by "ecclesiastical machinery" was reality—a reality that got them booted out for thinking that a return to local democracy was possible and desirable.

Did it matter that the clergy gained control of the Methodist Church? We believe that a number of critical changes were the direct result of this takeover.

Seminary-Trained Clergy

When Francis Asbury died in 1816 there was not a single Methodist college or seminary in America. It was not until 1847 that the Methodists opened a seminary. But then the rush for Methodist higher education was on. By 1880 there were, under official control of the Methodist Episcopal Church, 11 theological seminaries, 44 colleges and universities, and 130 women's seminaries and schools (W. W. Sweet, 1933, p. 333).

For the clergy, the educational standards were completely transformed. Not only were seminaries increasing in number and enrollment, but the educational requirements for all ministers were coming under closer scrutiny. As early as 1816, itinerants were given a recommended "course of study" by their conference, and a more experienced preacher in their local circuit would serve as a tutor; but by the mid- to late nineteenth century the apprentice program became a victim of the declining circuit system and there was increasing pressure from within the hierarchy to increase educational standards. As a result, the General Conference of 1844 authorized the development of a uniform course of study for all conferences; the local (lay) clergy were given a course of study in 1876; by the 1890s the General Conference passed legislation to ensure uniform examination procedures; and by 1900 a seminary education exempted the candidate from the course of study (Miyakawa, 1964; Rowe, 1971; Patterson, 1985). The training of clergy had gradually shifted from an informal apprenticeship program in the local circuits to a formal education at the national seminaries.

Why had this occurred? In part because of the expansion of higher education in the nation as a whole. But, in our judgment, in greater part because the larger, more affluent Methodist congregations desired educated clergy on a social par with Congregationalists, Episcopalians, and Presbyterians, and the clergy themselves desired the social status and increased pay that a well-educated clergy could obtain. As the itinerants were stationed, like the clergy of the old colonial mainline denominations, the argument soon followed that higher educational standards were

TABLE 5.1
Average Ministerial Salary, 1906

Denomination	Aver. salary
Southern Baptist Convention and	
Northern Baptist Convention	$536
Methodist Episcopal Church and	
Methodist Episcopal Church, South	$784
Congregationalists	$1,042
Presbyterian Church in	
the United States	$1,177
Episcopalians	$1,242
Unitarians	$1,653
Roman Catholics	$703
All	$663

SOURCE: Bureau of the Census (1910, vol. 1, pp. 94–97).

needed. In 1872 Alfred Brunson (a Methodist itinerant) argued that with the "old circuit system . . . we could repeat the discourse till we had perfected it; but now [with the station system], preaching to the same congregation every time, we must have a new subject, which requires a stock of knowledge to be laid in beforehand or extraordinary genius" (in Norwood, 1982, p. 402).

Where once it had been very easy to become a local Methodist minister and they were, therefore, in abundant supply, now it became difficult to do so, and clergy soon had the advantage in bargaining for wages and locations. By 1906 Methodist salaries were above the national average, and, if they had not yet caught up with those of the old mainline, they far surpassed the Baptists' remuneration (see Table 5.1).

Perhaps an even more drastic result of clergy control and the turn toward educated ministers was the toning down of doctrine and turning away from such vigorous marketing methods as revivals and camp meetings. At the dawn of the nineteenth century, Asbury described the Methodist camp meetings as "fishing with a large net" ([1852] 1958, vol. 3, p. 250). By the end of the century they too had been transformed. Sweet (1933, P. 333) reported, with obvious approval, that by 1880: "Many of the old camp-meeting grounds . . . were still in use, but rows of tents

SPECIMEN OF COTTAGES.

Martha's Vineyard near Bedford, Mass., was one of the many Methodist camp-meeting sites being transformed into "respectable middle-class summer resorts" (W. W. Sweet, 1933, p. 333). In addition to the well-crafted pews and preacher's stand, the resort had two hundred cottages by 1868—one fourth of them built in the summer of 1868—and a wide range of social entertainment, including croquet, swimming, fishing, sailing, and tea-making. On September 12, 1868, *Harper's Weekly* reported: "the thousands of people who frequent Martha's Vineyard at this season have more and fresher pleasures than those who summer at Newport or Long Branch. Here you see the latest fashions, and innocent flirtation is not unknown among the lads and lassies." (Courtesy of the Billy Graham Center Museum, Wheaton, Ill.)

were rapidly giving place to streets of frame cottages, and instead of the old-time camp-meeting revival, the religious services were now interspersed with lectures on semi-religious subjects. If there was less evidence of the old-time religious fervor, fewer shouts and hallelujahs, there also was less rowdyism. In fact, many of the old-time camp-meeting grounds were rapidly being transformed into respectable middle-class summer resorts with only a tinge of religion."

Peters (1985, p. 178) illustrates how quickly this transformation took place at the famous Ocean Grove Camp Meeting. "In 1872 the report from Ocean Grove to the *Guide to Holiness* had been, "Multitudes were sanctified wholly and many sinners were born into the Kingdom;" and in 1878, "Nearly six hundred . . . in converting, sanctifying and reclaiming grace." In 1894, however, the report said, "Several persons were at the altar and some were converted." The difference cannot be wholly a matter of reportorial accuracy.

Elsewhere Sweet (1944, p. 164) stressed how an educated clergy served as a "cool-headed leadership" exercising "a restraining influence on an overemotionalized company of people." He asserted that when there is "an educated minister in the pulpit, there is small chance that an extreme emotional revivalism will arise."

In Chapter 2 we suggested that religious doctrine often seems to become accommodated and secularized whenever it is delivered into the control of intellectuals. This may not always be the case, but it was surely true for the Methodists. When the intellectually promising students of American Methodism returned from their graduate training in the universities of Germany, they used their seats in the seminaries to challenge American Methodism's traditional notions of sin, conversion, and perfectionism (Peters, 1985). These challenges were quickly passed on to students of the seminaries, and the "course of study" underwent numerous revisions to accommodate the new insights (Norwood, 1982). The traditions of Methodism were being challenged not by the laity but by the ordained intellectuals.

In 1904, when Bishop Willard Mallalieu wrote the introduction to G. W. Wilson's book *Methodist Theology vs. Methodist Theologians*, he lamented that just as moral standards had been lowered to accommodate more worldly behavior, "theological standards of Christian experience [have been] adjusted to harmonize with a lukewarm, cold, or backslidden experience." American Methodism, according to the bishop, was rapidly becoming "unevangelical, un-Wesleyan, and un-Scriptural" (pp. 10–12). More than three decades later the president of the Iliff School of Theology, Charles Schofield (1939), reflected on the changes that had occurred with the Methodist clergy and their plans for evangelism. He noted that for the early Methodist preachers the problem of preaching was "vastly simplified," because "every sermon was an evangelistic sermon." The clergy's church planning had been consumed by evangelistic efforts: "By the time a man [the circuit rider] laid out and carried through a plan for from six to ten weeks of evangelistic preaching on each point of his circuit and made provision for camp meetings in the summer months, the year's program was pretty well filled out" (pp. 71–72). But all of this contrasted sharply with Schofield's view of evangelism and the role clergy should play in the newly formed Methodist Church:

> There has been, however, quite generally over the Church a sharp sub-sidence of enthusiasm for, and faith in, the evangelistic methods and ob-jectives to which our fathers gave themselves. . . . Perhaps this in part grows out of the fact that we have come to hold a more adequate conception of what is involved in real evangelism. . . . Today it is not anywhere nearly so easy to define what we mean by becoming a Christian. . . . We do not cherish the naive confidence in the complete adequacy of one momentary experience. (1939, pp. 73–74)

The intent of Schofield's essay was to argue in favor of increased evan-gelism, but his comments highlight why it is difficult for the secularized faiths to evangelize. Evangelism is no longer *the* mission of the church, the "adequacy" of sanctification is questioned, and the clear boundaries between Christian and non-Christian have faded. Compared with his ancestors, President Schofield lacked any clear message or sense of his mission. His confusion becomes poignant in the last sentence of the passage: "If we are to continue to be Christians at all, we must evange-lize" (p. 83). But he no longer could tell his seminarians whom to evan-gelize, or how.

Although these changes in the style and content of Methodism were not initiated by the people, many rank-and-file Methodists out in the pews (some now paying rent for the privilege) welcomed a more worldly Methodism and preferred pastors of the New School.

Worldly Methodists

John Wesley anticipated the day when most Methodists would not be lacking in worldly goods: "Religion must necessarily produce both in-dustry and frugality, and these cannot but produce riches. But as riches

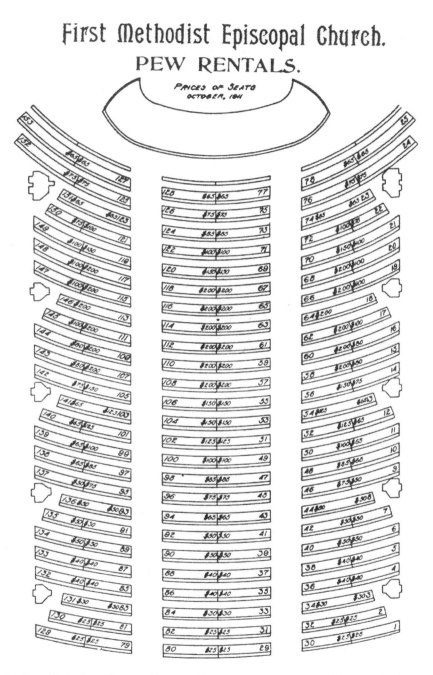

First Methodist Episcopal Church.
PEW RENTALS.

PRICES OF SEATS
OCTOBER, 1911

The First Methodist Church in Evanston, Illinois, was one example of the new dignity and status of Methodism. A pew rental chart for 1911 shows that the best seats went for $200 while seats in the last two rows sold for $25.

increase so will pride, anger, and love of the world in all its branches." Nor would it be possible to prevent the latter by preventing the former: "We ought not to prevent people from being diligent and frugal; we must exhort all Christians to gain all they can, and save all they can—this is, in effect, to grow rich. What way, then, can we take, that our money may not sink us into the nethermost hell? There is one way, and there is no other way under heaven. If those who gain all they can, save all they can, will likewise give all they can, then the more they gain, the more they grow in grace, and the more treasure they lay up in heaven" (in W. W. Sweet, 1933, p. 336).

But though some may well have heeded Wesley's advice about giving and about waiting to enjoy their treasure in the world to come, many Methodists didn't want to wait. Charles A. and Mary R. Beard sneered at Methodists who, in the 1890s, "fired by the ostentatious display of the plutocracy, crowded the hotels at Saratoga Springs and Long Branch, attended the opera, and made 'the grand tour' of Europe" (in W. W. Sweet, 1933, p. 337).

William Warren Sweet (1933), the dean of Methodist historians, agreed (without the sneer) that by the 1880s there were many rich Methodists determined to enjoy their wealth. He pointed to the rapidly rising scale of Methodist ministers' salaries, the building of costly churches, and the proliferation of pipe organs and paid choirs as the most obvious signs

TABLE 5.2
Value of Church Properties per Member, 1850 and 1906 (reported in denominational ratios)

Ratios	1850	1906
Episcopal/Methodist	7.2	3.5
Congregational/Methodist	4.1	2.3
Episcopal/Baptist	6.3	5.7
Congregational/Baptist	3.6	3.7

SOURCE: Calculated from denominational totals reported by the Bureau of the Census (1854, 1910)

NOTE: Each ratio represents the number of dollars of church property per member in one denomination divided by the number of dollars of church property per member in another denomination. The first row, for example, indicates that the Episcopalians had 7.2 times more dollars of church property per member than the Methodists in 1850.

of affluence. In 1850 the Episcopalians had 7.2 times more church property per member than the Methodists, but by 1906 this ratio dropped to 3.5 (see Table 5.2). The ratio between Methodists and Congregationalists similarly fell from 4.1 to 2.3. In contrast, the Baptists' church property per member in comparison with that of the Episcopalians and the Congregationalists showed little change.

In 1884 the trustees of Indiana Asbury University, Methodists all, agreed to rename the school De Pauw University in return for a large contribution by Washington C. De Pauw, a wealthy glass manufacturer and prominent Methodist layman. Given the theology that likely prevailed there at this time, the old bishop would probably have welcomed the name change.

Sweet (1944, pp. 163–164) also pointed with pride to the closing of the cultural and respectability gap between the Methodists and the old colonial mainline: "Clerical culture and learning were no longer a monopoly of the Congregationalists, the Presbyterians, and the Episcopalians. Education, refinement, and dignity now characterized the ministry and services of many Methodists . . . equally with those of the formerly elite churches. Indeed, the Methodists in the towns and cities by the end of the century began to get out the robes and prayer books which had been carefully put aside in the early years of the Church's independent existence, and many of them in form and ritual went far beyond Presbyterianism and Congregationalism."

Sweet knew about upscale Methodism firsthand. During his many years on the faculty of the University of Chicago Divinity School he often visited the famous First Methodist Church in nearby Evanston. The church served Northwestern University and Garrett Seminary, both Methodist institutions. From late in the nineteenth century until the 1960s the ushers at First Methodist wore swallowtail coats and its pews were rented on an annual basis by some of the most prominent Chicago families.

Although the Sunday morning services of early Methodists were orderly and generally exempt from the emotional freedoms reserved for the camp meetings, they were still informal gatherings that allowed spon-

The increasing affluence and size of the Methodist Episcopal Church is illustrated by its choice of buildings for the General Conference. Bishop Asbury held the 1790 meeting in a log cabin in Kentucky (top). But in 1888 the Methodists met in the Metropolitan Opera House in New York City. The *Frank Leslie Illustrated Newspaper* reported that the "cost of securing the building ($5,500)" was covered "by the sale of over fifty of the boxes at $100 each for the month, and the remainder at prices varying from $50 to $90, according to location." (Courtesy of the Billy Graham Center Museum, Wheaton, Ill.)

taneous responses of "Amen" or "Praise the Lord." According to Gerald McCulloh (1964, p. 636), as late as "1881 'formality' had been classed with 'worldliness' and 'improper amusements' as a peril to Methodism." But with an increasingly educated clergy and a more affluent membership, Sunday services began to display the formal liturgy and established ritual once reserved for the Episcopalians and Presbyterians. The 1905 *Hymnal* bears witness to this change: the "shouting Methodists" were now reciting responsive readings.

In addition to losing their distinctive style of worship and their uneducated clergy, they grew increasingly lax about enforcing the strict behavioral standards that once had been their hallmark (McCulloh, 1964). As the class meetings died out, there was no means to "administer the discipline" and little attempt to find a new avenue for enforcement. An article in the *Methodist Review* in 1898 illustrates the shift from strict standards of membership to more inclusive criteria: "We do not believe anything is gained by holding up the extreme penalty of excommunication for acts of doubtful character, or, at the worst, vanities or follies. . . . The church is not a punitive institution. It succeeds, not by casting out men, but by getting them in and developing all their capabilities for good" (Carroll, 1898, p. 183). The actual written standards for behavior changed only slowly. But by the turn of the century many Methodists could safely ignore the rules against such activities as playing cards, dancing, or attending the theater, horse races, and circuses. When, in 1924, the Methodists formally suspended their rules against these amusements, making them a matter of individual conscience, the announcement earned headlines in the *New York Times*. The eventual demise of class meetings not only limited the local church's ability to discipline existing members, the loss also reduced its ability to assimilate new members and screen out the lazy or uncommitted. Although Baptists and others often charged the Methodists with admitting people of questionable character and limited commitment, the Methodists' strict probationary system ensured that members would be held to high standards before being received as full members. During a probationary period of six months or longer, candidates were required to meet weekly with their classes where class leaders were directed to "instruct, exhort, and reprove." Giving weekly reports to the local pastor on the status of each probationary member, the class leader became a spiritual mentor and social support for the new recruit. Following the Civil War, however, the probationary system was gradually replaced by probationary classes. Placing more emphasis on instruction, little on support, and even less on accountability, many clergy welcomed this change because it reduced the dropout rate of probationers (Kirby, Richey, and Rowe, 1996; Wigger, 1998).

Thus we see the Methodists as they were transformed from sect to church. Their clergy were increasingly willing to condone the pleasures of this world and to deemphasize sin, hellfire, and damnation; this lenience struck highly responsive chords in an increasingly affluent, influential, and privileged membership. This is, of course, the fundamental dynamic by which sects are transformed into churches, thereby losing the vigor and the high octane faith that caused them to succeed in the first place.

But not all of the people drawn to Methodism had become rich, nor did all of them desire a more worldly and accommodated faith. And, as had Reverend Roberts and his Free Methodists at mid-century, they began to complain and to seek a return to old-time Methodist enthusiasm.

The Holiness Movement

Ironically, historians credit John Wesley as the founder of the Holiness Movement in reaction to what he perceived to be the worldliness and secularity of the Church of England. Eventually his commitment to such principles as "Christian Perfection" drove him from Anglicanism.

But the great American social movement that came to be known as the Holiness Movement arose within Methodism during the latter half of the nineteenth century and was, in large part, a call for return to Wesleyan principles. Linked closely to revivalism and camp meetings, the movement generally called for a reaffirmation of traditional Methodist theology and methods, placing special emphasis on the Wesleyan commitment to sanctification through baptism of the Holy Spirit. Just as the Methodist Episcopal Church began to deemphasize and to secularize their camp meetings, the Holiness Movement formed the National Camp Meeting Association for the Promotion of Holiness in 1867. The Holiness Movement was met with widespread enthusiasm and support by the Methodist laity and, at first, received cooperation from key bishops and clergy.

The result was rapid growth throughout the nation. By 1887 the national association reported holding sixty-seven national camp meetings as well as eleven Tabernacle meetings; and by 1892 the state and local holiness associations reported hosting 354 meetings for the promotion of holiness each week and maintained a list of 304 holiness evangelists. With the support of forty-one periodicals, and four publishing houses devoted exclusively to the publication of holiness materials, the growing strength of the movement became apparent to all—including the Methodist hierarchy (Peters, 1985).

The success of the movement soon brought increased criticism from the Methodist divines. As new bishops were appointed and segments of the Holiness Movement became more "radical," the movement was regarded by the Methodist hierarchy as a "sectarian" challenge like that of Roberts and his Free Methodists. Greatly concerned by the proliferation of holiness publications not under their control and by the immense number of camp meeting associations that were now independent of Methodist authority, the bishops began to express their criticism publicly. By the 1890s the Methodist hierarchy launched a serious counterattack on prominent Methodist clergy participating in the Holiness Movement.

The hierarchy's greatest fear, however, and the area over which they had the least control, was the proliferation of holiness evangelists who attracted the attention of the membership. Like the Methodist circuit rider of the early nineteenth century, these evangelists would preach whenever and wherever they were given the liberty to do so. Because many of these evangelists were not ordained or even licensed by the Methodist Church, and some were members of other denominations, the hierarchy had no means to control or regulate their behavior. They could discipline and reprimand their own clergy, but the holiness evangelists operated outside the formal structure of the church. The General Conference of 1894 described the situation: "We are confronted with a new condition. Evangelists are numbered by scores and hundreds, and multiply fast . . . all act without appointment or supervision in this special work" (in Peters, 1985, p. 146). To address this "condition" the *Discipline* of 1894 gave the Methodist clergy full authority and responsibility to "control the appointment of all services to be held in the Churches in his charge." The professional clergy could now determine when the evangelists should be given the liberty to preach; and in most areas, this liberty was denied.

In response, Holiness spokesmen began to call "all true holiness Christians to come out of Methodism's church of mammon" (Melton, 1989). And out they came; sect after sect. This rapid sect formation offers several important lessons. First, when growing religious groups begin to secularize, schisms often form as opponents seek to restore previous demands of the faith. Second, not all sect movements will grow.[3] Tenaciously holding to all past traditions, blocking all forms of organizational change

TABLE 5.3
Church of the Nazarene Membership, 1906–2000

Year	Members	Members per 1,000 population
1906	6,657	0.08
1916	32,359	0.32
1926	63,558	0.54
1936	136,227	1.06
1945	201,487	1.44
1955	270,576	1.64
1965	343,380	1.77
1975	441,093	2.04
1986	530,912	2.20
2000	663,264	2.25

SOURCES: Bureau of the Census (1941) and *Yearbook of American and Canadian Churches* (1988). We would like to thank Rich Houseal and the Nazarene Headquarters Research Center for providing the membership data for 2000.

and innovation, and often embedded in closed social networks, many of the sects remain small and obscure. Third, despite the decline of many small sects, the less secularized faiths still have a greater competitive capacity. By holding higher levels of member commitment, the sects generate the resources and enthusiasm needed for growth. Moreover, they appeal to a segment of the population abandoned by secularized faith. The Church of the Nazarene, typical of the Holiness sects that erupted from Methodism in the 1890s and early 1900s, offers one example (Table 5.3). As will be seen in Chapter 7, scores of new Holiness and Pentecostal sects have emerged in America since the 1890s and many have had spectacular growth curves.

The Design of Defeat

By the mid-nineteenth century the Methodists seemed to be hitting full stride. They were now the largest denomination in America, they had just opened their first seminary, and scores of new building projects were

Peter Cartwright on the Methodists Transformed

Writing in 1856, at the age of seventy-two and in the fifty-third year of his ministry, Peter Cartwright contrasts the Methodist Episcopal Church of the 1850s with the church of the early 1800s.

Clergy

A Methodist preacher in those days, when he felt that God had called him to preach, instead of hunting up a college or Biblical institute, hunted up a hardy pony of a horse . . . he cried, 'Behold the Lamb of God, that taketh away the sins of the world." . . . he went through storms of wind, hail, snow, and rain; climbed hills and mountains, traversed valleys, plunged through swamps, swam swollen streams, lay out all night, wet, weary, and hungry. . . . Under such circumstances, who among us would now say, "Here am I, Lord, send me"? (p. 243)

Dress

. . . When I joined the Church her ministers and members were a plain people; plain in dress and address. You could know a Methodist preacher by his plain dress as far as you could see him. The members were also plain, very plain in dress. . . . may we not well question whether we are doing right in the sight of God in adorning our bodies with all this costly and extravagant dressing? . . . would not the simple fund that might be created by disposing of the ornaments of the members of the Methodist Church alone, send the Gospel to hundreds of thousands. . . . (pp. 515–516)

on the horizon. Yet, a growing number of Methodists were expressing concern that the more refined church, promoted by Nathan Bangs and others, was losing its zeal. The complaints became so frequent the dissenters were labeled the "croakers" (Wigger, 1998).

Concerns were expressed by young and old, but the most prominent croakers included the celebrated circuit riders of early Methodism. Fiercely loyal to the church, and highly regarded by the membership, Peter Cartwright, Freeborn Garrettson, Charles Giles, James Quinn, and other itinerants published autobiographies expressing concern that Methodism's

(continued)

Prayer Meetings

Prayer meetings have accomplished great good, as practiced in the Methodist Episcopal Church; but are they not growing into disuse among us?... there have been fashionable objections to females praying in public, but I am sure I do not exaggerate when I say I have often seen our dull and stupid prayer meetings suddenly changed ... when a sister has been called on to pray....(p. 517)

Class Meetings

Class meetings have been owned and blessed of God in the Methodist Episcopal Church, ... For many years we kept them with closed doors, and suffered none to remain in class meeting more than twice or thrice unless they signified a desire to join the Church.... Here the hard heart has been tendered, the cold heart warmed with holy fire; But how sadly are these class meetings neglected in the Methodist Episcopal Church! ... is it any wonder that so many of our members grow cold and careless in religion, and finally backslide? ... And now, before God, are not many of our preachers at fault in this matter? (pp. 519–520)

Camp Meetings

I am sorry to say that the Methodist Episcopal Church of late years, since they have become numerous and wealthy, have almost let camp meetings die out. I am very certain that the most successful part of my ministry has been on camp-grounds. (p. 523)

climb to success was resulting in spiritual backsliding. John H. Wigger described the autobiographies as a "series of jeremiads, calling the church back to the zeal of its earlier, less refined days" (1998, p. 181). One of their chief concerns was the clergy's willingness to trade a once unfettered religious zeal for social status and educational refinement. Freeborn Garrettson cautioned that "the fall of the primitive Church began with the clergy; and should we fall, our declension will begin here" (1984, p. 31). He added that "it is better to have a pious, laborious, successful ministry, than to have wealth and ease without such a ministry." But their concerns were not confined to the ministry. They were also concerned with the decline of class meetings, love feasts, and camp meetings. They forecast that without the intimate social events so conducive to spiritual revival and discipline, the church would inevitably fall into decline (Wigger, 1998).

As the twentieth century dawned, the realization by many leaders of the Methodist Episcopal Church that they were not matching Baptist growth prompted a variety of responses. Some chose to emphasize that receipts from member contributions continued to rise quite rapidly. Others emphasized that a far more adequate and sophisticated theology now held sway and noted the immense progress toward more refined and respectable services (recall Sweet's evident relief that religious emotionalism had been brought under control). Some suggested that the whole past emphasis on conversion had been misplaced and that the church's emphasis should shift to social service, informed by the new science of sociology. There were also many comments that the slowdown was caused only by recent efforts to clean up local membership rolls—implying that growth by the Baptists and other evangelical groups was nothing more than sloppy bookkeeping.

But not everyone found these suggestions satisfactory. Speaking for those committed to old-fashioned Methodism with its emphasis on conversion, George W. Wilson bluntly rejected the prevailing views in *Methodist Theology vs. Methodist Theologians* (1904, pp. 329, 331): "a spiritual dearth has come over us [Methodists] which can not be removed by liberal giving, nor explained away by the theory that this is 'a transitional age,' or that we are 'cleaning up the Church records,' or that 'the trend of the times is towards ethics and sociology.' . . . Though the whole amount of our gifts increases yearly, it is in no reasonable proportion to the increase in our wealth."

Eight decades later, the Methodist bishop Richard B. Wilke chided his colleagues for fostering many of the same myths and deceptions. In *And Are We Yet Alive?* Wilke (1986, p. 17) reviewed the dismal declines in Methodist membership totals that had ensued in the 1960s and wrote: "What does this discouraging study of statistics mean? Some people say the situation isn't so bad as it seems. They argue that many congregations are vital and alive; millions of people are in worship; money keeps coming in . . . many church rolls have been 'cleaned.'" The bishop went on to note: "We've been cleaning the rolls for twenty years," but this simply means that "we are losing people all the time," and as long as this continues, "we will have to clean our rolls year after year" (p. 19). For those of his colleagues who responded that they didn't "believe in the numbers game" and who claimed to be more interested in the "quality, not the quantity of members," the bishop suggested they recall John Wesley's remarks in his *Journal* that any membership decline is a "sore evil," for growth is a sign of God's grace, "where the real power of God is, it naturally spreads wider and wider" (p. 15). The bishop wondered who could find anything resembling a "game" in such dismal numbers: in 1985 a third of the nation's Methodist churches had performed no baptisms, infant or adult; nearly two thirds had no membership training or confirmation classes; and nearly half had no list of potential new members.

But *why* this state of affairs? Bishop Wilke's answers are much like our own and were rather fully anticipated by Wilson in 1904—that the church had become too worldly to preach the messages and support the methods by which the Methodist miracle had occurred in the first place. Wilson (1904, pp. 333, 330) charged that "empty speculative babblings are uttered from pulpit, rostrum, and professor's chair, where positive truth should be uttered with power of the Holy Spirit resting on the speaker, convicting and not creating doubt . . . . Revivals are scarce. . . . [and] sermons are preached without a single appeal to the sinner to accept Christ Jesus now" Throughout his book Wilson argued that theologians and clergy were attempting to replace Christian experience and "spiritual impulses" with a respectable and consistent theology. For Wilson the result was: "Faith is circumscribed by finite, fallible, illogical reason (p. 329). And the blame for all this, in Wilson's view, should be placed on the clergy and especially upon the theologians in the seminaries. The church had fallen into the hands of a "self-seeking, hireling ministry, refusing to preach the whole Gospel." He rumbled on about "Christless leaders" and "looseness in examining the spiritual life of candidates for our ministry" (p. 342).

What was the alternative? Consider the more recent proposals Bishop Wilke (1986) made to reinvigorate Methodism:

> The overriding opinion held by laypeople and pastors alike is that the local church will thrive when the minister is enthusiastic, and it will founder when the minister is dry and lifeless.

> How can we energize our preachers for the challenge of the century before us?

> First, we focus on Jesus. . . . Preachers should burn, not burn out. They should shout, "I live; yet not I, but Christ lives within me!" (pp. 96–97)

The churches that are drawing people to them believe in sin, hell, and death. Jesus, who knew what he was talking about, explained them, experienced them, and conquered them. If there is no sin, we do not need a Savior. If we do not need a Savior, we do not need preachers. (p. 98)

Seminaries must fuel the faith of our new ministers. If they are only graduate schools, their graduates will be able to write term papers, but not to save souls. . . . Some wag has said that students enter seminary inspired to be evangelists and graduate aspiring to be seminary professors. (p. 99)

If we are to tackle the world for Christ, the seminaries must be fiery furnaces. The task is not to grant degrees, but to inflame the minds and hearts of a generation of preachers (p. 100).

Wilson would have liked these lines. If Peter Cartwright could have read them, he might easily have taken them to be his own.

The Baptist Triumph

Are all successful sect movements fated to "forget their errand into the wilderness," as Cotton Mather so aptly described the transformation of sects into churches? This question raises what is perhaps the most basic issue of social science—do humans have significant control of their destinies or are they essentially puppets dancing to the beat of the social forces that surround them? An either/or answer does not suffice. William Sims Bainbridge (1985) summed up our position when he wrote: "Do we make our history, or does it make us? Clearly, the answer is yes!"

In answer to our initial question, we can see that Methodist clergy and seminary professors always had (and have) the option of embracing the otherworldly faith of the Wesleys and Francis Asbury. But the underlying dynamic of sect-church theory is that social forces tend to influence religious preferences and opportunities. For an educated clergy, for example, the costs of remaining in a high tension sect are especially onerous and other options soon appear more attractive. When compared to their mainline professional counterparts, they often receive less pay and community respect, have fewer career options and less job security, while facing more stringent demands on their belief and behavior. The result: well-educated clergy are often the first to want reduced tension with the surrounding culture.

Thus, when seminary-trained clergy, often with advanced degrees, are in charge of denominational machinery, the transition from sect to church

FIGURE 5.4 Methodists and Baptists in the North as Percentage of Total Adherents, 1850–1926

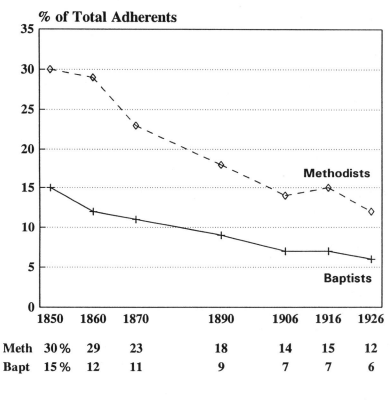

	1850	1860	1870	1890	1906	1916	1926
Meth	30%	29	23	18	14	15	12
Bapt	15%	12	11	9	7	7	6

-◇- **Meth**   —+— **Bapt**

***"North" Includes all states in the Northeast
and North Central census areas.**

tends to occur rapidly—as in the case of the Methodists. But when local clergy with little professional training and few professional ties have substantial power, the drift toward accommodation is delayed. This contrast helps to explain why only some Baptist groups were transformed into low tension churches. Unlike Methodists, whose regional bodies remained sufficiently alike so that they were eventually able to reunite (in 1939), the Northern and Southern Baptist branches became so different that the former was transformed from sect to church, while the latter maintained higher tension even though it went on to become the largest Protestant denomination in the United States. A brief examination of the fate of the Northern Baptists can be instructive.

The Secularization of Northern Baptists

Perhaps the most obvious difference between the Northern and Southern Baptists is that of membership growth. The Baptists' share of the religious market in the North showed a pattern of decline similar to that of the Methodists (see Figure 5.4). Although part of this decline can be explained by the rising numbers of Catholic and Lutheran immigrants, immigration does not explain the inability of the Northern Baptists to compete with other Protestants. Whereas the Baptists of the South made huge inroads on the Methodist share of the religious market between 1850 and 1926 (as we saw in Figure 5.2), the Baptists of the North fell into a decline that paralleled that of the Methodists.

The Baptists of the North and South soon differed on more than membership growth, however. At the turn of the twentieth century the Southern Baptists were still served by many untutored, unpaid farmer-preachers, who preached the "old-time" gospel to a relatively impoverished membership. In contrast, the overwhelming majority of Northern Baptist clergy were comparatively well paid graduates of seminaries where liberal theology held sway. The Northern Baptist membership was also increasingly more affluent.

In 1906 the average salary was $536 per year for all Baptist clergy and $784 for all Methodist clergy (see Table 5.1). But, broken down by specific denominations, the average annual salary for clergy from the Southern Baptist Convention was only $367, while the average salary for the Northern Baptist clergy was more than twice as high ($833)—higher even than that of Methodists in the North. These differences cannot be viewed as merely a product of the region, because the Methodists show relatively minor regional differences: $812 for the Methodist Episcopal Church and $714 for the Methodist Episcopal Church, South (Bureau of the Census, 1910).

In addition to their relatively high level of pay, the Baptist clergy of the North also could boast of their fine theological training. Even prior to the formation of the Southern Baptist Convention in 1845, Baptist seminaries were predominantly located in the North. Hayward (1836, p. 154) reports that in 1834–35 Baptist seminaries in the North enrolled 68 percent of all students attending Baptist seminaries, but only 36 percent of Baptist membership was located in the North. Even as late as 1916, when the membership of the Northern Convention was less than half that of the Southern Convention, the enrollments of the Northern Convention seminaries exceeded those of the Southern Baptist Convention by 40 percent (Bureau of the Census, 1919).[4] And just as had happened at the Methodist seminaries, the Northern Baptist seminaries gradually toned down their theology (Torbet, 1976). Hudson (1981, p. 280) judged that "all the northern Baptist seminaries were firmly in the liberal camp by the end of the [nineteenth] century." In 1915 Albert Henry Newman noted that "all of the older theological seminaries of the North have on their faculties scholars of the modern type who are outspoken in their acceptance of modernistic views of the Bible and of the evolutionistic philosophy, and no one of them . . . [has] a stalwart and aggressive advocate of the older conservatism" (p. 518).

Because most Baptist seminaries in the North were independently organized and thereby free of denominational control, they easily became a haven for the expression and development of liberal theology (Hudson, 1981). These developments did not go unnoticed by Baptists in the South. James J. Thompson (1982, pp. 71–72) reports that by the 1920s Southern Baptists had become very concerned about the lack of orthodoxy in the North, especially in seminaries such as the University of Chicago: "Southerners reserved their fiercest denunciations for the University of Chicago, charging that the once-orthodox Baptist school had become a 'satanic institution' harboring 'infidelity, atheism, rationalism, and materialism.'"

Another dramatic difference between the Northern and Southern Baptists was in the affluence of their churches. In 1906 the value of all church property owned by the Northern Baptist Convention was more than double that of the Southern Baptist Convention, despite the Northern Baptists' having only half as many members. Part of this contrast can be explained by regional differences in affluence as well as in real estate values and for this reason comparisons with other denominations are instructive. The Northern Baptist Convention's average of $70.92 of church property per member placed them above the Methodist Episcopal Church ($54.70 per member) and remarkably close to the Presbyterians ($82.07) and the Congregationalists ($90.34) (Bureau of the Census, 1910).

Like the Methodists, and the old colonial mainline denominations before them, the Northern Baptists had been transformed from sect to church.

As they entered the twentieth century their clergy overwhelmingly were paid, well-trained professionals, and their theology was becoming compatible with "modern" thought. But their market share was in decline.

Secularization and the Southern Baptists

Why weren't the southern Baptists transformed from sect to church as their Northern co-religionists were? We argue that structural features of the Southern Baptists, and their regional context, enabled them to offer strong resistance to secularization. Our argument rests on five basic points.

Initially, the most powerful tool for curbing secularization was the regional context of the Southern Baptists. The Civil War left the Southern Baptists representing an impoverished and shattered South. The Baptists seized this as an opportunity to become the primary organizational vehicle for sustaining a recusant Southern culture that clung to "traditional" views in political, racial, and social as well as religious spheres. Thus through the decades when the South remained an economically depressed internal colony and Southerners were the object of Yankee scorn, the sectlike qualities of the Southern Baptists were reinforced.

Second, Southern Baptist congregations were extremely democratic, believing that ecclesiastical power resided in all members (Wills, 1997).[5] The local laity hired and fired their preachers as they pleased and did not submit to any directives, theological or otherwise, from above. Local congregations retained the right to ordain ministers and voted annually on "whether to retain the pastor's services." In essence, the pastors were receiving one year "calls" or contracts to serve a congregation (Harvey, 1997, pp. 80, 175). This meant that the interests of the clergy could not be imposed upon the laity and that the will of the laity could, to a very considerable extent, be imposed on the clergy.

A third very significant fact of Southern Baptist life grows out of the independence of local congregations. The extreme version of this view was promoted by the powerful and well-organized Landmark Movement. Holding to the sovereignty of the local church, they did battle with any denominational organization that attempted to usurp local church authority, from missionary associations to seminaries (Baker, 1974; Harvey, 1997). It is not clear that Landmarkians ever were the majority in the Southern Baptist Convention, but their grass roots support was sufficient to fend off any limitations to local authority. The extreme independence and authority of the local churches made it difficult, if not impossible,

Ball Camp Baptist Church near Knoxville, Tennessee. (Courtesy of the Southern Baptist Historical Library and Archives, Nashville, Tenn.)

for the Southern Baptists to root out factions—including potential sect movements. Even substantial majorities in the Southern Baptist convention could not expel their opponents in the way that the Methodists expelled Benjamin Roberts and his Free Methodists or, later, the Holiness supporters. Dissidents were thus free to stay and fight for support from among rank-and-file Baptists. When the more sectlike dissidents are forced to leave a denomination, they leave behind a group in which the average member is less otherworldly than before the split. But such liberalization by expulsion and defection seldom took place among the Southern Baptists.

The fourth factor is that the Southern Baptists, urged on by dissident factions, never permitted their seminaries to emerge as independent organizations as did Northern Baptist seminaries. Although Southern Baptist seminaries were also prone to "modernism," this trend was held somewhat in check by the periodic dismissal of outspoken seminary professors. The most obvious was the firing of William H. Whitsitt from the presidency of Southern Seminary in 1899. Historians of American religion routinely refer to this as the Whitsitt Controversy, but it was the views of Whitsitt and his faculty, not the firing, that were controversial. For what was involved was not the martyrdom of a church historian because of his disagreement with rank-and-file Baptists over the historical validity of Landmarkian claims. Rather, what was involved was the takeover of the Southern Baptists' only seminary by a faculty who unanimously rejected *many* basic, traditional Christian tenets and who aggressively taught these unorthodox views to their students. That is, a group of religious intellectuals consciously attempted to "modernize" Southern Baptist theology, whether the membership liked it or not. Because the seminaries were never independent organizations, however, the seminary faculty was not able to re-create the denomination in their own image.

A final factor is that so many clergy remained bivocational local pastors, without seminary training and requiring little pay. This served to curb secularization and reduced the operating costs of local churches. Generally speaking, throughout the South the Baptist clergy received low salaries, when they received any at all. Consider an example offered by Victor Masters (1916, p. 98) of a Baptist farmer-preacher in Virginia who served two churches. Every Sunday he walked six miles to preach at one church and then walked five miles to the other. He also held three weeks of revivals yearly, while receiving an annual salary of $13.20. In order to live, this man farmed thirty acres of rented land, but was so poor he had to work part time for a neighbor in exchange for the use of a horse to till his field.

Among the Methodists a settled, professional clergy had largely replaced the local lay clergy by the 1880s, but even early in the twentieth century the Southern Baptists still had an abundance of farmer-preachers. Of all the active Southern Baptist pastors reporting their salaries to

Because Southern Baptists did not rely on a full-time professional clergy, they could support numerous small churches scattered across the countryside. Shown here is the Brier Creek Baptist Church in Wilkes County, North Carolina. (Courtesy of the Southern Baptist Historical Library and Archives, Nashville, Tenn.)

the 1916 census, 36 percent pursued full-time secular occupations. Of these, 71 percent were farmers.[6] By comparison, more than 98 percent of the active clergy in the Methodist Episcopal Church, South, earned their entire living from the church. This willingness to use bivocational clergy helps to explain why the Southern Baptists had a ratio of one minister for every 1.5 churches and for every 151 members, whereas the Methodist Episcopal Church, South, could supply only one minister for every 3 churches and for every 282 members. But even when Baptist clergy were not bivocational, they were seldom the products of seminaries. As late as 1930, when the Convention reported 23,731 churches, only 260 students were enrolled in "pastoral ministry" at Southern Baptist seminaries (Finke, 1994).

Like the upstart sects of the early nineteenth century, the Southern Baptists were not lacking for eager clergy, or held back by the inability of small rural churches to support a full-time minister, nor hobbled by the decisions of a central hierarchy. They could operate wherever a few gathered to worship—and they did.

Reorganizing Dixie

Even after Emancipation and the Civil War, many whites anticipated few changes in their local churches. In 1865, the Committee on the Religious Instruction of the Colored People of the Alabama Baptist State Convention explained that "the changed political status of our late slaves does not necessitate any change in their relation to our churches" (in Kolchin, 1997, p. 109).[7] Methodists of the South expressed similar sentiments, desiring to continue their ministry to blacks without significantly altering their status in the church (Gravely, 1994). But when it became clear that blacks wanted greater autonomy and whites wanted the status quo, both sides agreed that dividing churches along racial lines was desirable. The divisions that followed were remarkably amicable and rapid, with many churches recording the changes as a routine gain or loss of membership (Baker, 1974; Sparks 1994, 2001; Harvey, 1997). By 1870 the religious landscape for the freed slaves had been completely transformed.

The growth of the churches was spurred on by two powerful forces: the *conflicts* they faced with the dominant culture and the *competition* they faced from other churches. The freed slaves of the late nineteenth century took greater advantage of the unregulated religious market than any group in American history. Like the immigrant faiths, religious freedoms allowed African Americans to use the churches as institutional safe havens for supporting their members and their culture. E. Franklin Frazier explained that "organized religious life became the chief means by which a structured or organized social life came into existence" for the freed slaves ([1964] 1974, p. 36). Following the Civil War, the churches trained new leaders, mobilized political action, supported educational programs, provided supportive social networks, and developed mutual aid and fraternal associations (Nelson, Yokley, and Nelson, 1971; Nelson and Nelson, 1975; Lincoln and Mamiya, 1990). In Frazier's words the "church provided a refuge in a hostile white world" ([1964] 1974, p. 50).

The freed slaves were also greeted with a diversity of churches offering multiple expressions of the faith. The denominations of the North, both white and black, sent missionaries and money to start churches for the freed people, and the churches of the South responded quickly to these unwelcome intrusions. The result was intense and sometimes bitter religious rivalries (Barr, 1997; Gravely, 1994). Some of the most heated battles took place between Methodists. As the Methodist Episcopal Church, South, and the emerging Colored Methodist Episcopal Church (CME) fought to retain members, the African Methodist Episcopal Church (AME),

FIGURE 5.5 Rates of Religious Adherence for Blacks and Total Population, 1890–1926

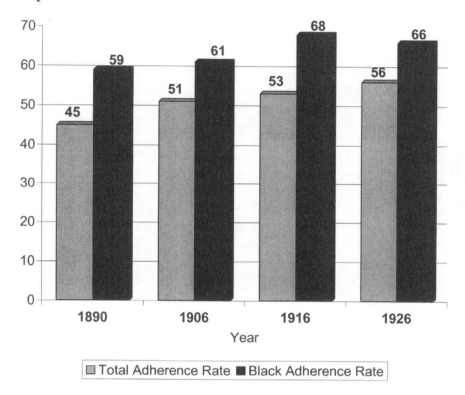

the African Methodist Episcopal Zion (AMEZ), and the Methodist Episcopal Church came from the North to seek members and churches. To add to the mix, the Union American Methodist Episcopal, the African Union Methodist Protestant, Congregational Methodist (Colored), Zion Union Apostolic, Methodist Protestant, and New Congregational Methodist would all form congregations for the freed slaves of the South (Bureau of the Census, 1894). An unaffiliated congregation of Methodist freed slaves was considered a "prize" and representatives of two or three Methodist denominations would often be recruiting the congregation at the same time. When this open competition was combined with churches serving as a "refuge" against a hostile environment, the level of religious involvement for black Americans quickly exceeded that of whites.

Figure 5.5 shows that the adherence rates for blacks exceeds whites by at least 10 percent from 1890 to 1926. These rates are based on the Bureau of the Census's detailed reports for all "Negro churches" from

FIGURE 5.6 Percentage of Black Population in Baptist, Methodist, and Other Denominations, 1890–1926

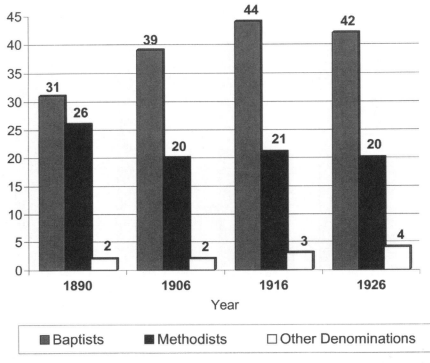

The Bureau of the Census's *Religious Bodies, 1906* would later conclude that the member estimate for the AMEZ denomination was too high in 1890.[8]

1890 to 1926, which included those affiliated with predominantly white denominations. Along with total membership, these reports offer rich details for each denomination. For example, only twenty-five years after the Civil War, ten denominations were formed entirely from "Negro" congregations and another nineteen denominations had at least one such congregation. Despite the large number of white denominations attempting to start churches for the freed slaves, however, the majority of the membership was found in the black denominations. In 1890, 51 percent of the black population belonged to the nine black denominations and only 8 percent to the predominantly white denominations. Of the predominantly white denominations, the Methodist Episcopal Church of the North was the only denomination with a sizeable membership.[9] By 1926 the percentage of the black population in white denominations was unchanged at 8 percent, but black denominations now enrolled 58.5 percent of the black population. The institutional growth of the black denominations is especially impressive when you consider that their sources of support where so few. Most members had few personal resources and, with the exception of those joining the Northern denominations, they could not appeal to a parent denomination or a home country for support.

The denominational families to which they belonged also began to shift. Prior to the Civil War the Methodists and Baptists were the only two denominations to make an effective appeal to the growing slave population. Although membership numbers for Baptists are few and far between, the Methodists seemed to have an edge in membership for the blacks of the South and the North, just as they did for the whites. By 1890, however, the Baptists had gained a very substantial edge over the Methodists and by the early twentieth century their rates were more than double the Methodists (see Figure 5.6). Despite receiving missionaries and support from the two black Methodist denominations from the North (the AME and the AMEZ), the Methodists could not keep pace with the Baptists in the South.

The autonomy and democratic structure of the local church proved to be a strong asset for the Baptists (Nelson and Nelson, 1975; Kolchin, 1997). Fearing the control of Southern whites and the intervention of Northern missionaries, Baptists offered freed slaves a local congregation with nearly complete autonomy and one where power was in the hands of the members. The congregations quickly reflected the religion of the people. In 1903 W.E.B. DuBois wrote that "three things characterized the religion of the slave—the preacher, the music, and the frenzy" (1971, p. 30). Baptist churches offered an abundance of all three. Facing few educational or ecclesiastical requirements, local clergy emerged who had experienced slavery, were involved in the invisible church of the past, and knew how to preach. Free of white supervision and the control of a centralized hierarchy, Baptist worship more fully incorporated the frenzy (or shouting) and the distinctive music of the freed slaves (Moore, 1981).

The organizational flexibility of the Baptist church also allowed thousands of new Baptist congregations to form in the late 1860s. Although some congregations continued to worship at the same church building as whites, and others relied on the assistance of Southern whites or Northern missionaries for securing buildings, many simply left their former churches and began their own churches without white "approval or assistance" (Sparks, 1994, p. 198; Harvey, 1997). Requiring no permission for starting a new church, and requiring only modest start up costs, new

A southern baptism. (Courtesy of the Billy Graham Center Museum, Wheaton, Ill.)

churches seemed to arise everywhere. When disagreements arose in the newly formed churches, church schisms would often occur, resulting in still more churches (Barr, 1997). By the late 1860s, the black Baptist churches began to form state associations similar to those of white Baptists and a successful national convention followed in 1886 (Lincoln and Mamiya, 1990). Even then, however, the autonomy of the local congregation was never threatened.

The hierarchical structure of the Methodist denominations initially caused delays and confusion for the freed slaves when it came to organizing local churches and choosing preachers. For a majority of the congregations their first step was to leave the Methodist Episcopal Church, South. The *Minutes of the Annual Conferences of the Methodist Episcopal Church, South,* reported 171,857 black members (and 35,909 probationers) in 1860 and the 1866 *Minutes* reported only 78,742 black members by the close of 1865 (Gravely, 1994). For existing congregations, some of the initial confusion over joining another denomination was due to the issue of property. Reviewing the history of the AME during the Reconstruction Era, James T. Campbell found that the disputes were often "three-sided, with the Methodist Episcopal Church, South holding deeds to buildings, the Methodist Episcopal Church, North claiming them by order from the Secretary of the Army, and the AME Church claiming them by dint of occupation" (1995, p. 57). But the greater concerns went far beyond property. After leaving an organization dominated by white Southerners, the remaining choices within the Methodist fold were denominations dominated by Northerners. Each of the options robbed them of some of the local autonomy and leadership granted to the Baptist congregations.

The AME was the most aggressive and successful Methodist denomination at attracting the churches of freed slaves, sending seventy-seven missionaries into the South between 1863 and 1870 (Walker, 1982). The first AME missionaries arrived in the summer of 1863 and on May 15, 1865, Bishop Daniel Payne personally organized the AME South Carolina Conference.[10] As the AME rapidly expanded, Bishop Payne worked tirelessly to increase the education of the clergy and to stamp out "heathen" practices in the churches. Payne stood firm on the literacy requirement for clergy and strongly discouraged religious practices such as corn songs and ring shouts. In his journal, Payne describes the "strange delusion that many ignorant but well-meaning people labor under."

> After the sermon they formed a ring, and with coats off sung, clapped their hands and stamped their feet in a most ridiculous and heathenish way. I requested the pastor to go and stop their dancing. At his request they stopped their dancing and clapping of hands, but remained singing and rocking their bodies to and fro. This they did for about fifteen minutes. I then went, and taking their leader by the arm requested him to desist and to sit down and sing in a rational manner. I told him also that it was a heathenish way to worship and disgraceful to themselves, the race, and the Christian name. ([1888] 1968, pp. 253–254)

But the concerns of Payne and other AME leaders over the freed slaves' manners, lack of literacy, and boisterous worship were not shared by many of their new members. The young pastor, so sharply admonished by Payne, responded, "sinners won't get converted unless there is a ring" (Payne, [1888] 1968, p. 254). After reviewing the history of the AME during the Reconstruction era, James T. Campbell concludes that "many former slave exhorters elected not to affiliate, lest they lose their standing" (1995, p. 62).

The structured Methodist hierarchy posed special problems for the other Methodist denominations as well. The leadership of the Methodist Episcopal Church, South, was slow in responding to the concerns of freed slaves, waiting until 1870 to form the Colored Methodist Episcopal Church (CME). Even then the CME was viewed by rival Methodist denominations as a "subservient body that did as the masters' church bid" (Dvorak, 1991, p. 167). The Methodist Episcopal Church of the North was well organized and well financed, but relied heavily on white clergy for missionaries and leadership. Finally, the AMEZ experienced many of the advantages and disadvantages of the AME. Their growth, however, was less uniform across the South, with 60 percent of their Southern churches concentrated in North Carolina and Alabama as late as 1890.

The efforts of the remaining denominations were sometimes impressive, but the results were modest. The Congregationalists directed the highly effective educational programs of the American Missionary Association, and invested heavily in missionary work to the freed slaves, but they established few churches, all of which relied on subsidies. Finding few blacks who could meet their educational requirements for the ministry, they relied on white clergy offering erudite preaching and formal worship. When combined with "paternalistic" practices and an appearance of "snobbishness," their extensive missionary efforts resulted in fewer than 7,000 members by 1890 (Richardson, 1994). With the exception of the Colored Cumberland Presbyterian Church, a similar pattern held true for the Presbyterians (Thompson, 1994) and most of the remaining denominations that were predominantly white and from the North.

The Baptists invited the free slaves to come as they were, and they did. The Methodists maintained a prominent position with the freed slaves, but they couldn't keep pace with the Baptists. Once again, the Methodists transformed, the Baptists triumphed.

Chapter 6

Why Unification Efforts Fail

In 1959, Eugene Carson Blake, a leader of the United Presbyterian Church who had just completed his term as president of the National Council of Churches, noted that the latest *Yearbook of American Churches* listed 258 separate denominations. Of course, he pointed out, the twenty-four largest of these bodies accounted for more than 80 percent of America's church members. Still, "even twenty-four churches . . . is entirely too many" (1959, p. 76).

Blake's solution was religious unity, to be achieved through what he referred to as the "ecumenical mission" of the churches—a mission to bring about mergers among the Protestant denominations. Blake's call for merger was not restricted to the liberal bodies, which he designated as the "old-line Churches." He wanted a real union. But he recognized that major resistance to ecumenism came from those "who style themselves as 'Bible-believing' Christians" and who embrace many "cultural crudities" (pp. 82, 77). Nonetheless, he suggested to his colleagues that they begin to cultivate leaders of "the conservative churches . . . to bring these sincere men out of theological isolation and personal provincialism" (p. 83). He acknowledged "the cleavage between unscholarly literal Biblical interpretation and scholarly higher criticism" (p. 83). But he warned that not all the "weaknesses of Biblical interpretation" were to be found among conservatives and concluded that through sincere study of the Bible the theological impediments to union could be overcome.

Blake's aims and observations, which appeared in an edited volume with the confident title *The Ecumenical Era in Church and Society*, were hardly novel. From the beginning, American pluralism has vexed many observers. How are people to be saved if they confront dozens of Christianities, each claiming it has the real truth? To William Warren Sweet ([1930] 1950, p. 424), "Our divisions are indeed the scandal of Christendom." And the solution has always been sought in unification. In 1827 Beecher warned that Finney's "new" form of revivalism must be stopped or "it will prevent the great evangelical assimilation, which is forming in the United States" (Beecher and Nettleton, 1828, p. 98). A decade later a number of religious leaders involved in the antislavery movement gathered in Syracuse "for the purpose of . . . adopting the most feasible methods, to annihilate the existing denominational distinctions." Their concern was that real unity could not be gained on the issue of slavery until the churches "abandon their exclusive creeds, and incorporate nothing in their articles that will shut off their fellowship with any true child of God" (in W. R. Cross, 1950, p. 280). Without a definition of a "true child of God," we cannot determine what Christian doctrines can be retained without excluding some from fellowship. But because in practical terms proposals of this sort reduce to a call to Unitarianism, it is not surprising that nothing came of this ecumenical effort.

Nor a century later, in the 1930s, was any progress toward unification actually in the offing, despite Sweet's ([1930] 1950, p. 424) pronouncement that "there is hope for a better day." True, Sweet was able to list an impressive number of mergers of American Protestant bodies since 1900. But these mergers had all taken place within narrowly defined denominational "families." Baptists had merged with Baptists, Presbyterians with Presbyterians, Lutherans with Lutherans, and Reformed with Reformed. All of this merging was capped by what Sweet called the "largest unification movement to take place in the United States" (p. 425), which, in 1939, joined three denominations: the Methodist Protestant Church, the Methodist Episcopal Church, South, and the Methodist Episcopal Church. The ecumenical aspect of such unions is hard to discover.

By the 1950s, nevertheless, despite the repeated failure of any real progress toward unity, it was so widely believed that massive mergers were at hand that a book was even published to explain ahead of time why it had happened: *The Social Sources of Church Unity*, by Robert Lee (1960). Among the many reasons cited by Lee, one of the most compelling was simple economics. All else being equal, it is incredibly inefficient to operate so many congregations. Surely even "Bible-believing Christians" could grasp this obvious fact.

In addition to more mundane justifications, proponents of religious unions have always condemned pluralism as sinful and unbiblical.[1] For example, during his stay in Boston, George Whitefield ([1756] 1969, p. 459)—a committed pluralist—severely antagonized local clergy when he claimed: "It was best to preach up the new birth, and the power of god-liness, and not to insist so much upon the form: for people would never be brought to one mind as to that; nor did Jesus Christ ever intend it."

Dr. Timothy Cutler immediately challenged Whitefield, "Yes, but He did." Cutler's proof: "Christ prayed, That all might be one, even as Thou Father and I are One" (p. 459). Incredibly, two centuries later this same claim was advanced in the pages of *The Annals of the American Academy of Political and Social Science* by Roswell P. Barnes (1960, pp. 136–137), a well-known Protestant who served as an executive both in the National and the World Council of Churches: "Basically, Christian unity is a given fact derived from a common belief in Jesus Christ as God and Savior. It is, therefore, not created by men, but gratefully acknowledged and mani-fested. It is furthered and developed by men as they progressively re-spond in obedience to what they believe to be God's will. Christ prayed for his followers of all time 'that they all may be one.' The ecumenical movement is essentially an expression of conviction, a matter of faith derived from biblical and theological authority."

That same year similar views were affirmed by the popular Jesuit theo-logian John Courtney Murray. Although Murray admitted that plural-ism was inevitable in democratic societies, he felt that there was no theological alternative but to conclude that "religious pluralism is against the will of God" (1960, p. 32). And European theologians, of course, have always known that American religious life is a tower of Babel. Hence Dietrich Bonhoeffer's (1965, p. 94) condescending jibe: "It has been granted to the Americans less than any other nation of the earth to realise on the earth the visible unity of the Church of God."

Sinful and inefficient it may be, but denominationalism continues to prosper in American life, while ecumenical movements have inevitably failed to achieve anything more than peripheral cartels such as the one currently vested in the National Council of Churches. Why is this the case? In reviewing the two major efforts at ecumenism in America dur-ing the twentieth century as well as several episodes of cartel formation, we test the proposition offered in Chapter 1: that pluralism is, as Father Murray recognized, the natural condition of any unregulated religious economy and that therefore voluntary ecumenical movements must fail. We also suggest that mergers involving major religious bodies will be limited to denominations already undergoing decline (with the possible exception of mergers within a denominational family).

Ecumenism and Country Life

In 1860 only one American in five lived in an urban community—that is, a community of more than 2,500 people. By the turn of the century two of five were urbanites and by 1920 more than half of all Americans lived in towns and cities. Although some portion of urban growth was caused by immigration, the bulk occurred because people deserted the countryside for the city.

In the wake of rapid urbanization a great deal of concern was expressed about the potential loss of many virtues and values associated with rural life. These concerns culminated in the appointment of a Commission on Country Life by President Theodore Roosevelt in 1908. The commission held thirty hearings throughout the country and distributed more than a half million questionnaires, of which slightly more than a hundred thousand were returned and partially tabulated. In 1909 the commission issued a report that was soon regarded as having "more influence on rural life in this country than any other document" (Sanderson, 1942, p. 712). Among its many recommendations, the commission proposed the creation of the agricultural extension service, initiation of massive agricultural research and training programs at the nation's land grant colleges and universities, and the inclusion of agricultural and home economics courses in the nation's high schools. Each of these proposals was soon put into effect, but these were only means to an end: the commission called for an all-out effort to "unite the interests of education, organization and religion into one forward movement for rebuilding of rural life" (in Sanderson, 1942, p. 712).

The mention of religion was not incidental. Rather, the importance of the rural church and the special relationship between religion and rural life were dominant themes for the early "Country Life Movement," and remained so when the American Country Life Association was founded in 1919 to continue the work started by the commission (Bowers, 1974; Madison, 1986; Wunderlich, 2002). Kenyon L. Butterfield, the founder and first president of the American Country Life Association and a leading member of Roosevelt's commission, was one of several who had published on the "country church problem" even prior to the commission's report (Butterfield, 1905). Butterfield went on to conduct and publish many additional studies of rural religion and, in 1921, was a founder of the Institute of Social and Religious Research in New York City. We shall have more to report about Butterfield and his associates at the Institute in a moment. But first, it is useful to consider the fundamental thesis that religion fares better among rural folk than it does among urbanites.

The Myth of Urban Irreligion

Since the dawn of recorded history, the city has been depicted as a precinct of sin and impiety. Whether the cities were Sodom and Gomorrah, Corinth and Rome, or New York and Chicago, observers have taken it for granted that city life not only encourages vice but also fosters skepticism and doubt—and that the pious life is easier in the hinterlands. John Lancaster Spalding wrote in 1880: "In the city neither the rich nor the poor can realize the infinite charm of the Christian ideal. The heart is troubled there, and God is not in the whirlwind of human passion" ([1880] 1967, p. 8).

Not only prophets and preachers regard the city as wicked and secular. Social scientists also assert that city life is corrosive of the moral order and that urban life is inevitably more permissive than life in the country. As Gideon Sjoberg (1960, p. 340) explained, urban religion sustains norms that "are generally permissive" because the "divergent, and often contradictory, roles, and the new technology ensures a continuous cycle of change, all of which requires flexibility of norms." Moreover, from Durkheim on, sociologists have been certain that the unavoidable tendency toward religious pluralism in cities weakens faith.[2] Indeed, Harvey Cox (1965, p. 1) flatly asserted that secularization has occurred because the "cosmopolitan confrontations of city living exposed the relativity of the myths and traditions men once thought were unquestionable." Similar views inspired Peter Berger's *The Sacred Canopy* (1967), an influential work in the sociology of religion.

Historians of religion have also affirmed the secular atmosphere of the city. American historians have taken it for granted that the city is especially inhospitable to Protestantism. Ahlstrom (1975, p. 194) claimed that one of the "particularly devastating consequences" of urbanization was that "large elements of the new urban population had no contact with any Protestant churches." Similarly, Robert Handy (1969, p. 90) noted: "There is wide agreement that Protestant churches have historically tended to be more at home in rural and town America than in the America of great cities."

But it just isn't so. The growth of cities increased religious participation, and even Protestant churches did better in the cities than in the hinterlands. Suppose the members of the commission (or any historian of

American religion since then) had consulted the 1906 report on religious bodies published by the Bureau of the Census (1910). What they would have found are the figures for 1890 and 1906, shown in Table 6.1. In both years the percentage of the population reported to be church members was substantially higher in the principal cities (those of 25,000 residents and larger) than in less urban areas. Moreover, the gap between city and country was increasing. The difference was not an artifact of denomination; when the 1906 figures are transformed into adherence rates, the rate for cities remains higher.

In fact, the gap between the countryside and the city is probably larger than indicated in Table 6.1. Because the rural totals included many small towns, where rates are also higher, the rates for rural areas are inflated. Indeed, when rural reformers sponsored by the Institute of Social and Religious Research conducted a national survey of 140 small towns (250–2,500 residents) in the early 1920s, they found a vast difference between the small town and the countryside. The percentage of the population affiliated with a church was far lower for those living in the country than it was for the villagers, regardless of region (see Table 6.2).

Why is religious mobilization higher in cities and towns? For one thing, it is easier for people to get to church—many farmers live a considerable distance from the nearest church. But the more important reason is that people in cities, and even in small towns, are more likely to have access to a church that is right for them. That is, the primary impact of religious pluralism is to provide a broad spectrum of specialized religious firms competing to attract and hold a segment of the market. Rather than

TABLE 6.1
Rural/Urban Comparisons in Church Membership (in percent)

	Church membership rate		Adherence rate*
	1890	*1906*	*1906*
Principal cities	37.9	46.9	56
Outside principal cities	31.2	36.3	50
Nationwide	32.7	39.1	51

SOURCE: Church membership rate from Bureau of the Census (1910, vol. 1, p. 70).
*The adherence rate includes children in the membership totals.

TABLE 6.2
Village/Countryside Comparisons in Church
Membership for 140 Villages, 1923

	Percentage of the population belonging to a church	
Region	*Village*	*Countryside*
Middle Atlantic	41	25
South	45	28
Middle West	33	26
Far West	21	14

SOURCE: Adapted from Brunner, Hughes, and Patten (1927, p. 183).

being a source of secularization and religious decline, pluralism strengthens religion.

The question remains, however, which religious groups were best suited to the urban environment. Is it true that Protestantism is inherently rural? An obvious way to settle that issue is to calculate the proportion of members resident in urban areas for the larger denominations (see Table 6.3). In 1926, Protestant bodies were about as urban as Catholics and most were far more urban than the nation as a whole (reflecting superior urban membership rates). Episcopalians were more urban than Catholics, and even the Lutherans and the Methodists outside the South were as urban as the nation as a whole. Keep in mind, too, that the apparent ruralism of Southern Methodists and Baptists reflected the fact that in 1926 two thirds of Southerners lived in rural areas, rather than any special affinity of these denominations for rural residents.

The Commission on Country Life was thus wrong to suppose that the health of religion, and especially of Protestantism, required the renewal of rural America. Even had the commission's members read these census data (and some of them probably did), however, they would not have changed course. Three years before the commission was appointed Butterfield explained that the "ideal solution of the country church problem is to have in each rural community one strong church adequately supported, properly equipped, ministered to by an able man—a church which leads in community service." (1905, p. 620). The agenda of

TABLE 6.3
Percentage of Church Membership in Urban
Areas, 1926

Denomination	Percentage membership urban
Protestant Episcopal	83.5
Roman Catholic	79.6
Presbyterian Church in the United States of America (Northern)	71.0
Congregational	69.3
Northern Baptist Convention	68.6
United Lutheran Church in America	67.3
Presbyterian Church in the United States (Southern)	59.9
Disciples of Christ	54.6
Methodist Episcopal Church	54.2
Evangelical Lutheran Synod Conference of America	53.6
African Methodist Episcopal	50.0
African Methodist Episcopal Zion	42.4
Colored Methodist Episcopal Zion	39.1
Negro Baptists	39.0
Methodist Episcopal, South	35.6
Southern Baptist Convention	28.0
All church members	64.4
All Americans	53.2

SOURCE: Calculated from Bureau of the Census (1930, vol. 1, pp. 82–90).

Butterfield and other rural reformers was not simply the renewal of rural religion or, indeed, of rural life. They had very firm notions about what *kind* of religion as well as what *kind* of social and economic philosophy they wanted rural Americans to embrace. In addition, many of their plans for rural America were based on misguided, and sometimes arrogant, assumptions.

The Myth of the Country Church Crisis

Two years after the Commission on Country Life offered its report, Warren H. Wilson (1911b, p. 677) informed readers of the *American Journal of Sociology* that "the growth of the cities has been in part at the expense of the country" and that "the community life in the country has generally been destroyed." But Wilson's main concern was the "decay of the country church," which he attributed to two causes. The first was the wasteful rural economy. Wilson claimed that progress toward renewing rural America could occur only if farmers ceased taking an individualistic approach and began to farm in more cooperative fashion. He also charged that the individualistic economic orientation of American farmers was reflected in their preference for competitive churches. This resulted in the second cause of the decline of rural churches, a "wasteful ecclesiastical economy." He explained: "The country church has been a mere means for distributing the hope of personal salvation. . . . Any small group of believers has been at liberty to build a meeting-house and maintain an organization. National denominations have been all too willing to support these competing congregations in the country community. We have, therefore, in almost all the older states too many country churches" (p. 681). Wilson warned that a "divided religious ministry . . . is fatal to the interests of religion" and proclaimed that "church unity . . . is forced upon the churches as a means of arresting the decay of religious institutions" (p. 688). Two years later, after a survey of churches in Indiana, Wilson (1913, p. 23) complained of widespread competition for members and new buildings and groused that "churches feel they are doing well if they can leave each other alone."

Wilson's conclusions on the necessity of church unity were based on two commonly held assumptions: first, that the growth of the cities led to the decline of the rural population, and second, that owing to the oversupply of rural churches, all denominations were being forced to close congregations and to subsidize others. These were simply the facts—"so well known" as to need hardly any discussion, according to Wilson (1911b). Nevertheless, both claims are false.

It is true that at the turn of the century urban areas were growing rapidly and that the *proportion* of the population living in rural areas was declining. In terms of absolute numbers, however, the population of rural America was *growing*, not declining, in this era. Consider that in 1890, 41 million people lived in rural America. In 1920 they numbered 51 million and by 1940 this total had risen to 57 million. Many young men and women were abandoning rural life in this period, of course, but the rate of natural increase in rural areas could sustain growth despite high rates of migration. Consequently, the closure of rural churches could not have been the result of a decline in the potential church population.

How could the reformers have been mistaken about the "fact" that rural churches were closing left and right? It depends on what kind of churches one counts. If we confine our attention to the mainline churches, Wilson's comments are not only accurate but prophetic. Between 1916 and 1926 the Presbyterian Church in the U.S.A. lost 826 churches (–8.5 percent), the Congregationalists dropped 872 (–14.8 percent), the Disciples lost 748 (–8.9 percent), and the Methodist Episcopal Church lost 3,185 (–10.9 percent). Many, if not most, of these losses were country and village churches.

But if we broaden our view to take in the entire landscape of rural American religion, the picture looks very different. Between 1916 and 1926 there was a *net increase* of 4,667 in the total number of American churches. The number of Lutheran and Catholic churches increased by 2,746, but this can account for only a modest part of the gain in churches. Given that the mainline churches mentioned above had lost 5,631 congregations, more than ten thousand new churches were needed to reach the new total. If the mainline was declining, someone else must have been quickly gaining. In addition to the Southern Baptists, who gained 1,178 churches, the "someones" included the Assemblies of God (+553 percent), Church of God (Cleveland, Tenn.) (+442 percent), Christian and Missionary Alliance (+169 percent), Church of the Nazarene (+577 percent), Churches of Christ (+656 percent), Free Will Baptists (+274 percent), the Pentecostal Holiness Church (+60 percent), and the Salvation Army (+310 percent). Only the last was an urban movement. The other growing denominations tended to be even more rural than those that were declining. The Southern Baptists, for example, increased their total number of churches by 5 percent, despite having more than 90 percent of their churches in rural areas.[3] Of the 553 new churches added by the Assemblies of God in this decade, approximately half were in rural areas. The "decay" of the country church was limited to the mainline: the evangelical Protestant sects still flourished.

If the rural population was increasing and new rural churches were opening, why did Wilson (1911b, p. 688) conclude that church unity is "forced upon the churches as a means of arresting the decay of religious institutions"? The answer: because the "respectable" churches were struggling for survival in the rural areas. As we saw in Chapters 3 and 5, churches relying on well-paid professionals are unable to survive in rural areas where only small congregations can be gathered. And in the early twentieth century the rural churches were small. Surveys conducted in 1920 showed that the average congregation in towns had 144 members, the average village church had 84 members, and the average country church only 46 (Morse and Brunner, 1923). According to Butterfield and his colleagues, an oversupply of rural churches had reduced the size of congregations so that most were made up of a tiny band of worshipers who could not even afford to pay the salary needed to secure an educated and qualified minister. Many congregations were forced to make do with uneducated locals or to share a pastor with several other congregations. Worse yet, many of these rural churches were subsidized by their denominations and therefore drained valuable home mission funds from more worthwhile causes. For mainline denominations, unity was a way of reducing subsidies, paying for full-time clergy, and uniting against the growing threat of sectarianism.

Thus an unacknowledged source of concern about the "wasteful ecclesiastical economy" was that the "respectable" denominations were not faring well in competition with the "emotional sects" (Brunner, 1927), who did not have to subsidize salaries in order to staff their rural churches. The actual country church crisis thus consisted of two factors: the decline of mainline churches and the growth of sectarian groups. For the rural reformers of the early twentieth century the sectarian churches were part of the problem, not the solution. Like the American Home Missionary Society of the early nineteenth century, not just any church counted—it had to be the right kind of church and served by the right kind of clergy.

But for all of the concern about the minister's training and salary, it is doubtful that rural congregations were much better off if they were served by a seminary-educated pastor—local farmer-preachers had long seemed adequate to the tasks at hand. Such an objection would have been dismissed as fatuous or heretical by the activists in the Country Life Movement, however. They knew what was wrong. Moreover, they knew how to fix it.

God's Sociology and Rural Ecumenism

In 1912, during the second quadrennial convention of the Federal Council of Churches—the forerunner of today's National Council of Churches— a dozen men committed to solving the problem of the rural churches met in Kenyon Butterfield's Chicago hotel room to form a rural section of the American Sociological Society (Madison, 1986). This section sought to encourage the denominations to create research departments with a primary emphasis on conducting massive surveys of rural churches and to formulate plans for renewal based on their results. This wedding of sociology and religious renewal had by then become commonplace—in 1900 the highly respected Charles E. Hayward had written: "The sociological movement is born of God, and is destined to be the mightiest power behind the Gospel the world has ever known" (in Madison, 1986, p. 647). And in 1911 Warren H. Wilson explained that though the home missions program of the churches had long been directed to the geographical frontier, now home missions "are based upon the discovery of a frontier no longer geographical, but sociological" (1911b, p. 682).

Butterfield, Hayward, Wilson, and a host of others, including Charles Otis Gill, Edmund deS. Brunner, Paul L. Vogt, and H. Paul Douglass, men with formal training in both theology and sociology, were soon conducting rural church studies across the country. Everywhere they made the same diagnosis: "cut-throat competition" (Burr, 1924) was destroying the rural church. In Wilson's (1911a, p. 35) words, "communities cannot be built out of competition: they must be dominated by union." He went on to condemn the belief commonly held by the "household farmer" that "country churches are maintained by competition." A highly influential report by Charles Otis Gill and Gifford Pinchot, published by the Federal Council of Churches, claimed in 1913: "With the whole world turning to combined or cooperative action as the basis of efficiency, the program of the country church continues to deal wholly with individuals, and hence remains defective and one-sided" (in Madison, 1986, p. 652).

Charles J. Galpin (1923, p. 287), a major figure in early rural sociology, thought even church architecture contributed to the cooperative spirit: "It is the small, weak, pastorless church, poorly located, which tends to surrender agriculture to destructive individualism. It is the strong church, with noble permanent architecture, properly located, with a capable resident pastor, which unifies agriculture: a unified agriculture, in time, matures the church." According to Benson Y. Landis (1922, p. 70), who served as editor of the *Yearbook of American Churches* for twenty-five years: "This weeding out process cannot begin too soon. Many churches deserve extinction. They are sectarian in spirit, lack community vision, and exist for the worship of a mere handful of individuals."

These authors seldom failed to remind readers that their conclusions were based on "scientific investigations" that were done not out of preconceptions or commitments "but simply to ascertain exact facts" (Madison, 1986). The cure for the rural churches was also justified in the name of science and efficiency. Landis (1922, p. 70) proposed that the solution to the "over-churching" of rural America was to "eliminate the large numbers of extra churches which are not worth what they cost." And the way to eliminate extra churches was to merge them into nondenominational Protestant community churches.

The campaign for rural ecumenism was given impetus by the Interchurch World Movement (IWM), founded in 1919. Under its auspices, sociologists intent on merging rural churches soon produced detailed plans and justifications for their cause. Under the direction of Edmund Brunner (and heavily funded by John D. Rockefeller, Jr.), the IWM published two volumes from its 1920 World Survey Conference that laid out specific guidelines for a minimum standard of efficiency: "There should not be . . . more than one church for one thousand . . . population. [At a minimum, each church must have] a resident pastor, adequate equipment for worship, religious education and community service; regular worship and preaching; purposeful pastoral visitation; adequate financial program; organized graded church school; enlistment and training of local leaders . . . adequate provision for recreation and social life; and definite, cordial cooperation with other churches of the community" (in Madison, 1986, p. 658).

Soon after this report was released, Landis expanded greatly on what he called the "Par Standard for Country Churches." Under his proposal a full-time pastor was to receive no less than $1,200 a year and a rent-free modern parsonage. In addition, all churches must have an organ (or at least a piano), toilets, a well-equipped kitchen, and a moving picture projector (or at least a stereopticon).

It seemed clear that the only way such standards could be met by rural churches required that small churches merge to create a larger "community church." The reformers suggested that mergers might be achieved in several ways. A denomination could withdraw from a community and merge its congregation with that of another denomination, which could return the favor by withdrawing from some other community. Or local churches could merge and maintain an affiliation with the denomination having the greater local support. A third option was to create a federated church within which individual members retained ties to various denominations.

But however it was to be done, rural church reformers were confident that church unity was the wave of the future and the salvation of rural churches and communities. Just as Robert Lee was to do nearly fifty years later, sociologists hurried to explain how it all would come to pass.

John Hargreaves (1914, pp. 258–259) wrote in the *American Journal of Sociology* that the rural churches would soon follow a trend of consolidation similar to that of rural schools. He predicted that: "The community churches of today are very few in number, but before ten years have passed they will be all over the land, and the countryside will have come to its own." A decade later, however, the 1926 religious census reported only 301 federated churches out of a total of 167,864 churches in rural areas. Country churches might be small, but they weren't merging.

Overchurching in Black America

Although the Institute of Social and Religious Research's attention to the African-American churches was comparatively modest, their conclusions offered a familiar refrain. Benjamin E. Mays and Joseph W. Nicholson's *The Negro's Church* produced a valuable history and overview of African-American churches, providing rich details and insights on the operation of local churches, but like other Institute publications they devoted several chapters to assess the "overchurching" problem and then offer solutions. Their solutions: merge churches, support a paid well-trained staff, and form comity agreements to reduce competition ([1933] 1969, p. 229).

For African-American churches, they suggested that the problem was not limited to rural areas. Assuming that a membership of five hundred was a minimum needed for an effective urban church, they found that every city in their study had excess churches, ranging from a 15 percent excess in Philadelphia to a 63 percent excess in Houston. In their final assessment, Mays and Nicholson ([1933] 1969, p. 219) concluded that the northern cities were "more poorly churched than overchurched." They found that in the five northern cities they studied "store-front and house churches are more numerous than churches with church buildings." Chicago was of special concern where 248 of the African-American churches, or 72 percent, were storefront and house churches. The problem, as the reformers saw it, was how to reduce the "enormous number" of store-front and house churches in the urban areas.

Like the problems identified by the rural reformers, the source of this urban "problem" is easily traced to the sectarian groups. Data from their twelve-city study showed that over 90 percent of the storefront and house churches were Baptist, Holiness, or Spiritualists. Using the same data, Table 6.4 shows that the vast majority of Holiness and Spiritualist congregations were meeting in homes or storefronts and nearly one third

Table 6.4

African-American Storefront and House Churches for Twelve Cities, 1931

	% Meeting in storefronts & homes	Number of congregations
Spiritualists	85.1	114
Holiness	70.8	339
Baptists	32.2	1,127
Methodists	14.9	369
Others	14.2	155
Total	36.9	2,104

SOURCE: Adapted from Mays and Nicholson ([1933] 1969, p. 313).

of the Baptists were. In contrast, only 15 percent of the Methodists and 14 percent of the remaining congregations were without a conventional church building. Notice that the Holiness churches, though still small in size, were nearly as numerous as the Methodists. These small churches would fuel the rapid growth of Holiness/Pentecostal movements for the remainder of the twentieth century.

Mays and Nicholson's greatest concern, however, was for the rural areas. They documented the rural churches' insufficient finances, lack of adequate worship, and poor facilities for social programs (94 percent were limited to one room), and lamented the lack of well-trained resident pastors. Of the 134 rural pastors they studied only 2 percent were college graduates (20 percent for the urban areas) and 58 percent reported only a grammar school education (27 percent in urban areas). When compared to urban churches, they explained, the poor training of the pastors combined with a high rate of illiteracy in rural areas "produced a larger proportion of other-worldly messages" (p. 249). They also reviewed the unique economic and demographic challenges facing the black rural churches, explaining that "croppers and renters move frequently, more frequently now than formerly" and that the number of black farmers was in decline.[4] Based on these assessments they called for social, educational, and economic reforms to help rural blacks (p. 275). But their attention always returned to the churches and here they echoed the theme of other reformers: the rural churches must merge.

Like the white churches, black churches failed to heed the reformers' advice on merging and they did not perceive that they had a problem with overchurching, or with being "poorly churched." Between 1916 and 1926, the census special report on "Negro Churches" found an increase from 39,592 to 42,585 congregations. And, like the white churches, not all denominations benefited from this growth. The AMEZ reported 250 fewer congregations (–9.2%), the CME reported a drop of 103 (–3.9%), and the AME reported a slight gain of 75 (+1.1%). But the Negro Baptists showed an increase of 868 congregations (+4.1%) and the newly formed Pentecostal sect, Church of God in Christ, reported 733 congregations. Mays and Nicholson were no doubt correct that many of the small struggling congregations would die out, but the growing denominations were capable of supporting small fellowships and rapidly beginning new ones. And, a few of the small storefront and house churches would become large and influential churches.

Barriers to Unification

Why didn't the rural churches obey the logic of efficiency and merge? The most important reason was that rural people did not think that they had too many churches or that a church lacking an organ was inadequate. When reformers noted with disdain that most rural clergy thought their primary job was to "preach and conduct weddings and funerals" rather than to pursue the liberal agenda of the social gospel, the great majority of rural Christians said "Amen" (Madison, 1986). No doubt the rural black pastors agreed their messages were more otherworldly and filled with passion than the educated urban pastors. But they and their members counted this as a virtue, not a vice. One rural pastor explained that "some fools can preach better than these educated men. I think our men drive too fast to the schools of theology and our students rush too rapidly. They will leave Jesus behind" (Mays and Nicholson, [1933] 1969, p. 248).

The reformers demanded that "the old efficiency which was reckoned in new converts and new congregations must be replaced by a new efficiency reckoned in social service" (Madison, 1986, p. 650). But they found that people went to church in search of salvation, not social service. Indeed, the reformers seemed to have nearly forgotten about religion altogether. Questions about the doctrinal basis for unification went virtually unasked, let alone answered, in the voluminous publications of the movement. To the extent that matters of doctrine were discussed at all they

SCORE CARD

(Concluded)

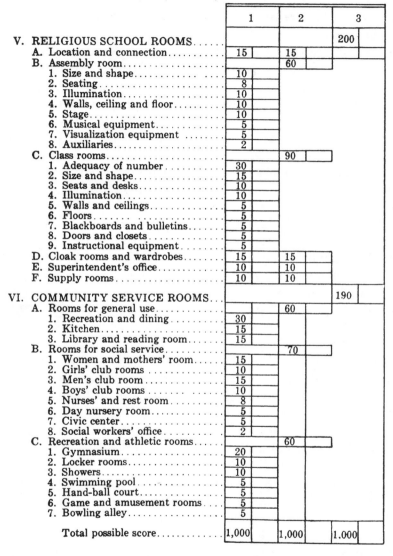

	1	2	3
V. RELIGIOUS SCHOOL ROOMS			200
A. Location and connection	15	15	
B. Assembly room		60	
1. Size and shape	10		
2. Seating	8		
3. Illumination	10		
4. Walls, ceiling and floor	10		
5. Stage	10		
6. Musical equipment	5		
7. Visualization equipment	5		
8. Auxiliaries	2		
C. Class rooms		90	
1. Adequacy of number	30		
2. Size and shape	15		
3. Seats and desks	10		
4. Illumination	10		
5. Walls and ceilings	5		
6. Floors	5		
7. Blackboards and bulletins	5		
8. Doors and closets	5		
9. Instructional equipment	5		
D. Cloak rooms and wardrobes	15	15	
E. Superintendent's office	10	10	
F. Supply rooms	10	10	
VI. COMMUNITY SERVICE ROOMS			190
A. Rooms for general use		60	
1. Recreation and dining	30		
2. Kitchen	15		
3. Library and reading room	15		
B. Rooms for social service		70	
1. Women and mothers' room	15		
2. Girls' club rooms	10		
3. Men's club room	15		
4. Boys' club rooms	10		
5. Nurses' and rest room	8		
6. Day nursery room	5		
7. Civic center	5		
8. Social workers' office	2		
C. Recreation and athletic rooms		60	
1. Gymnasium	20		
2. Locker rooms	10		
3. Showers	10		
4. Swimming pool	5		
5. Hand-ball court	5		
6. Game and amusement rooms	5		
7. Bowling alley	5		
Total possible score	1,000	1,000	1,000

The *Standards for City Church Plants* of the Interchurch World Movement included a ten-page introduction, a three-page "Score Card" (of which the final page is shown here), forty pages of detailed instructions on scoring, a six-page appendix offering sample specifications for pipe organs, and another fifteen-page appendix outlining the data to be collected before the actual scoring could begin. The organization also published a *Standards for Rural Church Plants*. These publications were offered "for use in measuring the adequacy of church and religious educational plants" (Interchurch World Movement, 1920). (Courtesy of the Billy Graham Center Museum, Wheaton, Ill.)

were dismissed as trivial—the "minutiae of creed"—or were condemned as "dogma" (Madison, 1986). Yet the reformers' own research studies found time and again that people cared a great deal about doctrine and about their differences over what Whitefield had identified as "the form" of belief and worship.

No matter what sociological theologians no longer believed, most rural Americans saw an important difference between adult and infant baptism and recognized that matters of great significance were involved in disputes over whether salvation was by faith alone or by a combination of faith and works. Never mind that scientific sociologists condemned those who clung to such outmoded ideas or castigated those who abandoned community churches for the "emotional sects"; rural America simply didn't care about such criticism (Brunner, 1927; Brunner, Hughes, and Patten, 1927; Madison, 1986).

Indeed, when reformers traveled forth to instruct rural congregations in these matters, it was they who were regarded as out of touch. An informant in Michigan told an investigator that "countryfolk would go to hell before they would leave their church" (in Madison, 1986, p. 666). And a farmer commented that she was "very weary of rural uplifters and country-life specialists who live in New York City. . . . If the city folks would only let us alone, there would be no rural problem" (in Jent, 1924, p. 126).

In the end, rural Americans were right. Perhaps the most amazing aspect about this whole interlude is that the essential good health of rural churches was staring the sociological reformers right in the face. Butterfield (1905, p. 620) recognized the benefits of religious choices for urban dwellers, but this didn't change his plans for the rural areas. In one paragraph he wrote that "in the city a person can usually find a denomination to his liking" and in the next he explained why rural churches should merge and that "church federation . . . promises large results." His commitment to a church with a well-trained church staff superseded all other concerns.

The Institute of Social and Religious Research's own data on rural communities showed that religious involvement was higher in communities with more religious options. Table 6.5 is adapted from one of the most influential works of the period, Brunner's *Village Communities* (1927). Where the IWM ideal of only one church per 1,000 population was met, only 27 percent of the population belonged to a church. In contrast, in the "lamentably overchurched" communities where four or more congregations competed for members, 43 percent of the population belonged. Similarly, the percentage enrolled in Sunday schools was more than twice

TABLE 6.5
Pluralism and Participation in Rural Areas, 1923–1925

	Number of churches per 1,000 population			
	One	*Two*	*Three*	*Four or more*
Percentage who belong to a church	27.4	36.0	34.8	43.4
Percentage enrolled in Sunday schools	15.8	22.3	25.2	37.4
Percentage with a resident minister	55.7	46.3	38.7	30.1

SOURCE: Adapted from Brunner (1927, p. 74).

as high in the "overchurched" communities as in those that conformed
to the ideal.

We hasten to note that Brunner was a competent statistician who was
entirely aware that far higher rates of participation obtained in the
"overchurched" communities. And although he didn't put it very generously, he did report this relationship: "Judged by these superficial tests
of their total impact on the community, competitive denominational
churches would seem to succeed in proportion to their relative number.
An organized church of each small sectarian group enlists more people
(1927, p. 73).

Brunner's own view; however, was that things were not really as they
seemed. He was quick to note that much of the "competition was not
so much among the established denominations" as it was between such
bodies and the "newer emotional sects." Thus he reasoned that church
unions could proceed among the respectable churches, and it mattered
little if the emotional sects held back. These he characterized as "on the
fringes" of the community and reduced to meeting "in tents, vacant stores,
halls, or homes." When such groups did have their own church buildings, these were "largely inexpensive structures." As to their clergy, they
usually were "untrained and poorly paid, if paid at all. Many are laymen." As to their membership, Brunner characterized them as a pathetic
lot, including one group he described as "a poor class of mixed blood
and of moronic intelligence" (1927, pp. 75–76).

High rates of church membership that included such riffraff were apparently not a significant trade-off for the elimination of overchurching. In the paragraph immediately following his admission that more churches meant more participation, Brunner returned to the theme that competition prevented the "concentration of forces" needed to provide the "minimum program of conventional church activities." He also noted that although his study was not able "to measure the spiritual effects of overchurching" these were known to be dire. Finally, Brunner kept returning to the issue of minister's pay and education, something he and his fellow reformers seemed to prize above all else: "[unified churches] were able to pay an unusually high salary to their ministers, thereby securing a higher than ordinary proportion of full-time resident ministers with a liberal education" (1927, p. 80).

Table 6.5 bears him out. Communities with few churches per 1,000 were more likely to have a resident, professional clergyman. But unless we are willing to assume that religion is somehow healthier where fewer people take part in it, then it is not at all obvious that professional clergy were a plus in rural America.

In any event, not even a God-given sociology was able to produce any significant ecumenical movement among rural American Protestants. The people who mattered, those who sat in the pews and paid the bills, didn't think anything was wrong with denominationalism—and they still don't.

The Mainline Cartel

The Federal Council of Churches was organized in Philadelphia by delegates from thirty-three Protestant denominations in 1908. The aims of the council were ecumenical and political. In its first public pronouncement, the council committed itself to a lengthy statement of political faith in which it called for enactment of a list of social reforms that included a minimum wage, pensions, disability payments, a reduced workweek, and the "most equitable division of the products of industry that can ultimately be devised"—all of which prompted Ahlstrom (1975, vol. 2, p. 72) to characterize the delegates as the "praying wing of Progressivism." On matters of religious faith the council was far less explicit, avoiding all mention of doctrine except for this reference in the preamble to its constitution: "the essential oneness of the Christian Churches of America, in Jesus Christ as their Lord and Saviour" (Ahlstrom, vol. 2, p. 271).

On the ecumenical agenda, the aims of the council included the re-

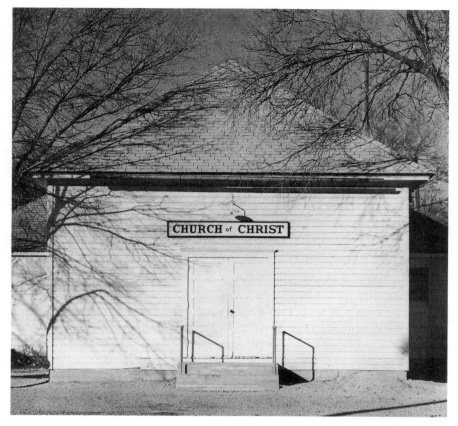

Built in 1914, this small church in rural Colorado would have received a poor rating by Interchurch World Movement standards. The Churches of Christ denomination did not condone the use of instrumental music in the worship service, were opposed to the "modern pastor," and discouraged anything that fostered pride and worldliness—including immodest church facilities. Yet the Churches of Christ had a net increase of 656 churches (+ 12%) between 1916 and 1926, with 86 percent of all their churches located in rural areas. (From Adams, 1970.)

placement of the many "redundancies" resulting from denominational competition with coordinated and consolidated activities conducted by interdenominational commissions and boards. Although the long-term goal was unification, in the meantime the council would allow Protestantism to speak with one authoritative voice.

Because many Protestant bodies, including the huge Southern Baptist Convention, did not belong to the council, it was never an "authentic voice of Protestantism," as Ahlstrom (1975, vol. 2, p. 272) pointed out.

Nor were the council's efforts to eliminate "needless" competition and duplications of effort among Protestant bodies really inclusive efforts at rationalization and unification. Instead, the council resorted to illusions based on cartel arrangements among its members. These were presented to the public as interdenominational and ecumenical in precisely the same way that, a century earlier, the American Home Missionary Society claimed to be serving unchurched areas that actually abounded in Baptist and Methodist congregations.

In the long run these cartels not only proved ineffective but probably harmed those denominations that entered into them. In the short run, however, some of these efforts were quite successful. Perhaps the most significant of these involved the way in which the council used a powerful cartel arrangement to restrict access to radio and television time so that, authentic or not, the public voice of American Protestantism tended to speak only the language of liberalism and ecumenism.

The Media Cartel

In 1960 a former executive of the National Council of Churches noted that having brought order to "the allocation of time *among themselves* on radio and television" was a major accomplishment of NCC members (Barnes, 1960, p. 137, emphasis added). He pointed out that "if it were not for the broadly representative National Council of Churches, there would be competition among the churches in radio and television broadcasting of religious programs."

But that same year the competition for media time that the council had worked so hard to prevent began to appear. The Federal Communications Commission, reversing its long-standing policy that only free air time counted toward radio and television stations' public service contribution, ruled that henceforth paid programming could be given public service credit. This decision, which received little attention when it was made, broke the cartel through which members of the National Council (and the Federal Council before it) had monopolized air time.

Ever since it began regulating radio stations in the 1920s, the Federal Communications Commission has classified religious programming as public service broadcasting. Because all stations are required to devote a minimum percentage of air time to public service and because the production costs of much religious broadcasting amount to little or nothing, stations have for decades found it attractive to offer free time to religious groups. Faced with dozens of groups seeking their free time, however, the stations sought guidance about whom to choose (White-head, 1982). Only one visible body claimed to represent a broad spectrum of the most "respectable" faiths—the Federal Council of Churches and its local chapters. Somehow these groups never suggested that free time go to evangelicals or other outsiders, preferring instead to keep it all for council members.

The council's monopoly on air time was further strengthened as it succeeded in persuading the national networks not to sell time for religious broadcasts. NBC never sold time to religious broadcasters, nor did ABC (which in its early days was a second NBC network, known as the Blue Network). CBS, which began in 1927, did sell time to religious broadcasters for its first several years, but ceased doing so in 1931. Only the Mutual Broadcasting System continued to sell commercial time to religious broadcasters and thus allowed evangelical Protestants their only national access to radio. But even with limited access the evangelicals produced the most popular religious shows on radio: Charles E. Fuller's "Old-Fashioned Revival Hour"; "The Lutheran Hour," sponsored by the Missouri Synod Lutherans; and the "Voice of Prophecy" which was produced by the Seventh-day Adventists. These shows attracted millions of listeners. Elsewhere on the network dial, however, American Protestantism was whatever the Department of Religious Radio of the Federal Council of Churches said it was. The council signed up many local stations to receive free religious programming in exchange for an agreement to refuse to sell air time to noncouncil denominations.

Noting that broadcasts by evangelical Protestants, "and others of the same stripe, have long been distasteful to liberal church leaders" (Crowe, 1944, p. 973), a campaign was mounted in 1944 through the auspices of the Federal Council to persuade the Mutual network to observe the cartel arrangement. The central claim was that only by discontinuing the sale of radio time to religious groups could the nation be spared the din of fundamentalism on the air waves (Whitehead and Conlan, 1978). The arrogant tones of this campaign can be seen in the accompanying excerpts from the *Christian Century*. In addition to the campaign against the Mutual radio "loophole," local committees of clergy were formed in many communities to seek similar policies at local stations. Miron A. Morrill (1945, p. 461) proposed that such committees should solve "this radio problem" by bringing sufficient pressure to bear so as to "claim our fair share of time over local radio stations, leaving national broadcasting to the Federal Council, which can do it better."

The campaign appeared to achieve rapid success when Mutual adopted

Walter A. Maier, the first speaker of the Lutheran Hour Radio Program, is seated behind a microphone in a St. Louis studio. The Lutheran Hour was first broadcast on October 2, 1930, and the Old Fashioned Revival Hour with Charles Fuller followed on October 3, 1937. Despite being banned from every major radio network by 1944, they remained popular radio programs through the use of syndication. (Courtesy of the Billy Graham Center Museum, Wheaton, Ill.)

new rules for paid religious programming, effective September 14, 1944. First, such programs could not run longer than thirty minutes. Second, no air time could be used to solicit funds to pay for the broadcasts. Third, paid religious programming would be aired only on Sunday mornings (when most of the regular listeners to Mutual's popular religious shows would be in church).

These changes appeared to have the full support of the Federal Communications Commission. When reviewing FCC actions prior to 1965, one of the commission's own members concluded that the "commission has established religion as a required element of broadcasting service and has applied this standard to mean such religion as meets the FCC definitions and notions of acceptability." Writing in the *George Washington Law Review* the Honorable Lee Loevinger (1965, p. 653) noted that the "content" of the religious programming was often more important than the time devoted to such programming. When complaints were made in the late 1940s and the 1950s that specific churches were receiving "exclusive or preferential broadcasting privileges," the commission held that

The Christian Century Campaign for "Good" Religious Broadcasting

February 4, 1942: "Religion on the Air"

. . . Dr. Fred Eastman . . . has been studying religious programs on Chicago radio. Seventeen stations submitted their religious programs to the analysis on which Professor Eastman reports. . . . Seventy-seven programs, filling 46 hours of broadcasting, were studied. Of these, 54 were Sunday programs. Of the Protestant programs, 61 per cent were found to be fundamentalist in character and this did not include the approximately 100 programs which are broadcast every week by the station owned by the Moody Bible Institute. . . . the report . . . emphasizes the fact that religious broadcasting is overloaded with talk, that much of it is on a low level of taste and artistic performance.

February 16, 1944: "Religious Radio Programs Need Much Improvement"

In most religious broadcasts there is too much talk—that is, preaching and exhortation—and too little use of other radio techniques of proved effectiveness, such as dramatization, forums, round table discussions and great music. The talk is not only excessive in quantity but, on average, not very good in quality. The religious program too often impresses the critical listener as being a cheap show, with too much sentimentality, too little artistry, and a too crude appeal for contributions. Some of the most blatant appeals for money seem to be most successful in getting it, to the point of making a few of these enterprises very profitable—which, it would seem, is a fact about the listening public quite as a much as a fact about the broadcasting evangelists. . . . A religious broadcast without a sermon might offer attractive and edifying possibilities.

March 22, 1944: "Mutual to End Radio Religious Begging"

. . . the Mutual Broadcasting System ruled that after next September 14 all religious programs over its network shall be forbidden to solicit funds. Just how much of a sacrifice Mutual was making is shown by its report for last year, which revealed that out of a total of $12,527,000 paid for time on the air, $3,367,000 came from seven religious broadcasters, most of whom have specialized in raising money

(continued)

by appeals during their programs ... *Old-Fashioned Revival Hour* led by Charles E. Fuller, spent $1,566,130 last year ... *The Lutheran Hour* (about $500,000 last year); the *Voice of Prophecy*, a Seventh Day Adventist program ($395,420); the *Young People's Church of the Air* ($395,420); and the *Wesley Radio League* ($172,384). The other leading chains—National, Columbia and Blue—have never permitted religious organizations to buy time or to ask for money.

August 23, 1944: "Religion on the Air," by Charles M. Crowe

Mutual's action will not remove the commercial type of program from the air—by which I mean the program whose time is paid for by the preacher or the church group. It already has been announced that *The Lutheran Hour*, the *Young People's Church of the Air* and the *Voice of Prophesy* (Seventh Day Adventist) will continue on the same network earlier in the day but without solicitation of funds. These programs evidently have a large enough clientele so that they can be supported by direct mail appeals for money to those who write in for free gifts or for copies of sermons. ...

The *Old Fashioned Revival Hour* and others ... will utilize a new network, the Associated Broadcasting Corporation, formed to handle such religious programs. ... Solicitation of funds will be permitted. ... This new network ... is composed in the main of smaller stations.

These programs and others of the same stripe, have long been distasteful to liberal church leaders, to much of the listening public and to network officials ... the new Mutual policy will serve only to intensify the problem. ... The network religious radio program racket, capitalized by independent superfundamentalist revivalists, will not be eliminated until Mutual goes the whole way and bans paid religious programs altogether, as the other networks have done.

The National Association of Broadcasters, leading radio trade organization, has been powerless thus far to establish or enforce regulations covering paid religious programs. Perhaps the only way such programs can be eliminated is by a ruling from the Federal Communications Commission against the sale of time for religious broadcasting, coupled with a parallel ruling requiring each station and network to give a specified minimum allotment of suitable time each week to religious programs.

such preferences could be "in the public interest." Such rulings quickly favored the council's attempts to monopolize all public service broadcasting.

Thus by the end of 1944 the council media cartel seemed in complete control of network religious broadcasting. But the loss of access to the Mutual network prompted evangelical Protestants to respond. Their first, and most dramatic, response was to buy time on scores of local stations across the nation, thus inventing syndication. That is, rather than offer a live feed to a hook-up of local stations as the networks did, transcriptions were sent to local stations to fill the time slot purchased from each. There were too many struggling local stations with too much time to sell for local clergy committees to be effective in promulgating policies against purchased time for religious broadcasts. The second response of evangelical Protestants was to organize the National Religious Broadcasters, which launched a vigorous campaign to redress inequities in radio access. In the long run this move was as significant as syndication, for eventually the NRB succeeded in influencing the FCC to count paid religious broadcasts as public service time. Still, for many years the evangelicals continued to be discriminated against in terms of media access.

The advent of television initially strengthened the grip of the liberal cartel over religious broadcasting (Hadden and Shupe, 1988). During the 1950s the Broadcasting and Film Commission of the National Council of Churches again tried to exclude the evangelicals from local access by campaigning in various states for a prohibition on paid religious broadcasting. But, as with radio, neither the council nor local clerical committees could gain substantial control over local television stations. In consequence, evangelicals bought time on local stations, and as they had pioneered on radio, they produced syndicated shows that were broadcast by hundreds of stations a week. By the 1970s evangelicals operated their own cable channels.

By being excluded from free radio and television time, the evangelicals were forced to develop the means to pay for their broadcasts. Hence, when the 1960 FCC ruling caused local stations to replace free religious time with paid broadcasts, this posed no new barrier to the evangelicals; their broadcasts had already attracted a substantial audience willing to send in contributions to keep the shows on the air. In contrast, the elimination of free time virtually silenced religious broadcasts by the council and its affiliated denominations. This is precisely what Adam Smith would have predicted. A free ride in terms of radio and television time meant that the NCC member bodies, like the established churches Smith had criticized two centuries earlier, were soon "reposing themselves upon their benefices" until they "were incapable of making vigorous exertion" ([1776] 1937, p. 740).

Ecumenism and Suburban Life

If urbanization ushered in efforts to merge America's rural churches, the suburbanization of the nation in the late 1940s and 1950s ushered in the greatest wave of ecumenical hoping and planning in the nation's history. And once again, a primary justification was efficiency.

As millions of Americans moved into sprawling new suburban communities, they created an immediate need for new churches. As the denominations struggled to form the thousands of new congregations and construct the new buildings needed, many influential spokesmen began to urge that nondenominational community churches were the obvious solution. Nor surprisingly, these were many of the same experts who had been ardent promoters of unified churches for rural America. As early as 1934 H. Paul Douglass, a major figure in the rural church movement and a leader at the Institute of Social and Religious Research, had called for a shift from interdenominational "competition" to alliances that would produce consolidated community churches all across the nation. The next year Douglass joined with Brunner (1935, p. 326) in proclaiming: "The movement for church unity is backed by powerful emotional and practical attitudes widely diffused throughout the nation, in all regions, among both clergy and laity and including persons of virtually all denominations."

In the 1940s the arguments about efficiency and about higher clergy salaries were joined to a potent new ideology concerning the necessary Christian response to the horrors of World War II: faced with a relentlessly evil world, Christians must finally abandon their selfish differences and achieve the "gathering" of "the whole world into one fellowship" (Visser t' Hooft, 1959, p. 29). Or, as William Warren Sweet put it:

> The most widely used term in American Protestantism since the end of World War II is the word "ecumenical"—world wide. Never before has world Protestantism been so conscious of its world obligation; the vast destruction, both spiritual and moral, wrought by the war has brought to American Protestantism especially, a new sense of mission. Out of the realization that Protestantism faces a world demanding a united front, there is emerging a World Council of Churches, largely under American Protestant leadership and inspiration. The war and its aftermath have done

much to bridge the chasm between American and European Protestantism and also between the several denominational members of the American Protestant family. Numerous church unions, which were hardly dreamed
of a generation ago, have been effected, and many others are in the offing. (1948, pp. 51–52)

It was soon common wisdom among major American religious com-
mentators that not only must the denominations unite, but they would
no longer face any substantial doctrinal stumbling blocks to merger. Back
in 1934 Douglass had claimed that his research showed "basic agreements
as far outweighing disagreements," and he expressed confidence that "a
few more years of frank discussions" among the denominations would
be all that was needed to resolve the remaining difficulties (in Douglass
and Brunner, 1935, p. 327). In similar terms, one of the most influential
books of the post-war period, Will Herberg's *Protestant-Catholic-Jew* (1960),
declared that the remaining denominational differences within Protestantism were organizational and ethnic, not doctrinal. Herberg took a
very hopeful view of ecumenical relations, not simply among Protestants,
but between Protestants and Catholics and even between Christians and
Jews.

In full agreement with Herberg, the Protestant writer Robert Lee (1960)
explained that a "common core Protestantism" had evolved in the place
of the old doctrinal diversities and disagreements. Sweet (1948) attributed this development to the shift away from denominationalism by the
leading American seminaries, which now recruited "increasingly interdenominational" faculties. The perceptions of doctrinal consensus were
even accepted by many of those, such as Marty (1959), who deplored
this state of affairs.

Sociologists were equally committed to the end of denominationalism. Richard D. Lambert (1960, p. 155) noted that "old doctrinal cleavages" had become "irrelevant in American thought today." The word
"denomination" did not even appear in the index of Gerhard Lenski's
(1961) widely read empirical study of religious effects, *The Religious Factor*.
Lenski was content to compare Protestants with Catholics and Jews, separating Protestants only on the basis of race, thus assuming that one kind
of Protestantism was pretty much like another.[5]

Peter Berger (1963, p. 89) was equally convinced that denominational
differences had become nothing more than "functionally irrelevant em-
bellishments and packaging," because American Protestant denominations had undergone a "process of intense product standardization." Berger
called upon the denominations to merge and to form "cartels," which

would rationalize competition among the denominations "by reducing the number of competing units by amalgamation and also by dividing up the market between the larger units that remain" (p. 87). Noting that American denominations were spending more than a billion dollars a year on the construction of new churches, Berger claimed that a "rational limitation of cutthroat competition" was an "economic necessity" (p. 84).

Within this intellectual climate, in 1960 the Consultation of Church Union was initiated by the Presbyterian Church in the U.S.A., the Protestant Episcopal Church, the Methodist Church, and the United Church of Christ (formerly the Congregationalists and the Evangelical and Reformed Church) for the purpose of planning the union of these four bodies. In 1966 the Presbyterian Church in the United States joined the group. The day of major mergers seemed at hand.

But the years passed, and somehow nothing ever seemed to come of these consultations. Moreover, the attempts at local unification efforts in order to replace denominationalism with community churches in the rapidly growing suburbs never seemed to come into their own. With the exception of nondenominational fundamentalist churches, which often did very well, people generally didn't seem to want to belong to a nondenominational church.

Meanwhile, in 1963 the first large-scale survey research studies of American religion were launched by Charles Glock and Rodney Stark. When the data were in they dealt a devastating blow to the notion of a common core American Protestantism. Indeed, it would have been difficult to conceive of greater doctrinal diversity and division than Stark and Glock (1965) reported in an article revealing what they called the "New Denominationalism."

Table 6.6 reprints a few of the key findings from this survey. In some of the denominations to the left of the table, only a minority of members expressed faith in major doctrines of the Christian tradition: only 41 percent of members of the United Church of Christ expressed unwavering faith in the existence of God. But at the right side of the table, overwhelming majorities express unwavering faith in the divinity of Jesus, in the Virgin Birth, in the Second Coming, and in the reality of the Devil. The data "indicate that the fissures which map what might well be called the 'New Denominationalism' fragment the very core of the Christian perspective. The new cleavages are not over such matters as how to worship God properly, but whether or not there is a God of the sort it makes any sense to worship; not over whether the bread and wine of communion

TABLE 6.6
The New Denominationalism, 1963

Doctrinal statements					Percentage responding affirmatively							
	U.C.C. (151)	Meth. (415)	Episc. (416)	D. of Christ (50)	Presb. (495)	Am. Luth. (208)	Am. Bapt. (141)	Mo. Luth. (116)	S. Bapt. (79)	Sects (255)	Total Prot. (2,326)	Total Cath. (545)
"I know God really exists and I have no doubts about it."	41	60	63	76	75	73	78	81	99	96	71	81
"Jesus is the Divine Son of God and I have no doubts about it."	40	54	59	74	72	74	76	93	99	97	69	86
It is completely true that "Jesus was born of a virgin."	21	34	39	62	57	66	69	92	99	96	57	81
Definitely, "Jesus will actually return to the earth some day."	13	21	24	36	43	54	57	75	94	89	44	47
It is "completely true" that "the Devil actually exists."	6	13	17	18	31	49	49	77	92	90	38	66

SOURCE: From Stark and Glock (1965).
NOTE: The Protestant churches represented are United Church of Christ (Congregationalists), Methodists, Episcopalians, Disciples of Christ, United Presbyterian Church, Lutheran Church in America and American Lutheran Church, American Baptist Church, Missouri Synod of Lutherans, and Southern Baptist Church. The numbers in parentheses represent the number of respondents.

become the actual body and blood of Christ through transubstantiation, or are only symbolic, but over whether or not Jesus was merely a man . . . In light of these findings it is difficult to account for the hopes and activities directed towards general ecumenicalism" (Stark and Glock, 1965, p. 14).

How was it possible that the experts could have been so wrong about the state of American denominationalism? We think they were entirely correct about the existence of a common core Protestantism, but failed to realize it was limited to a small select circle. Denominational differences *had* become irrelevant on Riverside Drive, at the famous divinity schools, and in the editorial offices of the *Christian Century*. But the members of this religious elite were not representative even of their own denominations, to say nothing of how out of touch they were with the evangelical Protestant majority. In America's suburbs and cities, as in its rural areas earlier in the century, denominationalism was regarded as neither a scandal nor an irrelevant embellishment; it was the backbone of religious commitment and participation.

In the end, the planned mergers never took place. Instead, the denominations most actively involved in talks of merger soon began to experience rapid declines in their membership. It is possible that when these bodies have become sufficiently weak, they will finally merge in an effort to forestall a complete collapse.

Shall the Weak Merge?

Bryan Wilson, Britain's leading sociologist of religion, has been a relentless advocate of the secularization thesis. Indeed, it would be very difficult to conceive of any fact or event (with the possible exception of the Second Coming) that would not strike Wilson as further proof that religion is rapidly on its way out. For example, not only does the decline in membership and attendance in Britain count in favor of secularization, but *so do the high rates* of membership and attendance in America: "the long recognized lack of depth of religious manifestations in the United States suggest that religion is in decline in both countries" (Wilson, 1966, p. 126). A few pages later he again notes "the generally accepted superficiality of much religion in American society" (p. 166).

During the 1960s Wilson drew his principal evidence for "the essential weakness of religious life" from the ecumenical movement. He argued that ecumenism could only become a "new faith" among clergy who need to have "something to believe in," having lost their ability to accept traditional Christian doctrines. The prospect of widespread denominational mergers, according to Wilson, could exist only if secularization had so eroded commitment that doctrinal differences no longer provided a reason to sustain separate organizations: "As the process of secularization has continued, so the differences between denominations have lost their social significance" (1966, p. 128). The vested interests of the clergy and the denominational bureaucracies in retaining separate organizations had faded because "the extreme weakness of religious commitment" threatened the continued survival of each religious organization. Thus Wilson advanced the proposition that "organizations amalgamate when they are weak" (p. 126).

Wilson's belief that all American denominations were on the brink of collapse was as misguided as his capacity to find religious depth only in solemn high church rituals. But, if the scope of his proposition is properly delimited, we are prepared to agree: strong organizations are seldom interested in merging—the urge to merge typically is prompted by weakness. Thus if substantial mergers do occur among Protestant denominations, these will be limited to the more secularized bodies.

Data offering strong support for this proposition were published by Douglass in 1935, based on a questionnaire study of 16,355 church members conducted in 1932 (Douglass and Brunner, 1935).[6] Among the items was one aimed at measuring support for ecumenism:

> If you had to decide now what religious people of the United States should do about church union—would you
>
> (1) Continue essentially the present system of separate denominations?
> (2) Unite the various church bodies into one church?
> (3) Adopt some form of permanent and binding federal union of denominations, after the analogy of the state and Federal Government in the United States? (p. 328)

Although the more liberal bodies were very overrepresented in the survey, only 31.7 percent of the respondents favored unification into one church. Moreover, among these were members of nonliberal bodies (particularly Southern Baptists and Missouri Synod Lutherans), whose idea of a unified church probably indicated not their willingness to make significant compromises, but their hope that others would see the light and embrace their creed. Another 30.3 percent selected the option of some sort of federal union (presumably a strengthened Federal Council of Churches), but with denominations retaining their autonomy. An

TABLE 6.7
Growth and Ecumenism, 1932 (in percent)

Protestant denominations	Net growth 1916–1926	% Rejecting ecumenism	Perceived differences
Missouri Synod Lutherans	51.1	89.5	75.7
Lutherans*	45.7	60,0	22.3
United Lutherans	43.9	51.4	15.0
Southern Baptists†	15.0	58.4	14.8
Presbyterian, U.S.	11.0	52.9	12.0
Episcopalians	3.8	40.2	14.3
Southern Methodists	2.6	40.3	8.7
Presbyterians, U.S.A.	1.4	20.9	7.1
Disciples of Christ	−2.7	24.7	12.0
Methodists	−5.3	23.1	9.1
Congregationalists	−6.1	21.1	6.7
United Brethren	−6.9	27.9	7.2
Reformed, America	−9.0	36.0	9.4
Reformed, U.S.	−10.2	14.7	5.8
Northern Baptists	−11.5	44.9	13.6
Methodists, Protestant	−12.3	34.2	7.6
Friends	−16.2	43.2	19.2
Evangelical Synod	−22.6	10.1	9.3

SOURCE: The data on "% rejecting ecumenism" and "perceived differences" are from Douglass and Brunner (1935, pp. 328, 260).
*All Lutherans except Missouri Synod and United Lutherans.
†The American Baptist Association was included in Southern Baptist totals for 1916, but not 1926. With the ABA included in the 1926 totals, the net growth for Southern Baptists was 19.4.

additional 4.5 percent selected more than one answer. And 33.5 opted for the denominational status quo.

These totals, however, mask immense variation among the Protestant bodies included in the sample (see Table 6.7). For example, 89.5 percent of Missouri Synod Lutherans and 58.4 percent of Southern Baptists preferred to stay with denominationalism (that is, they chose answer 1), as compared with 21.1 percent of Congregationalists and 10.1 percent of the Evangelical Synod. Only 7.5 percent of Missouri Synod Lutherans and 19 percent of Southern Baptists supported unification into a single church (answer 2), while 51.1 percent of Disciples of Christ and 39.9 percent of Methodists did.

If it is true that willingness to merge reflects organizational weakness, then we ought to expect that members of denominations that are doing well in the marketplace would be the ones most inclined to reject unification. To test this hypothesis, we turned to census data and calculated the rate of growth (or decline) for each of these denominations between 1916 and 1926. Because the nation's population grew by 15.1 percent during this decade, we subtracted the rate of growth (or decline) for each denomination from 15.1. Thus a denomination that scored zero would have grown by the precise amount of the population, thereby neither gaining nor losing in terms of market penetration. Denominations with positive scores had a net gain over and above simple population growth. Those with negative scores failed to keep pace with population growth.

Eight denominations had positive scores, and the majority of their members (51.7 percent) were opposed to any form of merger. But of the thirteen denominations with negative scores, the great majority (71.4 percent) favored some form of merger (see Table 6.7). There is a strong positive correlation (.79) between growth in market share and choosing to retain denominationalism. Members of growing denominations did not want to merge; those belonging to declining denominations did.

Douglass also helps us understand why the growing denominations were not predisposed to merge: they were inclined to see very substantial differences separating themselves from other denominations. Respondents were asked how willing they would be to enter into various relationships with members of other denominations. Among these relationships were: "Sending a child to their Sunday school; . . . receiving communion from their minister; . . . Uniting in observing their Holy Days; . . . Marrying a member of that church; . . . Having a burial service conducted according to their rites; . . . Acknowledging their church as a genuine church of Christ; . . ." (Douglass and Brunner, 1935, p. 259). These are nicely designed measures of social distance (and were a highly original contribution to survey research methods).

Denominations differed immensely on these measures. The Missouri Synod Lutherans scored at the top end of the scale, while the Reformed Church in the United States and the Congregationalists anchored the bottom end, seeing little to separate them from most other bodies (see Table 6.7). It is not surprising that denominations strongly committed to traditional confessions saw substantial differences between themselves and groups ready to waive doctrinal concerns. Douglass and Brunner, however, characterized all perceptions of differences as "prejudice" and claimed that "denominations which have the greatest prejudice strongly incline to vote for the existing denominational system, while those with the least prejudice are most strongly for union" (1935, p. 330). Although we do not accept these value judgments, we calculated that there was a strong positive correlation (.79) between degree of perceived religious difference and unwillingness to support unification in the data reported by Douglass and Brunner.

Our use of Douglass's data leads to the following conclusions:

1. Growing churches perceive substantial religious differences between themselves and others (which justifies their efforts to bring in new members).
2. Growing churches do not want to merge.
3. Churches that are shrinking see merit in mergers.

A question lingers: why did Douglass fail to report these relationships? It was not that they were unimportant. Given that one of the primary arguments for church unity was to increase the effectiveness and efficiency of religious organizations, membership growth and involvement were central matters. Nor could it have been that Douglass was an incompetent statistician, unfamiliar with rates or correlations. Douglass was quick to notice the strong correlation between "religious distance" and opposition to unity, and he published a scatterplot to illustrate this association. Nor could it have been that Douglass was unfamiliar with the religious census reports for 1916 and 1926 from which we took our data on membership growth or decline. He often cited these sources. Indeed, he knew very well that what he and his colleagues at the Institute of Social and Religious Research often referred to as the "respectable" denominations were losing members to what they called the "emotional sects" (Brunner, 1927). This awareness was a major element in his intense desire to end religious competition. Douglass valued church union far more than he valued the "minutiae of creed." He was supported by an institute and surrounded by colleagues dedicated to discovering how to achieve religious unification. Obviously, the sects were not about to discard their competitive ways. But it seemed equally obvious to Douglass and his friends that the reunification of Protestantism was the wave of the future. Thus Douglass wrote: "The present urban age still witnesses the backwash of sectarianism in certain quarters, especially in the less prosperous and more backward sections of the nation; but on the whole the age is distinctly dominated by integrative forces" (Douglass and

This photograph was taken at a Pentecostal Holiness Revival in 1932 near Kennett, Missouri. The twenty-three-year-old evangelist, Russell Ridgeway, reportedly baptized 400 persons as 10,000 more watched from the banks of the Mississippi. The back of the photograph reads: "'Ole man river' witnesses a wholesale baptism." (Courtesy of the Billy Graham Center Museum, Wheaton, Ill.)

Brunner, 1935, p. 257). If these characterizations were true, then it seemingly *had to be* that the "respectable" mainline bodies would soon bounce back and resume their historic role of cultural leadership.

Although we have focused on Douglass, he was by no means alone in viewing sectarianism as a temporary "backwash." Then, as now, there was considerable bias among scholars against the "emotional sects." As we noted earlier, Brunner (1927, pp. 75–76) described the emotional sects as being "organized on the fringe of the larger community" and was entirely willing to mention "mixed blood" and "moronic intelligence." If Brunner sounds like a bigot as well as an elitist, his colleagues in the Country Life Movement would not have noticed. Consider Warren H. Wilson's (1925, p. 58) assessment of these groups and of rural people in general: "among country people there are many inferior minds." He then displayed his contempt for an unregulated, that is to say free, religious economy: "the prevalence of revivalism among country people has a justification. Until a better administration of life is possible and the weak can be sifted from the strong, until we can lift the administration of popular institutions that are governed by public opinion out of the hand of the weak brother and the silly sister, we shall do well to use a method that steadies and arouses them and forbids them to express the impulses of the imbecile and moron. We must be content with the negative result which the old methods have given" (p. 58). It has been eighty years since these words were published. The temporary "backwash" of sect growth shows no signs of slowing down, and the "weak brother and the silly sister" still enjoy a good prayer meeting as much as ever.

In the final chapter we bring together many factors governing why some religious groups prosper, while others fail. Here our interest has been not in how organizations grow, but in attempts by some denominations to create cartels and thus to prevent the growth of new firms. We have also explored why the denominations that are doing best at a given moment are not prepared to support such cartels or to merge with others. Thus are ecumenical movements doomed. The most vigorous, growing, and significant organizations will not join, and a merger of failing groups cannot fulfill the essential ecumenical hope.

Chapter 7

Why "Mainline" Denominations Decline

If there is one urgent lesson we have learned from our historical studies of American religion it is this: anyone who plans to write about religious change in America should first consult Ecclesiastes 1:9, "The thing that hath been, it *is that* which shall be; and that which is done *is that* which shall be done: and *there* is no new *thing* under the sun." Unfortunately for the social sciences, verse 11 points out that there is "no remembrance of former *things*." Partly because we seldom work with historical materials, social scientists have tended to treat most religious changes as new things under the sun and to claim that any given movement is the product of unusual social conditions and the changing demands of the people. Ironically, even historians fall prey to this temptation, treating the specific era being studied as unique, or even a turning point for American religious history.

Since at least 1776 the upstart sects have grown as the mainline American denominations have declined.[1] And this trend continues unabated, as new upstarts continue to push to the fore. Consider that the Assemblies of God (2.6 million members) is larger than the Episcopal Church (2.3 million), or the American Baptist Churches in the USA (1.4 million), or the United Church of Christ (1.4 million). The Church of God in Christ (5.5 million) now outnumbers the National Baptist Convention, USA (5 million), National Baptist Convention of America (3.5 million), the African Methodist Episcopal Church (2.5 million), and the African Methodist Episcopal Church Zion (1.4 million). As for the Latter-day Saints, their

American membership now trails only that of the Roman Catholics, Southern Baptists, the United Methodists, and the Church of God in Christ.

These historical trends are not oddities of recent history. Rather, they reflect basic social forces that first cause successful religious firms to compromise their "errand into the wilderness" and then to lose their organizational vigor, eventually to be replaced by less worldly groups. The less regulated the religious economy, the more rapidly and thoroughly the process will occur. New groups arise with ease and immigrant faiths use local congregations as an institutional free space for organizing the faithful.

Most scholars interested in the subject see the religious condition of the United States, and of societies generally, as the product of unique, if periodic, cultural crises and eruptions. Thus, the preference is for ad hoc explanations that often amount to little more than identifying some eras as periods of religious excitement and others as periods of lethargy. Writing about the growth of "emotional sects" during the 1920s, Edmund Brunner first characterized this as a sudden and temporary annoyance, a mere "backwash," and then noted that "many theories were advanced to account for the rapid growth of this type of religion. . . . It was only a natural part of the westward movement; . . . it was a stab at modernism . . . it was part of the post-bellum state of mind" (1927, pp. 75–76). A few years later H. Paul Douglass and Brunner explained that this "backwash of sectarianism" was limited to the "less prosperous and more backward sections of the nation" (1935, p. 257). Both authors were convinced that the future of American religion lay securely in the hands of the mainline Protestants.

They were wrong, of course. And, in our judgment, so are most scholars who identify sudden shifts and eruptions in American religious history. In Chapters 2 and 3 we challenged claims about the first and second Great Awakenings, which we see as merely the routine activities of evangelists enthusiastically in pursuit of souls. We also reported that the "low ebb-tide of religion," as the end of the eighteenth century has typically been portrayed, was little more than the onset of hard times for the old colonial mainline.

To open this chapter we shall examine claims about major eruptions in American religion during the latter half of the twentieth century and show that these too are mainly in the eyes of the beholders. The "new" trends merely extend those of the past and are not new things under the sun. Then we explain more fully why the upstarts have a potential for growth and why costly religions can be so rewarding. Next we review why mainline churches succumb, by noting recent trends in American Catholicism. Finally, we offer future prospects for American religion.

Déjà Vu

Everyone knows that the latter part of the sixties turned into a "magical mystery tour" during which an explosion of cult formation and importation took place and that, for the first time, the cultural climate was right for faiths from the East, and especially from India, to make significant headway. It seemed equally clear that there was an eruption of evangelical growth and fervor. The conservative religions were suddenly growing rapidly as the mainline fell into decline. And, as the century came to a close, attention was drawn to the tight-knit religious communities appealing to new immigrants. The religious enclaves were bound by ethnicity, language, and a religious commitment that seemingly prevented them from assimilating into the larger culture. Upon closer inspection, however, none of these trends was new. To borrow a phrase, it was déjà vu all over again.

The Eastern Aspect and New Age

In their foreword to Part 1 of *The New Religious Consciousness*, Charles Y. Glock and Robert N. Bellah noted: "One of the most striking characteristics of the counterculture [of the sixties] and of the movements growing out of it is the influence of Asian religions. Of course, Americans have been interested in Asian religions for over a century, but the present period seems to differ from earlier ones both quantitatively and qualitatively. . . . Most important of all was the fact that Asian religions were attracting not only the curiosity of educated youth but also serious devotion and commitment" (1976, p. 1).

That same year Harvey Cox stressed the same points in his book *Turning East: The Promise and Peril of the New Orientalism*. Cox wanted to explain this phenomenon. Why was it happening? What did it all mean? In a 1983 interview he commented that Americans embraced Eastern faiths because "they've been maddened by a consumer culture." Cox continued: "In American society, I believe we're now in the late phase, the most deteriorated, decadent phase, of consumer capitalism. When I say 'consumer capitalism,' I don't mean simply the form of our economic life; I mean our whole culture . . . People's primal energies are fixated on commodities that are supposed to bring satisfaction of inner hungers. Through the suggestive and hypnotic power of the advertising indus-try, a direct connection is made from very basic and underlying needs and fears to material commodities which are touted as things which satisfy those needs; but of course they do not" (1983, p. 42). In conclusion, Cox noted a great irony, that though many critics charge that "vulnerable kids . . . are picked off the streets and brainwashed into the cults," it is only those who have not yet been brainwashed into the "existing distorted values of society" who are clear-headed enough to be "open to other life-patterns."

Underneath Cox's polemics one can detect a very common belief about the phenomenon in question: Indian religions arrived here in a sudden eruption and therefore they *must* reflect a serious cultural crisis. But such crises are, in fact, rare and have little, if anything, to do with the instance at hand.

Glock and Bellah were correct to note that there had been substan-tial interest in Indian and other Asian religions for more than a century. Gordon Melton (1987) has sketched the extensive involvements of Harvard professors and various proper Bostonians in Eastern religions during the latter part of the nineteenth century. The Boston Unitarian Church was responsible for the initial visits by Hindu teachers to the United States. According to Melton, the first of these was Protap Chundar Mozoomdar. In 1883 he gave his first American lecture in the Concord living room of the widow of Ralph Waldo Emerson. Other gurus soon followed.

In the wake of World War I, however, Congress passed very restric-tive immigration laws that effectively excluded all Asians and thereby limited authentic Eastern religious teachers to brief visits on tourist vi-sas. Thenceforth, Americans interested in exploring Eastern religion had to rely on books, travel abroad, or depend upon American teachers—some of whom pretended to be authentic Indians.[2]

In 1965 the exclusionary rules against Asian immigration were qui-etly dropped.[3] Before the year was out Swami Bhaktivedanta, founder of ISKCON, had become a resident of New York. Many other teachers of Eastern religion quickly followed, and some succeeded in attracting a following. It is their success that Cox and others were trying to explain. But it seems to us that there is much less here than meets the eye.

Given the existence of a sizable audience for books and periodicals dealing with "Eastern wisdom," it does not seem surprising that when talented gurus finally arrived and offered direct teaching they had little trouble finding at least some followers. Put another way, it was not so much that Eastern faiths suddenly struck a responsive chord in the American counterculture as that their growth had been artificially thwarted until then. With the barrier removed, normalization occurred. Given the structure of guru-based religions (Shinn, 1985), virtually each new guru who came to the United States founded a *separate* movement. Thus it took only a relatively small number of American converts to Hinduism to generate a substantial total of Hindu-based cult movements. Herein lies the explanation of the fact that an unusual number of the cult movements founded in the late sixties were of the Hindu variety. Whereas, only 7 percent of the groups founded during the fifties were based on Eastern faiths, 19 percent of those founded during the seventies were of the Eastern variety. The percentage declines to 12 in the 1990s, supporting the notion that the surge was simply a normalization of "frustrated" demand. The ability of a sudden influx of Eastern and Indian religious teachers to collectively round up a few thousand followers in the vast American religious economy was at most a blip, not an eruption.

Receiving equal attention with the rise of Eastern faiths, has been the New Age movement. Religion scholars have been highly attentive to this movement, with many regarding it as the truly important and lasting legacy of the earlier eruptions of new mysticisms (Burrows, 1987; Babbie, 1990; Robbins and Anthony, 1990).[4] In this they have been much abetted by the news media, for both the print and the electronic media uncritically pass along New Age press releases claiming that hundreds of thousands (perhaps millions) of Americans are sleeping in homemade pyramids and attending channeling classes. And judging from the shelf space devoted to anti–New Age materials in most Christian bookstores, the New Age is *the* cult threat of the moment.

Once again, we dissent. We believe that most people who can in any way be said to have responded to the New Age movement regard it as more of an amusement than a religion. Most are no more than casual dabblers in the various pseudoscientific activities and techniques promoted as New Age. Indeed, we suspect that for all but a handful of committed participants, the New Age movement is an audience cult (Stark and Bainbridge, 1985) and reflects interest levels on a par with reading astrology columns.[5]

Nor is the New Age Movement anything new. The term "New Age" is an old one, as is the practice of "channeling." In 1881 and 1882 John Ballou Newbrough, a New York spiritualist, "channeled" a manuscript later published as *Oahspe: A New Age Bible*. The phrase "New Age" was recurrent in the Theosophical Society at the turn of the century, and was commonly used by followers of Vedanta and the Rosicrucian Fellowship. During the 1950s, when "flying saucer cults" were popular, many spoke and wrote about the New Age that would begin when the "brothers from outer space" revealed themselves to the world. It was in the 1980s, however, that the term became widely known, largely owing to the publicity given to channelers such as J. Z. Knight and Kevin Ryerson by Shirley MacLaine (Melton, 1990).

Despite all the attention, the New Age Movement remains small and only loosely organized.[6] Admittedly, some people who report being Roman Catholics or Lutherans take part in the New Age audience. *But audiences do not constitute movements.* And even this audience is probably not all that large. According to *Ulrich's Periodicals Directory 2003*, paid circulation for the most popular New Age publication, *Body & Soul* (formerly the *New Age Journal*), was only 200,000. This rather modest audience, however, greatly overstates the number of people who are involved members. Consider that of the 29.6 million Canadians answering a census question on religious affiliation, only 1,530 selected New Age. It seems to us that the New Age is no more potent or relatively popular today than it was in the heyday of Theosophical Society, which claimed a total membership of 6,780 in 1926.

The New Immigrants

When country-of-origin quotas were abolished on October 3, 1965, the source of U.S. immigrants shifted east and south.[7] Immigration from Asia went from a modest 20,040 in 1965 to an average of nearly 150,000 per year in the 1970s and more than 280,000 per year in the 1980s and 1990s. Immigration from Latin America, especially Mexico, while sizable before 1965, rose sharply throughout the 1970s, and remained the largest current of immigration in the 1980s and 1990s at over 300,000 per year. Within forty years the new waves of immigrants transformed the foreign-born population in the United States. In 1960, about 75 percent of all foreign-born residents were born in Europe. By 2000, only 15 percent of the foreign-born were from Europe, 26 percent were from Asia, and 51 percent were from Latin America (U.S. Census Bureau, 2002a; U.S. Census Bureau, 2002b). Amidst all of these changes, however, many failed to notice that the new immigrant faiths developed congregations that were remarkably similar to the European immigrants of the past.

The most noticeable effect of this new wave of immigrants, and most alarming for many, is that world religions other than Christianity are being introduced to America. Islam, Buddhism, and Hinduism are making a presence throughout the nation. Although admittedly crude, the best recent estimates suggest that there are currently less than 2 million Muslims (1,209 mosques), about 2 million Buddhists (1,656 temples), and a little over 1 million Hindu adherents (629 temples) (Smith, 2002; Jones et al., 2002; Finke and Scheitle, 2004). To put these numbers in perspective, however, we should recall that from 1965 to 2000 over 23 million immigrants arrived in the United States and that some of the above adherents are native-born converts. The vast majority of the new immigrants involved in religion are forming Protestant and Catholic congregations. Even from nations where Christians are a minority, a disproportionate number of Christians emigrate and many immigrants convert to Christianity after they arrive. South Korea, for example, is 25 percent Christian, but a study of Chicago Koreans found that 52 percent were affiliated with Christian churches before emigrating and half of the remainder join Christian churches after arriving in the United States (Hurh and Kim, 1990; Chai, 1998). China holds only a small minority of Christians, yet the number of Chinese Protestant churches in the United States jumped from 66 in 1952 to 697 by 1994 (Yang, 1999). Latin Americans, the largest flow of immigrants, are overwhelmingly Protestant and Catholic.

Regardless of the immigrant religion being studied, whether it is Christian or another world religion, a growing volume of research documents the remarkable similarities of the new immigrant congregations with those of the past (Warner and Wittner, 1998; Yang, 1999; Ebaugh and Chafetz, 2000; Yang and Ebaugh, 2001a). Greeley noted that the Catholic parishes of the early immigrants simultaneously preserved a distinctive religious and ethnic subculture as they assimilated immigrants into the larger culture. The new immigrant congregations continue to do the same. Congregations teach the younger generations to speak the native language as they teach the older generations to speak English. They hold worship services in the native tongue and promote traditional rituals as they assist members in getting citizenship, jobs, and training. Whether the congregation was German at the end of the nineteenth century or Chinese at the dawn of the twenty-first, the immigrant congregations seek to reproduce portions of the old culture as they assimilate members into the new.

Like immigrant congregations before them, the new immigrants are also forced to compete in a religious market with no support from the state and where religious alternatives are many. Just as previous immigrants were forced to actively recruit new members and mobilize them to higher levels of commitment, the new congregations must do the same. When studying the Asian Indian community in Atlanta, John Fenton (1988, p. 179) reported: "in America, Hindu temples tend to become like other American voluntary associations, and in time will begin to resemble American synagogues and churches." How do they become like American congregations? Fenton explained that the "lay leadership is strong," temples financing is "broad-based," "cultural halls encourage non-religious activity," and the "priests perform a variety of functions not normal in India—junketing around the country to perform weddings, to do pujas, to teach children's schools, and so forth." He went on to explain that "visiting, 'circuit-riding' gurus do much the same and already function to some extent like pastoral counselors." The competitive market forces local congregations to be responsive to and reliant on the membership of the local congregation.

Unwittingly perhaps, the IRS also contributes to the organizational structure of new religions seeking tax-exempt status (Stark, 1987a). American tax laws induce new religious groups to formally organize and lay out the requirements for incorporation. Asking questions about fundraising, the place of worship, clergy's training and access to funds for personal use, familial relationships of the governing body, and the larger organizational structure, the IRS offers guidelines on what it means to be a religious organization in America.

One of the earliest conclusions of this emerging research on immigration was that immigrant faiths quickly organize into a congregational structure unfamiliar to their countries of origin (Warner, 1994). A part of this congregational structure is the development of a larger community for the immigrants. Dolan described the immigrant Catholic parish of the late nineteenth century as a "community institution" that included social, recreational, charitable, and religious activities and groups. The new immigrant congregations resemble the ethnic community institutions of old. When studying thirteen immigrant congregations in the Houston area, including a Hindu temple, two Buddhist temples, a Zoroastrian center, a Muslim mosque, a Greek Orthodox church, two Roman Catholic Churches, and five Protestant churches, Helen Rose Ebaugh and Janet Saltzman Chafetz (2000) found that eleven of the thirteen had a community hall or were in the process of building one. Twelve of the thirteen offered secular instruction such as native language classes for the children, English classes for the adults, or GED courses. And, though some of the congregations were small, with one being a storefront church, six had recreational facilities.

But the immigrants adapt more than the organizational structure, they also provide religious teachings that are relevant to the immigrant experience. Even when the immigrants are Catholic or Protestant, they bring a distinctive version to America. When discussing the immigrant leaders of the late nineteenth and early twentieth century, Timothy L. Smith (1978a, p. 1178) explained that pastors, rabbis, and lay religious leaders had to "make religion more personal by reinterpreting scriptures and creeds to allow ancient observances to serve new purposes." In the same way, leaders of new immigrant congregations are finding ways to combine old and new cultures with their religious traditions. For example, many Chinese Christians find that the family-oriented and theologically conservative teachings of evangelical Protestantism are congruent with Confucian principles so dominant in Chinese culture (Yang, 1998).

Supporting a tight-knit ethnic and religious community and often supported by conservative religious teachings, many of the new congregations generate high levels of member commitment. For the many sectarian (often Pentecostal) groups this might be expected, but even the ethnic congregations affiliated with mainline denominations show a similar trend. Within the Presbyterian Church (USA), 316 of 11,097 total congregations report a membership that is 80 percent or more Asian and 176 of these congregations (56 percent) report a membership that is 100 percent Asian. Not surprisingly, of the 273 congregations reporting a founding date, 91 percent were started after 1965.[8] Table 7.1 shows the striking differences between the Asian immigrant congregations and the average Presbyterian

TABLE 7.1
Member Commitment in Presbyterian Church (USA) Asian Congregations, 2002

	All Congregations	Asian Congregations
Average contributions per active member	$883	$1,680
Ratio of worship attendance and active membership	0.52	0.96
N =	11,097	207*

We would like to thank Ida Smith Williams and John Marcum of Research Services of the Presbyterian Church (USA) for providing the above data and for answering our many questions.

*The congregations omitted had missing data.

Church (USA) congregation. Average giving for an active member in a congregation was $883 in 2002. But the average nearly doubled to $1,680 for Asian congregations. The ratio between average Sunday worship attendance and the number of active members in a congregation is 0.52 for all Presbyterian Church (USA) congregations compared to 0.96 for Asian congregations. Additional research has shown that Asian members also donate more of their time outside of worship services. On every measure available, the level of commitment is far higher for the Asian congregations (Kim and Kim, 2001).

This commitment is fueled by a religious and social distinctiveness that goes far beyond ethnicity. The Presbyterian Panel Study of 1997–1999 and the Racial Ethnic Presbyterian Panel Studies conducted by the Presbyterian Church (USA) Research Services offer some striking contrasts. Whereas, 10 percent of Presbyterians agreed that "the Bible is an important piece of literature but largely irrelevant to our lives today," none of the 675 Korean Presbyterians responding to the survey agreed. Instead, 26 percent of Koreans hold the Bible as the "literally inerrant Word of God and a guide for faith and secular matters." The same striking differences are shown in the area of morality. When asked about heterosexual cohabitation outside of marriage, 82 percent of the Korean respondents highly disapproved compared to only 44 of white Presbyterians (Kim and Kim, 2001, pp. 85–87).[9]

Despite all of the obvious changes in immigration, the unregulated religious market continues to provide an institutional free space for new immigrants. A space that allows for the development of congregations uniquely capable of providing for the religious, cultural, and social needs of new immigrants, and remarkably similar to earlier immigrant churches.

The Evangelical Eruption

In 1972 Dean M. Kelley, an executive of the National Council of Churches, provoked a storm of controversy, especially among religious liberals, with his book *Why Conservative Churches Are Growing*. His first sentence noted: "In the latter years of the 1960s something remarkable happened in the United States: for the first time in the nation's history most of the major church groups stopped growing and began to shrink." Kelley was among the very first to attempt to explain what Martin Marty (1979, p. 10) would later describe as a "seismic shift" in American religion: the sudden and very steep membership declines that began to hit the mainline denominations during the sixties. Summing up the evidence of a series of graphs showing membership figures for a number of major denominations, Kelley noted that in the sixties the "strong upward curve weakens, falters, and tilts downward like a spent skyrocket" (p. 2). As the title of his book revealed, however, not *all* denominations had hit the skids. The evangelical Protestant bodies were still growing—many of them quite rapidly.[10]

What was going on? According to Marty (1976, p. 71) it was another cultural crisis: "mainline churches always have the advantage . . . [when] the official culture is secure and expansive . . . [but they] suffer in times of cultural crisis and disintegration, when they receive blame for what goes wrong in society but are bypassed when people look for new ways to achieve social identity and location. So they looked good in the 1950s as they looked bad in the 1970s." Kelley disagreed. He claimed that the mainline bodies were failing to offer credible religion, that they had become so accommodated to the secular culture that people could no longer satisfy their need for the sacred by attending services at their local Methodist, Congregationalist, Episcopalian, or Presbyterian Church.

As much as we admire Kelley's book, and his courage in writing it, we think the whole discussion of the sudden decline of the liberal denominations and the sudden "resurgence" of evangelical groups is based on a distorted historical perspective. Like Marty, Kelley was still trying to explain why this "sudden change took place in the 60s." Several years later Kelley (1984, p. 89) expressed continued confidence in his explanation of why the "conservatives" grew (as the "liberals" declined), but he confessed he was "less satisfied" that he had explained, "why it happened at this particular time in history [the 1960s]."

But did anything akin to an eruption take place? Kelley's skyrocket image to the contrary, what is involved here is a gradual trend that has been going on for at least two centuries. The notion of a "seismic shift" is based on the fact that it was only in the sixties that this trend was finally noticed. If we are correct, all efforts by Marty and others to link the fate of the liberal churches to the "cultural crisis of the 1960s" (Marsden, 1982, p. 156) are falsified by the inability of consequences to precede their causes in time.

When the crisis arrived, the consensus of church historians (and most sociologists) was that the decline of the liberal Protestant churches was a product of the sixties. For example, Winthrop S. Hudson claimed that the declines which "had begun in the 1960's . . . constituted a marked reversal after a century and a half of steady growth" (1981, p. 439). Likewise, Marty noted: "From the birth of the republic until around 1965, as is well known, the churches now called mainline Protestant tended to

TABLE 7.2

Market Shares of Religious Denominations per 1,000
Church Members, 1940–2000

	1940	1960	1980	2000	1940–2000 Percentage loss or gain
MAINLINE					
United Methodists	124.7	93.0	70.6	54.8	−56%
Presbyterian Church (USA)	41.7	36.4	24.3	16.6	−60%
Episcopal	31.4	28.6	20.7	15.3	−51%
Christian (Disciples)	25.7	15.7	8.7	5.4	−79%
United Church of Christ					
(Congregationalists)	26.5	19.6	12.9	9.1	−66%
EVANGELICALS					
Southern Baptists	76.7	85.0	100.9	104.9	+37%
Church of God in Christ	2.6	3.4	24.7	36.2	+1292%
Assemblies of God	3.1	4.4	7.8	9.9	+221%
Pentecostal Assemblies of					
the World	NA	0.4	3.7	9.9	+2375%
Church of God					
(Cleveland, Tenn.)	1.0	1.5	3.2	5.9	+501%
Church of the Nazarene	2.6	2.7	3.6	4.2	+63%
OTHER COSTLY RELIGIONS					
Mormons	12.0	13.0	20.9	30.8	+157%
Jehovah's Witnesses	NA	2.2	4.2	6.6	+200%

SOURCE: Calculated from multiple editions of the *Yearbook of American and Canadian Churches*. "Inclusive membership" estimates are used for all denominations except the Assemblies of God and the Presbyterian Church (USA). Due to a lack of "inclusive" estimates for earlier years, their rates are based on the smaller totals known as "full member" estimates. The 2000 rate for the Church of God in Christ is based on a 1991 membership estimate.

grow with every census or survey" (1979, p. 10). But in light of the two centuries of church statistics we have examined, it is obvious that a group can add members and still fail to keep pace with the growth of the population and of other religious firms.

The mainline denominations do not qualify as rockets that suddenly ran out of fuel in the sixties—their market shares were falling in the forties and fifties too, and throughout the century (see Table 7.2). In contrast, the evangelical groups—some of them rapidly becoming the new up-start sects of our era—do look like rockets. So much, then, for perceptions of a seismic shift or a sudden response to a cultural crisis. The speed of conservative growth and liberal decline will no doubt change from time to time, but the general trend has remained consistent for more than two centuries of American history. Thus, while it is true, as Hudson and Marty claim, that the total number of members of these mainline bodies increased regularly until the 1960s, each year they represented a smaller fraction of total church membership.

Even those without the slightest awareness of market share cannot long ignore an actual decline in numbers. And by the seventies the numbers were falling fast. Attempts to dismiss these declines as purely demographic (cf. Hoge and Roozen, 1979) or as symptomatic of the general decline in religiousness produced by modernity, fall apart when it is noted that *only some* religious bodies were losing out. And indeed, as Dean Kelley bravely noted, the conservative Protestant bodies were still growing.

There have been many attempts to explain this unwelcome fact away. Carl Bangs (1972) charged Kelley with using "deceptive statistics." Others suggested that Kelley had fallen into the trap of confusing quantity with quality—that though the evangelicals grow rapidly by "herding insecure and frightened masses together into a superficial conformity," it is the liberal churches who are the "faithful remnant of God's people whose prophetic courage and lifestyle will truly point the way" (Miller, 1978, p. 257). Others claimed that the growth of evangelical Protestant bodies was nothing but inflated membership roles caused by people who frequently hop from one sect to another, thus being counted again and again (Bibby and Binkerhoff, 1973, 1983). Some even suggest that it was all a function of disparities in absolute size, because it is easy for small evangelical sects to have high percentage rates of growth, but virtually impossible for large denominations to keep growing rapidly (Nelson and Bromley, 1988). This excuse not only ignored the fact that the nation's largest Protestant body, the Southern Baptist Convention, was among those growing in the 1970s, but also ignored the huge potential for growth that actually exists in the American religious economy.

Two cases are illustrative. Between 1960 and 1970 the Assemblies of God grew by 22.9 percent to reach a total membership of 625,027. This was one of the "small" groups, thereby able to grow fast, cited by Kelley's critics. Meanwhile, the United Church of Christ (formerly the Congregationalists) declined by 12.5 percent, to 1,960,608 members, between 1960 and 1970. In 2001 the Assemblies of God numbered 2,627,029 members and the United Church of Christ had only 1,359,105.[11] Does anyone really think that the advantage currently rests with the UCC, now that it has become the smaller group? It seems clear that the decline of the Protestant mainline is a long, steady trend. It is pointless to search the 1960s for the causes of a phenomenon that was far along by the War of 1812. But the question persists: Why do mainline faiths fail and why do the sects always overtake them?

Why the Upstarts Win, Again

By the time Kelley published his controversial book it was common knowledge that the mainline churches were shrinking. This realization had been dealt with in a number of ways. Some blamed it on secularization—religion is in retreat from modernity, probably never to recover. Others suggested that religion is not meaningfully reduced to membership counts; what matters is what is in people's hearts (and presumably that is beyond measure). Many proposed that the churches were badly in need of liberalization and modernization—that they must drop their unreasonable moral demands, which only drove people away.

Kelley's book stirred up so much controversy for many reasons. First, not only did he publicize the liberal losses, he accepted claims by conservative bodies of continued growth. Second, he was unwilling to brush this growth off as a momentary "backwash." Instead, he saw it as the key fact. Kelley said that the mainline churches were declining not because they asked too much of their members but because they asked too little. It was this position that antagonized so many of his critics.

Kelley argued that the flourishing conservative denominations:

> not only give evidence that religion is not obsolete and churches not defunct but they contradict the contemporary notion of an acceptable religion. They are not "reasonable," they are not "tolerant," they are not ecumenical, they are not "relevant." Quite the contrary!
>
> It is ironic that religious groups which persist in such "unreasonable" and "unsociable" behavior should be flourishing, while more "reasonable" and "sociable" bodies are not. It is not only ironic, but it suggests that our understanding of what causes a religious group to flourish is inadequate. Some dynamic seems to be at work which contradicts prevailing expectations. (1972, pp. 25–26)

Kelley outlined this dynamic in three propositions (italics omitted):

Strong organizations are strict. . . the stricter the stronger. (p. 95)

A strong organization that loses its strictness will also lose its strength. (p. 96)

Strictness tends to deteriorate into leniency, which results in social weakness in place of strength. . . . traits of strictness are harder to maintain in an organization than traits of leniency. (p. 96)

As Kelley knew they would, these propositions fueled many angry denials and attacks. Nearly a decade later he reported that his book "excited a certain amount of controversy, if not actual scandal, among those who thought such things were better off unannounced" (Kelley, 1984, p. 93). But he was unrepentant: "Despite all the howls of outrage and screams of annoyance, I am not aware that anyone has clearly disproved any of [his major theses]."

More recently, our own work and the work of Laurence Iannaccone has provoked heated reactions when we suggest that the high demands and distinctive boundaries of sect groups serve to generate the resources needed for growth. Below we more fully explain why a costly religion can be so rewarding.

The Rewards of a Costly Faith

First we should acknowledge the obvious. Not all sects grow. After collecting data on 417 American-born sects, Stark and Bainbridge (1985, p. 134) reported that "nearly a third of all sects (32 percent) reached their high-water mark on the day they began." Of the scores of sects spawned by the Baptists and Pentecostals, only a handful have been able to support sustained growth. Only one of the many Bible student groups that formed in response to the teachings of Charles Taze Russell went on to become the Jehovah's Witnesses. Many of the groups become so distinctive and so exclusive that they close themselves off from any opportunities for growth. For these and other reasons we will discuss below, most sect movements have remained small and obscure. Placing high demands on members and maintaining distinctive boundaries with the surrounding culture are not *sufficient* to explaining the vitality of religious organizations. Yet these are often *necessary conditions for vital religions*.[12] Over the past two hundred–plus years of American history it has been the costly sects that have shown the most rapid growth.

At first glance it seems paradoxical that when the cost of membership increases the net gains of membership increase too. This is necessarily the case, however, when the commodity involved is collectively produced and when increased costs result in increased levels of participation in collective action, for this results in a greater supply of collective goods (Iannaccone, 1992; Iannaccone, Olson, and Stark, 1995; Finke, 1997; Stark and Finke, 2000). An individual's positive experience in a worship service increases to the degree that the church is full, members enthusiastically participate (everyone sings and recites prayers, for example), and others express their positive evaluations of what is going on. Thus, as each individual member pays the cost of high levels of commitment, each benefits from the higher average level of participation thereby generated by the group. Or, to leave the realm of the immaterial, because Mormons are asked to contribute not only 10 percent of their income but 10 percent of their time to the church, they are able to lavish social services upon one another. Using conservative estimates, James T. Duke (1997) calculates that the average Mormon congregation (ward) receives 400–600 hours of voluntary labor per week, or the equivalent of ten to fifteen full-time employees. Thus are the rewards of Mormon membership made tangible.

The high membership costs and clear group boundaries produce these collective goods by example and exclusion. The example set by the typical member serves to increase the confidence and commitment of others. When members express confidence that their faith is true and effective, they affirm the beliefs of others. And, when the typical member displays a high level of commitment, others will be more willing to do the same. Exclusion results when high costs make membership sufficiently unattractive so as to chase away the apathetic, and in doing so make the rewards of belonging far more intense. A basic principle of collective action is that most will opt for a free ride if they can. Michael Hechter (1987, p. 27) explains: "Truly rational actors will not join a group to pursue common ends when, without participating, they can reap the benefit of other people's activity in obtaining them." Applying this principle to religious groups, Laurence R. Iannaccone (1992; 1994, p. 1188) noticed that religious groups are able to prevent free riding by requiring high costs of everyone so that "potential members are forced to choose whether to participate fully or not at all." The result is that high membership demands form a distinctive religious community with tight social networks and abundant resources.

We should be clear, however, that these high costs and clear boundaries are only possible when religions are based on beliefs in an exclusive God, active in the lives of the people. When religions conceive of God as distant, impersonal, and unresponsive, it is hard to justify why anyone should make significant sacrifices for their faith. For example, Duke (1997) explains that for each local Mormon congregation (ward) there are between 150 to 250 positions that are considered "callings" by the church. These callings are not merely requests to help out from the local bishop, they are considered callings from God. Such callings are taken seriously when the God is personal, responsive, and promises much in return.

But costs alone don't explain organizational growth. Many sects, cults, and communes have generated high member commitment without generating growth. A part of the answer is that religious organizations can make too many demands, just as they can make too few. Requiring members to withdraw from all secular opportunities, as some communes do, will clearly limit the growth of the organization. A second part is that religious groups must find ways of adapting to ever-changing environments, without compromising their core religious beliefs—beliefs that define their interactions or relationships with the supernatural. They must produce organizational innovations without compromising the faith.[13]

Generating Organizational Innovations

By seeking to revive the Anglican Church through the use of prayer and holiness, the early Methodists proposed a version of the faith that was far more costly to join than that of the traditional Church of England. When brought to America, this new faith fueled revivals and justified a level of commitment that couldn't be matched by mainline churches. But the early Methodists relied on more than a costly faith to ensure their growth. They developed and borrowed a series of innovations for promoting their emphasis on holiness living and experiential religion. Recall Francis Asbury adopting the camp meeting while mainline churches stood on the sidelines (see Chapter 3), John Wesley designing small groups called classes for monitoring spiritual growth, and Charles Wesley producing music for the masses. When combined with an organization relying on circuit riders preaching in the vernacular and using the latest printing technologies to promote their message, the Methodists produced an organization whose appeal to the people was unmatched.

Sects and para-church groups independent of mainline denominations continue to be sources of religious innovation. When Donald E. Miller (1997) studied congregations of the rapidly growing Calvary Chapel and Vineyard Fellowship, he found them developing innovations that paralleled those of the Methodists. New forms of worship with an infusion of fresh music, new strategies for founding new churches, new methods for recruiting members, and a renewed emphasis on small groups and Bible-centered teaching were all a part of the new upstart congregations. When combined with innovations developed by para-church groups like Campus Crusade for Christ or Promise Keepers and by the independent churches like Willow Creek, the American religious economy continues to generate new methods for appealing to the people (see Finke, 2004). Yet, the mainline denominations are seldom a source of such innovation and are often resistant to adopting such changes. Like the camp meetings of old, even the highly successful innovations face stiff resistance in the mainline.

So why do mainline churches resist? No doubt some of the roadblocks are due to differences in belief and theology. Innovations for spreading a plan for salvation are largely irrelevant if you have doubts about the plan. But the mainline denominations also face many organizational roadblocks for adopting change and one is administrative size. When the administrative sector of an organization expands, authority becomes more centralized and regulatory policies are standardized (Stark and Finke, 2000). The result is that organizational policies or administrative offices often block or discourage innovations. A second is that established religious organizations tend to mimic and conform to peer institutions (DiMaggio and Powell, 1983; Finke, 2004). Methodists sustained their most rapid growth when they were religious outsiders. The concern of Methodist jeremiads in the late nineteenth century (see Chapter 5) was that growing Methodist churches were mimicking the standards of others, seeking to be respectable in their eyes. Finally, professional clergy will be more restrained by the norms of the profession and the larger denomination than lay clergy, because they have more to lose—for example, denominational pension plans or future organizational appointments (Stark and Finke, 2000; Finke and Dougherty, 2002). The subtle irony is that as mainline denominations and their clergy conform to peer institutions they block changes that could stimulate growth at the very time they are revising core teachings that support belief and devotion. Simultaneously, they are discarding some of the most cherished church teachings as they refuse to make organizational adaptations (Finke, 2004).

In sharp contrast, the energetic young sects face few of the organizational restraints and they aren't lacking for commitment. When innovative adaptations are combined with the resources generated by a demanding and distinctive religion, the costly religions can become a "good bargain" for many. Over time, however, the religious groups will change. Some growing groups might increase membership costs over time and become less appealing, but most churches and sects do not. The recurring trend over the past two hundred years has been for "expensive" sects gradually to lower the costs of membership and, by doing so, to reduce the benefits of membership as well. Thus our attention must focus on why and how the reduction of tensions with the surrounding culture weakens religious organizations. Against this theoretical background, let us now examine the current situation of American Catholicism.

Recent Currents in American Catholicism

In the early 1960s, the American Catholic Church appeared as solid as ever. During the fifteen years following World War II, the church had undergone a new period of growth. From 1916 through the 1930s Catholic adherents had hovered between 150 and 160 per 1,000 population. But the combined effects of the baby boom and the resumption of immigration from Europe caused the Catholic market share to jump to 190 per 1,000 by 1950 and to 236 by 1960.

Then, in 1962, Pope John XXIII convened the Second Vatican Council, gathering all of the bishops of the Church in Rome to reassess and restructure doctrine and practice. The Italian word *aggiornamento*, which means updating, was used so often by the Pope to describe his aims to open the church to new ideas and influences that for a time it entered the vocabulary of the news media.

For four years the church fathers met periodically, making decisions that resulted in many far-reaching changes. The mass was no longer to be said in Latin, but in the local language. The faithful were no longer prohibited from eating meat on Friday. Many other prohibitions on Catholic behavior were also relaxed, and many traditions were greatly deemphasized. Moreover, the council stressed a new spirit of ecumenism. Melissa J. Wilde (2002) recently revealed that much of this new ecumenism was driven by a group of liberal bishops who met weekly at the hotel *Domus Mariae* to develop strategies and consensus for a "Protestant-friendly" agenda. Unlike the conservative bishops, who initially viewed organizing and consensus building outside of the official church structure as a threat to the Pope's authority, the liberal bishops organized early and viewed this as an opportunity for increased ecumenism. If, in the end, they did not achieve their every goal, the changes were far more dramatic than anyone had expected.

Although there were many within the church who did not greet these changes with open arms, the reactions from non-Catholics were almost universally enthusiastic. Martin Marty wrote:

> No feature of the Vatican Council was more reported upon than that which revealed Roman interest in non-Roman Christians; no aspects of the papal encyclicals of recent years were more enthusiastically greeted than those which carried the broadest Christian vision. . . . Think of the meaning of joint work in the areas of race relations and other ethical issues. Think of the missionary significance to the world when Christians re-evaluate their stands on issues of censorship, church-state relations, population growth, peace, with the whole of human need in view and the whole of Christian populace implied. (1964, pp. 107–108)

Noting that Pope John XXIII not only had called his bishops to a Vatican Council, but had at the same time appointed a Secretariat for Promoting Christian Unity, Marty remarked: "His action made John XXIII the most recognized ecumenical leader of his generation and made ecumenism a household word" (p. 108). Could a really successful ecumenical age be far away?

Oddly enough, Will Herberg—the Jewish spokesman who had played a major role in mounting the ecumenical movement of the 1950s—warned vehemently against too much aggiornamento. Speaking before a national convention of Catholics belonging to the Newman Apostolate, Herberg criticized the many Catholic intellectuals who urged the church to "slough off its old ways and bring itself up to date by adjusting itself to the spirit of the age. I say just the opposite: in all that is important, the Church must stand firm in its witness to the truth that is eternal and unchanging; it needs no updating. . . . If it is to remain true to its vocation, it must take its stand against the world, against the age, against the spirit of the age—because the world and the age are always, to a degree, to an important degree, in rebellion against God" (in Foy, 1966, p. 85). Herberg concluded by condemning many Catholics as *eager* for a crumb of recognition from the secular culture and . . . ready to swallow practically anything to get it" (p. 85). Herberg's remarks went almost unnoticed, being reported briefly in the 1966 *Catholic Almanac*. And for a little while some other things went almost unnoticed as well.

A primary symptom of the vigor of American Catholicism was its ability to generate religious vocations, to attract thousands of young Catholic men and women each year to a life of full-time dedication to the church. In 1966, as Vatican II ended, the American church was staffed as follows:

Diocesan priests	36,419
Religious priests	22,774
Brothers	12,255
Sisters	181,421
Seminarians	48,046

These totals were never again equaled, and sharply downward trends immediately ensued. In 1965 there were 10.6 seminarians for every 10,000 Catholics (see Table 7.3). After that the bottom fell out. By 2003 there were only 4,522 men enrolled in American Catholic seminaries, or a rate of 0.7 seminarians per 10,000 Catholics. Put another way, in the pre–Vatican II era, young Catholic males were fifteen times more likely to study for the priesthood than they are now.

TABLE 7.3

Number Enrolled in Catholic Seminaries per 10,000 U.S. Catholics, 1950–2000

Year	Total	Diocesan	Religious
1950	9.2	4.5	4.7
1955	10.1	4.9	5.1
1960	9.8	5.0	4.8
1962	10.5	5.4	5.1
1965	10.6	5.8	4.8
1968	8.4	4.7	3.7
1970	6.0	3.6	2.4
1976	3.5	2.3	1.2
1980	2.8	1.8	1.0
1986	2.0	1.3	0.7
1990	1.1	0.8	0.3
1996	0.8	0.5	0.3
2000	0.7	0.5	0.2

SOURCE: *Official Catholic Directory.*

Table 7.4

Number of Catholic Brothers and Sisters per 10,000 U.S.
Catholics, 1955–2000

Year	Brothers	Sisters
1955	2.7	47.5
1960	2.6	41.2
1965	2.7	39.4
1970	2.4	33.6
1975	1.8	27.8
1980	1.6	25.3
1985	1.4	22.1
1990	1.2	18.1
1995	1.1	15.3
2000	0.9	13.0

SOURCE: *Official Catholic Directory.*

There was also a rapid decline in brothers and sisters (see Table 7.4).
The total of 181,421 sisters and 12,255 brothers in 1966 had shrunk to
74,698 and 5,568 by 2003. The declines transformed virtually all Catholic institutions, most noticeably the schools. In 1966 over one half (51 percent) of the teachers in Catholic schools were sisters and another 9 percent
were priests or brothers. By 2003 all the religious combined for less than
6 percent of the teachers in Catholic schools.[14]

Just as the drop in seminary enrollments has resulted in a decline in
the number of priests, the decline in the number of sisters stemmed in
large part from a rapid decline in the number of women entering religious communities—from a total of 4,110 in 1965 to 1,486 in 1968 (Modde,
1974). In 1971 only 506 women entered a religious community—based
on reports from 274 communities representing 70 percent of the total
membership. These sudden declines were even more alarming given that
the large baby boom cohorts were coming of age in the late 1960s, which
greatly expanded the pool of potential recruits.

Finally, subsequent to Vatican II there was a substantial decline in the
proportion of Catholics attending mass during any given week. During
the 1950s more than 70 percent of American Catholics claimed weekly
attendance at mass. This continued into the early 1960s—71 percent told

the Gallup Poll in 1964 that they had been to church within the past seven days. But the next year, attendance at mass began a decline that continued until the mid-seventies, when it stabilized at slightly more than 50 percent (D'Antonio et al. 1989; Greeley, 1989). Reduced attendance, however, was not the only symptom of an apparent decline in Catholic commitment. The frequency of going to confession, participation in church activities, and even daily prayer fell sharply between 1963 and 1974 (Greeley, McCready, and McCourt, 1976). Church contributions, as a percentage of annual income, fell from 2.2 percent in 1963 to 1.1 percent in 1983 (Greeley and McManus, 1987). In general American Catholics displayed a serious drop in religious commitment, dating from the end of Vatican II.

Andrew M. Greeley and his associates (Greeley, McCready, and McCourt, 1976; Hout and Greeley, 1987; Greeley and McManus, 1987; Greeley, 1989) attribute this drop in lay commitment to the unpopular papal encyclical on birth control issued in 1968, *Humanae Vitae*. That may be true, but it can be only part of the story. As Greeley has argued, the encyclical was an attempt to impose higher costs in an area in which Catholics did not agree with their pontiff and were unwilling to accept his authority. Even prior to the encyclical, national surveys found that a majority of married Catholic women were not conforming to papal teachings on birth control (Ryder and Westoff, 1971).

But we will argue that the *decreasing demands* in other areas were as important, and probably more so, for reducing the commitment of Catholics. As Iannaccone (1994, p. 1204) has commented, the Catholic church "managed to arrive at a remarkable, 'worst of both worlds' position—discarding cherished distinctiveness in the areas of liturgy, theology, and life-style, while at the same time maintaining the very demands that its members and clergy are least willing to accept."

The distinctive sacrifices and stigmas of being Catholic were abandoned (without replacement) by the reforms of Vatican II. Recent declines in the vigor of American Catholicism reflect one more cycle of the sect-church process whereby a faith becomes a mainline body and then begins to wilt. Their "worst of both worlds" position is reminiscent of the position taken by mainline Protestants throughout American history.

Social and Cultural Assimilation

The vigorous era of the American Catholic "sect," covered in Chapter 4, was also an era during which Catholics tended to be immigrants and poor. This was still true in the 1940s. Writing in the *American Journal of Sociology*, Hadley Cantril (1943, p. 575) reported that the results of national survey studies "offer evidence for certain commonly known facts: Catholics are poorer and less educated than Protestants." But not for much longer. Reanalyzing data collected by Stouffer in 1955, Seymour Martin Lipset and Reinhard Bendix (1959) found that the difference between the occupational status of Protestants and Catholics disappeared when first- and second-generation immigrants were excluded. By the mid-1960s, when few first generation immigrants remained, there was little doubt that Catholics had achieved economic and educational parity with Protestants (Greeley, 1963, 1964; Glenn and Hyland, 1967; Alston, 1969). Today, because the Catholic population is so urban and non-southern, the average Catholic earns slightly more and has a job of slightly higher status than does the average Protestant.

If Catholics are no longer poorer than Protestants, they are no longer more prolific either. When reporting on recent trends in Catholic fertility in 1955, the demographer Dudley Kirk noted that "it is a matter of common observation that Catholic families . . . have more children than their non-Catholic neighbors" (p. 93). But in 1979 Charles F. Westoff wrote of "dramatic convergence of Catholic with non-Catholic" fertility (p. 239). From 1955 to 1975 the difference had gone from one of "common observation" to one of insignificance on a national survey of fertility.

In 1979 James McCarthy reported a substantial convergence in the divorce rates of Protestants and Catholics, although Catholics were still less likely to get divorced. Survey data from 1987 showed that nearly 60 percent of American Catholics think a good Catholic can ignore the "Church's teaching regarding divorce and remarriage" (D'Antonio et al., 1989). By 1999 the percent went even higher to 65 percent (D'Antonio et al., 2001). These changes removed major impediments to Protestant-Catholic marriages, and the church quietly removed another impediment when it ceased to require that a non-Catholic spouse agree to rear the children as Catholics. Consequently, a majority of American Catholics now agree that one can marry outside the church and still remain a "good Catholic" (D'Antonio et al., 1989). Not surprisingly, the intermarriage rate and the percentage marrying outside the church have been rising rapidly (McCutcheon, 1988; Alba, 1990; Kalmijn, 1991). Despite only minor changes in the percentage of the population that is Catholic, the percentage of weddings "witnessed by a Catholic priest" dropped from 20 percent of all marriages in 1970 to 13 percent in 1990 (Froehle and Gautier, 2000).

Meanwhile, another convergence took place. For generations, Roman

Catholics were overwhelmingly Democrats. As recently as the early 1970s Catholics still differed greatly from Protestants in terms of party identification. But this too is history (Bird, 1990). When we merged the first five years of the General Social Survey (1972–1976), we found that 64 percent of Catholics identified themselves as Democrats and only 21 percent were Republican. Less than thirty years later (1998–2002), 33 percent identified as Republicans and the percentage Democrat dropped 17 points to 47 percent.

As Catholics shed these distinctive cultural and social patterns, they also began to dismantle their parallel structure of institutions and organizations. In 1964 the *American Catholic Sociological Review* changed its name to *Sociological Analysis*. In 1970 the American Catholic Sociological Society changed its name to the Association for the Sociology of Religion. These changes did not go unremarked or without causing some hard feelings. Several former presidents of the organization, seeing no need for another secular sociological organization, resigned (Morris, 1989). But neither did sufficient numbers of Catholic sociologists wish any longer to encourage non-Catholic perceptions of parochialism. Similar changes took place in other Catholic professional societies. Between 1965 and 1970 the number of such associations listed in the *National Catholic Almanac* declined by 17 percent.

Religious Assimilation

But it wasn't only in the secular sphere that Catholics were becoming highly assimilated. Suddenly the mass was in English, and it proved to sound surprisingly similar to the ritual portions of services at high church Protestant bodies such as the Episcopalians and Lutherans. Moreover, the strict prohibitions against even entering a non-Catholic church building, let alone attending a non-Catholic wedding or funeral service, simply disappeared in the midst of the new ecumenism. Many Catholics thus began to have religious contacts with Protestants. Not only did the Catholic charismatic movement mirror Protestant Pentecostalism but the two were soon intertwined at the local organizational level.

An important aspect of assimilation involved the decision by the council to make meatless Fridays no longer mandatory, but to leave it to individual Catholics to discover and observe their own practices of penance. In Catholic nations this change may have mattered little, except to the fishing industry. But in a pluralistic setting the observance had been a clear cultural marker and social boundary. When Catholic teenagers at drive-ins on Friday nights counted down to midnight before ordering their burgers, everyone present was reminded who was Catholic and who was not. To waive this very visible rule necessarily raised serious questions about the basis of religious truth and institutional credibility. From the point of view of teenagers and even of some adults, the scrapping of meatless Fridays for Catholics appeared as radical as a decision by the Mormon Church to authorize cola and coffee drinking or one by the Southern Baptists to market beer. As William D'Antonio and his colleagues explained:

> this new norm regarding fasting also opened the door to independent thinking for the Catholic believer. The fact that eating meat on Friday was no longer considered a mortal sin raised for many Catholics the larger question about the attribution of sinfulness to other actions. It had, for many Catholics, a kind of "hole in the dike" effect. . . .
>
> In sum, the result of the changes of Vatican II was that Catholics began to believe that sin was perhaps not an objective phenomenon out there for all time, determined by some external unchanging authority, but highly situational and subject to legitimate redefinition over time. (1989, p. 17)

By the same token, when you inform your parishioners that it no longer is a sin to miss mass, you can expect fewer people in the pews on a given Sunday. Indeed, Catholics now attend church like Protestants. Before Vatican II, Catholics far surpassed Protestants in the proportion attending church *every* Sunday. But if the cutting point were dropped slightly, to the proportion attending several times a month, the Protestant and Catholic figures would be about the same (Stark and Glock, 1968). Once Catholics placed no more stress on attendance than Protestants do, their behaviors converged.

A final aspect of the religious assimilation of American Catholics is the secularization of Catholic higher education. Most Catholic colleges and universities were founded by religious orders or the local diocese, and were considered important components in the comprehensive Catholic subculture. But as Catholics became increasingly assimilated, many Catholic scholars wanted to break out of the ghetto of Catholic education. Speaking at the Catholic Commission on Intellectual and Cultural Affairs annual meeting in 1955, John Tracy Ellis, Professor of Church History at the Catholic University of America, charged American Catholics with a failure "to exercise commanding influence in intellectual circles" (in Power, 1972, p. 382). But not for much longer. With the increasing size and affluence of Catholic universities and the reforms of Vatican II, Catholic higher education became quite secularized. The laity were given partial or complete control of the boards of trustees, the number of lay administrators gradually increased, and new faculty were hired and promoted on the basis of secular standards of professional achievement (Greeley, 1969). The new style of Catholic university placed more stress on academic freedom and encouraged a greater diversity of research and scholarship (Annarelli, 1987). But the secular achievements of the new university were at the expense of the mission of the old, and many questions can be raised about how and whether these universities now differ from their secular counterparts (Gleason, 1967). They make substantial contributions to scholarship and professional training, but they are not good places for preserving the faith or for the encouragement of religious vocations. And this takes us back to the crisis in Catholic vocations.

The Religious

The ability of the Catholic Church to compete effectively in the free market American religious economy rested upon its ability to motivate sacrifice—on the willingness of thousands of men and women to take up lives of chastity, poverty, and obedience. Just as the Methodists and the Baptists could sustain churches on the frontiers, so could the Catholics. Nor did the Catholics lack for dedicated revival preachers. Moreover, Protestant sects for many years never matched the Catholics in offering religious roles to women, without whom American Catholics could never have sustained their institutional separatism.

The extraordinary decline in religious vocations therefore strikes at the very foundation of the church. Not only are far fewer young Catholics entering seminaries or joining religious orders, but many priests, monks, and sisters have been dropping out of the religious life. Prior to Vatican II the annual rate of those leaving the priesthood was about one in a thousand. But immediately after the council the rate shot upwards. During 1969, 2 percent of the nation's priests dropped out, or twenty of every thousand. The rate of priestly defections has declined since then, but has been holding steady at about seven per thousand (Schoenherr and Young, 1990). Sisters followed a similar pattern of defection, peaking in 1970 (Modde, 1974).

There has been an immense amount of research aimed at explaining why Catholic seminaries have been closing for lack of students and why men and women who took sacred, lifelong vows have so frequently been asking to be released from them. The consensus among researchers is that the *personal costs* of the Catholic religious life are too great for many to bear. Among the most frequently cited costs are celibacy, loneliness, unpleasant assignments, and, among the women religious, the subordinate role of women in the church (Fichter, 1968; Greeley, 1972; Schoenherr and Greeley, 1974; Ebaugh, 1977; Seidler, 1979; Seidler and Meyer, 1989). The question must arise, however, why only recently? These have been the costs of Catholic religious life for centuries. In 1962, as the council opened its first session, the seminaries were full of young men fully aware of the costs involved in the life they sought. The thousands of young women who took their vows that year knew full well what was expected of them as "brides of Christ." Costs alone cannot provide the answer, because the costs did not rise. Indeed, liberalization of the rules governing most religious orders would appear to have substantially reduced the personal sacrifices of belonging. And yet defection rates rose.

Faiths that impose high costs offset them by providing high levels of reward. Hence, when people cease choosing to sacrifice we must suspect that they no longer are getting a good deal—or at least that they no longer perceive the exchange as favorable. Because the sacrifices asked of American Catholic religious did not rise, their terms of exchange could have turned unfavorable only if there was a decline in the rewards entailed in the religious life.

Why would anyone want to become a priest or a sister? The first answer must involve religious motivation. The sacrifices involved are far too great for anyone who is not inspired by religious convictions to accept them. When Mother Teresa corrected a reporter who referred to her fellow sisters as social workers, saying "We are not social workers, we do this for Jesus," she expressed the inner conviction that makes sense of her life's work. Research on priests has always found that the primary motives and satisfactions are of a religious nature (Fichter, 1961; Schoenherr and Greeley, 1974; Verdieck, Shields, and Hoge, 1988).

But following Vatican II, Catholics began to redefine their faith and how it related to the church. Helen Rose Ebaugh (herself a former sister) argued in her 1990 presidential address to the Association for the Sociology of Religion that Vatican II caused an extraordinary shift away from a churchly faith based on clear doctrines and rules, backed by a strong, hierarchical institution, to a highly personalized faith. Ebaugh (1991, p. 7) believes that "the autonomy of individual conscience has replaced official pronouncements of morality" and that this in turn has led to a "selective Catholicism," in which people pick and choose which doctrines to accept and in which aspect of institutional life they wish to take part. This shift has been especially evident in young Catholics. A series of recent studies have confirmed that younger Catholics hold a weaker allegiance to their church (McNamara, 1992; D'Antonio et al., 1996; Hoge et al., 2001). James D. Davidson and his colleagues (1997) found that when Catholics were asked if they agreed that "the Catholic Church is the one true Church," 58 percent of those raised in the church prior to Vatican II (born before 1941) strongly agreed, whereas only 34 percent of those born from 1940–1960 and 30 percent of those born after 1960 strongly agreed.

Because intense otherworldliness is needed to motivate the religious, this cafeteria approach to religious doctrine and lack of confidence in the authority of the church creates a very special problem for the Roman Catholic Church. It is one thing to accept a life of sacrifice if one is certain that his or her actions are seen from above and they are serving the one true church. It is something else again to make great sacrifices on behalf of modernized doctrines and within a church that is one of many "true" churches. Put another way, to become the bride of Christ one must be utterly confident of Christ's personal awareness of you; otherwise it is a purely symbolic relationship. It is not at all clear that one can accept vows of celibacy and obedience on behalf of abstract ideas about virtue and goodness. We conclude that the crisis of vocations thus reflects a crisis of faith and the deep erosion of the power of traditional Catholic symbols and sacraments. Greeley (1982, p. 88) has expressed this point as well as anyone: "anyone save an academic or a bishop would have anticipated that, when you change that which was unchangeable for 1,500 years, you are going to create a religious crisis. Attempts to put together a new system of religious symbols were halfhearted, unplanned and, most of all, insensitive to the actual religious needs of the Christian people."

Although people take up the religious life primarily for religious reasons, it must not obscure the fact that they respond favorably to worldly, tangible rewards as well. Chief among these for Catholic religious have been status and power. The immense respect in which American Catholics held their priests and sisters in pre-Vatican days would be hard to exaggerate.[15] Ebaugh (1991, p. 8) has noted: "While the notion of papal infallibility strictly applied only to doctrinal pronouncements of the Pope, it carried for the laity the generalized notion that the Pope had the god-given authority to speak the truth in all matters, spiritual and temporal. The aura of authority filtered down through the hierarchical ranks such that bishops and local priests were also considered dispensers of truth even in the slightest matters of faith and morals." The power and authority of priests was a matter of specific Catholic doctrine. In 1888 Pope Leo XIII wrote: "It is indeed certain that in the Church there are two orders . . . the leaders and the people. The first order has the duty to teach, to govern, to guide men through life, and to fix rules for them; the duty of the other is to submit to the first, to obey, to carry out its orders and to pay it honor" (in Liebard, 1978, p. 1). The language was softened in the years that followed, but the "two orders" remained. The priest's authority was unquestioned, and he was conceived of as being set apart and above the people.

But after Vatican II, Peter Shannon (1967, p. 92), a past president of the Canon Law Society, wrote that "now we realize that the priest must be one with his people, not 'set apart' or 'above,' but united with, immersed in, a servant of his people." The role of the priest in the new church was still not clear, but the direction of change was obvious. Documents from the Second Vatican Council, such as the *Decree on the Apostolate of the Laity*, stated that lay people shared "in the priestly, prophetic and royal office of Christ," and called on secular priests to allow laity to "share actively in the life and action of His church," "in the liturgical life," and to "work in close cooperation" with the laity (in Liebard, 1978, pp. 220, 228–229).

The result was a profound loss of priestly power and authority. Paul F. D'Arcy and Eugene C. Kennedy, priests as well as psychologists, warned of the dangers:

> The aggiornamento has brought to priests not peace but a sword. Within the last year, as trumpets of new hope have been heard throughout the world, many priests have experienced deep and searing conflicts. Paradoxically, as unparalleled opportunities seem about to open for the Church, her priests have tasted a bitter harvest of self-doubt and frustration.
>
> The recurrent question among many serious priests concerns their own future. In a world of changed liturgy and emerged laymen, the function of the priest in relation to the Christian community is being examined. If it is true that many of the activities he now supervises . . . will gradually be assumed by an eager and better-prepared laity, what dimensions will his own work assume? (1965, pp. 228–229)

Joseph Fichter (1968) observed many of these same concerns when he asked priests if they attempted to interest boys in the priestly vocations. Fichter reports "a recurring theme is that the parish priests are themselves 'unsure' of their own role" (1968, p. 80). As a result of the confusion surrounding the priesthood, the parish priest, once a primary motivator for boys to enter the vocation, was less willing to "talk up" vocations and more willing to question his own.[16]

The uncertainty of diocesan priests in the mid-sixties was warranted. In the years that followed, the relationship between the laity and the priests did change. The reestablishment of the permanent diaconate, the growing number of parish councils, and the increasing role of the laity throughout the church reduced as well as changed the role of the priest. The laity were still dependent on the priest for the Eucharistic sacrament, but in many areas of administration, liturgy, and education the laity were filling roles previously reserved for priests or sisters.

This does not mean that the priests—especially the young priests—necessarily objected to the changes being implemented. Seventy-six percent reported that the inclusion of the laity in parish planning was occurring too slowly, and 65 percent thought that the pace of liturgical adaptations was "about right"—with 30 percent responding "too slowly" (Fichter, 1968). But their support for change did not ensure that they would remain in the priesthood. To the contrary, priests scoring high on "modern values" relating to the church and its teachings were more inclined to leave (Schoenherr and Greeley, 1974).

For the priesthood, the result of Vatican II was a reduction of benefits without a reduction of costs. Indeed, it soon became clear that while many of the former rewards of the priesthood were gone, one could attain many of the rewards that remained as a member of the laity and thus avoid the major costs of the traditional religious life, such as celibacy, entirely. No wonder many resigned and few signed up.

The changes for religious orders were equally striking. Three Council documents, in particular, impelled a revolution in the religious life. The first, *Lumen Gentium*, declared that *all* Christians were called "to holiness" simply by having been baptized, and those who pursued a religious vocation could no longer aspire to a superior state of holiness. Previously the Church had taught that priests and the religious were in a superior state of holiness. Now, despite their vows, they were just like everyone else. As Patricia Wittberg put it:

> The importance of this . . . statement cannot be stressed enough. *In one stroke, it nullified the basic ideological foundation for eighteen centuries of Roman Catholic religious life.* The traditional ideology had postulated . . . that only vowed members of religious orders could achieve true spiritual perfection. (1994, p. 214; italics in the original)

This change was especially devastating for women religious. Unlike men, they had never been granted ordination, and now their holiness was reduced to that of all other lay Catholics. The second document, *Gaudium et Spes* ("The Church in the Modern World"), revoked centuries of preference for withdrawal from the "sinful world" and proclaimed that it now was inappropriate for the religious to pursue a cloistered life, and that they should become full participants in the secular world. Indeed, this document stressed the need to modernize the entire lifestyle of the orders.

The third document, *Perfectae Caritatis* (usually referred to as the "Decree on the Up-to-Date Renewal of Religious Life") was released in October of 1965, just as the Council came to a close. Although it was quite vague on the outcomes expected or the methods used for renewal, a single sentence opened the door for dramatic revisions by religious orders, most of them by then primed for radical changes: "The manner of life, of prayer and of work should be in harmony with present-day physical and psychological conditions of the members" (quoted in Flannery, 1992, p. 613). Soon, entire orders abandoned their convents for a new life as scattered apartment dwellers, often without roommates, and dressed like everyone else.

The rewards that once distinguished nuns from lay people performing the same tasks were inherent in those aspects of the religious life which the orders would "update" or abandon: the separated life in a religious community, the daily devotions, the habit which resulted in instant recognition, and special treatment by a laity who acknowledged the greater holiness of the religious. With these rewards gone, nuns now compared themselves to others performing the same occupation and asked themselves, "Why?" Why be a nun in addition to being a teacher? What does a woman gain in return for her vows of celibacy, poverty, and obedience, if she lives alone in an apartment where her devotional life is not amplified by collective participation, and who acquires no special holiness thereby, while spending her working hours side-by-side with married women who now are officially seen as her equal in terms of virtue, but who are free from her obligations?

To sum up our view, many of the most distinctive aspects of Catholic liturgy, theology and practice, abandoned by the Council, turned out to have been crucial for generating and sustaining vocations, especially vocations sufficient to meet the high costs of Catholic religious life (Finke, 1997; Stark and Finke, 2000).

Appealing to New Immigrants

Despite the dismantling of Catholic institutions, a collapse in religious vocations, and eroding membership commitment, the American Catholic Church has continued to gain members. Fueled by a steady flow of immigrants, with high fertility rates, the percentage of Catholics in the population declined only slightly from 240 per 1000 in 1965 to 229 in 2003. With over 37 million Hispanics in the United States in 2002, and surveys reporting 50 percent and more identifying as Catholic, Hispanics and other immigrants represent a rapidly increasing portion of the church. Two major national polls recently found that 28–29 percent of Catholic respondents are now Hispanic and even conservative estimates place the percentage around 20 percent or above.[17] With immigration from Latin America exceeding 380,000 in 2000 and the fertility rate for Hispanics approximately 50 percent higher than the national rate, the church should be primed for continued growth.[18]

Even in this area of growth, however, the signs of a secularized institution are evident. In Chapter 4 we described American Catholicism of the late nineteenth and early twentieth centuries as an Irish sect movement. Producing an abundance of bishops and other religious, the Irish led a sect-like movement that drew clear moral and religious boundaries from the larger culture and aggressively sought out new immigrants. Once new immigrants enrolled, the church instilled a level of commitment that far exceeded anything imagined in the old country. But the accommodated and affluent Catholic Church of today has been slower to respond to the new immigrants and less able to build the ethnic Catholic enclave of the past (Díaz-Stevens and Stevens-Arroyo, 1998). The result is that the local parish does not serve as a hub for the ethnic community and Hispanic Catholics are getting involved at a level that is similar or slightly lower than other American Catholics.[19]

Although the rate of defection from Catholic parishes to conservative Protestant churches is still open for debate, several findings are clear (Greeley, 1988, 1994; Christiano, 1991; Hunt, 1998, 1999). First, the proportion of Protestant Hispanics is increasing as the proportion for Catholics declines. Greeley (1988, p. 62) has called these losses an "ecclesiastical failure of unprecedented proportions." Second, Protestant Hispanics hold higher levels of religious commitment than Catholic Hispanics. Whether the survey questions are about church attendance, prayer, or belief in the Bible, Hispanic Protestants report higher levels of religious activity and belief. Third, the higher level of commitment and the smaller congregations are generating more Hispanic leadership in the Protestant congregations. Since only 2 percent of American priests and 10 percent of the permanent (lay) deacons are Hispanic, there has been little Hispanic leadership in the local parish or the larger church (Froehle and Gautier, 2000).

Each of the survey findings reported above have been confirmed by research in local Hispanic congregations. When interviewing former Catholics at a Pentecostal church in Los Angeles, Luís León (1998, p. 188) found that they joined the church for a "feeling of belonging, the music, the message of security and control over life . . . friendship, and intimacy." A Hispanic woman living near the church offered a simple yet revealing answer on why she joined the Pentecostal church: "I came . . . because they invited me." When studying a Hispanic Catholic parish in Houston, Kathleen Sullivan (2000, p. 201) found that many Catholics converting to Protestantism felt "alienated" by the Catholic Church and reported that "Protestant churches were more willing than the Catholic Church to assist them in finding jobs and housing, developing the local knowledge, and making the connections needed to be successful in their new home." Even those who remained within the Catholic Church were not averse to visiting the Protestants. Sullivan explains that "some members . . . are Catholic on Saturday nights and equally Pentecostal, Methodist, or Baptist on Sunday morning." Hence, despite a promise for continued growth and holding an apparent advantage over other churches in attracting Hispanics, the American Catholic Church struggles to attract and hold new immigrants.

Future Prospects

Attracting new immigrants is one of many challenges facing the American Catholic Church. But the larger concern for both Catholics and mainline Protestants is how to regain their lost organizational vigor. This raises a series of questions. Can large and successful religious bodies resist the forces that typically transform sects into churches? Can the process be reversed? If the process is reversed, will organizational vitality return? We conclude by discussing the possibilities and prospects of such a reversal.

Future Prospects for Catholics

To suggest that the Catholic Church cannot reverse the trend would conveniently ignore nearly two millennia of church history. The Counter-Reformation of the fifteenth and sixteenth centuries reversed a long trend of moral laxity, institutional corruption, and spiritual apathy. When the renewal activities of new and existing religious orders, were combined with the organizational reforms of Pope Paul III and the Council of Trent (1534–1549), the church reaffirmed many moral teachings and doctrinal tenets. New catechisms, prayer books, and clerical education helped to clarify what it meant to be Catholic, and devotional practices and readings gave attention to spiritual renewal. But is even a modest version of such a renewal possible in the American Catholic Church? And, if so, would it make a difference? We will begin with the latter question first.

Earlier we argued that when the demands of community living, daily devotions, and the wearing of distinctive garb were dropped for women religious following Vatican II, many of the rewards of living in a religious community were eliminated and membership in orders declined. This suggests that retaining the traditional demands of community life should increase the appeal of a very costly commitment. A 1993 survey of religious communities by the Center for Applied Research in the Apostolate (CARA) allowed us to test this thesis (Finke, 1997; Stark and Finke, 2000). We found that religious orders retaining the more traditional demands had far more members in formation programs, more novices entering, and more sisters taking final vows (see Table 7.5). The differences are highly significant. Orders emphasizing the importance of religious houses and physical proximity have a new member rate that is over four times higher than those giving less emphasis to these aspects of community (107 to 23). Retaining the same spirituality since Vatican II and only training novices in their own community are also associated with sharply higher rates of recruitment. Note that we do not suggest that potential recruits are attracted to the high costs of community life, as if shopping for the most "expensive" order available. Rather, recruits tolerate these costs because they are attracted to the wealth of social and religious rewards provided by a stable community of religious life.

A similar finding is evident when we look at diocesan priests. Although a national survey of all American dioceses was not available, we did ask a group of expert observers to identify the ten most traditional and the

Table 7.5
Recruitment and Commitment to "Tradition" among 531 Catholic Women's Religious Orders (rates per 1,000 members)

Life in religious houses and in physical proximity rated as "extremely important."

	Yes	No
Number of novices in formation:	107	23
Number of novices entering in 1992:	48	6
Number taking final vows in 1992:	22	5

Order has changed its "spirituality" since Vatican II

	Yes	No
Number of novices in formation:	41	95
Number of novices entering in 1992:	15	43
Number taking final vows in 1992:	6	22

Novices are trained only by their own community

	Yes	No
Number of novices in formation:	120	40
Number of novices entering in 1992:	56	13
Number taking final vows in 1992:	21	10

SOURCE: A 1993 survey of religious communities conducted by the Center for Applied Research in the Apostolate (CARA).
NOTE: All differences are significant beyond 0.01.

ten most progressive dioceses. We explained that we were interested "primarily in the cultural context that has prevailed in the diocese over the past five years or so." To identify our set of traditional and progressive dioceses, we included only those named by six or more of the nine raters. This resulted in the six traditional and eight progressive dioceses shown in Table 7.6.[20] The differences are quite astonishing. The traditional dioceses are far more successful at attracting young men to the priesthood. Only Saginaw, Michigan, with the highest ordination rate (2.0) among the progressive dioceses, has a rate higher than any of the traditional dioceses. The traditional dioceses are about four times more productive of priests. Even if we delete Lincoln, Nebraska, the ratio favors the traditional dioceses by three to one, and there is no obvious reason

Table 7.6

Diocesan Culture and Ordinations per 100,000 Catholics[*]

TRADITIONAL	
Lincoln, Nebr.	10.6
Arlington, Va.	5.1
Bridgeport, Conn.	3.1
Scranton, Pa.	2.5
St. Louis, Mo.	1.8
Camden, N.J.	1.7
Mean =	4.1
Mean without Lincoln	2.8
PROGRESSIVE	
Saginaw, Mich.	2.0
New Ulm, Minn.	1.4
Albany, N.Y.	1.2
Milwaukee, Wisc.	1.0
Joliet, Ill.	0.6
San Francisco, Calif.	0.5
Rochester, N.Y.	0.3
Richmond, Va.	0.0
Mean =	0.9

[*]Data for 1994 and 1995

why this diocese, which has been much in the press for its bishop's traditional pronouncements, should be dropped. Indeed, Lincoln would seem be the truly compelling example in support of our position. Several colleagues have suggested that these findings are misleading because young men from elsewhere are attracted to seminaries in the traditional dioceses, thus inflating their rates. This might be so. If it is, surely the relative failure of the progressive dioceses similarly to attract outsiders simply supports our argument about the basis of Catholic vocations.

Other studies also suggest that recent recruits are attracted to the traditional rewards of religious vocations. Dean R. Hoge and Jacqueline E. Wenger's (2003, p. 69) 2001 survey of priests found that young priests are more willing to reintroduce pre–Vatican II practices and they "insist that the priest is distinct from the laity." When asked if "ordination confers on the priest a new status or a permanent character which makes him essentially different from the laity," 94 percent of the priests between the ages of twenty-five to thirty-five agreed, but only 69 percent of those from fifty-six to sixty-five agreed. Patricia Wittberg's (1997, p. 245) study of emerging new religious orders has found a consistent pattern with the new communities: "the majority stated that they were reviving ancient monastic or eremitical traditions." The wearing of a traditional habit was more common and community life received renewed emphasis.[21] Albert DiIanni (1993, p. 747) argues that the new religious orders are attracting vocations because they offer "intense community life and ritualized community structure, new practices of common prayer, and clear community goals."

Each of these examples suggests that reversing some of the changes following Vatican II does, in fact, make a difference. When the rewards for religious vocations are restored, more sign up. But does this mean that the American Catholic Church is seeking to reverse past trends and become more sect-like again? The bulk of the evidence would suggest otherwise. Below we review the unique organizational features of Catholicism and how each has served to deter secularization and promote renewal. In each case, however, we see little evidence for an impending reversal of trends.

First, the high cost of vocations screens out those with tepid commitment or a wavering faith. This higher level of commitment is significant, because efforts to reduce a church's tension with the surrounding culture often arise from the clergy. For the rapidly growing Protestant sects it was the educated clergy who sought to reduce the demands and distinctiveness of the movements. The high costs screen out those without the religious motivation needed to make major sacrifices on behalf of faith. This is clearly evident when we compare Catholic seminarians holding a vow of celibacy with those who do not. For those with a vow of celibacy, experiencing a "call from God" is most likely to be rated very important for selecting their profession. For those Catholic seminarians without a vow of celibacy (the laity), "intellectual interest in religious questions" receives the top ranking (Stark and Finke, 2000, p. 182). Once out of seminaries, Catholic priests continue to show more religious motivation by devoting more time to prayer than their Protestant peers, especially those in the mainline (Brunette-Hill and Finke, 1999; Finke and Dougherty, 2002). Thus, the high costs reserve Catholic vocations for those with a high level of religious commitment. The religious life requires more than an interest in theology or a passion for public speaking, it is a calling that demands sacrifice and devotion.

But regardless of the devotion of those in vocations, the question arises:

can the dwindling numbers continue to shape the life of the local congregation? Despite the relative success of traditional orders and dioceses in attracting new recruits, the overall trend remains an ongoing drop in new vocations. Even when compared to 1990, the 2003 totals for seminarians and newly ordained priests have dropped by over 25 percent, despite the growing membership of the church. Initially this reduction resulted in fewer priests at large parishes and other Catholic institutions. By the year 2000, however, this translated into 13 percent of all Catholic parishes (approximately 2,500 parishes) lacking a resident pastor (Froehle and Gautier, 2000).

This suggests that the only way the American Catholic Church can recruit the people needed to staff the institution is by *reducing the costs*. This means, of course, that many people holding jobs once performed by the religious will be lay members. It also means that the line between religious and lay will become very indistinct, just as the line between Protestant pastors and their members is slight. If the church takes this solution to the crisis of vocations, it also thereby becomes substantially more mainline—with all of the eventual consequences of such a shift.

The second major point to be recognized is that unlike most Protestant bodies in America, Catholicism is an international faith. Decisions made in Rome can have substantial impact on Catholicism in other nations. Some recent decisions have been meant to make the American church more otherworldly again and restore firmer hierarchical authority. Conservatives appear to outnumber liberals among American bishops once more, for example, and disciplinary actions have been taken against several liberal Catholic theologians who have challenged various doctrines of the church. Ignoring the cries of outrage from within the American Catholic Church, John Paul has clearly been trying to make the American church less mainline in terms of theology.

The most significant Vatican decisions, however, are not targeted at any one nation. They are pronouncements that address the international church. With Catholic membership increasing sharply in Latin America and Africa, as it declines in Europe and shows only modest gains in North America, the center of gravity is shifting South (Barrett, Kurian, and Johnson, 2001). When documenting this shift in detail, Philip Jenkins (2002, p. 196, 197) recently explained that the "hierarchy knows that the liberal issues dear to American or West European Catholics are irrelevant or worse to the socially traditional societies of the South." Even if Rome were willing to accommodate more fully to cultural standards, it would need to choose between cultures.

But regardless of the Pope and the larger hierarchy's position against liberalization, this does not ensure a change in the laity. The majority of rank-and-file Catholics in the United States and Europe seem to favor a much lower-tension faith. Changes in the hierarchy alone are not transforming the local church.

A third point is the Catholic Church's ability to retain sect movements within the fold. Internal renewal movements must always be taken into account when trying to read the future of American Catholicism. Currently there exists in the United States a large number of Catholic groups committed to a substantially higher-intensity version of their faith. Unlike sect movements within Protestant bodies, however, thus far the Catholic sect groups have remained within the formal structure of the church and no liberalization by defection has taken place. For doctrinal reasons these sect movements are determined to remain within the church. The Catholics most opposed to the liberalizing trends going on in the church are also those most committed to traditional Catholic doctrines concerning the Apostolic Succession and the One True Church. How can they defect to form a church lacking legitimacy?

But the most successful sect movements throughout the history of the church have been religious orders (Gannon, 1980; Stark and Bainbridge, 1985; Finke and Wittberg, 2000). Like Protestant sect movements, their messages of renewal and revival have often aroused mass movements. Unlike the sects, these movements are usually channeled within the church. Despite many new religious orders arising in recent years, however, the numbers within most of the orders remain small (Wittberg, 1997). Ironically, the Second Vatican Council's attempt at renewal has inadvertently handicapped one of the most effective and proven sources for doing so.

After considering all these possibilities, and acknowledging the unique organizational features of the Catholic Church, we think it unlikely that the American Catholic Church will be able to halt its transformation from an energetic sect into a sedate mainline body. For all the reasons we have discussed throughout this book, it would be surprising if the Catholic Church reversed its direction. But this prognosis by no means indicates that we expect it to disappear in the foreseeable future. After all, there are still 1.4 million Congregationalists (United Church of Christ) in our midst. What we do expect is that the American Catholic Church will behave like a member of the mainline. No longer in tension with the surrounding culture, the church will generate less commitment from its membership and will gradually fail to compete with a new generation of upstart sects.

Future Prospects for the Mainline

In recent work we have found that to the extent that people seek religion—and not all do—the demand is the highest for religions that offer close relations with the supernatural and distinctive demands for membership, without isolating individuals from the culture around them (Stark and Finke, 2000). Few want a religion that forces complete submission, requiring a life of isolation from secular society. Likewise, few want a religion whose God is so distant and powerless as to offer little assistance in daily living and few promises for the life hereafter. At either extreme of this continuum there is little opportunity for growth. Thus, as the God of the Protestant mainline becomes more distant, less powerful, and offers little direction for living, the mainline groups fall on the far end of the continuum with fewer potential members and more competitors.

This raises the question: Will the same market forces that tempt sects to drop some of their most onerous costs to secure growth also prompt mainline denominations to increase their tension with the larger culture? Just as the unregulated religious market offers few barriers for new up-starts, it offers no guarantees for the existing mainline. Churches that fail to attract members can *and do* go broke. For a time, mainline churches could ignore their rapid decline in market share because they continued to gain members; but for the last four decades the membership has declined and remaining members are getting older. How will the mainline respond?

Many prominent leaders within the Protestant mainline remain far removed and unconcerned with the beliefs of the people or the troubles of the local congregation. As his Newark diocese experienced severe membership losses, the now retired Episcopalian Bishop John Shelby Spong (1998, p. 227) tirelessly proclaimed that the Judeo-Christian conception of a conscious and concerned "theistic" God "is doomed to die, no matter how frantically or hysterically people seek to defend it. It will not survive." Many theologians at mainline Protestant seminaries would agree, and would go on to question the deity of Christ, the resurrection, and other beliefs held as essential Christian teachings by the laity. There are few signs that mainline leaders or seminaries are seeking to increase tension with the surrounding culture.

At the local congregation, however, evangelical pastors and laity are emerging and calling for a return to more traditional teachings. Based on past experiences, we would expect these traditionalists to be expelled, forming yet another sect. However, the new mainline evangelicals are not being kicked out. Ironically, the theological pluralism mainline evangelicals seek to eliminate has provided a barrier for their expulsion.[22]

One of the earliest evangelical mainline groups was the Good News movement founded by Charles W. Keysor in the United Methodist Church. In 1965 Keysor was asked to write an article for the Methodist ministers' journal, *New Christian Advocate*, outlining the central tenets of evangelical Methodists. After Keysor's essay "Methodism's Silent Minority" appeared he received over two hundred letters and phones calls from other Methodists, mostly pastors, lamenting their lack of contact with other evangelical Methodists and their feelings of being "cut off from the leadership of [their] church" (*Circuit Rider*, 1989, p. 6). So, less than a year later, Keysor launched *Good News* magazine. Incorporated as "A Forum for Scriptural Christianity" and seeking the revival of the United Methodist Church, *Good News* quickly became more than a magazine. By 1970 the *Good News* board sponsored their first national gathering, attracting 1,600 Methodists; and by 1976 they sponsored a newsletter for seminarians (*Catalyst*), published their own church school literature, launched efforts to promote evangelical delegates and statements at the General Conferences, established the Evangelical Missions Council, and promoted the founding of renewal groups at local conferences (Heidinger, 1992, pp. 14–19). As the circulation of the *Good News* magazine swelled to 20,000 and the growing list of services increased, many expected the young movement to split from the church like the Holiness groups of the past. But the leaders of the movement have consistently denied any desire to split from the denomination, insisting that they are "dedicated to the spiritual renewal and theological reform of our United Methodist Church" (*Circuit Rider*, 1989).

Nearly thirty years later, the Confessing Movement brought this effort to mobilize local clergy and congregations to an entirely new level. In 1994, ninety-two Methodist clergy, laity, bishops, and professors issued a Confessional Statement for the renewal and reform of the United Methodist Church, inviting others to support the statement. By 1996, 960 churches and 18,000 members signified support for the Confessional Statement. This support has continued to grow each year with 1,416 congregations, 3,975 pastors, and nearly 632,000 individuals supporting the Statement by the spring of 2002 (Confessing Movement, 2002, www.confessingumc.org). The Confessing Movement desires more than signatures; they also seek active participants for renewal, asking clergy and laity to "join" the movement to mobilize support and change in local conferences and congregations. They now have coordinators in sixty of the sixty-five United Methodist conferences.

A similar movement, the Confessing Church Movement, was started within the Presbyterian Church in 2001. Within one year 1,244 churches and 418,000 members from forty-five states had joined. The basic tenets of the movement mirrored those of other mainline evangelical groups: Jesus Christ alone is the way of salvation, the Bible is the infallible rule of faith and life, and God's people are called to holiness. Like other renewal movements, the Confessing Church Movement is not seeking to start a new denomination. To the contrary, it describes itself as a "growing, unstructured, grassroots, collection of independently gathered churches and individuals within the Presbyterian Church (USA) that have agreed to assert the reaffirmation of three basic confessional statements."[23] To date, the movement has no formal organization, constitution or bylaws.

We should also note that the clergy igniting these movements are not elderly pastors seeking a return to lost glory or past memories. A recent survey of Methodist clergy in a Midwestern conference found that the evangelical clergy are young, were often raised outside of the United Methodist Church, and have extensive social networks with other evangelicals. Over half of them attended evangelical seminaries and nearly 40 percent were involved in evangelical associations, such as Campus Crusade for Christ or InterVarsity Christian Fellowship, prior to attending the seminary (McKinney and Finke, 2002). Reversing the time-honored conflict between a "progressive" young clergy and their "reactionary" superiors, the Young Turks are seeking to free themselves from superiors committed to progressive theology.

The young clergy are calling for renewal and initial findings suggest that a renewal, of sorts, is underway. When the churches involved in the evangelical Willow Creek Association in 1996 were compared to those that were not, the affiliated congregations had far higher rates of attendance and financial giving. Of greatest significance is that the Methodist affiliated churches were *growing rapidly* in a declining denomination and the affiliated Presbyterians churches had curbed the decline. All of these changes were recorded in a brief three-year time span. Similar results were found when pastors in the Evangelical Fellowship (21 percent of all pastors assigned to congregations) of the Northern Indiana Conference were compared to other Methodist pastors in the conference. Over a two-year span, the congregations with a pastor in the Evangelical Fellowship increased in attendance and contributions as they slowed the loss of membership. The results were most striking when the evangelical clergy were young or the congregation had two or more pastors in the Evangelical Fellowship (Stark and Finke, 2000).

A final test compared clergy seeking to restore distinctive cultural boundaries with those trying to further reduce tension with the surrounding culture. The United Methodist Church's top legislative body added a statement to their Social Principles in 1996 stating: "Ceremonies that celebrate homosexual unions shall not be conducted by our ministers and shall not be conducted in our churches." Then on October 17, 1998, two prominent lay leaders from the California-Nevada Conference announced that they would be married at St. Mark's Methodist Church. The two women, along with their many supporters, offered this as an opportunity to celebrate their union and to challenge the existing policies of the United Methodist Church. They invited United Methodist pastors to show support for gay and lesbian marriages by serving as coofficiants at the wedding, whether in person or in absentia.[24]

The Confessing Movement and the Good News Movement were equally clear in their opposition to this union. A series of statements were released, but the most attention was given to a press conference held the day before the wedding by the Evangelical Renewal Fellowship (ERF), an informal fellowship of evangelical pastors and laity loosely aligned with the Confessing Movement. The president of the ERF described the couple as his friends, and asked fellow evangelicals not to disrupt the ceremony, but he was unequivocal in his opposition to the wedding, calling the relationship a sin and citing the Bible and the United Methodist's *Book of Discipline* as the foundations for his opposition.

These series of events placed the conference pastors into two distinct camps: pastors who sided with the ERF and sought more tension, and pastors who supported same-sex marriages and sought less tension—a large additional group included those who did not commit to either side. Once again, when the clergy's congregations were compared, the evangelical clergy showed growth in giving, attendance, and even membership, for pastors who had served in a congregation three years or longer. But the most dramatic changes were in congregations served by clergy seeking less tension with the culture. Congregations with "officiant" pastors showed sharp drops for all of the measures (Finke and Stark, 2001).

Returning to the questions posed at the beginning of this section, these results suggest that organizations' vitality can return when mainline congregations reverse the sect to church cycle and return to a less worldly faith. But can the young evangelical clergy and their congregants transform the larger denomination? Their initial impact is readily apparent. In addition to resurgence at the local level, they are striving to change national policies. The evangelical Methodists, who have been organized the longest, have already led efforts to affirm Jesus as the exclusive Lord and Savior, prevent the use of non-Trinitarian language in the liturgy, retain teachings that homosexuality is incompatible with Christian teachings, and have succeeded in having three evangelicals elected to a nine-member Judicial Council (the Methodists' version of a supreme court). President of the *Good News* magazine, James Heidinger, described the 2000 United Methodist General Conference as a "watershed" or turning point for the denomination and pronounced that evangelicals and centrists could now have a "genuine sense of hope for their church" (Heidinger, 2000).

Following the 2004 General Conference, however, the evangelical groups were less optimistic about a transformation. Despite their mounting support at the local level and an increasing influence on national policies, their unrelenting commitment to stay within the United Methodist Church began to waver. Heidinger acknowledged that the evangelical groups were "not going to sit down after another decade of dialogue and come to a mutually acceptable understanding" with liberal factions (Rutledge, 2004, p. 50). The president of the Confessing Movement, Bill Hinson, proposed that "the time has come when we must begin to explore an amicable and just separation that will free both sides from our cycle of pain and conflict" (Hinson, 2004). Although not speaking on behalf of the Confessing Movement, his comments revealed the doubts of evangelicals in their efforts transform the entire denomination.

These same efforts to return to traditional teachings are evident in Reform Judaism. This follows decades of discarding traditional teachings and practices. Responding to the emancipation of Jews in Europe early in the nineteenth century, Reform Judaism originated as a church movement (Steinberg, 1965). When given the opportunity to participate fully in civic and social life, many Jews found themselves prevented from doing so by the demands of orthodox observance. Kosher dietary restrictions, for example, prevented Jews from freely associating with gentiles just as their distinctive dress and appearance made them unacceptably unfashionable. Some Jews dealt with this problem by converting to Christianity. But, for many others who wished to retain some ties to their roots, the solution lay in a new form of Judaism that abandoned the "Law"—a Judaism freed from ethnicity (Steinberg, 1965; Stark, 2001). The extent to which Reform Jews rejected traditional observance was quite remarkable. During the early years they even refused to use the title of rabbi, instead referring to their clergy as "reverend." Indeed, as proclaimed by the Pittsburgh Platform, Reform Judaism rejected all aspects of orthodoxy which were:

> not adapted to the views and habits of modern civilization.
>
> We hold that all such Mosaic and Rabbinical laws as regulated diet, priestly purity and dress originated in ages and under the influence of ideas altogether foreign to our present mental and spiritual state.
>
> We recognize Judaism as a progressive religion, ever striving to be in accord with the postulates of reason. (Quoted in Steinberg, 1965, p. 125)

From these radical beginnings, Reform Judaism became progressively more liberal until it came to be regarded as a religion virtually devoid of conceptions of the sacred or of the supernatural—more philosophy than faith. And, as we have come to expect of the lowest tension faiths, Reform Jews came to display a pronounced lack of commitment: declining membership, poor attendance, waning contributions (Wertheimer, 1993).

Then in the aftermath of World War II, there was growing pressure from the Reform rank and file to reinstate certain traditional rituals in order to more fully identify with historic Judaism. In part this was a response to the horrors of the Holocaust and, in part, it stemmed from a growing membership of descendants of Jews from eastern Europe who were accustomed to a more traditional Judaism (the original Reform Movement began in Germany, and in America it had depended largely on German-American Jews). However, the Reform clergy would have no part of renewed observance. A leading rabbi explained in 1959 that "many [Reform Jews] seek comfort in the nostalgia of a romanticized Jewish past which never existed. We cannot lead our people forward by stumbling backward" (in Wertheimer, 1993, p. 11). In this same spirit, in 1955 the central policy committee ruled that traditional customs could not be observed at Bar Mitzvah and wedding ceremonies. But then, something changed. We suspect that a new generation of rabbis had rather more spiritual interests than did their predecessors. In any event, in 1979 the central policy committee reversed its 1955 ruling and acknowledged that such customs could now be observed "if a new generation finds them meaningful and useful in the practice of Judaism" (Wertheimer, 1993, p. 96).

And the new generation, clergy as well as laity, have found meaning in many of the orthodox religious observances and practices so vehemently discarded when the Reform Movement broke with Orthodoxy during the nineteenth century. There has been a marked increase in the use of Hebrew in services and "in many temples men don yarmulkes and prayer shawls, [and] kosher meals are prepared" (Wertheimer, 1993, p. 96). Meanwhile, a movement to reinstate the mikvah ritual bath following menstruation has been spreading among Reform women. In 2004, *Kosher Today* magazine reported that the U.S. kosher market has grown 15 percent annually for each of the last eight years. And so it has gone.

Like the Methodists, efforts to restore traditional teachings and practices are being led by the youth. Based on data from the 1990 National Jewish Population Survey (Kosmin and Lachman, 1993), there is a very strong reverse relationship between age and Jewish observance. For example, 61 percent of those aged eighteen to twenty-nine personally fasted on Yom Kippur compared to 44 percent of those over fifty. Among members of Reform Temples, those under thirty are far more likely than those over fifty to light Hanukkah candles, to attend Seder, to have had a Bar or Bath Mitzvah, or to buy kosher meat.

Finally, the move towards higher tension by Reform Jews also has reversed many years of declining membership. Between 1980 and 1998, the number of households enrolled in a Reform Temple had risen by 24 percent and the number of congregations has increased by 15 percent.

Yet, despite increasing numbers and a growing presence at national conventions, the mainline renewal groups remain a small minority within large and established bureaucracies. They have overcome several hurdles; many more remain. So can Methodists, or Presbyterians, or Reformed Jews, or any mainline denomination, successfully reverse the sect to church transformation? Maybe.

In Closing

This book began as an effort to describe and explain the churching of America—how it went from a nation in which most people did not belong to a church to one in which most people do. In pursuit of this goal, we found ourselves driven to dispute many received truths about American religion. The first of these is the portrayal of American religious history in terms of sudden shifts during which religiousness rises or falls willy-nilly in response to various cultural crises and social concerns. We find no basis for these claims, not in recent decades or in the past several centuries. What we do find to be the master trend of American religious history is a long, slow, and consistent increase in religious participation from 1776 to 1926—with the rate inching up slightly after 1926 and then hovering near 60 percent. We recognized that sudden shifts do occur in our religious economy, but these involve the rising and falling fortunes of religious firms, not the rise and fall of religion per se. Here we have been forced to dispute a second major misconception common to the general religious histories of America. Their authors have invariably managed to depict certain mainline Protestants as the winners, while a succession of sectarian challengers either slumped off into obscurity or mended their ways and joined the mainline. This is to tell the story entirely backwards.

But whatever we have managed to accomplish in terms of amending some of these basic notions about American religious history, we place far greater importance on our attempt to place this history within a dynamic sociological model. It is the idea of religious economies and the recognition of the sect-church process as its primary dynamic that we think justifies our efforts. In closing, we should offer a caveat about our theory on the fate of religious firms.

We do not believe that the sect-church process has the blind inevitability of Marx's dialectic or even of the wheel of karma. Humans are rational beings, not puppets enslaved to the strings of history, and always have the capacity to choose. What is history other than the record of the choices particular humans have made and the actions they have taken on the basis of their choices? The sect-church process appears so unstoppable because humans seem to have rather mixed motives when they make choices about religion. What we have in mind here is a sociological version of what John Wesley recognized as the inevitability of temptation.

Humans want their religion to be sufficiently potent, vivid, and compelling so that it can offer them rewards of great magnitude. People seek a religion that is capable of miracles and that imparts order and sanity to the human condition. The religious organizations that maximize these aspects of religion, however, also demand the highest price in terms of what the individual must do to qualify for these rewards. Moreover, because of the long-term exchange relations that religious organizations require, people are forever paying the costs in the here and now while most of the rewards are to be realized elsewhere and later. As a result, humans are prone to backslide, to get behind on their payments. As Mark put it, "The spirit truly is ready, but the flesh is weak" (14:38, King James translation). Thus, other things being equal, people will always be in favor of a modest reduction in their costs. In this fashion, humans begin to bargain with their churches for lower tension and fewer sacrifices. They usually succeed, both because it is those with the most influence—the clergy and the leading laity—who most desire to lower the level of sacrifice and because each reduction seems so small and engenders widespread approval. No doubt most Methodists were glad to be permitted to go to the circus, just as most Catholics probably welcomed the chance to skip mass from time to time. Thus does the sect-church process ensue.

There comes a point, however, when a religious body has become so worldly that its rewards are few and lacking in plausibility. When hell is gone, can heaven's departure be far behind? Here people begin to switch away. Some are recruited by very high-tension movements. Others move into the newest and least secularized mainline firms. Still others abandon all religion. These principles hardly constitute a wheel of karma, but they do seem to reveal the primary feature of our religious history: the mainline bodies are always headed for the sideline.

Appendix
Profile Tables, 1776 and 1850

TABLE A.1
Denominational Percentages by Colony, 1776, Based on
Number of Congregations

MAINE (*N* = 64)	
Congregationalist	60.9
Presbyterian	17.2
Episcopal	9.4
Baptist	7.8
Quaker	3.1
Lutheran	1.6
NEW HAMPSHIRE (*N* = 125)	
Congregationalist	63.2
Presbyterian	21.6
Baptist	8.8
Quaker	3.2
Episcopal	1.6
Other*	1.6
VERMONT (*N* = 20)	
Congregationalist	65.0
Presbyterian	10.0
Baptist	10.0
Episcopal	10.0
Other*	5.0

TABLE A.1 *(Continued)*

MASSACHUSETTS (N = 433)	
Congregationalist	71.6
Baptist	14.3
Quaker	4.2
Episcopal	3.7
Presbyterian	3.0
Methodist	0.2
Other*	3.0
RHODE ISLAND (N = 87)	
Baptist	57.5
Congregationalist	17.2
Quaker	12.6
Episcopal	6.9
Presbyterian	1.1
Moravian	1.1
Other*	3.4
CONNECTICUT (N = 310)	
Congregationalist	64.2
Episcopal	17.7
Baptist	9.4
Quaker	1.6
Presbyterian	1.3
Other*	5.8
NEW YORK (N = 220)	
Dutch Reformed	26.4
Presbyterian	15.9
Episcopal	15.5
Quaker	10.9
Lutheran	8.6
Baptist	8.2
German Reformed	4.5
Methodist	3.2
Moravian	2.3
Congregationalist	1.8
Roman Catholic	0.5
Other*	2.3

TABLE A.1 *(Continued)*

NEW JERSEY (N = 252)	
Presbyterian	30.5
Baptist	18.3
Quaker	15.5
Episcopal	11.5
Lutheran	9.5
Methodist	6.0
Dutch Reformed	3.2
German Reformed	2.4
Roman Catholic	2.0
Moravian	0.8
Congregationalist	0.4
PENNSYLVANIA (N = 535)	
Presbyterian	27.9
German Reformed	17.6
Quaker	15.3
Lutheran	9.7
Dutch Reformed	8.6
Episcopal	6.0
Baptist	4.9
Moravian	2.6
Roman Catholic	1.9
Methodist	0.2
Other*	54
DELAWARE (N = 67)	
Presbyterian	37.3
Episcopal	22.4
Quaker	19.4
Roman Catholic	9.0
Methodist	4.5
Baptist	4.5
Lutheran	1.5
Dutch Reformed	1.5
MARYLAND (N = 211)	
Episcopal	26.5
Roman Catholic	15.6
Presbyterian	14.2
Methodist	10.9

TABLE A.1 *(Continued)*

Quaker	10.9
German Reformed	7.6
Lutheran	7.1
Baptist	2.4
Moravian	1.0
Other*	2.8
VIRGINIA (N = 491)	
Episcopal	34.6
Baptist	29.9
Presbyterian	22.0
Quaker	7.1
Methodist	2.0
Lutheran	1.8
German Reformed	1.6
Roman Catholic	0.2
Other*	0.6
NORTH CAROLINA (N = 165)	
Presbyterian	28.5
Baptist	25.5
Quaker	18.2
Episcopal	14.5
German Reformed	7.2
Moravian	3.0
Lutheran	1.8
Methodist	1.2
SOUTH CAROLINA (N = 166)	
Presbyterian	31.3
Baptist	24.7
Episcopal	22.9
Lutheran	9.0
Quaker	4.8
German Reformed	2.4
Congregationalist	1.2
Other*	3.6
GEORGIA (N = 23)	
Baptist	30.4
Lutheran	21.7

TABLE A. I *(Continued)*

Presbyterian	13.0
Quaker	13.0
Episcopal	13.0
Congregationalist	4.3
Other*	4.3

SOURCE: See Table 2.2.
*Includes Separatist and Independent, Dunker, Mennonite, Huguenot, Sandemanian, and Jewish.

TABLE A.2

Denominational Adherents per 1,000 Population, 1850

NEW ENGLAND	
Maine (upstart ratio* = 2.80)	
Congregationalists	48
Episcopalians	2
Presbyterians	3
Baptists	89
Methodists	58
New Hampshire (upstart ratio = 1.33)	
Congregationalists	90
Episcopalians	3
Presbyterians	8
Baptists	82
Methodists	54
Vermont (upstart ratio = 1.35)	
Congregationalists	92
Episcopalians	8
Presbyterians	5
Baptists	56
Methodists	86
Massachusetts (upstart ratio = 1.03)	
Congregationalists	94
Episcopalians	7
Presbyterians	3
Baptists	58
Methodists	50
Rhode Island (upstart ratio 3.22)	
Congregationalists	32
Episcopalians	22
Presbyterians	0
Baptists	140
Methodists	34
Connecticut (upstart ratio = 0.80)	
Congregationalists	134
Episcopalians	32
Presbyterians	8
Baptists	58

TABLE A.2 *(Continued)*

Methodists	81
FORMER "MIDDLE COLONIES"	
New York (upstart ratio = 1.86)	
Congregationalists	13
Episcopalians	13
Presbyterians	51
Baptists	55
Methodists	88
New Jersey (upstart ratio = 1.95)	
Congregationalists	3
Episcopalians	12
Presbyterians	77
Baptists	47
Methodists	131
Pennsylvania (upstart ratio = 1.58)	
Congregationalists	1
Episcopalians	8
Presbyterians	67
Baptists	30
Methodists	90
Maryland (upstart ratio = 4.60)	
Congregationalists	0
Episcopalians	25
Presbyterians	19
Baptists	15
Methodists	189
Delaware (upstart ratio = 3.03)	
Congregationalists	0
Episcopalians	21
Presbyterians	48
Baptists	18
Methodists	191
FORMER SOUTHERN COLONIES	
Virginia (upstart ratio = 5.31)	
Congregationalists	0
Episcopalians	13
Presbyterians	32
Baptists	96

TABLE A.2 *(Continued)*

Methodists	143
North Carolina (upstart ratio = 8.19)	
Congregationalists	0
Episcopalians	4
Presbyterians	31
Baptists	129
Methodists	163
South Carolina (upstart ratio 4.88)	
Congregationalists	2
Episcopalians	12
Presbyterians	46
Baptists	136
Methodists	158
Georgia (upstart ratio = 16.13)	
Congregationalists	0
Episcopal	3
Presbyterians	21
Baptists	202
Methodists	173
FRONTIER: SOUTH	
Florida (upstart ratio = 5.33)	
Congregationalists	0
Episcopalians	11
Presbyterians	30
Baptists	77
Methodists	140
Alabama (upstart ratio 7.85)	
Congregationalists	0
Episcopalians	2
Presbyterians	34
Baptists	140
Methodists	143
Mississippi (upstart ratio = 6.32)	
Congregationalists	0
Episcopalians	2
Presbyterians	35
Baptists	107
Methodists	129

TABLE A.2 *(Continued)*

Louisiana (upstart ratio = 4.74)	
Congregationalists	0
Episcopalians	3
Presbyterians	8
Baptists	16
Methodists	36
Texas (upstart ratio = 6.67)	
Congregationalists	0
Episcopalians	1
Presbyterians	17
Baptists	29
Methodists	94
FRONTIER: BORDER	
Missouri (upstart ratio = 3.67)	
Congregationalists	0
Episcopalians	2
Presbyterians	30
Baptists	62
Methodists	56
Kentucky (upstart ratio = 5.93)	
Congregationalists	0
Episcopalians	2
Presbyterians	45
Baptists	168
Methodists	111
Tennessee (upstart ratio = 4.48)	
Congregationalists	0
Episcopalians	2
Presbyterians	60
Baptists	112
Methodists	164
Arkansas (upstart ratio = 5.42)	
Congregationalists	0
Episcopalians	0
Presbyterians	23
Baptists	52
Methodists	74
FRONTIER: NORTH	
Ohio (upstart ratio = 3.13)	
Congregationalists	9

TABLE A.2 *(Continued)*

Episcopalians	4
Presbyterians	59
Baptists	52
Methodists	174
Indiana (upstart ratio = 5.18)	
Congregationalists	1
Episcopalians	2
Presbyterians	48
Baptists	80
Methodists	180
Illinois (upstart ratio = 3.67)	
Congregationalists	8
Episcopalians	4
Presbyterians	44
Baptists	63
Methodists	141
Michigan (upstart ratio = 1.88)	
Congregationalists	11
Episcopalians	5
Presbyterians	24
Baptists	25
Methodists	52
Wisconsin (upstart ratio = 2.22)	
Congregationalists	15
Episcopalians	4
Presbyterians	12
Baptists	30
Methodists	40
Iowa (upstart ratio = 1.99)	
Congregationalists	11
Episcopalians	1
Presbyterians	18
Baptists	12
Methodists	47

SOURCES: The adherence rates were estimated from Bureau of the Census (1854) reports on the number of churches, the seating capacity of churches and the value of church property. See Finke and Stark (1986) for a complete discussion of the statistical procedures used to generate the estimates.

ˈThe upstart ratio represents the number of Methodists and Baptists for each Congregationalist, Episcopalian, and Presbyterian.

Notes

Preface

1. The comments from Greeley and Swierenga were taken from their reviews for the publisher.

Chapter 1   A New Approach to American Religious History

1. We should note, however, that Mark A. Noll's (2002) *The Old Religion in a New World* does offer an extended discussion on the effects of separating church and state.
2. Based on the General Social Survey the percentage reporting no religious preference doubled from 7 to 14 percent during the 1990s. Michael Hout and Claude S. Fischer (2003) attribute this change to demographics and a "symbolic statement" against the religious right.
3. A comparison of the 1926 census data for the city of Seattle with data collected in 1925 by the local church council gave strong support for the accuracy of the census data (Stark, 1992b).
4. In 1936 many evangelicals in the South and West refused to participate and by 1946 Jewish groups voiced special concern in the immediate aftermath of the Holocaust that all efforts to count or otherwise emphasize the Jewish presence could only inflame anti-Semitism.
5. To aid other scholars in assessing his data, Jernegan provided a detailed appendix which described his sources and methods. The opening paragraph reveals many of the primary sources used by Jernegan:

    The sources of information upon which the maps are based are many and varied. The principal original sources may be classified as follows: (a) records of individual churches, church books, minutes of meetings, letters, and other documents, commonly found among the archives of a church; (b) records of groups of churches organized as an association, presbytery, conference, council, coitus, ministerium, synod, etc.; (c) letters, diaries, journals, etc., particularly of clergy or of others directly concerned with the work of a church or group of churches. (1935, p. 49)

6. To estimate total adherents for denominations not counting children, we used the following equation: reported members × (total population ÷ (total population – children thirteen years and under)).

Chapter 2   The Colonial Era Revisited

1. Granted that Stiles believed the total population to be larger than that, placing the number of dissenters at 62,420. Thus he only claimed that 88 percent of New Englanders were Congregationalists. The actual proportion was closer to 13 percent.

2. For 1832 and 1841 not all diocese reported both the number of churches and the number of members. The 1832 average is based on eleven of the eighteen diocese and the 1841 average is based on eighteen of twenty-seven. With the exception of a few small missions, all diocese reported members and churches in 1860.

3. Although we admire the fine scholarship of these authors, we would disagree with their assumption of 480 adherents per church, even if we didn't have other data sources. Our informal tours of colonial churches reveal them to be exceptionally small. It would be difficult to seat one hundred people in most of those that either author has been in. As far back as good records go, American Protestants have always been optimistic builders—in 1890 Protestants averaged three seats per member nationwide (Finke and Stark, 1986).

4. In the words of Frederick Jackson Turner (1920), the "oldest west was the Atlantic Coast," and "the frontier towns of 1695 were hardly more than suburbs of Boston." Turner began his analysis of the significance of frontiers using Massachusetts of 1695 as his "early prototype."

5. Bailyn's extraordinary study is based on records made by British port officials, including 5,196 individuals leaving England and 3,872 leaving Scotland. Bailyn has managed to locate American records on many of these people, giving him the means for an immense study, only the first volume of which has appeared.

6. Muhlenberg later concluded that Pennsylvania, the colony with the most Lutherans and one of the highest rates of religious adherence, had "more necromancers . . . than Christians" (in Butler, 1990, p. 87).

7. Sometimes the liberal faction will leave, but usually those seeking higher tension lack the power to win the internal dispute, which is why the denomination had moved into lower tension in the first place.

8. For a complete explanation of why and how this occurs, see Stark and Bainbridge (1985, 1987).

9. For a discussion of religious declension and church membership in early New England, see Ahlstrom, 1975, vol. 1, pp. 208–210.

Chapter 3   The Upstart Sects Win America, 1776–1850

1. Some Congregational leaders still do not grasp the idea of market share. When discussing the process by which the Congregational and the Evangelical and Reformed Churches merged, Louis H. Gunneman (1977), a major figure in American Congregationalism, noted that the Congregationalists grew by 57,490 members between 1956 and 1960 while the Evangelical and Reformed grew by 33,681. He then acknowledged that these rates of growth fell far short of the national average for all churches during these years. Nevertheless, two sentences later he could write, "The obvious conclusion to be drawn is that during the time of the consummation of union both churches maintained rates of growth exhibiting high spirit and morale" (p. 59). This in 1977, after more than a decade of rapid membership declines.

2. Sweet (1976, p. 346) remarked that Beecher's account was dictated seventy years after the fact: "In his dotage, he constructed an exaggerated ash-heap of debauchery and irreligion at Yale." Beecher attributed the situation at Yale to the decay of religion in general.

3. Examination of Methodist membership statistics year by year does show a decline in six of the thirty-five years between 1776 and 1810. These could be noted as momentary ebb tides, but they cannot justify claims that religion fell on hard times for two decades or more. Moreover, we found no year during this period when Baptist membership declined. Careful regional studies of New York state and the city of Baltimore found no evidence of ebb tide during this time period (Bilhartz, 1986; Pointer, 1988).

4. For a more complete discussion of religious deregulation, see Finke (1990).

5. AHMS officials were entirely aware of the abundance of Methodists and Baptists in areas they sought funds to "church." More recently general historians, too, should have been aware of this fact, because it is a matter easily learned from denominational reports of the period, which are widely available.

6. For a complete account of the duties of the local exhorters, stewards, class-leaders, trustees, and local preachers, see Gorrie (1852).

7. Francis Asbury often referred to his circuit riders as "traveling bishops."

8. For example, Peter Cartwright helped to establish both McKendree and MacMurray Colleges and, while serving in the Illinois legislature, introduced the first bill to establish a state university (Miyakawa, 1964).

9. Cokesbury College was founded by the Methodists in 1787, but it burned to the ground in December of 1795. Asbury concluded that the "Lord called not Mr. Whitefield or the Methodists to build colleges." But Thomas Coke raised money for rebuilding, moved the school from Abingdon to Baltimore, Maryland, and changed the school to an academy rather than a college. But in December of 1796, the school was again destroyed by fire. With his typical candor, Asbury explained that "God loveth the people of Baltimore, and he will keep them poor, to make them pure" (as quoted in Bilhartz, 1986, p. 61).

10. See the 1871 *Baptist Quarterly* for a survey of Baptist opinion on an educated clergy.

11. Clearly the shortage persisted for many years. The 1820 *Minutes of the General Assembly* reported a total of 741 clergy and 108 licentiates for 1,299 congregations. Because some of the clergy did not hold congregational assignments and some congregations would have more than one pastor, the shortage was still severe.

12. When a circuit rider married he soon wanted to cease traveling and to "locate." This reduced the scope of his effect and made him far more expensive to sustain—he could no longer depend on the free meals and lodging often provided by families along the way, and soon had his own extra mouths to feed. Asbury frequently complained in his journals that women would get all his best traveling preachers.

13. In his day Asbury was thought to be the most famous man in the nation. He often received mail from abroad addressed to Francis Asbury, United States of America. Because he traveled a well-known itinerary from one conference meeting to another, the postal service prided itself in being able to deliver his mail.

14. For vivid details and a complete review of the religious experiences of Methodists and others in the nineteenth century, see Taves (1999). Also, for an account of the calls and messages Methodists received from God and the sounds they used in worship, see Schmidt (2000).

15. Lorenzo Dow, an eccentric Methodist itinerant, stated his case against Presbyterian Calvinism and their theological beliefs in predestination with the following jingle: "You can and you can't, you will and you won't, you'll be damned if you do, you'll be damned if you don't" (in Posey, 1965, p. 29).

16. See Cherry (1995) for an historical overview of divinity schools' struggles with intellect and piety.

17. We accept that instances of what might be classified as hysteria occurred during revival services—Finney provides quite complete descriptions of some. These symptoms, however, arose as a result of participation in a highly emotional service, and therefore cannot be claimed as a cause of the revival meeting. Moreover, nothing is explained by postulating some generalized angst or other equally vague psychological state as the precipitating cause of an awakening. We might just as well embrace the Zeitgeist as a major scientific force.

18. For a sample of the transforming powers attributed to the First Great Awakening, see Martin E. Marty's forward to McLoughlin's *Revivals, Awakenings, and Reform* (1978).

19. For a formal analysis of the functions of revival within religious organizations, see Stark and Bainbridge (1987).

20. The camp meeting was not the only major religious and social worship festi-

val of the early Methodists. For a more complete review of Methodist worship life, see Tucker (2001).

21. The 1851 totals include membership from the Methodist Episcopal Church and the Methodist Episcopal Church, South.

22. When Andrew Reed and James Matheson (1835a, vol. 1, p. 154) of England visited a worship service for slaves conducted by two black and two white preachers, they offered it as an experiment for testing the inequality of the races. They reported that "the experiment was undoubtedly in favour of the blacks. In sense and in feeling, both in prayer and address, they were equal to the whites; and in free and pointed expression much superior."

Chapter 4   The Coming of the Catholics

1. Notice, however, that these lumberjacks were not tithing.

2. It must be noted that Pope Leo had been misled to think that there had been massive defections, running into millions of members, to the Protestants.

3. Dolan (1978, p. 22) described a revival as an "occasion for a religious round-up of Catholics."

4. The religious orders were not alone in their outreach efforts, however. Aaron Abell (1960) reports that by 1908 thirty bands of diocesan priests were involved in missions to interested non-Catholics. Moreover, the laity often invited non-Catholics to attend church, especially during the time of a parish mission (Hennesey, 1981).

5. In the beginning Weninger preached four times a day in German during his missions. But, when his revivals attracted French- and English-speaking audiences he added sermons in these languages as well. Soon he was preaching as many as twelve times a day in three languages. He admitted that such a pace was "very taxing on the minister," but also noted that "the effect is far greater" (in Garraghan, 1984, p. 58).

6. Each car could seat about one hundred worshipers, and each was equipped with an organ and with living quarters for a missionary couple. When a chapel car arrived in a new town or village it was unhooked from the train and placed on a siding. Services were held nightly until a sufficient number had been gathered to found a new congregation, whereupon the chapel car was moved to another town. Despite relatively long stays in one place, each car traveled thousands of miles annually. In 1894 *Evangel*, a Baptist chapel car stationed in Minnesota, and *Emmanuel*, a Baptist car stationed in California, together logged 17,834 miles while the missionaries aboard delivered 1,313 sermons and held 207 prayer meetings (Mondello, 1987).

7. Female members of Catholic religious orders currently prefer to be called "sisters" or "women religious." We use the word "nun" in this chapter because it more accurately reflects common usage in the Catholic community during the era on which we are focusing.

8. Mission work in the United States was especially attractive for sisters who entered religious communities based in France, but did not have French citizenship. In France, unlike the United States, citizenship was required for teachers. Grace Donovan explains that "women of English, Irish, German nationalities who had entered congregations based in France were thereby relegated, no matter what their talents, to minor posts in schools" (1991, p. 196). In contrast, they were immediately given a wide range of teaching responsibilities in the new nation.

9. The convent school enrolled girls from upper-class Protestant and Unitarian backgrounds, but was located in a lower-class neighborhood. For congregational clergy and the neighborhood, the convent represented the threat of future "Catholic dominance" (Walch, 1996, p. 24).

Chapter 5   Methodists Transformed, Baptist Triumphant

1. Between 1860 and 1870 both Baptists and Methodists lost members due to the dislocations of the Civil War. Following the war the Methodist rate increased again, but they never regained their prewar level and failed to keep pace with the rapid Baptist gains.

2. As we will show later in this chapter, the increase in the Baptists' market share and the decline of the Methodists was similar for the black and white denominations. The trends hold regardless of the race of the churches.

3. After collecting data on 417 American-born sects, Stark and Bainbridge report that "nearly a third of all sects (32 percent) reached their high-water mark on the day they began" (1985, p. 134).

4. According to the 1916 census of religious bodies, the seminaries of the Northern Baptist Convention enrolled 997 students while the seminaries of the Southern Baptist Convention enrolled 708 students (including 220 females "preparing for missionary and social settlement work").

5. Although the administrative positions of deacon, elder, and pastor were typically limited to males, all members voted on matters of discipline and fellowship (Wills, 1997).

6. Unfortunately only 30 percent of all Southern Baptist ministers reported their salaries to the census, and therefore the exact percentage of ministers employed outside of the church is not known. But considering that farmer-preachers were most common in the rural South, where Landmarkism and resistance to central authorities were most prominent, the percentage employed outside the church was probably much higher than the 36 percent reported.

7. A similar opinion was expressed by the Southern Baptist Convention's Home Mission Board in 1891. They argued that "work among the colored people" should be increased and acknowledged that "to no people are we more deeply indebted than to them." But they went on to add that "nothing is plainer to any one who knows this race than its perfect willingness to accept a subordi-

nate place, provided that in that position of subordination it will receive justice and kindness" (in McBeth, 1990, pp. 286–287).

8. Despite a 34 percent increase in the number of AMEZ churches between 1890 and 1906, membership declined by 47 percent. Over reporting by the AMEZ in 1890, or a possible under reporting in 1906, might explain a portion of the sharp drop from 1890 to 1906 and the subsequent modest increase from 1906 to 1916.

9. The Methodist Episcopal Church reported 246,249 members and the Regular Baptists of the North were a distant second with 35,221members.

10. This was a personal victory for Payne. Thirty years prior, he was exiled from the Carolinas for "teaching colored children how to think and check" (in Richardson, 1976, p. 193).

Chapter 6   Why Unification Efforts Fail

1. If this position seems to echo the claims made on behalf of religious monopolies, keep in mind that the consequences of a fully successful ecumenical movement would be the creation of a religious monopoly.

2. An important exception is the work of Claude S. Fischer (1982). According to Fischer's subcultural theory, "urbanism bolsters ethnic and religious community, particularly if the group is small enough so that affiliation is difficult" (p. 202).

3. The American Baptist Association began in 1905, but did not officially split from the Southern Baptists until 1924. Because the ABA was included in the 1916 totals, we have included them in the 1926 totals to allow for a more accurate comparison.

4. Unlike the rural white population, the black population did plateau in the early twentieth century and began to decline in the 1930s. From 1930 to 1940 the rural black population declined by 10 percent. Most of this decline, however, would have occurred after Mays and Nicholson completed their research.

5. Marked denominational differences existed in Lenski's data. When these were pointed out by Babbie (1965), Lenski (1965) continued to claim that these were merely reflections of race, ethnicity, and region of birth.

6. Although the book is coauthored with Brunner, the chapters on church unity were apparently written by Douglass. The authors report, in the Preface, that "Dr. Brunner's contribution is confined to the rural sections, while Dr. Douglass is responsible for the rest of the volume" (1935, p. vii).

Chapter 7   Why "Mainline" Denominations Decline

1. Here, as throughout the book, we are referring to a declining share of all church adherents.

2. The popular mail-order guru Yogi Ramacharaka was actually an American named William Walker Atkinson (Melton, 1987).

3. In 1965 there were 467 immigrants from India, in 1966 there were 2,293, and Indian immigration now runs at over 30,000 per year.

4. From 1990 to 2003, the *Sociological Abstracts* alone found eighty-nine citations when searching for "New Age" and "religion." By contrast, during the same time period, there were only forty-one citations for the Jehovah's Witnesses, a religion with a rapid and sustained growth, and most of the citations were about legal cases involving the Jehovah's Witnesses, saying little or nothing about their religion. When the search was narrowed to "Jehovah Witnesses" and "religion" for 1990 to 2003 only twelve citations appeared.

5. Thomas Tweed (1999) offers a similar point for many Buddhist sympathizers in America, describing them as "Night-Stand Buddhists."

6. New Age groups suffer from ineffective leadership because when everyone is a "student," and everyone's ideas and insights are equally valid, then no one can say what must be done or who is to do what, when. The result is the existence of virtual nonorganizations—mere affinity or discussion groups incapable of action (Wagner, 1983).

7. The 1965 amendments to the Immigration and Nationality Act replaced country-of-origin quotas with a single quota for the Eastern and Western Hemisphere.

8. We would like to thank Ida Smith Williams and John Marcum of Research Services of the Presbyterian Church (USA) for providing the above data and for answering our many questions.

9. The sharp differences between the Korean churches and the larger Presbyterian Church (USA) have resulted in numerous tensions. Despite pressure from the PCUSA to ordain female elders, most Korean congregations prohibited the ordination of females until 1995 (Kim and Kim, 2001). The PCUSA continues to gain Korean congregations, but a growing number have affiliated with more conservative Presbyterians (Warner, 1994). The Korean Presbyterian Church in America reported 310 congregations in 2000, or approximately the same number of Korean congregations as the PCUSA.

10. Kelley was not the first to document this growth. In a little-noticed article in *Christianity Today*, Richard C. Wolf developed a series of tables documenting the rapid growth of conservative groups from 1900 to 1950. He concluded that the "more conservative groups have had greater success in enlisting members than have the more liberal groups" (1959, p. 6).

11. The Assemblies of God reports "full members" at 1,532,876 and "inclusive membership" at 2,627,029 in 2001. Even when we use the more conservative estimates, the Assemblies now outnumber the UCC.

12. In the social sciences there are few conditions or causes that are *sufficient* for explaining another event (i.e., the event always occurs when the cause is present). But this does not mean that the condition is not *necessary* for an event to occur. Our argument suggests that high costs alone don't explain growth,

but that high membership demands and distinctive boundaries are required for generating high levels of organizational vitality.

13. A series of recent publications recognize that some accommodation benefits organizational vitality while some does not (see Miller 1997; Smith, 1998; Sargeant, 2000; Carroll, 2000; Hoge, 2002; Miller, 2002; Dougherty, 2003).

14. Patricia Wittberg (2000) recently reminded us that these institutional transformations also changed the viability and mission of the orders that started these institutions. From schools to hospitals to social service agencies the declining numbers force them to surrender control of the very institutions they founded. This often results in a crisis of identity and mission for the orders as well as practical problems such as employment.

15. For a window into the extraordinary bonds between priests and their parishioners (and, indeed of the social rewards of the priesthood) of pre–Vatican II times, we recommend seeing Bing Crosby and Barry Fitzgerald in the 1944 Academy Award winning movie *Going My Way*. Before the film was released, Paramount held a special showing for the priests of Los Angeles. At the end of the movie, Paramount press agents were upset by the utter silence of the audience until they realized that the priests were too moved to speak and that there wasn't a dry eye in the house.

16. Dean Hoge (1987) reports that the level of encouragement priests provide for potential recruits to religious vocations declined sharply after the Second Vatican Council (as reported in a 1970 survey) and has increased slightly in the 1980s (based on a 1985 survey).

17. The 2001 American Religious Identification Survey of 50,281 residential households estimated that 29 percent of Catholics are Hispanic (Kosmin, Mayer, and Keysar, 2001) and the Center for Applied Research in the Apostolate's Catholic Poll estimated 28 percent. The 1999 Gallup Poll of Catholics (D'Antonio et al., 2001) and the General Social Surveys (2000 and 2002 combined) found 23 and 19 percent. The 1999 Gallup Poll and the General Social Surveys can be downloaded free of charge from the American Religion Data Archive (www.TheARDA.com).

18. Our attention has centered on Hispanics, due to the volume of Catholics entering from Latin America, but 3 percent of American Catholics report their ethnicity as Asian (Kosmin, Mayer, and Keysar, 2001).

19. Hoge et al. (2001), Froehle and Gautier (2000) and D'Antonio et al. (1996) find few differences between Hispanics and non-Hispanics in their samples. Using the 2000 and 2002 General Social Survey our own analysis found that Hispanic Catholics had slightly lower levels of involvement, but the differences were small. For example, 51 percent of Hispanic Catholics prayed daily or more and 56 percent of non-Hispanic Catholics did so. Thirty five percent of non-Hispanics attended mass about weekly or more compared to 27 percent for Hispanics.

20. For more details on this research, see Stark and Finke (2000).

21. Wittberg (1997, pp. 249–250) has pointed out that the "official Church has, to some extent, been backpedaling with respect to the equal status of 'the consecrated life' and the lay state." Recent Vatican documents, beginning with the 1983 Code of Canon Law, have implied that those in religious orders have a "holier" calling than the laity.

22. Evangelical renewal movements are proliferating within traditional mainline denominations. The American Baptist Church, Disciples of Christ, Episcopal Church, Evangelical Lutheran Church of America, the Presbyterian Church (USA), the United Methodist Church, and the United Church of Christ all have at least one active movement calling for renewal and a return to traditional teachings (McKinney, 2001; McKinney and Finke, 2002).

23. The confessional statements and quotes are taken from the Confessing Church Movement web site (http://www.confessingchurch.homestead.com).

24. The information on these recent events was taken from the United Methodist News Service (www.umc.org), billed as the "official news agency of The United Methodist Church."

Reference List

Abell, Aaron. 1960. *American Catholicism and Social Action: A Search for Social Justice, 1865–1950*. Garden City, N.Y.: Hanover House.

Adams, Robert Hickman. 1970. *White Churches of the Plains*. Boulder, Colo.: Colorado Associated Press.

Ahlstrom, Sydney E. 1975. *A Religious History of the American People*. Garden City, N.Y.: Image Books.

Alba, Richard D. 1990. *Ethnic Identity: The Transformation of White America*. New Haven: Yale University Press.

Alexander, June Granatir. 1987. *The Immigrant Church and Community: Pittsburgh's Slovak Catholics and Lutherans, 1880–1915*. Pittsburgh: University of Pittsburgh Press.

Alston, Jon P. 1969. "Occupational Placement and Mobility of Protestants and Catholics, 1953–1964." *Review of Religious Research* 10: 135–140.

Ammerman, Nancy Tatom. 1990. *Baptist Battles: Social Change and Religious Conflict in the Southern Baptist Convention*. New Brunswick, N.J.: Rutgers University Press.

Andrews, Dee E. 2000. *The Methodists and Revolutionary America, 1760–1800: The Shaping of an Evangelical Culture*. Princeton, N.J.: Princeton University Press.

Annarelli, James John. 1987. *Academic Freedom and Catholic Higher Education*. Westport, Conn.: Greenwood Press.

Appel, John, and Selma Appel. 1990. *Pat-riots to Patriots*. East Lansing, Mich.: Michigan State University.

Armstrong, O. K., and Marjorie M. Armstrong. 1967. *The Indomitable Baptists: A Narrative of Their Role in Shaping American History*. Garden City, N.Y.: Doubleday and Co.

Asbury, Francis. [1852] 1958. *Journal and Letters of Francis Asbury*. 3 vols. Nashville: Abingdon Press.

Asplund, John. 1790. *The Annual Register of the Baptist Denomination.*

Atkins, Gaius Glenn, and Frederick L. Fagley. 1942. *History of American Congregationalism.* Boston: Pilgrim Press.

Babbie, Earl. 1965. "The Religious Factor—Looking Forward." *Review of Religious Research* 7: 42–51.

———. 1990. "Channels to Elsewhere." In Thomas Robbins and Dick Anthony, eds., *In Gods We Trust.* 2d ed. New Brunswick, N.J.: Transaction Publishers.

Babcock, Rufus. 1841. "General Summary View of the Baptist Denominations in Each of the United States." *American Quarterly Register* (November): 184–186.

Bacon, Leonard Woolsey. 1897. *A History of American Christianity.* New York: Christian Literature Co.

Bailyn, Bernard. 1986. *Voyagers to the West: A Passage in the Peopling of America on the Eve of the Revolution.* New York: Knopf.

Bainbridge, William Sims. 1985. "Collective Behavior and Social Movements." In Rodney Stark, *Sociology.* Belmont, Calif.: Wadsworth Publishing Co.

Baird, Robert. [1844] 1969. *Religion in America; or an Account of the Origin, Progress, Relation to the State, [∞" Present Condition of the Evangelical Churches in the United States; with Notices of the Unevangelical Denominations.* New York: Arno Press.

Baker, Robert A. 1974. *The Southern Baptist Convention and Its People, 1607–1972.* Nashville: Broadman Press.

Baker, David P. 1992. "The Politics of American Catholic School Expansion, 1870–1930." In Bruce Fuller and Richard Rubinson, eds., *The Political Construction of Education: The State, School Expansion, and Economic Change.* New York: Praeger.

———. 1999. "Schooling All the Masses: Reconsidering the Origins of American Schooling in the Post-bellum Era." *Sociology of Education* 72: 197–215.

Bangs, Carl. 1972. "Deceptive Statistics." *Christian Century* 89: 852–853.

Barkun, Michael. 1986. *Crucible of the Millennium.* Syracuse: Syracuse University Press.

Barnes, Roswell P. 1960. "The Ecumenical Movement." *The Annals: Religion in American Society* 332: 135–145.

Barnhart, Joe Edward. 1986. *The Southern Baptist Holy War.* Austin: Texas Monthly Press.

Barr, Alwyn. 1997. "Black Urban Churches on the Southern Frontier, 1865–1900." *Journal of Negro History* 82: 368–383.

Barr, Josiah Henry. 1916. *Early Methodism under Persecution.* New York: The Methodist Book Concern.

Barrett, David B., George T. Kurian, and Todd M. Johnson. 2001. *World Christian Encyclopedia.* 2d ed. Oxford: Oxford University Press.

Beard, Charles A., and Mary R. Beard. 1930. *The Rise of American Civilization.* New York: Macmillan Co.

Beecher, Lyman. [1835] 1977. *Plea for the West.* New York: Arno Press.

Beecher, Lyman, and Asahel Nettleton. 1828. *Letters of the Rev. Dr. Beecher and Rev. Mr. Nettleton on the "New Measures" in Conducting Revivals of Religion.* New York: G. & C. Carvill.

Berger, Peter. 1963. "A Market Model for the Analysis of Ecumenicity." *Social Research* 30:77–93.

———. 1967. *The Sacred Canopy.* Garden City, N.Y.: Doubleday and Co.

———. 1979. *The Heretical Imperative: Contemporary Possibilities of Religious Affirmation.* New York: Doubleday and Co.

———. 1982. "From the Crisis of Religion to the Crisis of Secularity." In Mary Douglas and Steven M. Tipton, eds., *Religion and America: Spirituality in a Secular Age.* Boston: Beacon Press.

Berry, B., and J. Kasarda. 1978. *Contemporary Urban Ecology.* New York: Academic Press.

Bibby, Reginald W. 1978. "Why Conservative Churches Really Are Growing." *Journal for the Scientific Study of Religion* 2: 129–137.

Bibby, Reginald W., and Merlin B. Brinkerhoff. 1973. "The Circulation of the Saints." *Journal for the Scientific Study of Religion* 12: 273–283.

———. 1983. "Circulation of the Saints Revisited." *Journal for the Scientific Study of Religion* 22: 253–262.

Bilhartz, Terry D. 1986. *Urban Religion and the Second Great Awakening.* Cranbury, N.J.: Associated University Presses.

Billingsley, K. L. 1990. *From Mainline to Sideline.* Washington, D.C.: Ethics and Public Policy Center.

Bird, Steven. 1990. "The Blending of Catholic Political Behavior: Presidential Voting and Political Party Affiliation." Master's thesis, University of Washington.

Blake, Eugene Carson. 1959. "The American Churches and Ecumenical Mission." In Edward J. Jurji, ed., *The Ecumenical Era in Church and Society.* New York: Macmillan Co.

Bonhoeffer, Dietrich. 1965. *No Rusty Swords: Letters, Lectures, and Notes, 1928–1936.* New York: Harper & Row.

Bonomi, Patricia U., and Peter R. Eisenstadt. 1982. "Church Adherence in the Eighteenth-Century British American Colonies." *William and Mary Quarterly* 39:245–286.

Bonomi, Patricia. 1986. *Under the Cope of Heaven: Religion, Society, and Politics in Colonial America.* New York: Oxford University Press.

Bowers, William L. 1974. *The Country Life Movement in America, 1900–1920.* Port Washington, N.Y.: National University Publications.

Bruce, Dickson, Jr. 1974. *And They All Sang Hallelujah: Plain-Folk Camp-Meeting Religion, 1800–1845.* Knoxville: University of Tennessee Press.

Brunette-Hill, Sandi, and Roger Finke. 1999. "A Time for Every Purpose under Heaven: Updating and Extending Blizzard's Survey on Clergy Time Allocation." *Review of Religious Research* 41: 48–64.

Brunner, Edmund deS. 1927. *Village Communities.* New York: George H. Doran Co.

Brunner, Edmund deS., Gwendolyn S. Hughes, and Marjorie Patten. 1927. *American Agricultural Villages.* New York: George H. Doran Co.

Bryce, Mary Charles. 1986. "The Confraternity of Christian Doctrines in the United

States." In D. Campbell Wyckoff, ed., *Renewing the Sunday School and CCD*. Birmingham, Ala.: Religious Education Press.

Bureau of the Census. 1854. *Compendium of the Seventh Census*. Washington, D.C.: Government Printing Office.

———. 1894. *Eleventh Census of the United States: 1890*. Vol. 9. Washington, D.C.: Government Printing Office.

———. 1910. *Religious Bodies: 1906*. Vols. 1–2. Washington, D.C.: Government Printing Office.

———. 1919. *Religious Bodies: 1916*. Vols. 1–2. Washington, D.C.: Government Printing Office.

———. 1930. *Religious Bodies: 1926*. Vols. 1–2. Washington, D.C.: Government Printing Office.

———. 1941. *Religious Bodies: 1936*. Vol. 1. Washington, D.C.: Government Printing Office.

———. 1975. *Historical Statistics of the United States: Colonial Times to 1970*. Washington, D.C.: Government Printing Office.

Burns, James A. [1912] 1969. *The Growth and Development of the Catholic School System in the United States*. New York: Arno Press.

Burns, Jeffrey M. "The Parish History Project: A Descriptive Analysis of the Data." Cushwa Center for the Study of American Catholicism, University of Notre Dame.

Burr, Walter. 1924. "What's the Matter with the Rural Church?" In *Religion in Country Life: Proceedings of the Seventh National Country Life Conference*. New York.

Burrows, Robert. 1987. "A Christian Critiques the New Age." *Christianity Today* 16.

Butler, Jon. 1982. "Enthusiasm Described and Decried: The Great Awakening as Interpretative Fiction." *Journal of American History* 69: 305–325.

———. 1990. *Awash in a Sea of Faith: Christianizing the American People*. Cambridge, Mass.: Harvard University Press.

Butterfield, Kenyon L. 1905. "The Social Problems of American Farmers." *American Journal of Sociology* 10: 606–622.

Cameron, Richard M. 1961. *Methodism and Society in Historical Perspective*. Nashville: Abingdon Press.

Campbell, James T. 1995. *Songs of Zion: The African Methodist Episcopal Church in the United States and South Africa*. New York: Oxford University Press.

Cantril, Hadley. 1943. "Educational and Economic Composition of Religious Groups: An Analysis of Poll Data." *American Journal of Sociology* 48: 574–579.

Carroll, H. K. 1898. "Is Methodism Catholic?" *Methodist Review* 14: 177–186.

Carroll, Jackson W. 2000. *Mainline to the Future: Congregations for the 21ˢᵗ Century*. Louisville: Westminster John Knox Press.

Cartwright, Peter, 1856. *Autobiography of Peter Cartwright, the Backwards Preacher*. Edited by W. P. Strickland. New York: Carlton and Porter.

Casino, Joseph J. 1987. "From Sanctuary to Involvement: A History of the Catholic Parish in the Northeast." In Jay P. Dolan, ed., *The American Catholic Parish*. Vol. 1. New York: Paulist Press.

Chadwick, Owen. 1981. *The Popes and European Revolution*. Oxford: Clarendon Press.

Chai, Karen J. 1998. "Competing for the Second Generation: English-Language Ministry at a Korean Protestant Church." In R. Stephen Warner and Judith G. Wittner, eds., *Gathering in Diaspora: Religious Communities and the New Immigration*. Philadelphia: Temple University Press.

Chandler, Tertius, and Gerald Fox. 1974. *3000 Years of Urban Growth*. New York: Academic Press.

Cherry, Conrad. 1995. *Hurrying Toward Zion: Universities, Divinity Schools, and American Protestantism*. Bloomington: Indiana University Press.

Chiswick, Carmel Ullman. 1999. "Economic Adjustment of Immigrants: Jewish Adaptation to the United States." In Roberta R. Farber and Chaim Waxman, eds., *Jews in America: A Contemporary Reader*. Waltham, Mass.: Brandeis University Press.

Christianity Today. 1983. "The Historic Shift in America." 27 (August): 38–41.

Christiano, Kevin. 1987. *Religious Diversity and Social Change: American Cities, 1890–1906*. New York: Cambridge University Press.

———. 1991. "The Catholic Church and Recent Immigrants to the United States: A Review of Research." In Helen Rose Ebaugh, ed., *Vatican II and American Catholicism: Twenty-Five Years Later*. Greenwich, Conn.: JAI Press.

Circuit Rider. 1989. "The Good News Movement: Is it?" (April): 6–8.

Clark, Elmer T. 1952. *An Album of Methodist History*. New York: Abingdon–Cokesbury Press.

Cobbett, William. 1818. *Journal of a Year's Residence in the United States of America* (as excerpted in Powell, 1967).

Coke, Thomas. 1793. *The Life of the Rev. John Wesley*. Philadelphia: John Dickens.

Congregational Quarterly. 1866. "Editor's Table." 8: 308–311.

Cott, Nancy F. 1977. *The Bonds of Womanhood*. New Haven: Yale University Press.

Cox, Harvey. 1965. *The Secular City*. New York: Macmillan Co.

———. 1977. *Turning East: The Promise and Peril of the New Orientalism*. New York: Simon and Schuster.

———. 1983. "Interview." In Steven J. Gelberg, ed., *Hare Krishna, Hare Krishna*. New York Grove Press.

Cross, Barbara M., ed. 1961. *The Autobiography of Lyman Beecher*. Cambridge, Mass.: The Belknap Press of Harvard University Press.

Cross, Whitney R. [1950] 1982. *The Burned-Over District*. Ithaca: Cornell University Press.

Crowe, Charles M. 1944. "Religion on the Air." *Christian Century* 61: 973–975.

Curry, Catherine Ann. 1988. "Statistical Study of Religious Women in the United States." Available from George C. Stewart, Jr., P. O. Box 7, Fayetteville, N.C. 29302.

D'Antonio, William, James Davidson, Dean Hoge, and Ruth Wallace. 1989. *American Catholic Laity in a Changing Church*. Kansas City: Sheed and Ward.

D'Antonio, William, James Davidson, Dean Hoge, and Ruth Wallace. 1996. *Laity American and Catholic: Transforming the Church*. Kansas City: Sheed and Ward.

D'Antonio, William V., James D. Davidson, Dean R. Hoge, and Katherine Meyer. 2001. *American Catholics: Gender, Generation, and Commitment*. Walnut Creek, Calif.: AltaMira Press.

D'Arcy, Paul F., and Eugene C. Kennedy. 1965. *The Genius of the Apostolate*. New York: Sheed and Ward.

Davidson, James D., Andrea S. Williams, Richard A. Lamanna, Jan Stenftenagel, Kathleen Maas Weigert, William J. Whalen, and Patricia Wittberg. 1997. *The Search for Common Ground: What Unites and Divides Catholic Americans*. Huntington, Ind.: Our Sunday Visitor Publishing Division.

Deck, Allan Figueroa, S.J. 1989. *The Second Wave: Hispanic Ministry and the Evangelization of Cultures*. New York: Paulist Press.

Demerath, N.J., III, Peter Dobkin Hall, Terry Schmitt, and Rhys H. Williams, eds. 1998. *Sacred Companies*. New York: Oxford University Press.

Díaz-Stevens, Ana María, and Anthony M. Stevens-Arroyo. 1998. *Recognizing the Latino Resurgence in U.S. Religion*. Boulder, Colo.: Westview Press.

DiIanni, Albert. 1993. "Religious Vocations: New Signs of the Times." *Review for Religious* 52: 745–763.

DiMaggio, Paul J., and Walter W. Powell. 1983. "The Iron Cage Revisited: Institutional Isomorphism and Collective Rationality in Organizational Fields." *American Sociological Review* 48: 147–160.

Doherty, Robert W. 1967. *The Hicksite Separation*. New Brunswick, N.J.: Rutgers University Press.

Dolan, Jay P. 1975. *The Immigrant Church: New York's Irish and German Catholics, 1815–1865*. Baltimore: Johns Hopkins University Press.

———. 1978. *Catholic Revivalism: The American Experience, 1830–1900*. Notre Dame: University of Notre Dame Press.

———. 1985. *The American Catholic Experience: A History from Colonial Times to the Present*. Garden City, N.Y.: Image Books.

———., ed. 1987. *The American Catholic Parish*. Vols. 1–2. New York: Paulist Press.

Donovan, Grace. 1991. "Immigrant Nuns: Their Participation in the Process of Americanization." *Catholic Historical Review* 77: 194–208.

Dougherty, Kevin D. 2003. *Engaging and Expanding: How Boundaries and Adaptability Enhance Congregational Performance*. Dissertation, Purdue University.

Douglass, Paul F. 1939. *The Story of German Methodism*. Cincinnati: The Methodist Book Concern.

Douglass, Paul. 1964. "Bilingual Work and the Language Conferences." In E. S. Bucke, ed., *The History of American Methodism*. Vol. 2. Nashville: Abingdon Press.

Douglass, H. Paul, and Edmund deS. Brunner. 1935. *The Protestant Church as a Social Institution*. New York: Russell and Russell.

Dow, Lorenzo. 1849. *History of Cosmopolite or The Four Volumes of Lorenzo Dow's Journal*. 6th ed. Wheeling, Virginia: Joshua Martin.

DuBois, W.E.B. 1971. "Of the Faith of the Fathers." In Hart M. Nelson, Raytha Yokley, and Anne K. Nelson, eds., *The Black Church in America*. New York: Basic Books.

Duke, James T. 1997. "Church Callings as an Organizational Device in the LDS Church." Paper read at the annual meeting of the Association for the Sociology of Religion.

Dunn, Mary Maples. 1978. "Saints and Sisters: Congregational and Quaker Women in the Early Colonial Period." *American Quarterly* 30: 582–601.

Durkheim, Emile. [1897] 1951. *Suicide*. Glencoe, Ill.: Free Press.

Dvorak, Katharine L. 1991. *An African-American Exodus: The Segregation of the Southern Churches*. Brooklyn, N.Y.: Carlson Publishing.

Ebaugh, Helen Rose Fuchs. 1977. *Out of the Cloister: A Study of Organizational Dilemmas*. Austin: University of Texas Press.

———. 1991. "The Revitalization Movement in the Catholic Church." *Sociological Analysis* 52: 1–12.

Ebaugh, Helen Rose, and Janet Saltzman Chafetz. 2000. *Religion and the New Immigrants: Continuities and Adaptations in Immigrant Congregations*. Walnut Creek, Calif.: AltaMira Press.

Eighmy, John Lee. 1972. *Churches in Cultural Captivity: A History of the Social Attitudes of Southern Baptists*. Knoxville: University of Tennessee Press.

Ellis, John Tracy. 1956. *Documents of American Catholic History*. Milwaukee: Bruce Publishing Co.

———., ed. 1962. *Documents of American Catholic History*. 2d ed. Milwaukee: Bruce Publishing Co.

———. 1969. *American Catholicism*. 2d ed. Chicago: University of Chicago Press.

Ewens, Mary. 1978. *The Role of the Nun in Nineteenth-Century America: Variations on the International Theme*. New York: Arno Press.

Fenton, John. 1988. *Transplanting Religious Traditions: Asian Indians in America*. New York: Praeger Publishers.

Fialka, John J. 2003. *Sisters: Catholic Nuns and the Making of America*. New York: St. Martin's Press.

Fichter, Joseph H. 1961. *Religion as an Occupation: A Study in the Sociology of Professions*. Notre Dame: University of Notre Dame Press.

———. 1968. *America's Forgotten Priests: What They Are Saying*. New York: Harper & Row.

Finke, Roger. 1989. "Demographics of Religious Participation: An Ecological Approach, 1850–1980." *Journal for the Scientific Study of Religion* 28: 45–58.

———. 1990. "Religious Deregulation: Origins and Consequences." *Journal of Church and State* 32: 609–626.

———. 1994. "The Quiet Transformation: Changes in Size and Leadership of Southern Baptist Churches." *Review of Religious Research* 36: 3–22.

———. 1997. "An Orderly Return to Tradition: Explaining Membership Growth in Catholic Religious Orders." *Journal for the Scientific Study of Religion* 36: 218–230.

———. 2004. "Innovative Returns to Tradition: Using Core Beliefs as the Foundation for Innovative Accommodation." *Journal for the Scientific Study of Religion* 43: 19–34.

Finke, Roger, and Kevin Dougherty. 2002. "The Effects of Professional Training: The Social and Religious Capital Acquired in Seminaries." *Journal for the Scientific Study of Religion* 41: 103–120.

Finke, Roger, and Christopher Scheitle. 2004. "Accounting for the Uncounted: Computing Correctives for the 2000 RCMS Data." Unpublished manuscript.

Finke, Roger, and Rodney Stark. 1986. "Turning Pews into People: Estimating Nineteenth-Century Church Membership." *Journal for the Scientific Study of Religion* 25: 180–192.

———. 1988. "Religious Economies and Sacred Canopies: Religious Mobilization in American Cities, 1906." *American Sociological Review* 53: 41–49.

———. 2001. "The New Holy Clubs: Testing Church-to-Sect Propositions." *Sociology of Religion* 62: 175–189.

Finke, Roger, and Patricia Wittberg. 2000. "Organizational Revival from Within: Explaining Revivalism and Reform in the Roman Catholic Church." *Journal for the Scientific Study of Religion* 39: 154–170.

Finney, Charles Grandison. [1835] 1960. *Lectures on Revivals of Religion*. Cambridge, Mass.: Harvard University Press.

Fischer, Claude S. 1982. *To Dwell among Friends: Personal Networks in Town and City*. Chicago: University of Chicago Press.

Flannery, Austin P., ed. 1975. *Documents of Vatican II*. Grand Rapids, Mich.: Eerdmans Publishing.

———. ed. 1992. *Vatican Council II: The Conciliar and Post Conciliar Documents*. Grand Rapids, Mich.: Eerdmans Publishing.

Flynt, J. Wayne. 1981. "Southern Baptists: Rural to Urban Transition." *Baptist History and Heritage* 16: 24–34.

Foy, Felician A., ed. 1965. *National Catholic Almanac*. Paterson, N.J.: St. Anthony's Guild.

———. ed. 1966. *National Catholic Almanac*. Garden City, N.Y.: Doubleday.

Franklin, Benjamin. [1868] 1916. *The Autobiography of Benjamin Franklin*. Garden City, N.Y.: Garden City Publishing Co.

Frazier, E. Franklin. [1963] 1974. *The Negro Church in America*. New York: Schocken Books.

Frey, Sylvia R. 1991. *Water from the Rock: Black Resistance in a Revolutionary Age*. Princeton: Princeton University Press.

Frey, Sylvia R., and Betty Wood. 1998. *Come Shouting to Zion: African American Protestantism in the American South and British Caribbean to 1830*. Chapel Hill: The University of North Carolina Press.

Froehle, Bryan T., and Mary L. Gautier. 2000. *Catholicism USA: A Portrait of the Catholic Church in the United States*. Maryknoll, N.Y.: Orbis Books.

Galpin, Charles Josiah. 1923. *Rural Life*. New York: Century Co.

————. 1925. *Empty Churches: The Rural-Urban Dilemma*. New York: Century Co.

Gannon, Thomas M. 1980. "Catholic Religious Orders in Sociological Perspective." In Ross P. Scherer, ed., *American Denominational Organization: A Sociological View*. Pasadena, Calif.: William Carey Library.

Gardner, Robert G. 1989. "The Statistics of Early American Baptists: A Second Look." *Baptist History and Heritage* 24: 29–44.

Garraghan, Gilbert J. 1984. *The Jesuits of the Middle United States*. Vol. 2. Chicago: Loyola University Press.

Garrettson, Freeborn. 1984. *American Methodist Pioneer: The Life and Journals of the Reverend Freeborn Garrettson, 1752–1827*. Rutland, Vt.: Academy Books.

Gaustad, Edwin S., ed. 1982. *A Documentary History of Religion in America to the Civil War*. Grand Rapids, Mich.: Eerdmans Publishing.

————. 1987. *Faith of Our Fathers: Religion and the New Nation*. San Francisco: Harper & Row.

Gaustad, Edwin S., and Leigh E. Schmidt. 2002. *The Religious History of America*. rev. ed. New York: HarperCollins Publishers.

Gill, Anthony J. 1998. *Rendering Unto Caesar: The Roman Catholic Church and the State in Latin America*. Chicago: University of Chicago Press.

Gleason, Philip. 1967. "American Catholic Higher Education: A Historical Perspective." In Robert Hassenger, ed., *The Shape of Catholic Higher Education*. Chicago: University of Chicago Press.

————. 1973. "Coming to Terms with American Catholic History." *Societas* 3: 305.

————. 1987. *Keeping the Faith: American Catholicism Past and Present*. Notre Dame: University of Notre Dame Press.

Glenn, Norval, and Ruth Hyland. 1967. "Religious Preference and Worldly Success: Some Evidence from National Surveys." *American Sociological Review* 32: 73–85.

Glock, Charles Y., and Robert N. Bellah, eds. 1976. *The New Religious Consciousness*. Berkeley: University of California Press.

Gordon-McCutchan, R. C. 1981. "The Irony of Evangelical History." *Journal for the Scientific Study of Religion* 20: 309–326.

————. 1983. "Great Awakenings." *Sociological Analysis* 44: 83–95.

Gorham, B. W. 1854. *Camp Meeting Manual: A Practical Book for the Camp Ground*. Boston: H. V. Degen.

Gorrie, P. Douglass. 1852. *Episcopal Methodism. As It Was and Is*. Auburn: Derby and Miller.

————. 1890. *History of the Methodist Episcopal Church in the United States*. Keystone Publishing Co.

Goss, C. C. 1866. *Statistical History of the First Century of American Methodism*. New York: Carlton and Porter.

Gravely, William B. 1994. "The Social, Political, and Religious Significance of the Formation of the Colored Methodist Episcopal Church (1870)." In Donald G. Nieman, ed., *Church and Community Among Black Southerners, 1865–1900*. New York: Garland Publishing.

Gray, Mark M., and Mary L. Gautier. 2003. "Latino Catholic Leaders in the United

States." A report for the Center for Applied Research in the Apostolate, Georgetown University, Washington, D.C.

Greeley, Andrew M. 1963. "Influence of the 'Religious Factor' on Career Plans and Occupational Values of College Graduates." *American Journal of Sociology* 68: 658–671.

———. 1964. "The Protestant Ethic: Time for a Moratorium." *Sociological Analysis* 25: 20–33.

———. 1969. *From Backwater to Mainstream.* New York: McGraw-Hill.

———. 1972. *The Catholic Priest in the United States: Sociological Investigations.* Washington, D.C.: United States Catholic Conference.

———. 1974. *Ethnicity in the United States: A Preliminary Reconnaissance.* New York: John Wiley and Sons.

———. 1977. *The American Catholic: A Social Portrait.* New York: Basic Books.

———. 1979. "Ethnic Variations in Religious Commitment." In Robert Wuthnow, ed., *The Religious Dimension: New Directions in Quantitative Research.* New York: Academic Press.

———. 1982. "The Failures of Vatican II after Twenty Years." *America,* February 6, pp. 86–89.

———. 1988. "Defection among Hispanics." *America,* July 30, pp. 61–62.

———. 1989. *Religious Change in America.* Cambridge, Mass.: Harvard University Press.

———. 1994. "The Demography of American Catholics: 1965–1990." In *The Sociology of Andrew Greeley.* Atlanta: Scholars Press.

Greeley, Andrew M., William C. McCready, and Kathleen McCourt. 1976. *Catholic Schools in a Declining Church.* Kansas City: Sheed and Ward.

Greeley, Andrew M., and William McManus. 1987. *Catholic Contributions: Sociology and Policy.* Chicago: Thomas More Press.

Greeley, Andrew M., and Peter H. Rossi. 1966. *The Education of Catholic Americans.* Chicago: Aldine.

Grund, Francis. 1837. *The Americans in Their Moral, Social and Political Relations* (as excerpted in Powell, 1967).

Gunneman, Louis H. 1977. *The Shaping of the United Church of Christ.* New York: United Church Press.

Gustafson, David A. 1994. "A Confessional Lutheran Encounters American Religion." In Marvin A. Huggins, ed., *Missionary to America: The History of Lutheran Outreach to Americans.* Minneapolis: Augsburg Fortress Publishers.

Guttentag, Marica, and Paul F. Secord. 1983. *Too Many Women?* Beverly Hills, Calif.: Sage Publications.

Hadden, Jeffrey K. 1969. *The Gathering Storm in the Churches.* Garden City, N.Y.: Doubleday and Co.

Hadden, Jeffrey K., and Anson Shupe. 1988. *Televangelism Power and Politics on God's Frontier.* New York: Henry Holt and Co.

Hall, Timothy D. 1994. *Contested Boundaries: Itinerancy and the Reshaping of the Colonial American Religious World.* Durham, N.C.: Duke University Press.

Hammond, Phillip. 1993. "A review of *The Churching of America, 1776–1990: Winners and Losers in Our Religious Economy.*" *Sociology of Religion* 54: 318–319.

Handy, Robert T. 1969. "The City and the Church: Historical Interlockings." In Kendig Brubaker Cully and F. Nile Harper, eds., *Will the Church Lose the City?* New York: World Publishing Co.

———. 1977. *A History of Churches in the United States and Canada.* New York: Oxford University Press.

Hardt, Philip F. 2000. *The Soul of Methodism: The Class Meeting in Early New York City Methodism.* Lanham, Maryland: University Press of America.

Hargreaves, Robert. 1914. "The Rural Community and Church Federation." *American Journal of Sociology* 20: 249–260.

Harrison, Paul M. 1959. *Authority and Power in the Free Church Tradition.* Princeton: Princeton University Press.

Harvey, Paul. 1997. *Redeeming the South: Religious Cultures and Racial Identities among Southern Baptists, 1865–1925.* Chapel Hill: The University of North Carolina Press.

Hatch, Nathan O. 1989. *The Democratization of American Christianity.* New Haven: Yale University Press.

Hayward, John. 1836. *Religious Creeds and Statistics of Every Christian Denomination in the U.S.* Boston: John Hayward.

Hechter, Michael. 1987. *Principles of Group Solidarity.* Berkeley: University of California Press.

Hefley, James C. 1983. "The Historic Shift in America." *Christianity Today* 27: 38–41.

Heidinger, James V. 1992. "25 Years of Vision." *Good News* (March/April): 14–19.

———. 2000. "Cleveland Brings Reason for Hope." *Good News Magazine,* November 14, http://www.goodnewsmag.org/magazine.

Hempton, David. 1984. *Methodism and Politics in British Society, 1750–1850.* Stanford: Stanford University Press.

———. 1988. "Methodism and the Law, 1740–1820." In A. Dyson and E. Barker, eds., *Sects and New Religious Movements, Bulletin of the John Rylands Library.* 70: 93–107.

Hennesey, James. S.J. 1981. *American Catholics.* New York: Oxford University Press.

Herberg, Will. 1960. *Protestant-Catholic-Jew.* Garden City, N.Y.: Doubleday and Co.

Heyrman, Christine Leigh. 1997. *Southern Cross: The Beginnings of the Bible Belt.* New York: Alfred A. Knopf.

Hinson, Bill. 2004. "A Statement of Conscience." Address given at the United Methodist Decision Breakfast at the General Conference of the United Methodist Church, May 6, Pittsburgh, Pa. (www.confessingumc.org).

Hoge, Dean R. 1987. *Future of Catholic Leadership: Responses to the Priest Shortage.* Kansas City: Sheed and Ward.

———. 2002. "Core and Periphery in American Catholic Identity." *Journal of Contemporary Religion* 17: 293–302.

Hoge, Dean R., William D. Dinges, Mary Johnson, and Juan L. Gonzales. 2001. *Young Adult Catholics: Religion in the Culture of Crisis.* Notre Dame, Indiana: University of Notre Dame Press.

Hoge, Dean R., and David A. Roozen, eds. 1979. *Understanding Church Growth and Decline, 1950–1978.* New York: Pilgrim Press.

Hoge, Dean, and Jacqueline E. Wenger. 2003. *Evolving Visions of the Priesthood.* Collegeville, Minn.: Liturgical Press.

Hooker, Elizabeth R. 1931. *Hinterlands of the Church.* New York: Institute of Social and Religious Research.

Horgan, Paul. 1975. *Lamy of Sante Fe.* Toronto: McGraw-Hill.

Hout, Michael, and Claude S. Fischer. 2003. "Why More Americans Have No Religious Preference: Politics and Generations." *American Sociological Review* 67: 165–190.

Hout, Michael, and Andrew M. Greeley. 1987. "The Center Doesn't Hold: Church Attendance in the United States, 1940–1984." *American Sociological Review* 52: 325–345.

Hudson, Winthrop S. 1965. *Religion in America.* 1st ed. New York: Charles Scribner's Sons.

———. 1981. *Religion in America.* 3d ed. New York: Charles Scribner's Sons

Hunt, Larry L. 1998. "The Spirit of Hispanic Protestantism in the United States: National Survey Comparisons of Catholics and Non-Catholics." *Social Science Quarterly* 79: 828–845.

———. 1999. "Hispanic Protestantism in the United States: Trends by Decade and Generation." *Social Forces* 77: 1601–1623.

Hurh, Won Moo, and Kwang Chung Kim. 1990. "Religious Participation of Korean Immigrants in the United States." *Journal for the Scientific Study of Religion* 29: 19–34.

Iannaccone, Laurence R. 1990. "Religious Practice: A Human Capital Approach." *Journal for the Scientific Study of Religion* 29: 297–314

———. 1991. "The Consequences of Religious Market Regulation: Adam Smith and the Economics of Religion." *Rationality and Society* 3: 156–177.

———. 1992. "Sacrifice and Stigma: Reducing Free-Riding in Cults, Communes, and other Collectives." *Journal of Political Economy* 100 (2): 271–292.

———. 1994."Why Strict Churches are Strong." *American Journal of Sociology* 99: 1180–1211.

Iannaccone, Laurence R., Daniel Olson, and Rodney Stark. 1995. "Religious Resources and Church Growth." *Social Forces* 74: 705–731.

Interchurch World Movement. 1920. *Standards for City Church Plants.* New York: Interchurch Press.

James, Larry M. 1988. "Biracial Fellowship in Antebellum Baptist Churches." In John B. Boles, ed., *Masters and Slaves in the House of the Lord.* Lexington: University of Kentucky Press.

Jenkins, Philip. 2002. *The Next Christendom: The Coming of Global Christianity.* New York: Oxford University Press.

Jent, John W. 1924. *The Challenge of the Country Church*. Nashville: Sunday School Board of the Southern Baptist Convention.

Jernegan, M. W. 1916. "Slavery and Conversion in the Colonies." *American Historical Review* 21: 504–527.

———. 1931. *Laboring and Dependent Classes in Colonial America, 1607–1660*. Chicago: University of Chicago Press.

———. 1932. "Colleges, Universities, and Churches, 1775–1890." In Charles O. Paullin, ed., *Atlas of Historical Geography of the United States*. Washington, D.C.: Carnegie Institution.

Johnson, Benton. 1963. "On Church and Sect." *American Sociological Review* 28: 539–549.

Johnson, Charles A. 1955. *The Frontier Camp Meeting: Religion's Harvest Time*. Dallas: Southern Methodist University Press.

Johnson, Douglas W., Paul R. Picard, and Bernard Quinn. 1974. *Churches and Church Membership in the United States: An Enumeration by Region, State, and County*. Washington, D.C.: Glenmary Research Center.

Jonas, Thomas J. 1988. *The Divided Mind: American Catholic Evangelists in the 1890s*. New York: Garland Press.

Jones, Dale E., Sherri Doty, Clifford Grammich, James E. Horsch, Richard Houseal, Mac Lynn, John P. Marcum, Kenneth M. Sanchagrin and Richard H. Taylor. 2002. *Religious Congregations and Membership in the United States 2000: An Enumeration by Region, State and County Based on Data Reported for 149 Religious Bodies*. Nashville, Tenn.: Glenmary Research Center.

Kalmijn, Matthijs. 1991. "Shifting Boundaries: Trends in Religious and Educational Homogamy." *American Sociological Review* 56: 786–800.

Kelley, Dean. 1972. *Why Conservative Churches Are Growing*. New York: Harper and Row.

———. 1984. "Why Conservative Churches Are Still Growing." In Patrick H. McNamara, ed., *Religion: North American Style*. Belmont, Calif.: Wadsworth Publishing Co.

Kim, Kwang Chung, and Shin Kim. 2001. "The Ethnic Roles of Korean Immigrant Churches in the United States." In Ho-Youn Kwon, Kwang Chung Kim, and R. Stephen Warner, eds., *Korean Americans and Their Religions*. University Park: The Pennsylvania State University.

Kirby, James E., Russell E. Richey, and Kenneth E. Rowe. 1996. *The Methodists*. Westport, Conn.: Greenwood Publishing.

Kirk, Dudley. 1955. "Recent Trends of Catholic Fertility in the United States." In Milbank Memorial Fund, *Current Research in Human Fertility*, pp. 93–105.

Kolchin, Peter. 1997. *First Freedom: The Responses of Alabama's Blacks to Emancipation and Reconstruction*. Westport, Conn.: Greenwood Press.

Kosmin, Barry A., and Seymour P. Lachman. 1993. *One Nation Under God: Religion in Contemporary American Society*. New York: Harmony Books.

Lambert, Frank. 1990. "'Pedlar in Divinity': George Whitefield and the Great Awakening, 1737–1745." *Journal of American History* (December) 77: 812–837.

————. 1999. *Inventing the "Great Awakening."* Princeton: Princeton University Press.

————. 2003. *The Founding Fathers and the Place of Religion in America.* Princeton: Princeton University Press.

Lambert, Richard D. 1960. "Current Trends in Religion: A Summary." In *The Annals: Religion in American Society* 332: 146–155.

Land, Kenneth C., Glenn Deane, and Judith R. Blau. 1991. "Religious Pluralism and Church Membership: A Spatial Diffusion Model." *American Sociological Review* 56: 237–249.

Landis, Benson Y. 1922. *Rural Church Life in the Middle West.* New York: Institute of Social and Religious Research.

Larkin, Emmet. 1972. "The Devotional Revolution in Ireland, 1850–1875." *American Historical Review* 77: 625–652.

Lee, Robert. 1960. *The Social Sources of Church Unity.* New York: Abingdon Press.

León, Luís. 1998. "Born Again in East L.A.: The Congregation as Border Space." In R. Stephen Warner and Judith G. Wittner, eds., *Gatherings in Diaspora: Religious Communities and the New Immigration.* Philadelphia: Temple University Press.

Lenski, Gerhard. 1961. *The Religious Factor.* Garden City, N.Y.: Doubleday and Co.

————. 1965. "Comment." *Review of Religious Research* 7: 51–53.

Leonard, Bill J. 1990. *God's Last and Only Hope: The Fragmentation of the Southern Baptist Convention.* Grand Rapids, Mich.: Eerdmans Publishing.

Liebard, Odile M. 1978. *Official Catholic Teachings: Clergy and Laity.* Wilmington, N.C.: Consortium.

Lincoln, C. Eric, and Lawrence H. Mamiya. 1990. *The Black Church in the African American Experience.* Durham, N.C.: Duke University Press.

Lipset, Seymour Martin, and Reinhard Bendix. 1959. *Social Mobility in Industrial Society.* Berkeley: University of California Press.

Liptak, Dolores. 1989. *Immigrants and Their Church.* New York: MacMillan Publishing.

Littell, Franklin. 1962. *From State Church to Pluralism.* Chicago: Aldine Publishing.

Loevinger, Lee. 1965. "Religious Liberty and Broadcasting." *George Washington Law Review* 33: 631–659.

Lowry, James A. 1989. "Selected SBC Trends." *The Quarterly Review* 49: 51–61.

McBeth, Leon. 1982. "Expansion of the Southern Baptist Convention to 1951." *Baptist History and Heritage* 17: 32–43.

————. 1990. *A Sourcebook for Baptist Heritage.* Nashville: Broadman Press.

McBrien, Richard P., ed. 1995. *The HarperCollins Encyclopedia of Catholicism.* New York: HarperCollins Publishers.

McCarthy, James. 1979. "Religious Commitment, Affiliation, and Marriage Dissolution." In Robert Wuthnow, ed., *The Religious Dimension: New Directions in Quantitative Research.* New York: Academic Press.

McClellan, Albert. 1985. "The Southern Baptist Convention, 1965–1985." *Baptist History and Heritage* 20: 7–24.

McCulloh, Gerald O. 1964. "The Theology and Practices of Methodism, 1876–1919." In E. S. Bucke, ed., *The History of American Methodism*. Vol. 2. Nashville: Abingdon Press.

McCutcheon, Alan L. 1988. "Denominations and Religious Intermarriage." *Review of Religious Research* 29: 213–227.

McKinney, Jennifer. 2001. *Clergy Connections: The Impact of Clergy Networks on Evangelical Renewal Movements*. Ph.D. Dissertation. Department of Sociology and Anthropology. West Lafayette, Ind.: Purdue University.

McKinney, Jennifer, and Roger Finke. 2002. "Reviving the Mainline: An Overview of Clergy Support for Evangelical Movements." *Journal for the Scientific Study of Religion* 41: 771–783.

McLoughlin, William G. 1971. *New England Dissent, 1630–1833: The Baptists and the Separation of Church and State*. Vols. 12. Cambridge, Mass.: Harvard University Press.

———. 1978. *Revivals, Awakenings, and Reform*. Chicago: University of Chicago Press.

———. 1983. "Timepieces and Butterflies: A Note on the Great-Awakening–Construct and Its Critics." *Sociological Analysis* 44: 103–110.

McNamara, Patrick. 1992. *Conscience First: Tradition Second*. Albany: State University of New York Press.

Madison, James H. 1986. "Reformers and the Rural Church, 1900–1950." *Journal of American History* 73: 645–668.

Marsden, George M. 1982. "Preachers of Paradox: The Religious New Right in Historical Perspective." In Mary Douglas and Steven M. Tipton, eds., *Religion and America: Spirituality in a Secular Age*. Boston: Beacon Press.

Martin, David. 1990. *Tongues of Fire: The Explosion of Protestantism in Latin America*. Oxford: Basil Blackwell.

Marty, Martin E. 1959. *The New Shape of Religion*. New York: Harper & Brothers.

———. 1964. *Church Unity and Church Mission*. Grand Rapids, Mich.: Eerdmans Publishing.

———. 1970. *Righteous Empire: The Protestant Experience in America*. New York: The Dial Press.

———. 1975. "Vice and Virtue: Our Moral Condition." *Time*, October 27.

———. 1976. *A Nation of Behavers*. Chicago: University of Chicago Press.

———. 1979. "Foreword." In Dean R. Hoge and David A. Roozen, eds., *Understanding Church Growth and Decline, 1950–1978*. New York: Pilgrim Press.

———. 1984. *Pilgrims in Their Own Land: 500 Years of Religion in America*. New York: Penguin Books.

———. 1991. "Never the Same Again: Post-Vatican II Catholic-Protestant Interactions." *Sociological Analysis* 52: 13–26.

Masters, Victor. 1916. *Country Church in the South*. Atlanta: Home Mission Board of the Southern Baptist Convention.

Mays, Benjamin E., and Joseph W. Nicholson. [1933] 1969. *The Negro's Church*. New York: Arno Press.

Mead, Sidney E. 1956. "From Coercion to Persuasion: Another Look at the Rise of Religious Liberty and the Emergence of Denominationalism." *Church History* 25: 317–337.

———. 1973. "By Puritans Possessed." *Worldview* 16: 49–52.

———. [1963] 1976. *The Lively Experiment: The Shaping of Christianity in America.* New York: Harper and Row.

Melton, J. Gordon. 1978. *The Encyclopedia of American Religions.* Wilmington, N.C.: McGrath.

———. 1987. "How New Is New? The Flowering of the 'New' Religious Consciousness since 1965." In David G. Bromley and Phillip E. Hammond, eds., *The Future of New Religious Movements.* Macon, Ga.: Mercer University Press.

———. 1988. "Testing the Truisms about the 'Cults': Toward a New Perspective on Nonconventional Religion." Paper presented at the annual meetings of American Academy of Religion, Chicago.

———. 1989. *The Encyclopedia of American Religions.* 3d ed. Detroit: Gale Research.

———. 1990. *New Age Encyclopedia.* Detroit: Gale Research.

Miller, Donald E. 1997. *Reinventing American Protestantism.* Berkeley: University of California Press.

Miller, Kent D. 2002. "Competitive Strategies of Religious Organizations. *Strategic Management Journal* 23: 435–456.

Miller, Paul M. 1978. "Yes, Dean Kelly [*sic*], there has been growth." *Gospel Herald,* March 28.

Miller, Perry. 1935. "The Contribution of the Protestant Churches to Religious Liberty in America." *Church History* 4: 57–66.

Minutes of the General Assembly of the Presbyterian Church, 1789–1820. Philadelphia: Presbyterian Board of Publication, 1847.

Miyakawa, T. Scott. 1964. *Protestants and Pioneers.* Chicago: University of Chicago Press.

Modde, Margaret Mary, O.S.F. 1974. "A Study of Entrances and Departures in Religious Communities of Women in the United States, 1965–1972." As reported in the 1975 *Catholic Almanac.*

Mondello, Salvatore. 1987. "Baptist Railroad Churches in the American West, 1890–1946." In Carl Guarneri and David Alvarez, eds., *Religion and Society in the American West.* New York: University Press of America.

Moore, David O. 1981. "The Withdrawal of Blacks from Southern Baptist Churches Following Emancipation." *Baptist History and Heritage* 16: 12–18.

Moore, R. Laurence. 1986. *Religious Outsiders and the Making of Americans.* New York: Oxford University Press.

Morgan, Edmund. 1961. "New England Puritanism: Another Approach." *William and Mary Quarterly* 18: 236–242.

Morrill, Miron A. 1945. "Will Churches Surrender Sovereignty?" *Christian Century* 62: 460–461.

Morris, Loretta M. 1989. "Secular Transcendence: From ACSS to ASR." *Sociological Analysis* 50: 329–349.

Morse, Hermann N., and Edmund deS. Brunner. 1923. *Town and Country Churches in the United States*. New York: Institute of Social and Religious Research.

Muhlenberg, Henry. 1959. *The Notebook of a Colonial Clergyman*. Philadelphia: Fortress Press.

Murray, John Courtney. 1960. *We Hold These Truths: Catholic Reflections on the American Proposition*. New York: Sheed and Ward.

Nash, Gary B. 1988. *Forging Freedom: The Formation of Philadelphia's Black Community, 1720–1840*. Cambridge: Harvard University Press.

Nelson, E. Clifford, with Theodore G. Tappert, H. George Anderson, August R. Suelflow, Eugene L. Fevold, and Fred W. Meuser. 1980. *The Lutherans in North America*. Philadelphia: Fortress Press.

Nelson, Hart M., and Anne Kusener Nelson. 1975. *Black Church in the Sixties*. Lexington: University of Kentucky Press.

Nelson, Hart M., Raytha Yokley, and Anne K. Nelson, eds. 1971. *The Black Church in America*. New York: Basic Books.

Nelson, Lynn D., and David C. Bromley. 1988. "Another Look at Conversion and Defection in Conservative Churches." In David G. Bromley, ed., *Falling from the Faith*. Newbury Park, Calif.: Sage Publications.

Nettles, Tom J. 1981. "Southern Baptists: Regional to National Transition." *Baptist History and Heritage* 16: 13–23.

Neuhaus, Richard John. 1987. *The Catholic Moment*. San Francisco: Harper & Row.

Newman, Albert Henry. 1915. *A History of the Baptist Churches in the United States*. 6th ed. New York: Charles Scribner's Sons.

Nickerson, Michael G. 1983. "Historical Relationships of Itineracy and Salary." *Methodist History* 21: 43–59.

Niebuhr, Richard H. 1929. *The Sources of Denominationalism*. New York: Henry Holt.

Noll, Mark A. 2002. *The Old Religion in a New World: The History of North American Christianity*. Grand Rapids, Mich.: Eerdmans Publishing.

Norwood, Frederick A. 1982. *Sourcebook of American Methodism*. Nashville: Abingdon Press.

Oates, Mary J. 1980. "Organized Voluntarism: The Catholic Sisters in Massachusetts, 1870–1940." In Janet Wilson James, ed., *Women in American Religion*. Philadelphia: University of Pennsylvania Press.

O'Callaghan, E. B., ed. 1855. *Documents Relative to the Colonial History of the State of New York*. Vol. 5. Albany, N.Y.: Weed, Parsons, and Co.

O'Connell, Eugene. [1853] 1956. "Letter to Father Moriarty." In John Tracy Ellis, ed., *Documents of American Catholic History*. Milwaukee: Bruce Publishing Co.

The Official Catholic Directory. 1950–1990. P. J. Kenedy and Sons.

Olmstead, Clifton E. 1961. *Religion in America: Past and Present*. Englewood Cliffs, N.J.: Prentice-Hall.

Olson, James S. 1987. *Catholic Immigrants in America*. Chicago: Nelson-Hall.

O'Malley, John. 1993. *The First Jesuits*. Cambridge, Mass.: Harvard University Press.

Orsi, Robert A. 1985. *The Madonna of 115th Street: Faith and Community in Italian Harlem*. New Haven: Yale University Press.

Patterson, L. Dale. 1985. "Improvement in Methodist Ministerial Education at the End of the Nineteenth Century." *Methodist History* 23: 68–78.

Patterson, W. Morgan. 1979. "Baptist Growth in America: Evaluation of Trends." *Baptist History and Heritage* 14: 16–26.

Paullin, Charles O. 1932. *Atlas of the Historical Geography of the United States*. Washington, D.C.: Carnegie Institution, and New York: American Geographical Society.

Payne, Daniel Alexander. [1888] 1968. *Recollections of Seventy Years*. Nashville, Tenn.: Publishing House of the AME. Sunday School Union.

Perko, F. Michael, S.J. ed. 1988. *Enlightening the Next Generation: Catholics and Their Schools, 1830–1980*. New York: Garland Press.

Peters, John Leland. [1956] 1985. *Christian Perfection and American Methodism*. Grand Rapids, Mich.: Francis Asbury Press.

Petersen, William. 1962. "Religious Statistics in the United States." *Journal for the Scientific Study of Religion* 1: 165–178.

Phares, Ross. 1964. *Bible in Pocket, Gun in Hand*. Lincoln: University of Nebraska Press.

Pies, Timothy Mark. 1986. "The Parochial School Campaigns in Michigan, 1920–1924: The Lutheran and Catholic Involvement." *Catholic Historical Review* 72: 222–238.

Pointer, Richard W. 1988. *Protestant Pluralism and the New York Experience: Study of Eighteenth-Century Religious Diversity*. Bloomington: Indiana University Press.

Pollock, John. 1972. *George Whitefield and the Great Awakening*. Belleville, Mich.: Lion Publishing.

Powell, Milton B., ed. 1967. *The Voluntary Church: Religious Life, 1740–1860, Seen through the Eyes of European Visitors*. New York: Macmillan Co.

Power, Edward J. 1972. *Catholic Higher Education in America*. New York: Appleton-Century-Crofts.

Presbyterian Board of Publication. 1847. *Minutes of the General Assembly, 1789–1820*. Philadelphia: Presbyterian Board of Publication.

Protestant Episcopal Church. 1832. *Journal of the Proceedings of the Bishops, Clergy, and Laity of the Protestant Episcopal Church in the United States of America in a General Convention*. New York: Protestant Episcopal Press.

———. 1841. *Journal of the Proceedings of the Bishops, Clergy, and Laity of the Protestant Episcopal Church in the United States of America in a General Convention*. New York: Swords, Stanford, and Co.

———. 1861. *The Church Almanac for the Year of our Lord*. New York: The Protestant Episcopal Tract Society.

The Quarterly Review. 1990. Vol. 50 (4): 62.

Raboteau, Albert. 1978. *Slave Religion: The "Invisible Institution" in the Antebellum South*. New York: Oxford University Press.

Reed, Andrew, and James Matheson. 1835a. *A Narrative of the Visit to the American Churches*. Vol. 1. New York: Harper and Brothers.

———. 1835b. *A Narrative of the Visit to the American Churches*. Vol. 2. London: Jackson and Walford.

Reichley, A. James. 1986. *Religion in American Public Life*. Washington, D.C.: Brookings Institution.

Richardson, Harry V. 1976. *Dark Salvation: The Story of Methodism as It Developed Among Blacks in America*. Garden City, N.Y.: Anchor Press/Doubleday.

Richardson, Joe M. 1994. "The Failure of the American Missionary Association to Expand Congregationalism Among Southern Blacks." In Donald G. Nieman, ed., *Church and Community Among Black Southerners, 1865–1900*. New York: Garland Publishing.

Richey, Russell E. 1991. *Early American Methodism*. Bloomington: Indiana University Press.

Richey, Russell E., Kenneth E. Rowe, and Jean Miller Schmidt. 2000. *The Methodist Experience in America: A Sourcebook*. Vol. 2. Nashville: Abingdon Press.

Ritchie, Carson I.A. 1976. *Frontier Parish*. London: Associated University Presses.

Robbins, Thomas, and Dick Anthony, eds. 1990. "Introduction." In *In Gods We Trust*. 2d ed. New Brunswick, N.J.: Transaction Publishers.

Rogers, James R. 1910. *The Cane Ridge Meeting-house*. 2d ed. Cincinnati: Standard Publishing Co.

Roof, Wade Clark, and William McKinney. 1987. *American Mainline Religion: Its Changing Shape and Future*. New Brunswick, N.J.: Rutgers University Press.

Rose, Royce A. 1983. "The Rural Church: Not Gone, But Forgotten." *Baptist History and Heritage* 18: 44–46.

Rowe, Kenneth E. 1971. "New Light on Early Methodist Theological Education." *Methodist History* 10: 58–62.

Rutledge, Kathleen K. 2004. "Pondering a Divorce." *Christianity Today* 48: 50–52.

Ryder, Norman B., and Charles F. Westoff. 1971. *Reproduction in the United States, 1965*. Princeton: Princeton University Press.

Sanders, James W. 1977. *The Education of an Urban Minority: Catholics in Chicago, 1833–1965*. New York: Oxford University Press.

Sanderson, Dwight. 1942. *Rural Sociology and Rural Social Organization*. New York: John Wiley and Sons.

Sargeant, Kimon Howland. 2000. *Seeker Churches: Promoting Traditional Religion in a Nontraditional Way*. New Brunswick, N.J.: Rutgers University Press.

Schaff, Philip. 1855. *America: A Sketch of Its Political, Social, and Religious Character*. Cambridge: The Belnap Press.

Scherer, F. M. 1970. *Industrial Market Structure and Economic Performance*. Chicago: Rand McNally and Co.

Schmidt, Leigh Eric. 2000. *Hearing Things: Religion, Illusion, and the American Enlightenment*. Cambridge, Mass.: Harvard University Press.

Schneider, Herbert W. 1952. *Religion in Twentieth-Century America*. Cambridge: Harvard University Press.

Schoenherr, Richard A., and Andrew M. Greeley. 1974. "Role Commitment Processes and the American Catholic Priesthood." *American Sociological Review* 39: 407–426.

Schoenherr, Richard A., and Lawrence A. Young. 1990. *The Catholic Priest in the U.S.: Demographic Investigations.* Final report for the United States Catholic Conference, Washington, D.C.

Schofield, Charles Edwin. 1939. *We Methodists.* New York: Methodist Publishing House.

Seidler, John. 1979. "Priest Resignations in a Lazy Monopoly." *American Sociological Review* 44: 763–783.

Seidler, John, and Katherine Meyer. 1989. *Conflict and Change in the Catholic Church.* New Brunswick, N.J.: Rutgers University Press.

Shannon, James P. 1957. *Catholic Colonization on the Western Frontier.* New Haven: Yale University Press.

Shannon, Peter M. 1967. "Future Laws for the Secular Priest." In Gerard S. Sloyan, ed., *Secular Priest in the New Church.* New York: Herder and Herder.

Shaughnessy, Gerald. 1925. *Has the Immigrant Kept the Faith.* New York: Macmillan Co.

Shaw, Stephen J. 1987. "The Cities and the Plains, a Home for God's People." In Jay P. Dolan, ed., *The American Catholic Parish.* Vol. 2. New York: Paulist Press.

Shiels, Richard D. 1981. "The Feminization of American Congregationalism, 1730–1835." *American Quarterly* 33: 45–62.

Shinn, Larry D. 1985. "Conflicting Networks: Guru and Friend in ISKCON." In Rodney Stark, ed., *Religious Movements: Genesis, Exodus, and Numbers.* New York: Paragon.

Shurden, Walter B. 1980. "Documents on the Ministry in Southern Baptist History." *Baptist History and Heritage* 15: 45–54.

Sjoberg, Gideon. 1960. *The Preindustrial City.* New York: Free Press.

Slayton, Robert A. 1986. *Back of the Yards: The Making of a Local Democracy.* Chicago: University of Chicago Press.

Smith, Adam. [1776] 1937. *The Wealth of Nations.* New York: Modern Library.

Smith, Christian, with Michael Emerson, Sally Gallagher, Paul Kennedy, and David Sikkink. 1998. *American Evangelism: Embattled and Thriving.* Chicago: The University of Chicago Press.

Smith, Daniel Scott. 1985. "The Dating of the American Sexual Revolution: Evidence and Interpretation." In John F. Crosby, ed., *Reply to Myth: Perspectives on Intimacy.* New York: John Wiley.

Smith, Timothy. 1957. *Revivalism and Social Reform in Mid-Nineteenth-Century America.* New York: Abingdon Press.

Smith, Timothy L. 1978a. "Religion and Ethnicity in America." *American Historical Review* 83(5): 1155–1185.

———. 1978b. "Lay Initiative in the Religious Life of American Immigrants, 1880–1950." In John M. Mulder and John F. Wilson, eds., *Religion in American History.* Englewood Cliffs, N.J.: Prentice-Hall.

———. 1983. "My Rejection of a Cyclical View of 'Great Awakenings' in American Religious History." *Sociological Analysis* 44: 97–101.

Smith, Tom. 2002. "Religious Diversity in America: The Emergence of Muslims, Buddhists, Hindus, and Others." *Journal for the Scientific Study of Religion* 41: 577–585.

Sobel, Mechal. 1979. *Trabelin' On: The Slave Journey to an Afro-Baptist Faith*. Westport, Conn.: Greenwood Press.

Spalding, John Lancaster. [1880] 1967. "The Country and the City, 1880." In Robert D. Cross, ed., *The Church and the City, 1865–1910*. New York: Bobbs-Merrill Co.

Sparks, Randy J. 1994. *On Jordon's Stormy Banks: Evangelicalism in Mississippi, 1773–1876*. Athens, Ga.: University of Georgia Press.

Sparks, Randy J. 2001. *Religion in Mississippi*. Jackson: University Press of Mississippi for the Mississippi Historical Society.

Spong, John Shelby. 1998. *Why Christianity Must Change or Die*. San Francisco: HarperSanFrancisco.

Stark, Rodney. 1971. "The Economics of Piety: Religion and Social Class." In Gerald W. Thielbar and Saul D. Feldman, eds., *Issues in Social Inequality*. Boston: Little, Brown and Co.

———. 1985. "Church and Sect." In Phillip E. Hammond, ed., *The Sacred in a Secular Age*. Berkeley: University of California Press.

Stark, Rodney. 1987a. "Correcting Church Membership Rates: 1971 and 1980." *Review of Religious Research* 29: 69–77.

———. 1987b. "How New Religions Succeed: A Theoretical Model." In David G. Bromley and Phillip E. Hammond, eds., *The Future of New Religious Movements*. Macon, Ga.: Mercer University Press.

———. 1991. "Antioch as the Social Situation for Matthew's Gospel." In David L. Balch, ed., *Social History of the Matthean Community: Cross-Disciplinary Approaches to an Open Question*. Minneapolis: Augsburg-Fortress.

———. 1992a. "Epidemics, Networks, and the Rise of Christianity." *Semeia* (issue edited by L. Michael White).

———. 1992b. "A Note on the Reliability of Historical U.S. Census Data on Religion." *Sociological Analysis* 53: 91–95.

———. 1992c. "Do Catholic Societies Really Exist?" *Rationality and Society* 4: 261–271.

———. 1996. *The Rise of Christianity: A Sociologist Reconsiders History*. Princeton: Princeton University Press.

———. 2001. *One True God: Historical Consequences of Monotheism*. Princeton: Princeton University Press.

———. 2003. *For the Glory of God: How Monotheism Led to Reformations, Science, Witch-hunts, and the End of Slavery*. Princeton: Princeton University Press.

Stark, Rodney, and William Sims Bainbridge. 1980. "Networks of Faith: Interpersonal Bonds and Recruitment to Cults and Sects." *American Journal of Sociology* 85: 1376–1395.

———. 1985. *The Future of Religion: Secularization, Revival, and Cult Formation*. Berkeley: University of California Press.

———. 1987. *A Theory of Religion*. New York and Bern: Peter Lang.

Stark, Rodney, William Sims Bainbridge, Robert D. Crutchfield, Daniel Doyle, and Roger Finke. 1983. "Crime and Delinquency in the Roaring Twenties." *Journal of Research in Crime and Delinquency* 20: 4–23.

Stark, Rodney, and Roger Finke. 1988. "American Religion in 1776: A Statistical Portrait." *Sociological Analysis* 49: 39–51.

———. 2000. *Acts of Faith: Explaining the Human Side of Religion*. Berkeley: University of California Press.

Stark, Rodney, and Charles Y. Glock. 1965. "The New Denominationalism." *Review of Religious Research* 7: 8–17.

———. 1968. *American Piety*. Berkeley: University of California Press.

Stark, Rodney, and Laurence R. Iannaccone. 1991. "Sociology of Religion." In Edgar F. Borgotta, ed., *Encyclopedia of Sociology*. New York: Macmillan Co.

———. 1992. "Cult and Sect Movements within Religious Economies." In David C. Bromley and Jeffrey K. Hadden, eds., *Handbook of Cults and Sects in America*. Greenwich, Conn.: JAI Press.

Stark, Rodney, and James C. McCann. 1993. "Market Forces and Catholic Commitment: Exploring the New Paradigm." *Journal for the Scientific Study of Religion* 32: 111–123.

Steinberg, Stephen. 1965. "Reform Judaism: The Origin and Evolution of a Church Movement." *Review of Religious Research* 7:1–8.

Stephenson, George M. 1926. "The Background of the Beginnings of Swedish Immigration, 1850–1875." *The American Historical Review* 31: 708–723.

Stone, Barton. 1910. *A Short History of the Life of Barton W. Stone*. Appended to James R. Rogers, *The Cane Ridge Meeting-house*. Cincinnati: The Standard Publishing Company.

Stout, Harry S. 1986. *The New England Soul: Preaching and Religious Culture in Colonial New England*. New York: Oxford University Press.

Sullivan, Kathleen. 2000. "St. Mary's Catholic Church: Celebrating Domestic Religion." In Helen Rose Ebaugh and Janet Saltzman Chafetz, eds., *Religion and the New Immigrants: Continuities and Adaptations in Immigrant Congregations*. Walnut Creek, Calif.: AltaMira Press.

Sundberg, Walter. 1993. "A review of *The Churching of America, 1776–1990: Winners and Losers in Our Religious Economy*." *First Things* (June/July): 55–57.

Swanson, Merwin. 1977. "The 'Country Life Movement' and the American Churches." *Church History* 46: 368–369.

Sweet, Douglas H. 1976. "Church Vitality and the American Revolution: Historiographical Consensus and Thoughts toward a New Perspective." *Church History* 45: 341–357.

Sweet, William Warren, ed. 1920. *The Rise of Methodism in the West: Being the Journal of the Western Conference, 1800–1811*. New York: Methodist Book Concern.

———. [1930] 1950. *The Story of Religion in America*. New York: Harper & Row.

———. 1933. *Methodism in American History*. New York: Methodist Book Concern.

———. 1939. *Religion on the American Frontier, 1783–1850: The Congregationalists*. Chicago: University of Chicago Press.

———. 1944. *Revivalism in America*. New York: Charles Scribner's Sons.

———. 1946. *Religion on the American Frontier, 1783–1840: The Methodists*. Chicago: University of Chicago Press.

———. 1947. *Religion in Colonial America*. New York: Charles Scribner's Sons.

———. 1948. "The Protestant Churches." *The Annals* 256: 43–52.

———. 1952. *Religion in the Development of American Culture, 1765–1840*. New York: Charles Scribner's Sons.

———. 1964a. *Religion on the American Frontier, 1783–1840: The Baptists*. New York: Cooper Square Publishers.

———. 1964b. *Religion on the American Frontier, 1783–1840: The Presbyterians*. New York: Cooper Square Publishers.

Szafran, Robert F. 1976. "The Distribution of Influence in Religious Organizations." *Journal for the Scientific Study of Religion* 15: 339–350.

Taves, Ann. 1986. *The Household of Faith: Roman Catholic Devotions in Mid-Nineteenth-Century America*. Notre Dame: University of Notre Dame Press.

———. 1999. *Fits, Trances, and Visions: Experiencing Religion and Explaining Experiences from Wesley to James*. Princeton: Princeton University Press.

Taylor, John. 1843. *History of Ten Baptist Churches*. Frankfort, Ky.: J. H. Holeman.

The Testimony of an Association of Ministers Convened at Marlborough, January 22, 1744, against the Reverend George Whitefield and His Conduct. 1745. Boston, Mass.: T. Fleet.

The Testimony of the President, Professors, Tutors and Hebrew Instructor of Harvard College in Cambridge, against the Reverend Mr. George Whitefleld and His Conduct. 1744. Boston, N.E.: T. Fleet.

Tharp, Clifford J. 1985. "A Study of the Forced Termination of Southern Baptist Ministers." *The Quarterly Review* 46: 50–56.

Thernstrom, Stephan. 1980. *The Harvard Encyclopedia of American Ethnic Groups*. Cambridge, Mass.: The Belknap Press of Harvard University Press.

Thompson, Ernest Trice. 1994. "Black Presbyterians, Education, and Evangelism after the Civil War." In Donald G. Nieman, ed., *Church and Community Among Black Southerners, 1865–1900*. New York: Garland Publishing.

Thompson, James J. 1982. *Tried as by Fire: Southern Baptists and the Religious Controversies of the 1920s*. Macon, Ga.: Mercer University Press.

Thompson, Robert C. 1974. "A Research Note on the Diversity among American Protestants: A Southern Baptist Example." *Review of Religious Research* 15: 87–92.

Tipton, Steven M. 1982. "The Moral Logic of Alternative Religions." In Mary Douglas and Steven M. Tipton, eds., *Religion and America: Spirituality in a Secular Age*. Boston: Beacon Press.

Tocqueville, Alexis de. [1835] 1969. *Democracy in America*. Garden City, N.Y.: Anchor Books.

Torbet, Robert G. 1963. *A History of the Baptists*. Valley Forge, Pa.: Judson Press.

————. 1976. "Baptists of the North." In James E. Wood, Jr., ed., *Baptists of the American Experience*. Valley Forge, Pa.: Judson Press.

Tucker, Karen B. Westerfield. 2001. *American Methodist Worship*. New York: Oxford University Press.

Turner, Frederick Jackson. 1920. *The Frontier in American History*. New York: Henry Holt and Co.

Turner, James. 1985. *Without God, Without Creed: The Origins of Unbelief in America*. Baltimore: Johns Hopkins University Press.

Tweed, Thomas A. 1997. *Retelling U.S. Religious History*. Berkeley: University of California Press.

————. 1999. "Night-Stand Buddhists and Other Creatures: Sympathizers, Adherents, and the Study of Religion." In Duncan R. Williams and Christopher S. Queen, eds., *American Buddhism: Methods and Findings in Recent Scholarship*. Richmond, Great Britain: Curzon Press.

Tweed, Thomas A., Grant Wacker, Jon Pahl, Valerie H. Ziegler, and William D. Dinges. 2002. "Teaching the Introductory Course in American Religion." *Religion and American Culture* 12: 1–30.

U.S. Census Bureau. 2002a. *Statistical Abstract of the United States, 2002*. 122nd ed. Washington, D.C.: U.S. Census Bureau.

————. 2002b. "Population Division, Ethnic & Hispanic Statistics Branch." http://www.census.gov/population/www/socdemo/foreign/p20-534.html

Verdieck, Mary Jeanne, Joseph J. Shields, and Dean R. Hoge. 1988. "Role Commitment Processes Revisited." *Journal for the Scientific Study of Religion* 27: 524–535.

Villeneuve, Alphonse. 1891. "Les Etats-Unis d'Amerique et l'emigration." *Siècle*, tome 2, année.

Visser t' Hooft, W. A. 1959. "The Gathering of the Scattered Children of God." In Edward J. Jurji, ed., *The Ecumenical Era in Church and Society*. New York: Macmillan Co.

Vogt, Paul L. 1917. *Introduction to Rural Sociology*. New York: D. Appleton and Co.

Wagner, Melinda Bollar. 1983. "Spiritual Frontiers Fellowship." In Joseph H. Fichter, ed., *Alternatives to American Mainline Churches*. New York: Rose of Sharon Press.

Walch, Timothy. 1996. *Parish School: American Catholic Parochial Education from Colonial Times to the Present*. New York: Crossroad Publishing.

Walker, Clarence E. 1982. *A Rock in a Weary Land: The African Methodist Episcopal Church During the Civil War and Reconstruction*. Baton Rouge: Louisiana State University.

Walker, Williston. 1894. *A History of the Congregational Churches in the United States*. New York: Christian Literature Co.

Wamble, G. Hugh. 1976. "Baptists of the South." In James E. Wood, Jr., ed., *Baptists and the American Experience*. Valley Forge, Pa: Judson Press.

Warner, R. Stephen. 1988. *New Wine in Old Wineskins: Evangelicals and Liberals in a Small-Town Church*. Berkeley: University of California Press.

———. 1994. "The Place of the Congregation in the Contemporary American Religious Configuration." In James P. Wind and James W. Lewis, eds., *American Congregations*. Vol. 2. Chicago: University of Chicago Press.

Warner, R. Stephen, and Judith G. Wittner, eds. 1998. *Gathering in Diaspora: Religious Communities and the New Immigration*. Philadelphia: Temple University Press.

Weber, Herman C. 1927. *Presbyterian Statistics through One Hundred Years: 1826–1926*. Presbyterian Board of Christian Education.

Weber, Max. 1946. *From Max Weber: Essays in Sociology*. Edited by H. H. Gerth and C. Wright Mills. New York: Galaxy.

Weis, Federick Lewis. 1936. *The Colonial Clergy and the Colonial Churches of New England*. Society of the Descendants of the Colonial Clergy. Massachusetts.

———. 1938. *The Colonial Churches and the Colonial Clergy of the Middle and Southern Colonies, 1607–1776*. Society for the Descendants of the Colonial Clergy. Massachusetts.

———. 1950. *The Colonial Clergy of Maryland, Delaware, and Georgia*. Society for the Descendants of the Colonial Clergy. Massachusetts.

———. 1955. *The Colonial Clergy of Virginia, North Carolina, and South Carolina*. Society for the Descendants of the Colonial Clergy. Massachusetts.

Welch, Kevin. 1983. "Community Development and Metropolitan Religious Commitment: A Test of Two Competing Models." *Journal for the Scientific Study of Religion* 22: 167–181.

Welch, Michael R., and John Baltzell. 1984. "Geographic Mobility, Social Integration, and Church Attendance." *Journal for the Scientific Study of Religion* 23: 75–91.

Wertheimer, Jack. 1993. *A People Divided: Judaism in Contemporary America*. New York: Basic Books.

Westoff, Charles F. 1979. "The Blending of Catholic Reproductive Behavior." In Robert Wuthnow, ed., *The Religious Dimension*. New York: Academic Press.

Whitefield, George. [1756] 1969. *George Whitefield's Journals*. Gainesville, Fl.: Scholars' Facsimiles and Reprints.

Whitehead, John. 1982. *The Second American Revolution*. Westchester, Ill.: Crossway Books.

Whitehead, John, and John Conlan. 1978. "The Establishment of the Religion of Secular Humanism and Its First Amendment Implications." *Texas Tech Law Review* (Winter): 1–66.

Whitney, Arthur P. 1951. *The Basis of Opposition to Methodism in the Eighteenth Century*. New York: New York University Press.

Wigger, John H. 1998. *Taking Heaven by Storm: Methodism and the Rise of Popular Christianity in America*. Urbana: University of Illinois Press.

———. 2001. "Fighting Bees: Methodist Itinerants and the Dynamics of Methodist Growth, 1770–1820." In Nathan O. Hatch and John H. Wigger, eds., *Methodism and the Shaping of American Culture*. Nashville, Tenn.: Kingswood Books.

Wilde, Melissa J. 2002. *Reconstructing Religion: A Sociological Analysis of Vatican* II. Ph.D. Dissertation. Department of Sociology. Berkeley: University of California.

Wilke, Richard B. 1986. *And Are We Yet Alive?* Nashville: Abingdon Press.

Wills, Gregory A. 1997. *Democratic Religion: Freedom, Authority, and Church Discipline in the Baptist South, 1785–1900.* New York: Oxford University Press.

Wilson, Bryan. 1966. *Religion in Secular Society.* London: C. A. Watts.

Wilson, George W. 1904. *Methodist Theology vs. Methodist Theologians.* Cincinnati: Press of Jennings and Pye.

Wilson, John F., ed. 1965. *Church and State in American History.* Boston: D. C. Heath and Company.

———. 1993. "A review of *The Churching of America, 1776–1990: Winners and Losers in Our Religious Economy.*" *Journal of Church and State* 35: 618–619.

Wilson, Warren H. 1911a. *The Church of the Open Country: A Study of the Church of the Working Farmer.* New York.

———. 1911b. "The Church and the Rural Community." *American Journal of Sociology* 16: 668–693.

———. 1913. *A Rural Survey in Indiana.* New York: Department of Church and Country Life of the Board of Home Missions of the Presbyterian Church in the U.S.A.

———. 1923. "The Church and the Country Life Movement." *Journal of Social Forces* 2: 23–28.

———. 1925. *The Farmer's Church.* New York: Century Co.

Wissel, Joseph. 1886. *The Redemptorist on the American Missions.* New York: John Ross and Son.

Wittberg, Patricia. 1994. *The Rise and Fall of Catholic Religious Orders.* Albany: SUNY Press.

———. 1997. "Deep Structure in Community Cultures: The Revival of Religious Orders in Roman Catholicism." *Sociology of Religion* 58: 239–259.

———. 2000. "Declining Institutional Sponsorship and Religious Orders: A Study of Reverse Impacts." *Sociology of Religion* 61: 315–324.

Wolf, Richard C. 1959. "Religious Trends: 1900–1950." *Christianity Today* 3: 3–6.

Wood, James R., and Mayer N. Zald. 1966. "Aspects of Racial Integration in the Methodist Church: Sources of Resistance to Organizational Policy." *Social Forces* 45: 255–265.

Wunderlich, Gene. 2002. "The Community Idea in American Country Life." *Agriculture and Human Values* 19: 81–85.

Wuthnow, Robert. 1973. "Religious Commitment and Conservatism: In Search of an Elusive Relationship." In Charles Y. Glock, ed., *Religion in Sociological Perspective.* Belmont, Calif.: Wadsworth Publishing Co.

———. 1976. *The Consciousness Reformation.* Berkeley: University of California Press.

———. 1978. *Experimentation in American Religion.* Berkeley: University of California Press.

Wuthnow, Robert, and Kevin Christiano. 1979. "The Effects of Residential Mobility on Church Attendance." In Robert Wuthnow, ed., *The Religious Dimension: New Directions in Quantitative Research.* New York: Academic Press.

Wyneken, Friedrich Conrad Dietrich. [1843] 1982. *The Distress of the German Lutherans in North America.* Translated by S. Edgar Schmidt and edited by R. F. Rehmer. Fort Wayne, Ind.: Concordia Theological Seminary Press.

Yang, Fenggang. 1998. "Chinese Conversion to Evangelical Christianity." *Sociology of Religion* 59: 237–258.

———. 1999. *Chinese Christians in America: Conversion, Assimilation, and Adhesive Identities.* University Park: The Pennsylvania State University Press.

Yang, Fenggang, and Helen Rose Ebaugh. 2001a. "Transformation in New Immigrant Religions and Their Global Implications." *American Sociological Review* 66: 269–288.

———. 2001b. "Religion and Ethnicity Among New Immigrants: The Impact of Majority/Minority Status in Home and Host Countries." *Journal for the Scientific Study of Religion* 40: 367–378.

Yearbook of American and Canadian Churches. 1988. Edited by Constant H. Jacquet. Nashville: Abingdon Press.

Young, Jacob. 1857. *Autobiography of a Pioneer.* Cincinnati: Cranston and Curt's.

Zelinsky, W. 1961. "An Approach to the Religious Geography of the United States: Patterns in 1952." *Annals of the American Association of Geographers* 51: 139–193.

Index

ABC (Associated Broadcasting Corporation), 219, 222
advertisements, 89
Advocate, The (periodical), 161
affluence, 47, 161, 162, 165, 169, 171–175, 179, 180, 184, 185
Africa, 273
African Americans, 32, 298n22, 302n5; and Baptists, 99, 101, 102–103, 105, 106, 192, 193–194, 196, 300n2; clergy, 103, 106, 193, 194; and Methodists, 99–103, 104–106, 190–193, 194–196, 300n2. *See also* slavery; slaves
afterlife, 46
agriculture, 200, 208. *See also* farmers
Ahlstrom, Sydney, 2, 7, 47, 49, 58, 119, 201, 216, 217
AHMS (American Home Missionary Society), 66–67
Alabama, 149; Baptists in, 190; circuit riders in, 81; Methodists in, 100, 196; religious adherence in, 70; sex ratio in, 69
Alemany (archbishop), 149
Alexander, June Granatir, 138
Allen, Richard, 101–102, 104
alliances, 155, 224
American Almanac, 77, 117
American Catholic Sociological Society, 145, 259
American Country Life Association, 200
American Home Missionary Society, 2, 207, 218

American Indians, 19, 81, 99
American Journal of Sociology, 205, 210, 257–258
American Missionary Association, 196
American Quarterly Register, 59–60
American Sociological Society, 208
America (Schaff), 6
Anglican church, 75, 251; clergy of, 29–30, 39, 54, 62–63, 75. *See also* Church of England; Episcopal churches
archbishops, 124, 147, 148
Arizona, 121, 149
Arkansas, 66, 69–71, 100
Asbury, Francis, 77, 79, 83, 84, 96–97, 105, 112, 131, 172, 298n13
Asia, 304n18; immigrants from, 240–244; religions from, 237–240
Asplund, John, 29
Assemblies of God, 206, 235, 246, 247, 303n11
assimilation, 155, 174, 241, 259
Association for the Sociology of Religion, 145, 259, 262
Association of Statisticians of American Religious Bodies, 22
associations: professional, 145; voluntary, 65–67, 138–139, 190, 194
Atkinson, Elizabeth, 91
Atlas of the Historical Geography of the United States (Paullin), 18–19, 27
attendance at services, 243–244, 256–257, 260, 277, 278, 280, 302n19
authority, 263–264, 273

Europe *(continued)*
123, 142, 240, 253, 280; Lutherans in,
151; Protestants in, 225; religious
adherence in, 10. *See also names of
specific countries*
Evangelical Church, 15, 226
Evangelical Fellowship, 277–278
Evangelical Missions Council, 276
Evangelical Renewal Fellowship (ERF), 278
Evangelical Synod, 15, 230
Evangelical United Brethren, 159–160
evangelism and evangelists, 9, 88, 89, 233;
Catholic, 125, 126; egalitarianism of,
105–106; growth of, 6, 206, 237, 245–247;
mainline, 275–278, 304n22; Methodist,
169, 175, 279; Protestant, 206, 223, 228,
243, 276–278; and radio, 219, 223;
urban, 90, 92. *See also* Asbury, Francis;
Cartwright, Peter; Finney, Charles
Grandison; Whitefield, George
experience, 86, 103, 168, 169, 181, 251
expulsion and excommunication, 163, 174

faith, 10, 45, 46, 103, 108, 214; and camp
meetings, 94, 96; of Catholics, 262, 264;
high-tension, 45; rational, 47; *vs.*
theology, 84–85, 87; weakening of, 53,
201
families, 133, 138, 243, 258. *See also* children
farmers, 107, 208, 211; as preachers, 96, 184,
188–189, 207, 300n6
Federal Communications Commission
(FCC), 218, 220, 222, 223
Federal Council of Churches, 207, 208, 216–
218, 219, 223
Fenton, John, 242
fertility, 257, 258, 267
Fichter, Joseph, 264–265
Finney, Charles Grandison, 87, 88, 89–92,
97, 107, 108, 198
firings of clergy, 186, 188
Fischer, Claude S., 301n2
Fleming, Thornton, 96–97
Florida, 69–70, 100
food, 259–260, 279–280, 281
France, 119, 300n8
Frank Leslie Illustrated Newspaper, 172
Franklin, Benjamin, 48, 51–52, 89
Frazier, E. Franklin, 190
Free African Society, 101
freedoms, religious, 3, 6–7, 11–12, 55, 60
freethinkers, 60

Frey, Sylvia R., 103, 105
Friends. *See* Quakers
front groups, 65–67
frontiers, 71, 79, 296n4; awakenings on, 88;
and camp meetings, 97, 99; Catholics
on, 144, 148–149; missions to, 66, 74,
208; Presbyterians on, 75, 87; religious
adherence on, 71; sociology of, 34–38;
upstart sects on, 72–73
Fuller, Charles E., 219, 220, 222
fundamentalism, 219, 221, 222, 226
funerals, 212, 259

Galpin, Charles J., 208
Galpin, Horace, 66
Gardner, Robert, 101
Garraghan, Gilbert J., 127, 130
Garrettson, Freeborn, 178–179
Garrick, David, 51
Gaustad, Edwin S., 39
gender, 37. *See also* men; sex ratios; women
General Association, 65
Georgia, 27, 52, 242; African-American
Methodists in, 100; clergy in, 49, 81;
Episcopalians in, 43, 75; religious
adherence in, 30, 31, 70; sex ratio in, 37,
69
German Reformed church, 28, 31, 32–33,
39, 77
Germany, 40, 123, 152, 168
Gibson, Edmund, 68
Giles, Charles, 178
Gill, Charles Otis, 208
Glock, Charles Y., 226–227, 237, 238
God, 47, 86, 107, 128, 275; exclusivity of,
250–251; existence of, 226–227
gold rush, 71, 149
Good News movement, 276, 278
Gorham, B. W., 98, 116
Goss, C. C., 113–115
Graham, Billy, 88
Great Awakenings, 3, 49, 59, 87–88, 89
Greeley, Andrew M., 119, 241, 257, 263,
267
Grund, Francis, 4, 11, 12
Gunneman, Louis H., 297n1
gurus, 239, 242, 302n2

Handy, Robert, 201
Hargreaves, John, 210
Harper's Weekly, 81, 167
Harvard, 53, 54, 87, 107, 238;

About the Authors

ROGER FINKE is professor of sociology and religious studies at the Pennsylvania State University and serves as the director of the American Religion Data Archive (www.TheARDA.com).

RODNEY STARK was for many years professor of sociology and comparative religion at the University of Washington. In 2004 he became University Professor of the Social Sciences at Baylor University.